Oxfordshire Friendly Societies, 1750-1918

The Oxfordshire Record Society
Oxfordshire Friendly Societies, 1750-1918

Edited by

Shaun Morley

Volume 68

2011

First published in Great Britain 2011
By Oxfordshire Record Society
c/o The Secretary,
Shaun Morley, Tithe Corner, 67 Hill Crescent,
Finstock, Chipping Norton, OX7 3BT

Registered Charity No. 209808

British Library Cataloguing in Publication Data
A catalogue record for this book is available from the British Library
ISBN 978 0 902509 73 3
Printed and bound in Great Britain by Information Press Ltd
www.informationpress.com

Table of Contents

Foreword

For some readers, this volume on friendly societies will at first sight irresistibly recall the Donald McGill cartoon of about 1950 which shows an elderly and irascible gentleman sitting up in his hotel bed remonstrating with a hapless member of staff. 'Here, what's all that noise going on downstairs?' he enquires. 'They're holding an Oddfellows' Ball, Sir', comes the reply. 'Well, if he makes all that row about it, why the devil don't they let him have it back?'

From the perspective of the twenty-first century, the world of Victorian friendly societies can seem even more curious. With their heyday behind them, there are perhaps now only a few hundred left in the country. It would as a result be all too easy to see them as a historical irrelevance. Historians of Oxfordshire might be forgiven for falling into this trap more readily than most, for it has long been believed that the county was almost uniquely impoverished when it came to the provision of friendly societies. A series of studies has assumed that a lack of Oddfellows, Foresters, and other national organisations meant an absence of friendly societies more generally throughout Oxfordshire.

As Shaun Morley triumphantly shows in this calendar, these sorts of assumptions are completely wrong. Friendly societies could be found in almost every village across the county, and their importance was more than just a consequence of their ubiquity. They brilliantly illustrate the hopes and fears of the period in which they were founded, with societies established to pay militia fines, deal with agricultural violence, and even cope with hailstones, as well as to provide a basic form of social insurance. They also reveal the strong associational life of the times, and the bands, banners, and celebrations that helped sustain it.

This calendar, then, takes the reader right to the heart of nineteenth-century Oxfordshire. It will be, I hope, of real value not just to those interested in parish history or the development of friendly societies in general, but also to anyone who wants to understand the every-day lives of the Victorians. At a time in which we are constantly being asked to think about the so-called 'Big Society', in which voluntarism and localism are intended to replace the supposedly heavy hand of the state, here too is a reminder that there is nothing new under the sun. We have, it turns out, been here before.

Oxford, October 2011

William Whyte
Editor of the Oxfordshire Record Society

Editor's Preface

This volume collates a significant amount of information concerning the friendly societies of pre-1974 Oxfordshire in a format that is hoped will lead to the easier identification of sources relating to each society and encourage further research on the principal organized associational form for the labouring man in nineteenth century Britain. The nature of this volume is that as soon as it is published I hope that new records, artefacts and information will come to light. To that end, an addendum will be maintained at the Oxfordshire Record Society website at **www.oxfordshire-record-society.org.uk.** This volume would not have been possible without the help, assistance, encouragement and guidance of many individuals. Dr Kate Tiller has been a guiding hand in much of my formal studies whilst I have received great encouragement and opportunities from those at the Department for Continuing Education of the University of Oxford, especially Adrienne Rosen, Chris Day, and Mark Smith. Staff at several archives have been both courteous and helpful in locating original material, especially at Oxfordshire Record Office and Oxfordshire Studies, the Bodleian Library, Oxfordshire Museum Service, Roger Logan at the Foresters' Heritage Trust, the People's History Museum, and Berkshire Record Office. While the automated search and ordering system at the National Archives ensures contact with people is kept to a minimum, it is no less efficient.

Many local history societies have shown great interest in this topic and several have opened their archives for me to locate original material. In particular, I would like to express my thanks to Margaret Fissenden of Weston on the Green, Martin Greenwood of Fringford, Pat Cox of Great Milton, Jenny Dodds at Thame Museum, Wendy Pearse of the Wychwoods Society, Maureen Hicks of the Sibfords Society, and many members of Finstock Local History Society.

William Whyte, the general editor of Oxfordshire Record Society has been extremely supportive in the production of this volume and his suggestions to improve the content and presentation, and his eagle-eye to identify corrections, have been invaluable. However, as is normal, it is my wife and history-widow, Beverley, who has tolerated my endless hours in archives and on the computer. To all I extend my sincere thanks.

Shaun Morley

List of abbreviations

Abbreviation	Description
AOD	Ancient Order of Druids
AOF	Ancient Order of Foresters
AOS	Ancient Order of Shepherds
Assistant Commissioner	Sir George Young, the Assistant Commissioner for Southern and Eastern Counties for the Royal Commission for Friendly and Benefit Building Societies (1874)
BicA	Bicester Advertiser
BanA	Banbury Advertiser
BBFS	Bath and Bristol Friendly Society
BG	Banbury Guardian
BH	Bicester Herald
BA	Bicester Advertiser
BOA	Berkshire and Oxfordshire Advertiser
Bodl.	Bodleian Library
BPP	British Parliamentary Papers
BuckA	Buckingham Advertiser
CBS	Catholic Benefit Society
CCAWMBS	Cirencester Conservative Association Working Men's Benefit Society
CNDM	Chipping Norton Deanery Magazine
COETSBS	Church of England Temperance Sick and Burial Society
Commission	Sir Stafford Northcote was the chairman of the Royal Commission for Friendly and Benefit Building Societies from 1871 to 1874, supported by seven other members.
DDM	Deddington Deanery Magazine
DMUOOF	Derby Midland United Order of Oddfellows
FINBSFS	Friend in Need Benefit and Sick Fund Society
HA	Kinch's Henley Advertiser
HC	Henley Chronicle

HOO	Hearts of Oak
HS	Hospital Sunday
HSOS	Henley and South Oxfordshire Standard
IIOOFSLU	Improved Independent Order of Oddfellows, South London Unity
IMBFS	Independent Mutual Brethren Friendly Society
IOOFMU	Independent Order of Oddfellows, Manchester Unity
IORSU	Independent Order of Rechabites, Salford Unity
JOJ	Jackson's Oxford Journal
LFI	London Friendly Institution
LG	London Gazette
LVFS	Liverpool Victoria Friendly Society
NA	National Archives
NAIUOOF	Nottingham Ancient Imperial United Order of Odd Fellows
NDFS	National Deposit Friendly Society
NIOOF	National Independent Order of Oddfellows
OCBBG	Oxford Chronicle & Berks & Bucks Gazette
OCCPA	Oxfordshire County Council photographic archive
OHC	Oxfordshire History Centre (the combined Oxfordshire Record Office and Oxfordshire Studies Library)
OF	Unspecified Oddfellows branch
OIJ	Oxford Illustrated Journal
OMS	Oxfordshire Museum Service
OSOT	Order of the Sons of Temperance
OT	Oxford Times
PLMR	The Guardian or Poor Law Monthly Register (Banbury)
PSD	Petty Session Division
Registrar	The Registrar of Friendly Societies (until 1875), then the Chief Registrar of Friendly Societies
SON	South Oxfordshire News
TG	Thame Gazette
UPI	United Provident Institution
UPNBS	United Patriots National Benefit Society

VCH	Victoria County History
WE	Witney Express
WG	Witney Gazette
WT	Wallingford Times

Oxfordshire Friendly Societies, 1750-1918
Introduction

The far-reaching network of friendly societies that had developed by the end of the nineteenth century throughout Britain significantly influenced those who promoted and implemented the beginning of the welfare state in the twentieth century. When considered alongside the Poor Law and other elements of parochial welfare provision, they provided a proto-welfare state at a time of increasing intervention by government. The most visible sign of the existence of an extensive number of friendly societies is in the form of photographs and newspaper accounts of their annual club days which received considerable attention from the mid nineteenth-century onwards. Club day, often associated with the annual feast, was the most celebrated day of the year for many communities. The overall structure of the day was formulaic but each place had its unique characteristics. The day commenced with members gathering at the club headquarters at c.9.00 a.m. where the consumption of alcohol commenced for the non-temperance societies. Dressed in best clothes and wearing the club colours in the form of ribbons or a rosette, the group assembled, having been joined by the distant members, those who had moved away from the area. Some 'mischievous proceeding' could take place, such as at Chadlington where people were tied in their houses, gates were lifted off their hinges and thrown in the brook, and knockers and bells rung or pulled off.[1]

A band, hired for the day, would appear and with the members paraded to church where the vicar would deliver divine service for a small fee. Congregating outside the church, the band and members moved off and perambulated the area calling at substantial houses where a gift of money or goods was expected. The streets were lined with family and non-members, and as the nineteenth century progressed, an increasing number of tourist visitors. Dinner for the members and a few invited guests, including the vicar and some other selected local elites, was held at the club headquarters. The club room was decorated with the local flowers or foliage of choice. At Stonesfield it was peonies, at Chesterton, laburnum, at Wendlebury, lilac, at Hethe, rhododendrons and azaleas, and at Finstock it was horse chestnut. Occasionally, alternative provision in the form of a tea was made for members' wives and children, as reported at Churchill in 1882.

An account of the current state of the society was delivered, either as separate business, or as part of the after-dinner celebration, as well as a number of other speeches. After 1884 Members of Parliament were regular attendees at club dinners following the extension of the male franchise when 60 per cent of labourers were able to vote. It provided an opportunity to canvass amongst a new class of voter although friendly societies were largely non-political. The dinner was followed by further music from the band and perhaps another march to other parts of the area. Contemporary reports show that from 1840s an increasing number of stalls were attracted by club day, either selling goods such as cherries or gingerbread, or providing entertainment like swings and roundabouts. The celebrations were a whole-day affair, often described as a red-letter day, which frequently extended late into the evening with alcohol consumption continuing for much of the day. Howkins (1973)[2] explores how traditional village feasts, especially at Whitsun, were consumed by friendly society club days and a clear example can be seen at Kirtlington. In c.1859 the club day of the Kirtlington Provident Friendly Society (Kirtlington 403) moved from Easter Monday to Trinity Monday, the day of the traditional Lamb Ale,[3] and from then on friendly society activities dominated the proceedings. The Kirtlington Lamb Ale was one of the numerous village feasts celebrated in spring, pagan festivals with many dating from the late medieval period that had been incorporated into the religious calendar. Club days breathed new life into many such feasts.

Friendly societies held a special place within the community and they were embraced by the labouring classes and supported by the elite. They were not simply co-operatives to share the burden of insurance against sickness and burial but were mutually beneficial to the members whilst also having the effect of reducing the burden upon the poor rate. Members of a friendly society received sickness benefit from the club and hence a much reduced rate of support from the Overseer of the Poor, and after 1834 the Poor Law Union. Every settlement in Oxfordshire had access to a friendly society that gave a sense of belonging to its members, a feeling of independence, stability in changing times, exposure to true democratic principles in the form of one-man, one-vote for all its members and provided a focus for the foremost event in the calendar with the annual club feast. Insurance through mutual aid was important but the impact of the development of friendly societies was both a consequence of change and a catalyst for it.

The earliest friendly societies were local in nature and formed by groups of men as mutual societies whereby the payment of a regular, defined subscription gave insurance against loss of wages through sickness, the cost of burial and occasionally other issues that may have impact on the health or life of the member such as superannuation in old age, payment for lying-in for any female members or the provision of a militia substitute. This latter benefit awarded the member a set sum, normally £5 or £10, with which to buy a substitute if they were selected for militia service. Each society had its own articles or rules that governed the management and administration of the society, including the conditions under which benefit would be paid, but the rules provided much more than that. They defined the conditions of inclusion as a member and a code of conduct that could exclude members from joining or render them liable to a fine or expulsion if they breached the rules.

Friendly societies appeared in the Edinburgh area in the early seventeenth century and developed independently in London.[4] Industrial and mining areas in the north of England, Cornwall, and south Wales were the first to embrace these new societies that had similarity to but no continuity with the medieval guilds. The agricultural counties were slower to adopt this form of club and the first known society in Oxfordshire appeared with the formation of the Witney Friendly Society (Witney 712) on 29 September 1750, Michaelmas Day. This society was limited to 100 members whose age at joining was required to be less than 30 years, meeting at the Crown Inn and King's Head. The Woodstock New Friendly Society (Woodstock 743) is the next oldest society known in the county, established in 1757 and the following years saw societies established in the main towns of Oxford and Banbury. An advertisement for the Elderly Society of Oxford (Oxford 488) in *Jackson's Oxford Journal*, on 2 December 1858 stated that benefit clubs lately established in the county saw people excluded due to a maximum age of entry of 35 years. Only two clubs are currently known to pre-date the Elderly Society and their maximum age at joining was 30 years. The suggestion of 'lately established' clubs indicates the presence of other, as yet unknown societies in Oxfordshire. Other rural societies identified included the Poor Man's Club at Watlington, (Watlington 674) established 1759 and the Kidlington Friendly Society (Kidlington 395) in 1760. In all, 57 societies have been identified that were established before 1800. An insight into the position of friendly societies in Oxford in 1762 can be gleaned from a letter to *Jackson's Oxford Journal* that highlighted the presence of 14 box clubs in the city.[5] The term 'box club' referenced the method of securely retaining the funds and books of the society in a locked box held at the club house.

The basic principles of the function of a friendly society were relatively standard but they differed greatly in form. They lend themselves to categorization as has been undertaken by the Royal Commission of 1874 and historians alike. Clubs could be registered or unregistered; they could be permanent societies or divide their funds after a pre-determined time; they could be independent, have branches or be a branch of one of the large local societies; they could be defined by gender or youth with both female and juvenile societies; or they could be an affiliate of one of the national societies that spread to Oxfordshire from 1836. These affiliated orders grew largely from the industrial north of England. The largest nationally became the Independent Order of Oddfellows, Manchester Unity (IOOFMU).

A continual problem for researchers of friendly societies is the poor survival of primary records and the widespread nature of repositories. Some records of those societies that enrolled with Clerk of the Peace (from 1793) or registered with the Registrar of Friendly Societies (from 1846) survive in The National Archives (TNA). Stored under series FS, many early files simply contain a copy of the rules of the club, in manuscript and later printed form, but some have correspondence, notification of change of headquarters and details of dissolution. The latter records frequently include lists of members at the time of the division of the assets when the society ceased. Yet many societies remained registered when in fact they had ceased many years before because there was no requirement to notify the authorities of the cessation of a society. Errors were remarkably common with some societies being given two registration numbers, the misfiling of papers was frequent and information substantially out of date. However, the records do provide an invaluable source.

Many copies of Oxfordshire friendly society rules, enrolled at the Quarter Sessions, were not forwarded to the Registrar of Friendly Societies as required and they remained filed with the Clerk of the Peace.[6] Series QSD/R/1-43 at the Oxfordshire History Centre, formerly the County Record Office (OHC) contains manuscript and printed rules of some of the earliest enrolled societies in the county, 20 of which do not feature in TNA records. This had led to a significant under-reporting of the early establishment of societies in the county where actual enrolment was 66 per cent higher than reported in parliamentary papers. The statistics presented in Parliamentary Papers consequently need close scrutiny and careful interpretation.

The OHC also contains many individual documents relating to friendly societies and affiliated order branches amongst its collections. It is also the home of two of the three substantial sets of records relating to independent societies. The most comprehensive are the records of the Stonesfield Friendly Society (Stonesfield 626), covering all aspects of the society for its entire 147 years of existence from 1765 to 1912.[8] The records of the Filkins Friendly Society, also known as the Red, White and Blue club (Filkins 286), are also deposited at the OHC and provide a wide range of administrative and membership records for the late-nineteenth and early-twentieth century.[9]

Oxfordshire Studies library and the Bodleian Library all hold records, primarily copies of printed rules whilst some remain in private hands, such as local history societies or with private individuals. A significant set of records of the Weston on the Green Friendly Society are held by the local history society (Weston on the Green 680).

One set of papers at Berkshire Record Office is also of interest. The records of the Reading Savings Bank (D/EX/1044/7) contain sets of rules for those friendly societies that deposited their funds with them, including seven societies from south Oxfordshire. Records of affiliated orders are similarly dispersed. The Oddfellows have recently made available a large amount of material on-line at *www.oddfellows.co.uk*, including directories, magazines and reports. The Foresters' Heritage Trust have an extensive museum and archive, containing a wide range of documentary records and material culture, such as banners, boxes, and photographs,[10] with details of holdings at *www. aoforestersheritage.com*. However, records of individual affiliated branches for Oxfordshire can also be found in OHC and the Bodleian Library.

The formal records of friendly societies provide detailed evidence concerning their management, administration and progress and a general review of friendly society records can be obtained in existing literature.[11] Social history requires additional context and information to enable a fuller picture and sound conclusions to be drawn. It is the informal sources that can provide the breadth and depth of detail concerning social interaction, simmering tensions, dishonestly, the role of alcohol and a variety of other issues of historical interest. Almost 5,000 reports from 16 different newspapers, two deanery magazines, and a variety of other printed sources have enabled a much fuller picture of the social history of Oxfordshire friendly societies to be developed than for any other county. Of the 196 unregistered friendly societies in this calendar, 155 were identified from these sources alone. Together with the primary source material, including the surprising amount of correspondence

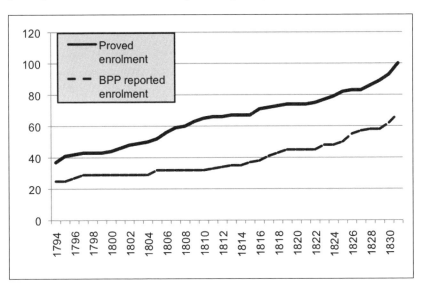

Figure 1 - Comparison of reported enrolment in Parliamentary Papers with actual, Oxfordshire 1793-1831[7]

contained within the Registrar's files at TNA a holistic picture of the extent and nature, form and function of the variety of societies can be established. This has led to the identification of the 755 Oxfordshire societies that existed up to 1918. However, there are many others that remain hidden or are yet to be discovered. The calendar provides a comprehensive list of primary sources for each identified society.

Gosden's *The Friendly Societies in England, 1815-1875,* and Cordery's *British Friendly Societies, 1750*-1914 are the only two publications dedicated to an overview of English or British friendly societies.[12] They rely largely on formal reports of the Registrar, Parliamentary Papers, on affiliated order records, and on contemporary writing. Insufficient attention is given to primary source material from friendly society records themselves. Neave, in his regional study of the East Riding (excluding Kingston upon Hull) makes wide use of all available material and provides an excellent contrast to Oxfordshire.[13] East Riding towns and villages were dominated by a variety of affiliated orders and had a much lower proportion of both registered and unregistered independent clubs. Similar to Oxfordshire in its rural nature, East Riding's population was almost two-thirds that of Oxfordshire's in 1801, rising steadily to over three-quarters in 1901. Neave's detailed study of the area revealed 362 friendly societies, including affiliated order branches, between 1750 and 1912. This Oxfordshire calendar highlights more than double the number of societies in the same period.

A further useful source for the investigation of friendly societies is the series of British Parliamentary Papers, but with many caveats. As well as the under-reporting of enrolled societies already identified, the reports contain many errors and omissions in the detail. This was partly caused by the use of source data from parishes, townships, or individual friendly societies, but also by errors within the Registrar's office. The earliest such report was compiled through answers to a standard set of 18 questions reported in 1804.[14] Each parish or township in the country was required to complete the questionnaire for the year to Easter 1803 on various aspects of the poor law, but in addition each was asked to report on the number of friendly societies present in their place and the number of resident members of any society. The consolidated report identified 65 societies in Oxfordshire with a membership of 4,679, an average of 72 per club. The calendar in this volume has identified with certainty 34 of these clubs and many more will be present in the calendar although they cannot positively be matched.

A further parliamentary report in 1818 required townships to state the number of friendly society members (but not the number of societies) present for the years 1813, 1814, and 1815.[15] During this period membership increased 3.7 per cent from 5783 to 5998, and demonstrated an increase of 28 per cent since the 1803 survey. However, it was the 1830s that saw the start of four decades of rapid growth in the number of societies and membership, peaking in 1860s when there were 218 independent societies or branches in Oxfordshire. The total membership of societies is difficult to assess with no repetition of the questions asked in the 1818 report. Unregistered clubs rarely reported their membership and registered societies only reported their membership to the Registrar at infrequent intervals. Any attempt to estimate the number of friendly society members would contain a substantial degree of speculation. However, in 1892 Henry Pocock, a labourer of Great Milton commented that, 'Almost all of the men in the village belong to one or the other [friendly society]'[16]. The number of clubs thus seems to have remained largely static until 1912.

The formation of a friendly society was a relatively simple affair. A meeting was usually called at a prospective club headquarters at the instigation of the vicar or other member of the local elite, or simply of the residents themselves. An agreement upon the rules was reached and they were then prepared, in manuscript form in the early years and in a printed poster form by the early-nineteenth century. There is evidence that rules from neighbouring societies were used as a basis for a new society's rules although some local variation was generally included. For example, there were five societies in Oxfordshire that included the benefit of a militia substitute. This was a local rule with all five societies being in four of the most southerly parishes of the county (Eye and

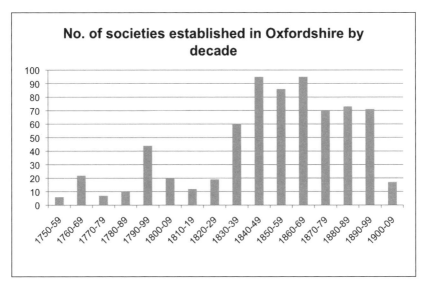

Figure 2 - Number of friendly societies established by decade in Oxfordshire, 1750-1910

Dunsden 269, Goring 310, Goring 311, Whitchurch 695, and Woodcote 725) and was likely to have been copied from club rules of neighbouring Berkshire. In the mid-nineteenth century the Registrar of Friendly Societies issued a suggested template but it was always in the gift of members to shape their own.

A limited number of copies of manuscript rules were made and they were posted on the wall of the club room where they could be consulted when necessary. New members were required to read them or have them read over. As printing techniques improved and costs decreased, most societies produced printed posters, and then rulebooks with a copy provided at a small fee for each member. The rules were an important aspect of the club and as well as providing the framework for governance, financial contributions and benefits of membership, they also set out the behavioural code. General exclusions from membership included soldiers and sailors, those with existing serious medical issues or who had a felony conviction. Rules followed a similar pattern but rarely were they identical, with local issues or concerns being included. The 1857 rules of the Stokenchurch Friendly Society (Stokenchurch 624) excluded bargemen although the village is far from a navigable canal or river, and the 1854 rules of the Fountain of Friendship Benefit Society (Adderbury 9) excluded colliers and miners. These exclusions may have been copied from rules in other parts of the country but were probably as a result of experience where a member of a local society had migrated and taken on that occupation as a distant member, but through sickness, injury or death had become an undue burden. Exclusions from benefit were extensive including any injury caused through drunkenness, fighting, gaming, wrestling, or through the contraction of venereal disease. Injury from sports were also regularly excluded such as back-swording or later, football.

There is no evidence of any complex ritual to accept new members into independent friendly societies. They were generally no more complicated than 'crowning' which involved holding a large can of beer upon the head of the person to be admitted whilst he was lustily cheered, before and after which he was expected to take draught of the contents.[17] The affiliated orders, large national organizations composed of an affiliation of semi-independent branches, were somewhat different with initiation ceremonies being akin to pure fraternal, charitable organizations such as the Masons. Extensive regalia, secret passwords, a hierarchy of membership reinforced by written 'lectures' or ceremonies and other elements were similar to Freemasonry and distinguished affiliated orders from independent societies, something that may have been alien to many labourers in rural areas. Contemporary criticism of money spent on beer by labouring members was not mirrored with criticism made on such practices and their inherent additional cost.

One group of people that were not generally explicitly excluded, but could not be members unless the rules stated, were women. In Oxfordshire, few societies permitted female members and the number of totally female societies numbered just three until two Oxford societies were established in the early 1880s (Oxford 462 and 547) and the last decade of the nineteenth century when female lodges of the affiliated orders were established. The Banbury Female Friendly Society (Banbury 44) was a pioneer, established on 1 October 1805 through the endeavours of Mrs Mary Longe of North Bar Street and was open for women aged between 16 and 45 to join. No man was permitted to enter the club room and only the vicar could attend club day. Collections to establish the society were made as far as Oxford[18] and it continued for at least 20 years as an autonomous society. The painted flag of the club was still in use in 1879, by the Hanwell Friendly Society. Another all-female society was very different in nature. The Whitchurch Women's Friendly Society (Whitchurch 698) was an annual dividing society, established in 1860 under the control of the Rector, the Rev. E. Moore.[19] Dividing societies were a particular type of friendly society, established for a limited period of normally terms of three, five or seven years after which the remaining funds were divided amongst the surviving members. The Whitchurch society was open to married women aged between 18 and 40 at joining, and unmarried women over 21, paying benefit for sickness, burial, and lying-in after childbirth. However, unlike male dividing societies where the division was made in money, the end of year division was made in tickets to be spent on clothing. The Shipton Female Friendly Society (Shipton under Wychwood 570) lasted at least 42 years from 1860. Just 22 of the 755 societies were open to both male and female members, but membership was rarely equal. Married women could join the Bloxham Friendly Society (established 1850, Bloxham 116) but they required the written permission of their husband to join. Only male members could vote on club issues so they held their wife's vote as well.

There were two types of membership, with honorary members making a regular, often annual, subscription but were not entitled to receive benefit. These were local men, and occasionally women, who wished to demonstrate their support for the club. They were of a position that did not need the security of insurance against sickness and were frequently farmers, well-off tradesmen, clergy and people of similar financial and social standing. The rules of each society determined the status of honorary members in the management, voting or other administration. Only rarely did the honorary members control the society by having a majority vote or total control. Kidlington Friendly Society (Kidlington 396) was an exception and their honorary members were large in number, 31 in 1868, and they held a separate club dinner from the rest.[20] The benefit members were those who paid a regular, pre-determined subscription and in return received the defined benefits only after a period set by the rules. This period differed between six months and three years and once served the member was declared a 'free' member and entitled to receive benefits.

A few societies, especially in the earlier years, required new members to demonstrate a minimum weekly income or be from a particular occupation. The Reform Mechanics Society (Henley on Thames 356) was open to mechanics earning a minimum of 16s a week in 1834. Printers, plumbers or 'anyone in a trade of a dangerous or pernicious nature' were excluded.[21] New members of the Wheatley Tradesmen's Hand in Hand Benefit Society (Wheatley 693) were required to earn 12s a week in 1845. However, most societies were open to all, subject to acceptance by existing members through a simple majority vote. That vote was by a show of hands, by the use of black and white balls, or peas and beans to vote against or for the prospective member.

Whilst the formation of a friendly society was often encouraged by one of the local elite, decision making and management of the club was invariably left in the democratic hands of the members. Only in a few cases did control of the society exist outside the membership. The Studley and Horton Benefit Society (Horton cum Studley 382) was under the control of the trustees who had to approve rule changes and any division of funds. Trustees were appointed to guarantee the funds of the society held by the treasurer. The Launton Provident Society (Launton 410), founded in 1863 by the Rev. C. Coker, was under the control of the vicar and honorary members, whilst the vicar had a veto on all aspects of the Kidlington Friendly Society (Kidlington 396), established 1839, until this was reversed after a protracted court case in 1878 (see appendix 2, Crimes 107). The patrons of the Fountain of Friendship Benefit Society (Adderbury 9) were the Warden and Fellows of New College, Oxford. They directed that at least one half of the directors and trustees were chosen from the honorary members, so controlled the club. However, over 95 per cent of societies held the democratic principle which gave each benefit member a vote, albeit the votes of permitted female members were often transferred to their spouse. In general, honorary members were excluded from voting so all major decisions were in the hands of the benefit members. They could decide to change rules, to divide all or a proportion of the funds of the society, or to dissolve it. Registered societies were governed by legislation and the rules of the Registrar. In theory, unregistered societies had no such limitation although any member could seek redress through the courts if they believed they had been financially disadvantaged.

In most cases, the labouring classes held a majority of the membership of the independent clubs. Agricultural labourers were normally the largest group of members in small towns and villages whilst craftsmen also comprised a substantial proportion of members. Analysis of membership of Stonesfield

Friendly Society (Stonesfield 626) for 1881 identifies that 59 per cent were from the labouring classes and 29 per cent craftsmen, representing in excess of three-quarters of all craftsmen in the village. In some places, two societies existed for those from different social groups. The Steeple Aston Friendly Society, established 1831 was also known as the Tradesmen's Society (Steeple Aston 615), whilst the Lower Heyford and Steeple Aston Friendly Society (Steeple Aston 614), established in 1836 was also known as the Labourers' or Poor Man's club, even though there was no such distinction within the club rules.

The affiliated orders were a significant component of the national picture but were rather slower to gain hold in Oxfordshire. The largest were the Independent Order of Oddfellows Manchester Unity (IOOFMU)[23] and the Ancient Order of Foresters (AOF). The IOOFMU were the largest of a number of affiliated orders utilising the word 'oddfellows' and the early history of 'oddfellowship' remains largely clouded. Some affiliated orders claimed a long lineage with the IOOFMU maintaining descent from Roman times whilst the AOF professing the longest descent of all, from Adam!

There were many fraternal organizations that used the term 'oddfellow' in their title in the eighteenth century but they were not friendly societies in the recognized sense of providing mutual insurance benefit for members against sickness and burial. The earliest evidence of an oddfellows' lodge in

Figure 3 - The percentage of members from each occupational group, Stonesfield Friendly Society, 1881[22]

Oxfordshire is the County of Oxford Loyal Independent Lodge of Odd Fellows (Oxford 477), established in 1804 (being branch number 25), and known from 1812 as the Oxford Loyal and Independent Order of Odd Fellows. This lodge existed until at least 1822 at various public houses in the city. The Loyal Wellington Lodge (Banbury 75), branch number 27 of an independent lodge of oddfellows was established at the Cock Inn, Banbury in 1817 and another lodge existed at The Blenheim, St Ebbe's in 1833 (Oxford 466). There is no evidence these were anything other than fraternal societies, membership clubs similar in nature to the Masonic lodges, but they have been included in the calendar for completeness due to the uncertainty of their status. There is no evidence of their part in a wider organization other than the reporting of a branch number implies.

The IOOFMU were formed in 1810 and they were the first affiliated order in Oxfordshire when the Bud of Friendship Lodge (Witney 704) was established in 1836 and followed two years later by the Loyal Good Intent Lodge (Oxford 506). Branches of the IOOFMU were termed lodges and were an affiliation with a high degree of independence. They belonged to geographically based districts, with the Banbury and Oxford Districts comprising many of the Oxfordshire lodges although districts were established at Witney and Woodstock for a short time. The early affiliated lodges struggled to establish themselves. Twenty-three lodges of the IOOFMU were formed in the county between 1836 and 1850, but 14 were dissolved within ten years of their establishment and only six of them remained in existence into the twentieth century.

The Ancient Order of Foresters (AOF),[24] founded in 1834, had a slower start but demonstrated greater resilience. Branches of the AOF were termed courts and again held a high degree of independence. Each affiliated branch chose whether to join a district where funds were combined to increase financial resilience, or could remain fiscally independent. The districts differed from that of the IOOFMU in that they were not strictly geographical. Branches could choose to join a district outside their area if they wished. Whilst local districts existed at Banbury and Oxford, eight Oxfordshire courts joined the popular and wealthy London United District. Court Old House at Home (Horley 370) was established in 1846 and Court Isis (Oxford 479) in 1849. The Foresters developed rapidly in terms of the number of new branches and few failed so by 1867 the number of AOF Courts exceeded IOOFMU in Oxfordshire and remained in the majority as seen in figure 4. The Foresters provided a more affordable friendly to agricultural labourers with the IOOFMU having higher entry fees,[25] and so were more popular in a largely rural county.

Other affiliated orders, such as the Independent Order of Rechabites, Salford Unity (IOORSU), a temperance movement, had an early presence with the Chipping Norton Tent being established in 1840 (Chipping Norton 192). They

failed to grow in Oxfordshire at a substantial rate and in 1883 the Order of the
Sons of Temperance (OSOT), an international movement established in the
United States and first seen in England in 1849, exceeded their number in the
county. The annual meeting of the different affiliated orders was normally held
during Whitsun week. The Annual Moveable Conference of the IOOFMU, the
governing body of the IOOFMU, was held in Oxford between 24 May and 29
May 1847 and again between 30 May and 4 June 1898.[26] Neither conference
had any impact on increasing the number of lodges in the county, and three
years after the first conference in Oxford seven lodges dissolved.

The early societies were independent and unregulated and it was not until
the Friendly Societies Act of 1793, known as George Rose's Act after the
promoter of the bill, that government showed legislative interest. This was
permissive legislation in that it allowed friendly societies to enrol their rules
and amendments with the Clerk of the Peace in return for defined benefits
but like all subsequent legislation, registration was never compulsory. One
of the main benefits for enrolled societies was that they were recognized as
corporate bodies and could litigate should they unlawfully lose funds, such as
by defalcation or embezzlement by a club official. For unregistered societies,
the only recourse was to take action for larceny, a difficult offence to prove
with the club officials lawfully holding money on behalf of members, and only
misapplying it after they had gained lawful possession.

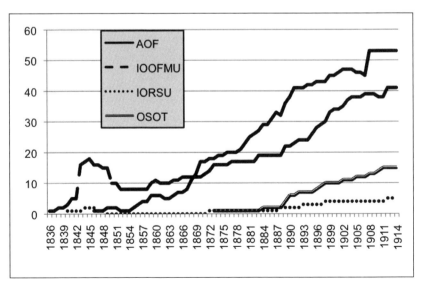

**Figure 4 - The number of branches of the main four affiliated orders in
Oxfordshire, 1836-1912**

Thirty-seven societies in Oxfordshire enrolled their rules in 1794. However, many remained unregistered and in 1803 at least 26 per cent of societies recorded in the British Parliamentary Papers, Abstract of Answers and Returns did not register. There were numerous legislative changes throughout the nineteenth century, each further regulating those societies that chose to register. After 1829 a barrister-at-law, John Tidd Pratt, was required to confirm the rules of registered societies were in conformity with the law before enrolment by the Clerk of the Peace and 1846 saw the establishment of the office of The Registrar of Friendly Societies, filled by Pratt. His department took possession of those rules enrolled with the county Clerks of the Peace between 1846 and 1855. John Tidd Pratt was a colossus of the friendly society movement from 1829 until his death in 1870. He was a national figure and shaped its development. From 1855, Pratt as Registrar was required to submit an annual report to Parliament, a series of reports that contain a wealth of information on those registered societies that submitted their returns. Pratt is known to have visited Oxfordshire in his official capacity on two occasions, firstly in December 1859 when he spoke on the subject at a public meeting and again in July 1864 when he visited Leafield to arbitrate in an acrimonious dissolution of the Old George Benefit Society (Leafield 415).

The most significant development came with the Royal Commission to Inquire into Friendly and Benefit Building Societies that presented its final report in 1874, leading to further legislation the following year. Assistant Commissioners toured the county and Sir George Young, whose area of responsibility was the southern and eastern counties of England, visited Oxfordshire in early 1872.[28] Young examined two areas in detail, Oxford City and Banbury and its hinterland, including the villages in Banbury Poor Law Union. In Oxford, the Assistant Commissioner reported six local clubs, one branch of a London society, and six branches of affiliated orders. All independent societies reported upon were registered and there must be some question whether unregistered societies were sought out. Oxford was in contrast to the Banbury Union area, where many of the village and town clubs reported upon were unregistered. Twenty-three of the settlements in the Banbury Union had a friendly society based in their parish but distribution was not even. Swalcliffe and South Newington, with an 1871 population of 356 and 372 respectively, did not have their own societies but many Swalcliffe residents were members of the Sibford Benefit Friendly Society (Sibford Gower 576).[29] All other parishes without a society had populations below 310. In contrast, residents of Hornton with a population of 500 in 1871, had access to four societies in the village; one Foresters court, one registered club, one unregistered dividing society, and a branch of a registered society based at Mollington. These four clubs had a combined membership of 80.

In Oxfordshire, unregistered societies maintained a significant presence throughout the nineteenth century. The Assistant Commissioner reported that the Banbury Union district was 'swarming with local clubs of a good average character', many of which were registered but the number unregistered was also large.[30] For the county as a whole, the overall level of unregistered societies was between 18 per cent and 21 per cent between 1850-1890. The villages in the Banbury Poor Law Union had 24 per cent of societies that were unregistered.[31] The south of Oxfordshire had far fewer societies in total and a lower proportion of unregistered societies than either the north or west of the county. Oxford itself has revealed most societies to be registered independent clubs or affiliated orders. Rural areas also had a higher percentage of unregistered clubs than the larger towns.

Friendly Societies in Banbury Poor Law Union 1872					
	Banbury	Rural parishes	% in rural parishes	Total	% total
Registered	5	22	67%	27	64%
Unregistered	1	8	24%	9	21%
Affiliated	3	3	9%	6	14%

Figure 5 - Friendly societies recorded by the Assistant Commissioner in Banbury Poor Law Union, 1872[32]

County societies were a particular type of registered society. In many places in England, a large number of the county elite supported a county friendly society. Their nature was one of strict control by appointed club officials from the honorary members and there were no democratic principles for the benefit members built into their rules. They were largely a southern phenomenon and in 1872 including Hampshire and Berkshire. Oxfordshire had one attempt at a county-wide society with the Oxfordshire Friendly and Medical Society (Charlbury 178) and it was open to anyone residing in the whole county. Its long list of trustees, including the Earl of Macclesfield, Lord Norreys, Viscount Villiers, Lord Churchill, and Sir George Dashwood signify the county elite nature of the honorary member support. It was not successful, developing only two small branches at Charlbury and Finstock and achieving a maximum membership of 95 in 1863. The South Oxfordshire Friendly Society (Henley on Thames 359) with a maximum of 145 members and the Central Oxfordshire Friendly Society (Oxford 469) with membership of over 300 for several years, run along county society lines, were only marginally more successful. Whilst the latter was larger than most independent clubs, it was small compared to many affiliated branches and a tiny proportion of overall membership. An editorial comment in *Jackson's Oxford Journal* on 3 August 1889 perhaps summed up the position in Oxfordshire. 'The main drawback of establishing a County Society in Oxfordshire is the existence of village clubs in a dubious state', referring to the generalized perception of fraudulent club officials, the regular division of funds and reforming of societies, and the technically insolvent state of many of them.

Thirty-three of the identified societies in Oxfordshire were branches of a larger friendly society, each based outside the county. These branches were financially integrated as one society, unlike the affiliated orders where the branches retained a degree of financial and administrative autonomy. In many cases, it is unclear why they spread to Oxfordshire but was likely to have been due to the local connection of an individual with the parent society. The earliest were six branches of the London Friendly Institution (LFI), established between 1825 and 1850 at Bicester, Eynsham, Fringford, Oxford, Witney and Woodstock. The society had been established in 1824 in the City of London and progressed to have nine branches in Middlesex and Surrey, a branch in Portsmouth and the Oxfordshire contingents. The LFI first advertised for members in *Jackson's Oxford Journal* between October 1825 and January 1826 and it remained relatively strong with the Oxford and Bicester branches continuing until at least 1900. The United Provident Institution (UPI), a registered society from Finchley, Middlesex, established a branch at Bicester in 1847, with a sub-branch at Chesterton in 1879. It was the largest of the 26 UPI branches in 1880 and by 1906 was the only branch outside London, with one-third of the total membership. One of the most controversial societies was the Independent Mutual Brethren Friendly Society (IMBFS), established in Middlesex in 1873. It expanded rapidly, including six branches in Oxfordshire between 1879 and 1884. However, its turbulent existence saw its officers prosecuted by the Registrar for three consecutive years from 1881 and a valuation showed a deficiency of nearly £150,000 against liabilities according to standard actuarial tables. An investigation into the society by the Registrar, published to Parliament in 1887, saw the end of the society.[33] A final, more successful society with branches was the Compton Pilgrims, a small village society from Berkshire that expanded greatly and had four branches in Oxfordshire.[34] Whilst friendly societies with branches were popular in some places, the independent club with members retaining control of their local society remained the dominant form until the early twentieth-century.

One area of friendly society development that has been given little attention is the growth of juvenile societies. All were associated with an affiliated order branch or an independent parent society, and were introduced after the Friendly Societies Act 1875 set a minimum age of membership at 16. This led directly to the growth of societies just for young members. Juvenile societies were especially important in bringing young people into a club where the main membership was ageing, hoping the young person would transfer from the juvenile to the main society when meeting the required age. Some independent clubs saw the need to attract young boys by involving them in the village club at an early age to compensate for the number of young men migrating from rural areas. Without new, young members a society was likely to rapidly become insolvent. The minimum age was relaxed soon after its introduction but juvenile societies continued to grow, with the Noble Juvenile Friendly Society (Caversham 157) of the AOF accepting children as young as three years of age and the independent Brookhampton Hand and Heart Juvenile Friendly Society (Stadhampton 590) taking members between 6-16 years before they moved on to the full society.

The headquarters of a friendly society was an important characteristic that helped define the nature of a club. The characteristics of the building, its primary use, and whether there was a bespoke club-room facility all added to a club's distinctive attributes. The headquarters was the place of meeting for members, of paying their subscription, where the books and assets of the society were retained and also the home base for the annual club day festivities. All societies identified in Oxfordshire before 1800 had a public house as their headquarters but as the century progressed the importance of public houses as a headquarters of choice reduced, although remained the favoured option for over two-thirds of clubs. The increased use of schools and other public buildings such as chapels or town halls was partly a feature of an increasing

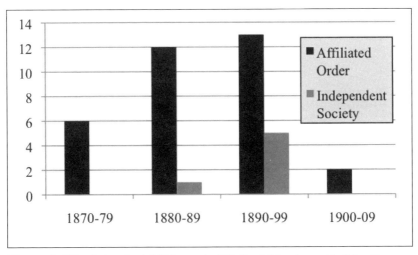

Figure 6 - The date of establishment of Oxfordshire juvenile friendly societies

temperance movement but also represented the availability of buildings suitable to hold a meeting. Not all societies that met at a school or other public building objected to alcohol consumption.

The link between a landlord and the friendly society was mutually beneficial. The landlord, who would often be an honorary members of the society or a club officer, provided the room for the meeting and retained the box in which the books, papers and assets, including cash, were retained. This feature provided a popular name for such societies as box clubs. The box would be secured by a number of locks with differing keys, frequently three or five in number and each retained by a club officer. Only when all were present could it be opened. As well as a room and retention of the box, the landlord was required to provide additional facilities and sometimes these were subject to a specific club rule. The landlord of the Fox Inn, home of the Union Society of Chipping Norton in 1836, was required to provide pens, ink and a fire.[35] In return, members were often required to pay 3d in addition to their monthly or quarterly subscription as 'wet rent' on club nights. In exchange for this sum, tokens were given by the landlord and exchanged for beer as the meeting progressed, providing a guaranteed income. The 1828 rules of the Stokenchurch Friendly Society (Stokenchurch 626) stated,

> The room wherein the society meet, shall be kept in decent order, and shall have in it a clock, watch, or hour-glass, by which the society is to regulate its time of sitting. And from Michaelmas to Lady Day a fire and candles shall be ready at the appointed time of meeting, in default of which the Inn-keeper shall forfeit one shilling.[36]

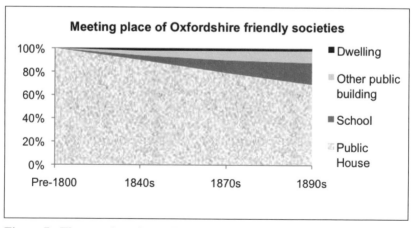

Figure 7 - The meeting place of Oxfordshire friendly societies, 1750-1900

There was increasing opposition to wet rent and it began largely to die out by mid-century. Friendly societies, with their connection to public houses and association with alcohol consumption were a prime target for the temperance movement of the nineteenth century, promoting the reduced use of alcohol. Several societies required members to 'sign the pledge', included a rule of meeting away from a public house or otherwise actively discouraged alcohol consumption by its members. One of the earliest was the United Christian Benefit Society of Banbury (Banbury 84), established in 1836. Like other clubs, they were non denominational. The Thame Temperance Provident Society (Thame 650), established in 1850, and the Nephalites (Watlington 668), established in 1861, were a non-sectarian, tee-totallers' club promoting alcohol abstinence. Other societies were formed at Primitive Methodist chapels such as the Refuge Friendly Society (Mollington 441). The Independent Order of Rechabites, Salford Unity, and the Order of the Sons of Temperance were two affiliated orders who promoted total abstinence. Henley Congregational Benefit Society (345), established in 1839, held the monthly meetings at the vestry of the congregational chapel 'to avoid the temptations of the ale-house' but the annual dinners were held at a public house.[37] The Holy Guild and Friendly Society of St Joseph and Our Blessed Lady (Heythrop 364), open only to Roman Catholics, expelled members if they were found 'tipsy' four times within twelve months with increasing fines up to that point.

Comment on alcohol consumption was regularly made in publications such as newspapers and deanery magazines, making the link to violence and unruly behaviour. Rarely did this lead to direct confrontation but in 1887 Finmere club day (Finmere 287) was disrupted when the Salvation Army paraded on a temperance agenda. They were themselves confronted by the Skeleton Army, an informal anti-temperance movement and the *Bicester Advertiser* reported that a 'serious disturbance was avoided by the sagacity of the Police'.[38] The intervention of the Police prevented any skirmish and the Salvation Army withdrew. The Skeleton Army were first active in 1881 in London and their sole purpose was to obstruct Salvation Army meetings and marches. There was no formal structure to their organization but a group of that name was active in Oxford and several of their band appeared before the City Court in November 1882.[39] The origin of the group that appeared in Finmere is unknown but was likely to have been the group that was especially active in Buckingham during that period.

The size of the clubhouse was a limiting factor for the society. In many cases buildings were adapted or bespoke clubhouses built to accommodate the club. A purpose-built club room was constructed in 1891 at The Bell Inn for the unregistered Long Hanborough Sick and Benefit Society (Hanborough 325), large enough to hold 200 people.[40] Otherwise, a move to a larger building or the formation of another society at a rival public house was the result, but this did not always go smoothly. Richard Hicks, the landlord of the Red Lion in Summertown had invested a considerable amount of money to enlarge the public house to provide room for the Summertown Benefit Society (Oxford 540) but was taken to court in January 1860 when he refused to give up the club box containing the books and assets of the club. The society had moved its headquarters to the parochial school-room at the end of 1859. Hicks was ordered to give up the box but the justices also ordered the society to pay him compensation (see appendix 2, Crimes 125).

The most popular day of the week for the regular club meeting was Monday evenings (58 per cent) followed by Tuesday evenings (18 per cent). Other weekdays were far less popular although many affiliated orders chose Saturday (16 per cent). The frequency of meetings varied between monthly (54 per cent) and quarterly (44 per cent).

One aspect of popular culture that grew alongside, if not hand in hand, with friendly societies was brass bands. The brass band movement developed in the first quarter of the nineteenth century and the end of the Napoleonic wars in 1815 saw many soldiers return to civilian life having gained experience of musical instrument playing. The first brass bands set a standard of being showy with highly coloured uniforms and having processional and ceremonial functions.[41] This early development was largely restricted to the better off and better educated of the working class, often supported financially by elites or employers who saw a works band as a symbol of their benevolence. Pure brass bands developed in the 1840s and 1850s. Mass production techniques, the relative cheapness and abundance of raw materials and the removal of tariffs led to increased competition in manufacturing and retailing. Instruments became affordable and brass bands became ubiquitous with almost every village and town having their own band at some time during the Victorian era.

The hiring of a brass band for club day music was essential for the wider celebration. It is recorded that a parade of Oddfellows in Glossop, Derbyshire was led by a band in 1816 and another at Farnworth, Greater Manchester in 1838.[42] The earliest recorded deployment of a band at a friendly society club day in Oxfordshire was at Burford in 1836 when the local band played for the Burford Friendly Society (Burford 143), followed by Benson in 1839 when the Thame Band played. Club day in Banbury saw five bands in their annual parade in July 1840. The most popular bands were deployed throughout Whitsun week. 'There is no single week in the whole year in which brass bands are in greater demand'.[43] In 1877, Titcombe's Witney Brass Band played at Stanton Harcourt, Longworth (Wiltshire), Minster Lovell, Hailey, and Leafield on consecutive days,[44] providing useful income to supplement the purchase of instruments and defray other expenses. The rise of friendly societies and brass bands can be viewed side by side in the development of leisure, the use of leisure time, the increasing confidence of the labouring classes, greater mobility, and development of independent thought. The heyday of Brass Bands mirrored that of friendly society feasts. Appendix 3 records the 266 bands deployed at friendly society club days and other associated events.

The traditional club feast with a band and parade largely died out in the middle-sized and large towns such as Witney, Bicester, Thame, and Henley by the end of the 1860s. Banbury club feast saw just three societies parade in 1856 and the decline caused comment in the local newspaper that the glory of club days had departed and, 'This was once a day of considerable account but with the establishment of village clubs it has greatly declined'.[45] In 1852 it was reported that Chipping Norton club feast was, 'A visible decline on former occasions',[46] and by 1860 Witney Whitsun week was quiet in town, occasionally 'virtually deserted' due to town-folk's attendance at village club days.[47] A decade later, Thame clubs were not even engaging a band for entertainment. However, this tradition continued in the small towns and villages where members were more willing to expend additional money on a dinner and entertainment that included a parading band, thus attracting large crowds from the towns. Here, the club feast remained a significant event into the late nineteenth century and in many villages until the early twentieth century, supported by local tourism. Watlington, Burford, and Deddington persisted with thriving club feasts.

The timing and cause of the demise of town club feasts was dictated by local circumstances. In Banbury, where the club feast was traditionally held on the first Tuesday of July, members could not spare time off work, such as those employees at the Britannia foundry and works in 1861,[48] an indication of the total reliance on wage labour. Only during the more popular Whitsun holiday period could the workers attend a club feast. The extension of the railways made leisure travel easier and relatively cheap and at Shipton under Wychwood, trains made additional stops at the local station to enable visitors to attend club day. However, the impact of the railways on village clubs drew contrasting contemporary observation. The *Bicester Advertiser* reported in 1882 under its Kirtlington report that, 'The railway is the real aggressor in curtailing village feasts and festivals', whilst the following year the *Banbury Guardian*, reporting on Deddington, commented, 'Railways and their cheap pleasure and Sir John Lublock's Bank Holiday have done much towards availability of village club feasts'.[49] Overall, they seemed to enable travel to the benefit of club days outside the main towns and certainly rural club days continued to flourish.

In many of the larger towns, fetes run by affiliated order branches became the focus of club celebration with only the occasional attempt to resurrect a parade but with little long term success. However, parades and friendly societies attained one last period of popularity in towns, providing entertainment and a visible spectacle in the 1890s when Hospital Sunday was introduced. Societies from the hinterlands congregated each with their own hired band on Whit Sunday and paraded through the town, collecting money for the Radcliffe Infirmary and Oxford Eye Hospital. This was added to any locally collected money and was donated to the respective hospitals. After 1900, funds were largely collected by house to house donation and the proceeds donated to cottage hospitals or nursing associations, again curtailing the spectacle of the parade.

Place	Dates active
Bampton	1903
Charlbury	1894-1900
Chipping Norton	1894-1900
Cowley, Iffley, Littlemore and Sandford	1892-1894
Eynsham	1890
Headington	1892-1899
Kidmore and Peppard	1909
Oxford	1890
Standlake	1900
Thame	1903-1906
Witney	1890-1899
Watlington	1901
Woodstock	1894

Figure 8 - Period of activity of Hospital Sundays

Friendly societies were also instrumental in organising a variety of other leisure activities, especially the affiliated orders. The Oddfellows' and Foresters' fetes became the normal mode of public celebration for friendly societies but the railway also provided opportunity for long distance day trips. In 1880s there were annual day excursions from Oxford for members and their families to Portsmouth and the Isle of Wight with the Great Western Railway, and to Liverpool, Blackpool, and Southport with the Great Northern. Henley members visited Windsor by train as tourism established a place in the life of the majority. The rail network had been instrumental in providing the opportunity for members and their families to travel but it was the friendly societies that seized that opportunity with extensive, day-long excursions.

This detailed calendar of Oxfordshire friendly societies has identified a substantial number of unusual societies and interesting stories. Bampton was the location of the registered office of a national society for legal clerks (Bampton 36) whilst the Fighting Cocks Inn at Thame was the headquarters of a society for Poor Law relieving officers and workhouse masters (Thame 653). Some bizarre societies were registered under the legislation, such as the Banbury Hail Storm Assurance Association (Banbury 47), established in 1849 but dramatically coming to an abrupt end in 1851 when a devastating hailstorm in north Oxfordshire and south Warwickshire wiped out crops and the funds of the society. Many more can be seen in the calendar but it was the independent club in town and village, offering insurance against sickness and death that was the backbone of friendly society development, later supported by affiliated order branches.

A total of 188 incidents involving friendly societies of crime, dishonesty, disputes or the interface with the law have been identified in Oxfordshire between 1833 and 1906, largely through court reports in newspapers. These are summarized in Appendix 2 and display a wide array of issues. Various themes have been identified including defalcation and embezzlement by club officials, disturbances at club day and disputes over the non-payment of benefit. The varying punishments and approaches to justice can be viewed, as well as the personal view of the Justices on occasions. One-third of all cases relate to members taking their club to court for non-payment of benefit or an appeal against exclusion from the club and 83 per cent of all such cases were found in favour of the member. Twenty-two cases of theft or embezzlement by officials are recorded and a harsh lesson was seen at the True Britons Friendly Society (Chinnor 189) in 1858. A three-year dividing box club, when the members removed their assets from the box held at the Royal Oak public house they discovered a £41 gold bar wrapped in cloth had been replaced by a piece of lead of the same shape. It appears a former steward of the club had misappropriated the gold and emigrated to America (see appendix 2, Crimes 46). Such cases were not confined to independent village clubs. In 1870, William Thurland, secretary of the respectable College Servants' Provident Society (Oxford 474), absconded with over £500 of club funds and a small amount from the College Servants' Benefit Society (Oxford 473). Thurland was cook and manciple of New College as well as being a city councillor for East Oxford (see appendix 2, Crimes 127).

A further third of cases involving friendly societies appearing before the courts related to assaults and drunkenness. Many were minor in nature but Bodicote club day was the scene of two serious riots within 20 years, the second on Whit Friday 1844. Approaching 50 men from Banbury and Northamptonshire attended club day and rioted for three hours causing a 'scene of riotous drunkenness' (see appendix 2, Crimes 26).[50]

The 1911 National Insurance Act has been generally accepted as the reason for the demise of all but the largest friendly societies. The Act relied upon these large societies to administer the payment of sickness benefit from July 1912 in the absence of any government agency to do so. Nine registered societies dissolved in 1912 and 16 the following year. However, the Oxfordshire research has identified that at least 30 independent societies continued until after the outbreak of the Great War and at least twelve continued beyond 1918. Unregistered clubs at Fifield and North Leigh existed into the 1920s (Fifield 284 and North Leigh 448) whilst of the registered clubs, Sibford Gower survived until 1944 (Sibford Gower 576) leaving Stratton Audley Benefit Society (Stratton Audley 629) as the last independent club in the county until it too dissolved in 1948. The discontinuity of the Great War ended club day parades and celebrations but it was not the end. Unregistered, annual-dividing friendly societies continued in the name of slate clubs, so called because the accounts of the society were kept on a chalk board at the local public house. Slate clubs provided the same benefit as friendly societies and continued widely until after World War II, although the annual celebration was changed to Christmas when the distribution of surplus funds and the club dinner took place.

From this brief introduction, the importance of friendly societies to nineteenth-century life is established. They provide a fertile ground for historical study. This current volume is the most ambitious and complete listing of any county or substantial region yet published. It is hoped that it will inspire further detailed work on the nature of societies by social and economic historians, local and family historians and those interested in fields of history such as medical history or welfare. It is disappointing that only one of the few existing studies of individual societies or of a county assessment in Oxfordshire stands up to the rigours of examination. The detailed study of more local societies, supported by material yet to be discovered, would add richness to our understanding of the importance of these institutions in the late eighteenth and nineteenth-century Oxfordshire. Within the calendar are a myriad of stories waiting to be told in full and placed in their historical context. The establishment of the Subscription Fire Engine Society (Steeple Aston 616) in 1831 in response to the 'Swing Riots', a significant period of a rural protest movement, or the obvious class tensions played out between honorary and benefit members for control of the Kidlington Friendly Society (Kidlington 396) are two such opportunities.

Since Gosden's *The Friendly Societies in England*, published in 1961, Oxfordshire has been viewed as a backwater in friendly society development, a position that has been restated by subsequent writers. However, the underestimation of registered societies in formal records, the lack of recognition of the existence of county societies, and the dismissal of unregistered clubs miscalculate the strength of the movement in the county. Oxfordshire developed societies at a much faster rate than has hitherto been recognised and many chose not to obtain voluntary registration. This volume in the *Oxfordshire Record Society* series re-balances that position and sets out Oxfordshire's place within the national picture of friendly society development.

Footnotes

[1] JOJ, 17 April 1852.
[2] Alun Howkins, 'Whitsun in 19th Century Oxfordshire', p.19, *History Workshop Pamphlet, No. 8* (Oxford 1973).
[3] BA, 28 May 1880; Howkins (1973), p.5.
[4] Simon Cordery, *British Friendly Societies, 1750-1914* (Basingstoke 2003), p.20.
[5] JOJ, 22 May 1762.
[6] OHC, QSD/R/28 – a note states that many transcripts had not been forwarded to the Registrar, and it referenced a minute book of the County Records Joint Committee, pp.66 and 104. However, this minute book cannot be located in OHC.
[7] BPP 1831-32, XXVI (90), p.21.
[8] OHC, STON I-V, records of the Stonesfield Friendly Society.
[9] OHC, The records of the Filkins Friendly Society were awaiting indexing at the time of publication and were filed under Accession 5658, R 8-52.
[10] The Foresters' Heritage Trust is located at 29-33 Shirley Road, Southampton, SO15 3EW.
[11] Roger Logan, *Friendly Society Records*, (Bury 2000); David Neave, *Mutual Aid in the Victorian Countryside, 1830-1914*, (Hull 1991), pp.107-112.
[12] P.J.H.J. Gosden, *The Friendly Societies in England, 1815-1875*, (Manchester 1963); *British Friendly Societies, 1750-1914* (Basingstoke 2003).
[13] David Neave, *Mutual Aid in the Victorian Countryside, 1830-1914*, (Hull 1991).
[14] BPP, 1803-04 XIII, *Abstract of Answers and Returns under Act for procuring Returns relative to Expense and Maintenance of Poor in England*.
[15] BPP, 1818, XIX, *Abridgement of Abstract of Answers and Returns relative to Expense and Maintenance of Poor in England and Wales*.
[16] Parliamentary Archives, SAM/A/4, p.10.
[17] Islip Friendly Institution, BA, 18 May 1894.
[18] JOJ, 19 October 1805.
[19] OHC, PAR 287/13/F3/1.
[20] Alun Howkins, 'Whitsun in 19th Century Oxfordshire', p.19, *History Workshop Pamphlet, No. 8* (Oxford 1973), pp.23-25. Howkins describes the organization of the Kidlington Friendly Society, including the control by the vicar and honorary members. From this he draws the conclusion a considerable number of village friendly societies were managed that way and that the 'local ruling class' held influence in all clubs. This view is now shown not to be the case and the example of Kidlington was totally atypical. This was a view challenged by David Neave, *Mutual Aid in the Victorian Countryside, 1830-1914*, p.89, and confirmed by this calendar of Oxfordshire Friendly Societies.
[21] TNA, FS 1/576/50, rulebook of 1834

[22] OHC, STON I/i/a/1, membership book of Stonesfield Friendly Society

[23] For a history of the IOOFMU see Daniel Weinbren, *The Oddfellows 1810-2010: 200 years of making friends and helping people*, (Lancaster 2010)

[24] Audrey Fisk reviews the development of the AOF in Oxfordshire in *Mutual Self-Help in Southern England, 1850-1912* (Southampton, 2006). She aims to assess the spread of Foresters in Southern England, not the natural stronghold of the affiliated orders. Fisk was joint historian of the AOF, and she drew most of her material from the Foresters' archives. She reports Oxfordshire as having the lowest development of new lodges in any southern county and Fisk chose Oxfordshire for the purposes of in-depth examination as a contrast to other counties where take up was better. She reports just four courts opened in the county before 1860 and only two in the 1860s. However, these statistics are far from accurate and the examination of AOF directories, supported by newspaper and other accounts demonstrate eight AOF lodges opened before 1860 and no less than nine in the 1860s as detailed in this calendar and Appendix 6. Fisk also undertakes a cursory examination of registered clubs, using selected files in TNA. Unfortunately, her conclusions fail to recognise the importance of independent clubs and she significantly misinterprets the number of village societies and their relationship with town clubs.

[25] Audrey Fisk, *Mutual Self-Help in Southern England, 1850-1912* (Southampton, 2006), p.13.

[26] Daniel Weinbren (2010), p.328-329.

[27] BPP, 1803-04 XIII.

[28] BPP, 1874, XXIII (c.997), *Friendly and Benefit Building Societies' Commission. Report of the Assistant Commissioners. Southern and Eastern Counties of England (Sir George Young)*.

[29] BG, 12 June 1879.

[30] BPP, 1874, XXIII (c.997), pp.103-104.

[31] The Assistant Commissioner reported a much higher percentage of unregistered clubs, but seven of those he reported were in fact registered.

[32] BPP, 1874, XXIII (c.997), pp.103-104.

[33] BPP, 1887, LXXVI (c.4988).

[34] Malcolm Bee, 'A friendly society case study: the Compton Pilgrims Benefit Society', *Southern History*, 11 (1989), pp.69-89.

[35] Rulebook of the Union Society of Chipping Norton (1836), TNA, FS 1/576/61.

[36] Rulebook of Stokenchurch Friendly Society (1828), TNA, FS 1/574/1.

[37] JOJ, 6 June 1857.

[38] BA, 3 June 1887.

[39] JOJ, 2 December 1882.

[40] JOJ, 23 May 1891.

[41] Arthur R. Taylor, *Brass Bands*, (St Albans, 1979), pp.17-18.

[42] Ibid, pp.9-11.

[43] WG, 8 June 1876.

[44] WG, 24 May 1877.

[45] BG, 6 July 1848.

[46] JOJ, 10 June 1852.

[47] JOJ, 27 May 1890.

[48] BG, 4 July 1861.

[49] BA, 9 June 1882 and BG, 24 May 1883.

[50] BG, 13 June 1844.

Calendar of Oxfordshire Friendly Societies

The following entries are a calendar of identified friendly societies in the pre-1974 county of Oxfordshire. The societies and branches included in the calendar include:

- All friendly societies whose rules were enrolled with the Clerk of the Peace for Oxfordshire

- All societies allocated a registration number for Oxfordshire by the Registrar of Friendly Societies from 1-392 (excluding 389)[1]

- All branches of affiliated order friendly societies

- All organizations identified as friendly societies by the payment of sickness, burial or other related benefit

- Branches of independent friendly societies

- Juvenile branches of affiliated order and independent friendly societies

- Oddfellows lodges in Oxfordshire pre-1836 (whether or not sickness, burial or other benefit payments were apparent)

There is a standard layout of each entry.

Place Name: This is based upon township or settlement and not ecclesiastical or civil parishes. The latter changed in many cases during the nineteenth century, especially with the formation of chapelries and new parishes by division. Oxford includes the parishes of St Clement's, St Thomas's, St Aldate's, Holywell, and St Giles's. Individual friendly societies are listed in alphabetical order within each place.

Friendly societies and members in 1802/3 and membership 1813/14/15: This information is from two British Parliamentary reports, and shows the reported number of friendly societies present in each place, together with the

---

[1] The Registrar allocated register number 389, and 392 onwards to Working Men's Clubs, Specially Authorized Loan Societies and Agricultural Credit Societies. Oxfordshire 228 was Lillingstone Lovell Friendly society, a village in Buckinghamshire that until 1844 was a detached part of Oxfordshire under the control of the royal manor of Kirtlington. The friendly society was established in 1860 but given an Oxfordshire registration number in error by the Registrar.

number of friendly society members resident for the period Easter 1802 to Easter 1803, and the number of friendly society members resident in each place for the three years from 1813-1815.[2]

Any issues of general interest concerning the township or settlement will be noted here. There then follows all societies whose headquarters were in the identified place. Each society is consecutively numbered throughout the entire calendar and in alphabetical order within each place. When cross-referenced, a society is identified by the name of the place followed by the consecutive number (e.g. Bampton 37 is the Tadpole Club).

Name: The name of the society, including in parentheses alternative names that were sometimes used. Where a name is fully within parentheses, the actual name of the club is unknown. **Status:** Either Enrolled (with the Clerk to the Justices [1794-1846]), Registered (with the Registrar of Friendly Societies [1846-onwards]), or unregistered. The Oxfordshire registration number will be included where appropriate. **Type:** Either Permanent friendly society and including qualifiers of Female or Juvenile where appropriate, Dividing Society (including years between division of funds where known), the name of the Affiliated Order of which it was a branch or a number of other classifications such as Burial, Cattle or Benevolent Society. Where the classification is given as just friendly society, its exact type cannot be ascertained. **Branch No.** The branch number of the affiliated order. **Established:** Either date of establishment or date first known to exist. **Registered:** If a registered or enrolled society, the date registered or enrolled. **Dissolved:** The date the society dissolved, ceased to exist or was last known to exist. **Headquarters:** Location of either the registered office of an enrolled or registered society, or the headquarters. Round parentheses indicate a definite start or end date, whereas square parentheses indicate the earliest or latest known date the headquarters was at that location. When only one year is known the date is enclosed by round parenthases. **Anniversary/feast day:** The day or date of the annual celebration.

Minimum age at entry and **Maximum age at entry**: The age at which new members could join the society. On the formation of a new society, different ages to those stated in the rules were sometimes applied to achieve sufficient members to establish the society. **Membership**: The number of benefit members at key years in the societies' history, including the earliest known, the maximum and minimum numbers and latest date known. **Primary Sources:** Brief description, location, and reference numbers of primary records in

---

[2] *Abstract of Answers and Returns under Act for procuring Returns relative to Expense and Maintenance of Poor in England*, BPP 1803-04, XIII and *Abridgement of Abstract of Answers and Returns relative to Expense and Maintenance of Poor in England and Wales*, BPP 1818, XIX

archives or other repositories. **Notes:** Key events or interesting aspects in the history of the club. Reference to 'The Registrar' means the Registrar, or after 1875 the Chief Registrar of Friendly Societies. Reference to the 'Assistant Commissioner' means Sir George Young, the Assistant Commissioner for the Southern and Eastern Counties of England of the Royal Commission appointed to inquire into friendly and benefit building societies that reported in 1874 (BPP 1874, XXIII, (c.997)).

Calendar of Oxfordshire Friendly Scoieties

Adderbury

No. of friendly societies and members 1802/3 – 2, 133
No. of members of a friendly society 1813/14/15 – 146, 130, 146
Notes: The traditional club feast attracted a large influx of visitors during 1890s (BG, 4 June 1891) and continued at Adderbury until after 1900. (See also appendix 2, Crimes 3).

1.   Adderbury Amicable Friendly Society, also Adderbury Benefit Society

Status: Enrolled, OXF 59   **Type:** Permanent friendly society
Established: 12 May 1802   **Registered:** 11 June 1836   **Dissolved:** 1893
Headquarters: White Lion Inn [1814-1820), Wheatsheaf Inn (1821-1864), Red Lion Inn (1864-1893)
Anniversary/feast day: First Wednesday in June
Minimum age at entry: 15 (from 1867) **Maximum age at entry:** 30 (from 1814), 35 (from 1867)
Membership: 44 in 1870, 49 in 1878, 35 in 1880, 31 in 1884, 21 in 1885, 12 in 1893
Primary Sources: Manuscript rules, 1814, rulebooks of 1836 and 1867, TNA, FS 3/319/59; TNA, FS 4/42/56; BPP 1874, XXIII, (c.997), p. 115.
Notes: In 1872 the Assistant Commissioner reported that members were agricultural workers and tradesmen. He also stated that when at the Wheatsheaf Inn on an unknown date, the club owned some houses but sold them for £110 and then divided the funds. The society started afresh having dispensed with some of the old members when it moved to the Red Lion in 1864. There had been several new members and funds were in a better state after it had removed to there. It paid £3 per annum for rent of the club-room. (BPP 1874, XXIII, (c.997), p.115). (See also appendix 2, Crimes 1).

Adderbury Benefit Society – see Adderbury Amicable Friendly Society, Adderbury 1

2.   **Adderbury Friendly Society, also Red Lion Friendly Society**

Status: Enrolled   **Type**: Permanent friendly society
Established: 1 January 1769   **Registered:** 1794   **Dissolved**: Last known 1805
Headquarters: Red Lion (1769-1794]
Anniversary/feast day: First Wednesday in June
Maximum age at entry: 35
Primary Sources: Manuscript rules, 1 January 1769, OHC QSD/R/1; Oxon. Cal. QS iii, p. 615.
Notes: Rules amended 4 December 1804 and recorded at Epiphany Quarter Sessions, 1805.

3.   **Adderbury Friendly Society**

Status: Registered, OXF 184   **Type**: Friendly society
Established: Earliest known 1820   **Registered:** 1820   **Dissolved**: Last known 1820
Primary Sources: TNA, FS 4/42/184; TNA, FS 2/9
Notes: There are no substantive records in TNA, only being present in indexes, which show the headquarters as Red Lion (1855) and Mr John Wyatt's (1876). An undated handwritten note from John Wyatt stating he had 'nothing to do with any friendly society whatsoever' appears in the index (TNA FS 4/42/184). The society was probably closed before 1855 but continued in the index. It is possible this is the same society as Adderbury 2 but was given a new registered number by error as reported in the Parliamentary reports.

4.   **Adderbury Juvenile Foresters Friendly Society**

Status: Juvenile branch of an affiliated order, registered, OXF 374 **Type**: AOF
Established: 1885   **Registered:** 1891   **Dissolved**: post 1918
Headquarters: Bull Inn (1885-1890), Girls' Schoolroom (1891-1918)
Anniversary/feast day: First Wednesday in June
Minimum age at entry: 8, 3 from 1908 **Maximum age at entry**: 18
Membership: 12 members in 1885, 30 in 1893, 40 in 1910.

5.   **Adderbury Loyal Friendly Society**

Status: Unregistered   **Type**: Friendly society

Established: First known 1910   **Dissolved:** Last known 1910
Headquarters: Coach and Horses (1910)
Anniversary/feast day: First Wednesday in June
Notes: The only reference to this society was in the *Banbury Guardian*, 2 June 1910.

6.   Adderbury Mutual Friendly Society

Status: Unregistered   **Type:** Annual dividing friendly society until 1845, then Permanent friendly society
Established: 1836   **Dissolved:** 1900
Headquarters: Coach and Horses [1859-1900)
Anniversary/feast day: First Wednesday in June
Membership: Over 100 in 1859, 96 in 1873, 88 in 1879, 76 in 1884, 61 in 1890, 49 in 1895, 36 in 1900
Primary Sources: BPP 1874, XXIII, (c.997), pp. 115-116.
Notes: In 1872 the Assistant Commissioner reported it was the largest club in Adderbury. It was an annual dividing society but in 1845 Mr Hawkins, a tailor, was appointed secretary and he insisted that annual division ceased and it became permanent. There was pressure to divide, mostly from the agricultural workers who could out-vote the officers. Hawkins made attempts to get members to pay for the feast but they refused and it was paid from club funds. The feast cost the club 5s a head, £25 in total and lasted two days. The club had many members who were quarrymen (BPP 1874, XXIII, (c.997), pp. 115-116).

7.   Adderbury West Sick Club

Status: Unregistered   **Type:** Friendly society
Headquarters: White Hart
Notes: Mentioned but not referenced in Nicholas Allen, *Adderbury - A Thousand Years of History*, Banbury Historical Society v.25, (Banbury, 1995).

8.   Court Hand and Heart

Status: Branch of an affiliated order **Type:** AOF **Branch no.** 6599
Established: 1879   **Registered:** 5 January 1855   **Dissolved:** post 1918
Headquarters: Bell Inn (1879-1918)
Anniversary/feast day: First Wednesday in June
Membership: 12 members in 1879, 38 in 1885, 43 in 1890, 88 in 1893, 106 in 1900, 135 in 1905, 150 in 1910
Notes: Banbury District of AOF.

9.   Fountain of Friendship Benefit Society

Status: Registered, OXF 145   **Type:** Permanent friendly society
Established: 1854   **Registered:** 5 January 1855   **Dissolved:** 1912
Headquarters: Endowed Free School (1854-1912)
Anniversary/feast day: First Wednesday in June
Minimum age at entry: 14 **Maximum age at entry:** 50
Membership: 79 in 1862, 56 in 1866, 27 in 1871, 45 in 1874, 45 in 1880, 63 in 1885, 54 in 1891, 59 in 1896, 59 in 1905, 33 in 1912
Primary Sources: Rulebook of 1854, TNA, FS 3/320/145; TNA, FS 4/42/145; Rulebook of 1854, Bodl. G.A. Oxon 8° 1308(3); BPP 1874, XXIII, (c.997), p.116.
Notes: The society was started by a local clergyman and was open to male and female members. The patrons of the society were the Warden and Fellows of New College, Oxford. At least one half of the directors and trustees were chosen from the honorary members, so they controlled the club. The only occupational exceptions for admission contained in the rules were colliers and miners, who could only become members of the deferred annuity fund of the society. Members were prohibited from subscribing to sickness benefit greater than their average weekly earnings. No sick benefit was payable to female members for the four weeks following childbirth but lying-in benefit could be purchased for an additional 6d per week, excepting unmarried women. On claiming sickness benefit, members could not leave home without the written permission from the medical officer, and when given, the time absent was limited to between 6.00 a.m. to 8.00 p.m. from 1st April to 1st October, otherwise 8.00 a.m. to 5.00 p.m. The rules permitted the appointment of agents and the incorporation of other societies (Bodl. G.A. Oxon 8° 1308(3)). The Assistant Commissioner reported in 1872 that one member had been chronically sick for ten years and had received £200 from the club. There was no provision in the rules for any reduction of benefit after a specified time but eventually they were changed to award half pay. The case was taken to the County Court and was found in favour of the club. The secretary, Mr Butler, a grocer, described in 1872 the pressure from members for the club to pay for some of the feast. That year he charged an extra amount to members for his preparation of the quinquennial returns and then gave it back to the club for payment of the band to help defray the amount spent on club day from club funds (BPP 1874, XXIII, (c.997), p.116.). In 1888 the society purchased between seven and eight acres of land for allotments for the members at a cost of £516, including conveyancing (BG, 7 June 1888).

Hook Norton and Adderbury Sick Club – see Hook Norton 362

Ironstone Works Sick Club – see Hook Norton 362

Red Lion Friendly Society – see Adderbury Friendly Society, Adderbury 2

10.   Tradesmen's Beneficial Society

Status: Registered, OXF 122   **Type:** Permanent friendly society
Established: 3 May 1847   **Registered:** 25 September 1847   **Dissolved:** 1894
Headquarters: Royal Oak Inn (1847-1894)
Anniversary/feast day: First Wednesday in June
Maximum age at entry: 30
Membership: 36 in 1855, 35 in 1860, 25 in 1865, 29 in 1870, 32 in 1877, 32 in 1884, 26 in 1891, 19 in 1894
Primary Sources: Rulebook of 1847, TNA, FS 3/319/122; TNA, FS 4/42/122; BPP 1874, XXIII, (c.997), p.116.
Notes: The society had ceased attending divine service with the other clubs on club day by 1861, although taking part in the other celebrations. They last paraded in 1873. In 1872 it was reported by the Assistant Commissioner that Mr Tustian was secretary. The club had never divided and no funds were spent on beer. The society stopped paying a member who was sick but was away from home for twelve nights and was intoxicated. The case went to court and was found against the society who was required to pay his benefit (BPP 1874, XXIII, (c.997), p.116.) It ceased to exist in 1894 but was formally dissolved by the Registrar in 1896. (See also appendix 2, Crimes 2).

Alvescot

No. of friendly societies and members 1802/3 – None
No. of members of a friendly society 1813/14/15 – None
Notes: Traditional club day continued at Alvescot until at least 1903 with a parade and church attendance.

11.   (Alvescot Friendly Society)

Status: Unregistered   **Type:** Dividing friendly society
Established: First known 1894   **Dissolved:** Last known 1914
Headquarters: Plough Inn [1903]

Anniversary/feast day: Whit Monday
Membership: 74 members in 1894
Notes: In 1894, a tea was held on club day at the vicarage after the usual celebrations (WG, 19 May 1894). In 1903 it was reported the society was over 50 years old, claiming continuity since the Victoria Friendly Society (Alvescot 14) was formed in 1860 and indicating the existence of an earlier, unregistered society (WG, 6 June 1903).

12.   Royal George Friendly Society

Status: Unregistered   **Type**: 7-year dividing friendly society
Established: 21 April 1867   **Dissolved**: 6 April 1874
Headquarters: Royal George (1867-1874)
Anniversary/feast day: Whit Monday

13.   Royal George Friendly Society

Status: Unregistered   **Type**: 7-year dividing friendly society
Established: 6 April 1874   **Dissolved**: Last known 1874
Headquarters: Royal George (1874)
Anniversary/feast day: Whit Monday
Notes: The society was established on the dissolution of Alvescot 12 on the same terms as that society (JOJ, 28 March 1874).

14.   The Victoria Friendly Society

Status: Unregistered   **Type**: 7-year dividing friendly society
Established: 28 May 1860   **Dissolved**: 21 April 1867
Headquarters: Plough Inn (1860-1867)
Anniversary/feast day: Whit Monday
Primary Sources: Rulebook of 1860, OHC, PAR 6/17/A1/1
Notes: Orange and blue ribbons were worn by members on club day.

Ambrosden

No. of friendly societies and members 1802/3 – None
No. of members of a friendly society 1813/14/15 – 5, 5, 5

15.   Amicable Society of Tradesmen

Status: Enrolled, OXF 181   **Type**: Permanent friendly society

Established: 19 July 1817 **Registered:** 1818 **Dissolved**: Last known 1818
Headquarters: Turners Arms (1817-1818)
Anniversary/feast day: Third Tuesday in June
Maximum age at entry: 35
Primary Sources: Rulebook of 1818, TNA, FS 1/579/161 and Bodl. G.A. 900(30); TNA, FS 4/42/161; OHC Oxon. Cal. QS iii, p.647
Notes: The society had a maximum of 101 members and provided superannuation of 5s a week at age 65, and 7s a week at age 70.

Arncott

No. of friendly societies and members 1802/3 – None
No. of members of a friendly society 1813/14/15 – None
Notes: The traditional club feast continued until at least 1914.

16.   Arncott Benefit Society

Status: Registered, OXF 328   **Type:** Permanent friendly society
Established: 1875   **Registered:** 1875   **Dissolved:** 1925
Headquarters: Plough Inn (1875-1925)
Anniversary/feast day: Whit Tuesday
Minimum age at entry: 16 Maximum age at entry: 45
Membership: 63 in 1876, 76 in 1880, 108 in 1885, 133 in 1891, 77 in 1899, 92 in 1905, 91 in 1910, 88 in 1914
Primary Sources: Valuations, annual returns and dissolution documents, TNA, FS 15/577; undated rulebook c.1875, Bodl. G.A. 8° 1255(3).
Notes: The rules stated payment for sickness benefit was stopped if a member was resident in the workhouse (Bodl. G.A. 8° 1255(3)). The society was approved as a provisional scheme under National Insurance Act 1911. A valuation for 1911 showed the society was insolvent from an actuarial point of view. A letter of 3 August 1923 from the accountant and auditor called for drastic reform given the large and growing deficiency (TNA, FS 15/577). It also stated most members were involved in agriculture. The members of the society marched to Ambrosden each year to attend the parish church on club day.

17.   Arncott Friendly Institution, also Arncott Friendly Society

Status: Registered, OXF 216   **Type**: Permanent friendly society
Established: 1 June 1858   **Registered:** 2 May 1859   **Dissolved**: 1875
Headquarters: Plough Inn (1858-1860]

Anniversary/feast day: Whit Tuesday
Minimum age at entry: 16 Maximum age at entry: 45
Primary Sources: Rulebook of 1859, TNA, FS 1/581/216; TNA, FS 4/42/216

> **Arncott Friendly Society** – see Arncott Friendly Institution,
> Arncott 17

Ascott under Wychwood

No. of friendly societies and members 1802/3 – None
No. of members of a friendly society 1813/14/15 – None

18.   Ascott under Wychwood Benefit Club

Status: Unregistered   **Type**: Friendly society
Established: 1863   **Dissolved**: 1881
Anniversary/feast day: Third Tuesday in July
Notes: The society never enrolled and became weaker over time. The club was dissolved in 1881 and funds divided between existing members (CNDM, May 1881). The location of the headquarters is unknown.

19.   Ascott under Wychwood Friendly Society

Status: Registered, OXF 35   **Type**: Friendly society
Established: First known 1834   **Registered:** 10 May 1834   **Dissolved**: Last known 1834
Headquarters: Swan Inn (1834)
Primary Sources: TNA FS 4/42/35
Notes: The main Registrar's file is absent in TNA although indicated in the index at FS 1/575/35.

20.   Ascott under Wychwood Friendly Society

Status: Registered, OXF 200   **Type**: 5-year dividing friendly society
Established: 21 July 1857   **Registered:** 29 January 1858   **Dissolved**: 1863
Headquarters: Churchill Arms Tavern (1857-1863)
Anniversary/feast day: Third Tuesday in July
Membership: 27 members in 1863
Primary Sources: Rulebook of 1858, TNA FS 1/581/200; TNA FS 4/42/200; TNA FS 2/9

Milton, Shipton and Ascott United Provident Society – see
Shipton under Wychwood 565

Aston and Cote

No. of friendly societies and members 1802/3 – None
No. of members of a friendly society 1813/14/15 – None
Notes: Traditional club day of the Aston Friendly Society (Aston 22) continued
until at least 1913.

21.   Aston Friendly Society

Status: Registered, OXF 159   **Type**: Permanent friendly society
Established: 25 March 1808   **Registered:** 8 October 1811   **Dissolved**: Last
known 1811
Anniversary/feast day: Whit Monday
Minimum age at entry: 14 **Maximum age at entry**: 40
Primary Sources: Rulebook of 1811, TNA FS 1/579/159; TNA FS 4/42/159
Notes: New members were admitted by a vote by existing members, submitting
a bean (for) or pea (against). The rules described it as a society for Aston and
Cote (TNA FS 1/579/159).

22.   Aston Friendly (Benefit) Society

Status: Unregistered   **Type**: 5-year dividing friendly society
Established: 3 June 1844   **Dissolved**: Last known 1913
Headquarters: Schoolroom (1906)
Anniversary/feast day: Whit Tuesday (Whit Wednesday in 1890)
Membership: 105 members in 1897
Notes: Club dinner was held in Mr Kirby's barn in 1890 (WG, 31 May 1890).

23.   Aston Self-Help Club

Status: Unregistered **Type**: Friendly society
Established: 1881   **Dissolved**: 1884
Headquarters: Lamb Inn (1881-1884)
Anniversary/feast day: Whit Tuesday

24.   Universalist Friendly Society

Status: Unregistered   **Type**: 7-year dividing friendly society

Established: March 1844   **Dissolved**: Last known 1847
Headquarters: Red Lion (1844-1847)
Anniversary/feast day: Whit Friday
Minimum age at entry: 14 **Maximum age at entry**: 40
Membership: Almost 40 members in 1844
Notes: The divine service for the club on club day, 1844 saw the largest congregation at church since its consecration (JOJ, 8 June 1844). The society was subject to embezzlement of £3 by Richard Waite in 1847 (see Appendix 2, Crimes 4).

Aston Rowant

No. of friendly societies and members 1802/3 – None
No. of members of a friendly society 1813/14/15 – None

25.   Hand in Hand Friendly Society

Status: Unregistered   **Type**: Friendly society
Established: 1853   **Dissolved**: Last known 1865
Headquarters: Lambert Arms [1858-1865)
Anniversary/feast day: Whit Monday
Membership: Over 90 members in 1865

Bampton

No. of friendly societies and members 1802/3 – 2, 129
No. of members of a friendly society 1813/14/15 – 121, 123, 122
Notes: The Primrose League proposed forming a benefit society in Bampton 1886, and a committee was formed to draw up the rules. However, there is no indication a society was actually established (JOJ, 6 November 1886). In 1898, *Jackson's Oxford Journal* reported on Bampton that 'To those who remember these societies in days gone by there seems to be a great falling off, both in attendance of members themselves and also in interest taken in these gatherings by the inhabitants generally' (JOJ, 4 June 1898).

26.   Bampton branch of IMBFS

Status: Branch of a registered society **Type**: Permanent friendly society
Established: 1 June 1881   **Dissolved**: Last known 1881
Membership: 12 members enrolled on establishment of the branch

27.   Bampton Friendly Society

Status: Enrolled   **Type**: Friendly society
Established: 3 July 1795   **Registered:**   **Dissolved**: Last known 1804
Anniversary/feast day: Whit Monday
Primary Sources: Oxon. Cal. QS iii, p.615
Notes: Rules of 6 April 1804 were enrolled at the Epiphany Quarter Session, 1805.

28.   Bampton Friendly Society, also Bampton Old Club

Status: Registered, OXF 52   **Type:** 7-year dividing friendly society
Established: 1810   **Registered:** 1810   **Dissolved:** 1872
Headquarters: Talbot and Fleur de Lis alternately [1837-1867], Elephant and Castle (1871-1872)
Anniversary/feast day: Whit Monday (Whit Wednesday in 1846, Whit Tuesday in 1847)
Minimum age at entry: 14 (1810), 12 (1827) Maximum age at entry: 36, 45 (from 1827), no new members (from 1830), 35 (from 1837)
Membership: 36 in 1810, 100 in 1841, 100 in 1855, 120 in 1858, 120 in 1864, 99 in 1871
Primary Sources: Manuscript rules of 1810, rulebooks of 1813 and 1827, TNA, FS 1/576/52; TNA, FS 4/42/52
Notes: 36 members signed the articles of incorporation in 1810. To vote on the enrolment of a new member, peas and beans were used to determine acceptance. A bean was 'for' and a pea 'against' a proposed member (FS 1/576/52). The hay harvest prevented many villagers from attending club day in 1846 (BG, 4 June 1846). A new flag was made for the society by Mr Stevens of King & Stevens, containing the words, 'Love the brotherhood, fear God, honour the King' (JOJ, 10 June 1843). The society purchased just over 9 acres of land in 1849, a field called 'California' near to the town and it was allotted for the use of members to be occupied as gardens. Selection for use of the allotment was by a ballot (JOJ, 27 January 1849). The land was advertised for sale in JOJ on 27 April 1872 at the dissolution of the society. In 1866 it was reported that funds of the society had reduced due to a large amount of sickness (JOJ, 6 April 1867).

Bampton Old Club - see Bampton Friendly Society, Bampton 28

29.   Bampton Self-Help Society

Status: Unregistered   **Type**: 3-year dividing friendly society
Established: 1881   **Dissolved**: 1890
Headquarters: Lamb Inn (1881-1890)
Anniversary/feast day: Whit Monday
Notes: A 3-year dividing society that re-formed in 1890 as a registered club
(Bampton 37).

30.   Bampton Self-Help Society

Status: Registered, OXF 369   **Type:** 5-year dividing friendly society
Established: 1890   **Registered:** 11 February 1890   **Dissolved:** 1912
Headquarters: Lamb Inn (1890-1912)
Anniversary/feast day: Whit Monday
Minimum age at entry: 16 Maximum age at entry: 40
Membership: 51 members in 1891 32 in 1899, 24 in 1905, 12 in 1912
Primary Sources: Rulebook of 1890, TNA, FS 3/322/369; FS 4/42/369
Notes: The rules permitted a maximum membership of 999 (TNA, FS
3/322/369). The society had insufficient funds to hold a dinner or hire a band
by 1907 (WG, 25 May 1907), and dissolved on 21 September 1912 with £3
funds.

31.   Court Alexandra

Status: Branch of an affiliated order, OXF 296 **Type**: AOF **Branch no.** 5298
Established: 1869   **Registered:** 30 March 1869   **Dissolved**: 1869
Headquarters: Fleur de Lis (1869)
Minimum age at entry: 18 **Maximum age at entry**: 40
Primary Sources: Rulebook of 1869, TNA, FS 1/582/296; TNA, FS 4/42/296
Notes: North Wiltshire district of AOF. The Court was reported as being
established in the Executive Council Report of AOF, April 1869, p.10 but it is
not reported upon after that date and does not appear in any annual directories.

32.   Court The Bush

Status: Branch of an affiliated order   **Type**: AOF **Branch no.** 8000
Established: 1891   **Dissolved**: Post 1918
Headquarters: New Inn (1891-1918)
Anniversary/feast day: Whit Tuesday

Membership: 52 members in 1895, 51 in 1901, 151 in 1905, 144 in 1910
Notes: Oxford District of AOF. There was an announcement of a juvenile branch of this Court (Bampton 33).

33.   Court The Bush, Juvenile branch,

Status: Juvenile branch of an affiliated order **Type**: AOF
Established: 1895   **Dissolved**: Last known 1895
Notes: Formation of the juvenile branch of Court the Bush (Bampton 32) was announced as due in July 1893 (WG, 15 June 1895) but there is no record of its establishment in the Foresters' Heritage Trust archives.

34.   [The Eagle Club]

Status: Unregistered   **Type**: Friendly society
Established: First known 1885   **Dissolved**: Last known 1885
Headquarters: The Eagle (1885)
Anniversary/feast day: Whit Monday

35.   England's Glory Lodge

Status: Branch of an affiliated order **Type**: IOOFMU **Branch no.** 3436
Established: 1843   **Dissolved**: 1847
Headquarters: Fleur de Lis (1843-1847)
Anniversary/feast day: Whit Monday, Whit Tuesday (1847)
Membership: 24 members in 1844, 17 in 1846
Notes: Oxford District (1844-45) and then Faringdon District (1846) of IOOFMU.

> **Law Clerks Mutual Benefit Society** – see The Legal Provident Institution, Bampton 36

36.   The Legal Provident Institution, also Law Clerks Mutual Benefit Society

Status: Registered, OXF 358   **Type**: A specially authorized collecting society
Established: 1886   **Registered:** 2 December 1886   **Dissolved**: 1892
Headquarters: Bampton
Anniversary/feast day: On a day in Easter week
Minimum age at entry: 16 **Maximum age at entry**: 45
Primary Sources: Rulebook of 1886, TNA, FS 3/322/358; FS 4/42/358

Notes: The society was a national society and was open to clerks of barristers, conveyancers, special pleaders, and solicitors, and clerks in all public law courts and offices. Benefit was for sickness, death, and for assistance (by registration) to enable members out of work to gain employment. If a member left the profession, they could continue to be a member. Members could receive a pension at 65 years of 9s a week. The annual meeting of the society was during Easter week at a place to be agreed in England. J.J. Smith of Bampton was appointed secretary at the inauguration of the society (JOJ, 19/6/1886). A letter of 11 January 1892 from John James Smith of Shaftesbury Hall Chambers, Bournemouth states the society was not successful and it ceased to exist 'long ago' (FS 4/42/358).

37.   The Tadpole Club

Status: Unregistered   **Type**: Friendly society
Established: First known 1843   **Registered:**   **Dissolved**: Last known 1844
Headquarters: Trout Inn, Tadpole Bridge (1843-1844)
Anniversary/feast day: Whit Tuesday
Membership: 60 members in 1843
Notes: At the removal of the cloth after dinner, *Non Nobis Domine*, a Latin hymn, was chanted by the members.

38.   The Victoria Club

Status: Registered OXF 152   **Type:** 7-year dividing friendly society
Established: 1850   **Registered:** 19 May 1851   **Dissolved:** 1857
Headquarters: Horse Shoe Inn (1850-1857)
Anniversary/feast day: Whit Monday
Minimum age at entry: 8 Maximum age at entry: 40
Membership: Commenced with 15 members, 43 members at dissolution in 1857
Primary Sources: Rulebook of 1851, TNA, FS 1/579/152; TNA, FS 4/42/152
Notes: Rule 15 stated that at the funeral of a member, all club members were required to attend, 'walking two and two as their names stand in the club book' (TNA, FS 1/579/152). The society dissolved and immediately reformed as Bampton 39.

39.   The Victoria Club

Status: Registered, OXF 196   **Type**: 14-year dividing friendly society, changed to 7-year dividing friendly society in 1864

Established: 1857   **Registered:** 4 August 1857   **Dissolved:** 1904
Headquarters: Horse Shoe Inn (1857-1871), Wheatsheaf Inn, Mill Street (1871-1901), New Inn (1901-1902]
Anniversary/feast day: Whit Monday
Membership: 80 members in 1857, 83 in 1860, 127 in 1865, 71 in 1870, 86 in 1874, 109 in 1877, 60 in 1880, 35 in 1885, 31 in 1899, 14 in 1904
Primary Sources: Rulebook of 1857 and substantial rule changes from 1864, TNA, FS 3/320/196; TNA, FS 4/42/196
Notes: This was a re-formed society from a club of the same name (Bampton 38). The original rules of 1857 permitted the division of two-thirds of funds after 14 years. However, the rules changed from a 14-year to 7-year dividing society in 1864 and two-thirds of funds were divided then. The society was dissolved on 20 August 1904 with 14 members and £15 16s 2d.

Banbury

No. of friendly societies and members 1802/3 – 3, 278
No. of members of a friendly society 1813/14/15 – 479, 508, 536
Notes: Banbury club feast was traditionally held on the first Tuesday in July, a day observed as a midsummer holiday by the artisans of Banbury. The friendly society parade was in order of seniority of club by age. In 1843, the *Banbury Guardian* reported that club day had never passed off so well, with no rioting and not a single charge (BG, 8 July 1843) but by 1846 it was said, 'The glory of club days has, in a great measure departed' (BG, 9 July 1846), citing the growth of village clubs as the cause. The traditional parade had been abandoned by 1860s and it was replaced by a joint Oddfellows and Foresters fete, held at Bodicote Grange. In 1874 over 2,000 people attended the fete (BG, 9 July). (See also appendix 2, Crimes 7).

40.   Banbury Amicable Society

Status: Enrolled   **Type:** Permanent friendly society
Established: 15 March 1794   **Registered:** 1794   **Dissolved:** Last known 1794
Maximum age at entry: 36
Primary Sources: Manuscript rules of 1794, OHC, QSD/R/2
Notes: The rules of the society permitted a maximum of 81 members.

41.   Banbury Cross Female Lodge

Status: Branch of an affiliated order **Type:** IOOFMU **Branch no.** 7800

Established: 1903 **Dissolved:** Post 1914
Headquarters: Cadbury Memorial Hall (1903-1912]
Membership: 31 members in 1905, 35 in 1907, 56 in 1910, 227 in 1913
Notes: Banbury District of IOOFMU.

42.   Banbury Cross Subordinate Division

Status: Branch of an affiliated order **Type:** OST **Branch no.** 994
Established: 1902 **Dissolved:** Last known 1910
Headquarters: Cadbury Memorial Hall (1905-1910)
Membership: 62 members in 1905, 93 in 1910

43.   Banbury District of IOOFMU

Status: Affiliated Order district, OXF 147   **Type:** IOOFMU
Established: 1852   **Registered:** 25 March 1852   **Dissolved:** Post 1918
Headquarters: White Hart Inn [1855-1875]
Anniversary/feast day: First Tuesday in July
Minimum age at entry: 16 Maximum age at entry: 45
Membership: In 1875 there were 773 members of the IOOFMU in the
Banbury District lodges
Primary Sources: Blank lodge rules for Banbury District, Bodl. G.A. 8°
635(2); undated rulebook of Banbury District Widows and Orphans Fund,
Bodl. G.A. 8° 635(3); Rules dated 1846, Bodl. G.A. 8°635(4); Banbury District
Branch AGM report 1886, OHC, O127/A/10
Notes: This society was the district lodge of the IOOFMU, and ran a district
Widows and Orphans fund.

44.   Banbury Female Friendly Society

Status: Enrolled, OXF 183   **Type:** Permanent friendly society
Established: 1 October 1805   **Registered:** 1805   **Dissolved:** Last known
1825
Headquarters: North Bar Street (1805-1825)
Anniversary/feast day: First Tuesday in July
Minimum age at entry: 16 **Maximum age at entry:** 45
Primary Sources: TNA, FS 4/42/183
Notes: This was the first all-female society and one of only five in the county
until the last decade of the nineteenth century when women's branches of
affiliated orders were established. The founder of the club was Mrs Mary
Longe of North Bar Street, Banbury. The rules of the society were published in

Herbert (1948), p.129. An admission fee of 2s 6d entitled the member to a rule book, a blue bow, and a wand. The blue bow had to be worn on the member's left side at club days and other events. All members resident within 15 miles were required to attend the club day. No man was admitted to the club room or on feast day except for the vicar. In October 1805 there was a collection for this society in Oxford (JOJ, 19 October 1805). The club dinner was held at the White Lion Inn in 1825 (JOJ, 23 July 1825). The society's painted flag was made by Messrs Chayney and Gublin, Banbury in 1808 (BG, 5 June 1879), and was later used by the Hanwell Amicable Society (Hanwell 326).

45.   Banbury Friendly Society

Status: Enrolled, OXF 186   **Type:** Friendly society
Headquarters: Plough Inn
Primary Sources: Undated rulebook and amendments, TNA, FS 1/580/186; TNA, FS 4/42/186; TNA, FS 2/9
Notes: The society was enrolled before 1855 (TNA, FS 2/9) but no other details are recorded.

46.   Banbury Friendly Societies Medical Association

Status: Registered, OXF 364   **Type:** Society for medical assistance
Established: 1888   **Registered:** 1888   **Dissolved:** Last known 1910
Headquarters: 7 New Land (1888-1910)
Membership: 4,110 members in 1891, 3,779 in 1910
Notes: Open to members of friendly societies in Banbury giving greater access to medical treatment.

47.   Banbury Hail Storm Assurance Association

Status: Enrolled, OXF 136   **Type:** Friendly society
Established: 1 May 1849   **Registered:** 20 June 1849   **Dissolved:** Last known 1851
Headquarters: Red Lion Inn (Hotel) (1849-1851)
Primary Sources: Rulebook of 1849, TNA, FS 1/579/136; TNA, FS 4/42/136
Notes: The object of this society was 'for the mutual assurance against loss by hailstorms'. It was open to all farmers whose land was within twelve miles of Banbury and provided insurance against damage to crops caused by hail storms. A tremendous thunderstorm in south Warwickshire was reported in June 1851 and the society suffered considerable losses (JOJ, 28 June and 5 July 1851). There is no mention of the society after this date and it appears this

storm ended the society in favour of larger institutions such as the Norwich Hail Storm Insurance Society. A letter of 8 October 1878 was returned to the Registrar marked 'no such society' (TNA, FS 4/42/136).

48.   Banbury Juvenile Foresters Friendly Society

Status: Juvenile branch of an affiliated order, OXF 359 **Type**: AOF
Established: 1886   **Registered:** 1886   **Dissolved**: Last known 1910
Headquarters: Temperance Hall (1886-1910)
Membership: 95 members in 1887, 104 in 1891, 82 in 1895, 51 in 1900.
Notes: A Juvenile Society for Court Prince of Wales (Banbury 65) and Court Royal Crown (Banbury 67).

49.   Banbury Mutual Cattle Assurance Association

Status: Enrolled, OXF 134   **Type**: Annual dividing cattle assurance society
Established: 1 May 1848   **Registered:** 19 July 1848   **Dissolved**: 1898
Headquarters: National School (1855), Red Lion Hotel [1873-1895]
Anniversary/feast day: Last Tuesday in April or first Tuesday in May
Membership: 190 members in 1863
Primary Sources: Rulebooks of 1848 and 1873, TNA, FS 3/319/134; TNA, FS 4/42/134; BPP 1874, XXIII, (c.997), p. 107
Notes: The object of the society was to insure against loss of cattle from pleuro-pneumonia or similar diseases. It was open to all within twelve miles of Banbury. Membership cost was 1s per head of cattle per annum. The society was cancelled by request on 15 June 1900, having dissolved in 1898. In 1872, 3-4,000 cattle were insured. A 'special club' was started at the time of the cattle plague (BPP 1874, XXIII, (c.997), p. 107).

50.   Banbury and Neithrop Clothing Society

Status: Enrolled, OXF 135   **Type**: Annual dividing benevolent society
Established: 1849   **Registered:** May 1849   **Dissolved**: 13 March 1935
Headquarters: National School (1855-1878), Cherwell British School (1905-1910]
Anniversary/feast day: Second or third Saturday in October
Membership: 426 members in 1876, 560 in 1905, 611 in 1910, 222 in 1934, 281 in 1936
Primary Sources: Rulebook of 1849, TNA, FS 15/1042
Notes: Members were divided into subscribers and donors. Subscribers had to pay 4d per week from the end of March to the end of September and

tickets were given out on the last Monday in September to the value of their subscription plus a proportionate amount subscription from honorary donors. At a meeting on the second or third Monday in October clothing was laid out and members selected them to the value of their ticket. New members were required to receive a recommendation from an existing subscriber or donor member. The society was 'for the very poor and not those who could take care of themselves'. On 13 March 1935 a request to cancel the registration of the society was made on the grounds that all members had withdrawn from the society and there were no funds remaining.

51.   Banbury Refuge for the Afflicted

Status: Enrolled, OXF 92   **Type:** Permanent friendly society
Established: 1844   **Registered:** 1 January 1845   **Dissolved:** Last known 1852
Headquarters: Infant Schoolroom, Church Passage (1845-1852)
Anniversary/feast day: First Tuesday in July
Minimum age at entry: 14 Maximum age at entry: 45
Membership: 54 members in 1846, 44 in 1850
Primary Sources: Rulebook of 1852, TNA, FS 1/578/92; undated rulebook, Bodl. G.A. 8° 635(6); TNA, FS 4/42/92
Notes: Open to male and female members of the Borough of Banbury. Members of Banbury Mutual Aid society could be members but no other Friendly society member could belong. The club day was described as 'The annual tea meeting'. The maximum age of joining was 60 until there were ten members of the society, then a maximum of 45. Lying-in benefit was paid to female members. Subscriptions were mostly from the labouring classes (JOJ, 11 July 1846). A burial society was also attached to this club.

52.   Banbury Sick Fund Society

Status: Enrolled, OXF 91   **Type**: Permanent friendly society
Established: 1846   **Registered:** 6 January 1846   **Dissolved**: Last known 1846
Headquarters: Talbot Inn (1846)
Anniversary/feast day: Easter Monday
Minimum age at entry: 18 **Maximum age at entry**: 30
Primary Sources: Rulebook of 1846, TNA, FS 1/578/91 and Bodl. G.A. 8° 635(5); TNA, FS 4/42/91

Notes: A society for sickness, blindness, lameness, and deafness. All members were required to be a member of the Banbury Society. A returned envelope of 3 January 1867 to the Registrar stated the society was dissolved.

53.   Banbury Working Man's Co-operative Friendly Society

Status: Enrolled, OXF 151   **Type:** Permanent friendly society
Established: 1851   **Registered:** 11 October 1851 **Dissolved:** 1852
Headquarters: Store Room, Church Lane (1851)
Primary Sources: Rulebook of 1851, TNA, FS 1/579/151; TNA, FS 4/42/151; TNA, FS 2/9
Notes: The object of the society was 1. To improve the social and domestic conditions of members, 2. To encourage honesty and fair dealing. This was to be achieved by 'raising sufficient capital to establish stores for enabling them to purchase food, firing, clothes, or other necessities, or the tools, implements or materials of their respective trades or calling'. Members could purchase up to five shares and if sick or unemployed, they could withdraw expenses. There was also death benefit with the capital paid to widow or children (TNA, FS 1/579/151). A note in TNA, FS 2/9 states the society was 'Not for sickness'. In 1852 the annual meeting was at the Star Inn but it ceased to exist after that time with the formation of a new club, the United Britons Friendly Society (Banbury 83).

54.   The Beneficial Society

Status: Enrolled, OXF 15   **Type:** Permanent friendly society
Established: 7 July 1806   **Registered:** 1838   **Dissolved:** Last known 1843
Headquarters: Cock Inn [1838-1843)
Anniversary/feast day: First Tuesday in July
Maximum age at entry: 30, 35 after 1838
Primary Sources: Rulebook of 1838, TNA, FS 1/574/15 and Bodl. G.A.8° 635(12); TNA, FS 4/42/15
Notes: The society had a maximum membership of 101 and provided superannuation at age 65 (TNA, FS 1/574/15). In 1840 it was said to be the oldest established club in Banbury (JOJ, 11 July 1840) but had only limited members by 1843 (JOJ, 8 July 1843).

55.   British Queen Benefit Society

Status: Enrolled, OXF 133   **Type:** Friendly society
Established: First known 1849   **Registered:** 1849   **Dissolved:** 1849

Headquarters: White Hart Inn, Cow Fair (1849)
Primary Sources: Rulebook of 1849, Bodl. G.A. 8° 635(9); TNA, FS 2/9/133
Notes: This society was formed by some dissident members of the British Queen Lodge, IOOFMU (Banbury 72). It amalgamated with that lodge on an unspecified date (TNA, FS 2/9/133).

56.   Britannia Works Sick Fund

Status: Unregistered   **Type**: Shop club
Established: First known 1871   **Dissolved**: Last known 1871
Headquarters: Samuelson & Co., Britannia Works, Banbury
Anniversary/feast day: First Tuesday in July
Membership: 650 members in 1872
Primary Sources: Rules of 1871 printed in BPP 1874, XXIII, (c.997), pp.107, 112)
Notes: This was a mutual aid society for employees of Samuelson's iron foundry, a shop club. It was compulsory and membership ceased if an employee left. The members contributed fortnightly. It accumulated up to £100 annually for division, but this was changed with payments lowered so there was far less balance at year end. A member could draw a maximum of one years' benefit for sickness. Samuelson's made no contribution to the club.

57.   Cadbury Tent

Status: Branch of an affiliated order **Type**: IORSU **Branch no.** 134
Established: 1872   **Registered:** 1872   **Dissolved**: Last known 1910
Headquarters: Temperance Hall [1887-1910)
Membership: 86 in 1905
Notes: The society had a juvenile branch (Banbury 69).

58.   Christian Mutual Benefit Society

Status: Enrolled, OXF 143   **Type**: Permanent friendly society
Established: 7 June 1854   **Registered:** 1854 **Dissolved**: Last known 1855
Headquarters: Primitive Methodist Chapel (1853-1855)
Anniversary/feast day: Whit Wednesday
Minimum age at entry: 18 **Maximum age at entry**: 45
Primary Sources: Rulebook of 1855, TNA, FS 4/42/143
Notes: The meeting place was the Primitive Methodist Chapel, or any other place agreed except inns and public houses. Membership of the society was for religious or conscientious persons of every denomination. There were different

classes of benefit and no-one received benefit greater than five-sixths of their weekly wage. (TNA, FS 1/579/143). The annual meeting was a public tea.

59.   (Conservative) Friendly Society

Status: Enrolled, OXF 54   **Type**: Permanent friendly society
Established: 15 October 1837   **Registered:** 8 October 1837   **Dissolved**: 1857
Headquarters: White Hart Inn (1837-44), Buck & Bell Inn (1844-1853), White Hart Inn (1853-1857)
Anniversary/feast day: First Tuesday in July
Maximum age at entry: 40
Membership: 93 in 1844, 95 in 1856
Primary Sources: Rulebook of 1837, TNA FS 1/576/54 and Bodl. G.A. 8° 635(10); TNA FS 4/42/54; BPP 1874, XXIII, (c.997), p.106-7
Notes: The society had a maximum of 100 members who had to reside within three miles of Banbury on admission (FS 1/576/54). It was one of the three principle clubs in Banbury in 1843 (JOJ, 8 July 1843). The society was mostly made up of artisans and shopkeepers. It had many honorary subscribers and was political, formed in opposition to the Reformers Friendly society (Banbury 79). The society broke up in 1857, having divided £800 between its members a few years earlier. It re-formed as a new society, Banbury 60. (See also appendix 2, Crimes 6).

60.   Conservative Friendly Society

Status: Registered, OXF 156   **Type**: Friendly society
Established: 1857   **Registered:** 12 February 1857   **Dissolved**: 1867
Headquarters: White Hart Inn (1857-1867)
Anniversary/feast day: First Tuesday in July
Maximum age at entry: 35
Membership: 88 members in 1860, 91 in 1864
Primary Sources: Rulebook of 1857, TNA, FS 1/579/156; TNA, FS 4/42/156; BPP 1874, XXIII, [c.997], p.106
Notes: At the time of joining, a member had to live within three miles of Banbury. The rulebook of 1857 states the society was formed in 1837 indicating continuity from Banbury 59. The society had £500 loaned on mortgage, but it was called in and divided amongst the members. However, a run of four or five years of sickness by ten to twelve old men led to funds falling very low and the society consequently broke up (BPP 1874, XXIII, (c.997), p.106). It re-formed as a new society, Banbury 61.

61.   Conservative Friendly Society

Status: Registered, OXF 283   **Type**: Permanent friendly society
Established: 1867   **Registered:** 31 October 1867   **Dissolved**: 5 January 1885
Headquarters: (Old) George Inn (1867-1880]
Anniversary/feast day: First Tuesday in July
Maximum age at entry: 35
Membership: 29 members in 1867, 27 in 1871, 22 in 1877, 13 in 1885.
Primary Sources: TNA, FS 1/582/283; TNA, FS 4/42/283; BPP 1874, XXIII, (c.997), pp.106-107)
Notes: Re-formed from society Banbury 60. The Assistant commissioner noted in his report that this was a new society and was not political. In general, friendly societies avoided party politics and the Reformers Friendly Society (Banbury 79) and previous incarnations of the Conservative Friendly Society were exceptions to that general rule. The society was formed after the old Conservative Society divided its funds and dissolved. The secretary, Mr Miles stated in 1872 that the average age of members was 50 years (BPP 1874, XXIII, [c.997]), pp.106-107). It was dissolved in 1885 with 13 members and £95. (See also appendix 2, Crimes 8).

62.   Constitutional Friendly Society

Status: Enrolled   **Type**: Permanent friendly society
Established: 28 November 1758   **Registered:** 1794   **Dissolved**: Last known 1794
Anniversary/feast day: First Tuesday in July
Maximum age at entry: 35
Primary Sources: Manuscript rules of 3 March 1794, OHC, QSD/R/3
Notes: The rules stated the society could have a maximum of 141 members.

63.   Constitutional Union Friendly Society

Status: Enrolled **Type**: Permanent friendly society
Established: 21 March 1794   **Registered:** 1794   **Dissolved**: Last known 1794
Headquarters: Blue Boar (1794)
Anniversary/feast day: Whit Monday
Primary Sources: Manuscript rules of 1794, OHC, QSD/R/4

Notes: The rules stated the society could have a maximum of 41 members and they must live within ten miles of Banbury. Labourers and manual servants were excluded from membership. The society had a superannuation benefit of 3s a week from age 65, increasing to 4s 6d from 70 years.

64.   Court Loyal Britannia

Status: Branch of an affiliated order, OXF 224 **Type**: AOF **Branch no.** 3112
Established: 1859   **Registered:** 11 October 1856   **Dissolved**: 1862
Headquarters: Star Inn, High St (1859-1861), Plough Inn, Cornhill (1862)
Anniversary/feast day: First Tuesday in July
Minimum age at entry: 18 **Maximum age at entry**: 45
Primary Sources: Rulebook of 1859, TNA, FS 1/581/224; FS 4/42/224
Notes: The branch was not affiliated to any AOF District. Members had to be in receipt of earnings of at least 16s a week.

65.   Court Prince of Wales

Status: Branch of an affiliated order **Type**: AOF **Branch no.** 2805
Established: 1856   **Registered:** 1856   **Dissolved**: Post 1918
Headquarters: Prince of Wales, Grimsbury (1856-1918)
Anniversary/feast day: First Tuesday in July
Membership: 94 members in 1864, 117 in 1865, 156 in 1867, 226 in 1872, 308 in 1880, 346 in 1890, 385 in 1900
Notes: Warwickshire Central District of IOOFMU (1856-1876), then Banbury District (from 1876). Several years during 1860s the society held a large ball at the Corn Exchange. In 1870s a joint fete was held with the Oddfellows at Bodicote Grange, home of Sir Bernhard Samuelson (BG, various dates).

66.   Court Queen Mary

Status: Branch of an affiliated order **Type**: AOF **Branch no.** 9437
Established: 1912 **Dissolved**: Post 1918
Headquarters: Cadbury Memorial Hall (1912–post 1918)
Membership: 136 members in 1912
Notes: Banbury District of AOF.

67.   Court Royal Crown

Status: Branch of an affiliated order, OXF 289   **Type**: AOF **Branch no.** 5156
Established: 1868   **Registered:** 1868   **Dissolved**: Post 1918

Headquarters: Crown Inn, Bridge Street (1868-post 1918)
Minimum age at entry: 18 **Maximum age at entry**: 45
Membership: 36 members in 1871, 67 in 1874, 94 in 1878, 125 in 1886, 156 in 1890, 184 in 1900, 271 in 1905, 335 in 1910
Notes: Warwickshire Central District of AOF (1868-1876) Banbury District (1876-post 1918)

> **Derby United Smiths Society** - see Whitesmiths club, Banbury 86

68.   Friendly Society of Shag Weavers

Status: Enrolled   **Type**: Permanent friendly society
Established: 2 April 1774   **Registered:** 1794   **Dissolved**: Last known 1794
Headquarters: The Bear (1794)
Anniversary/feast day: Last Friday in July
Maximum age at entry: 40
Primary Sources: Manuscript rules of 1794, OHC, QSD/R/5
Notes: A new society of plush weavers was formed in 1822 (Banbury 78).

69.   Forward Juvenile Tent

Status: Juvenile branch of an affiliated order   **Type**: IORSU **Branch no.** 1499
Established: First known 1897   **Registered:** 1897   **Dissolved**: Last known 1910
Headquarters: Cadbury Memorial Hall (1910)
Membership: 102 members in 1910
Notes: A Juvenile Society of the Cadbury Tent, IORSU (Banbury 57).

70.   Fountain of Liberty Lodge

Status: Branch of an affiliated order **Type**: IOOFMU **Branch no.** 3311
Established: 1843 **Dissolved**: 1846
Headquarters: Weaver's Arms (1843-46)
Anniversary/feast day: First Tuesday in July
Notes: Part of Banbury District of IOOFMU (1844-1846). The members dissolved the society in 1846 and joined the Weavers Arms Friendly society (Banbury 85).

71.   General Beneficial Society

Status: Enrolled, OXF 127   **Type**: 3-year dividing friendly society
Established: 1847   **Registered:** 30 November 1847 **Dissolved**: Last known 1847
Headquarters: Wesleyan Schoolroom (1847)
Anniversary/feast day: First Tuesday in February
Minimum age at entry: 21
Primary Sources: Rulebook of 1847, TNA, FS 1/579/127; TNA, FS 4/42/127
Notes: Open to male and female members. The objects of the society were 1. To assist members to apprentice their children, 2. To buy tools for their children when out of apprenticeship, 3. To provide clothing, furniture, etc. The officers of the society were required to be male and live in Banbury or Neithrop. Shares were purchased at 3d a week or multiples thereof. The three year division was of the profits of the society only. A public tea and entertainment was held at the annual meeting.

72.   (Loyal) British Queen Lodge

Status: Branch of an affiliated order, OXF 123 **Type**: IOOFMU **Branch no.** 2429
Established: 1840   **Registered:** 1840   **Dissolved**: post 1918
Headquarters: White Horse Inn, High Street [1841- 1846], White Hart Inn, High Street [1850-1918)
Anniversary/feast day: First Tuesday in July (after 1866). Anniversary dinners held at various times of the year
Membership: 36 in 1841, 60 in 1842, 105 in 1844, 62 in 1850, 88 in 1855, 141 in 1865, 231 in 1875, 342 in 1886, 430 in 1895, 553 in 1905, 670 in 1914
Primary Sources: BPP 1874, XXIII, (c.997), pp.104-105
Notes: Part of Edmonscote District of IOOFMU, Warwickshire (1841-1842), and then Banbury District (1844-post 1918). An account of the lodge and district is given in the report of the Assistant Commissioner (BPP 1874, XXIII, [c.997], pp.104-105). The British Queen Benefit Society (Banbury 55) was formed by some dissident members in 1849 but they re-joined the lodge at a later unknown date. (See also appendix 2, Crimes 5).

73.   Loyal British Queen Lodge Juvenile Branch

Status: Juvenile branch of an affiliated order, OXF 366 **Type**: IOOFMU
Established: 1889   **Registered:** 1889   **Dissolved**: Post 1918

Headquarters: 10 Queen St, Banbury (1889], 10 Spring Cottages (1899-1902], 23 Broad St [1905-1910]
Minimum age at entry: 5 **Maximum age at entry**: 16
Notes: A Juvenile Society for the British Queen Lodge (Banbury 72).

74.   Loyal Good Intent Lodge

Status: Branch of an affiliated order **Type**: IOHCMU **Branch no.** 6893
Established: 1889 **Dissolved**: Post 1918
Headquarters: Plough Inn (1890-1901], Angel Inn, Market Place [1905-1918)
Membership: 48 members in 1892, 62 in 1895, 79 in 1897, 153 in 1901, 256 in 1910
Notes: Banbury District of IOOFMU.

75.   Loyal Wellington Lodge

Status: Unregistered   **Type**: Independent Lodge of Oddfellows **Branch no.** 27
Established: 1817   **Dissolved**: Last known 1843
Headquarters: Cock Inn [1839-1843)
Anniversary/feast day: Last Friday in August
Notes: It is not known what order of Oddfellows the society belonged to although its use of a branch number indicates an affiliation or a branch relationship with a larger organization. This was likely to be an Oddfellows lodge that was a fraternal organization and may have had connection with the County of Oxford Loyal Independent Lodge of Odd Fellows (Oxford 477) that had branch number 25.

76.   Millwright Arms Friendly Society

Status: Unregistered   **Type**: Friendly society
Established: First known 1843   **Dissolved**: Last known 1843
Headquarters: Millwright Arms (1843)
Notes: A benefit society with a limited number of members (JOJ, 8 July 1843).

77.   Mutual Aid Burial Society

Status: Unregistered   **Type**: Burial society
Established: Earliest known 1872   **Dissolved**: Latest known 1872
Membership: 220 members in 1872
Primary Sources: BPP 1874, XXIII, (c.997), p.104

Notes: Upon the death of a members, all others paid a 1s levy. It was open to male and female members.

78. The New Society of Plush Weavers

Status: Unregistered **Type**: Permanent friendly society
Established: 7 October 1822 **Dissolved**: Last known 1838
Headquarters: Reindeer Inn (1822)
Anniversary/feast day: First Tuesday in July
Membership: 21 members in 1838
Primary Sources: Report of Commissioners on Hand Loom Weavers, BPP 1840, XXIV, pp.333-335.
Notes: Members of the society had to be plush weavers and was for relief of members during sickness and for burial, and to subscribe to the infirmary. Apprentices to members could also belong, paid for by the master. The rules of the society were produced in Pamela Horn, 'The New Society of Plush Weavers', *Cake and Cockhorse*, (1968), V.3, No.11, pp.199-202.

> **Old Friendly Society** – see The Weavers Arms Friendly Society, Banbury 85

79. Reformers Friendly Society

Status: Enrolled, OXF 16 **Type**: Permanent friendly society
Established: 1837 **Registered:** 22 March 1838 **Dissolved**: June 1867
Headquarters: Reindeer Inn, White Horse Inn (1844-1856], Buck and Bull Inn [1860-1862), Plough Inn (1862-1867)
Anniversary/feast day: First Tuesday in July
Maximum age at entry: 35
Membership: 55 in 1844, 67 in 1856, 78 in 1861, 90 in 1866
Primary Sources: Rulebook of 1862, TNA FS 1/574/16; TNA FS 4/42/16; BPP 1874, XXIII, (c.997), p.106-7
Notes: The Conservative Friendly society at Banbury (Banbury 59) was formed as a political club in opposition to the Reformers Friendly society (BPP 1874, XXIII, (c.997), p.106-7). It was one of the three principle clubs in Banbury in 1843 (JOJ, 8 July 1843). In 1854, the editorial of the *Banbury Guardian* urged changing the name of the society due to its political nature (BG, 6 June 1854). The society had 65 members and assets of £82 3s 5d at dissolution and 19 members had been sick for the previous year. A letter dated 17 June 1867 from John Ward, secretary, explained that the payment to sick members was excessive. He stated that, 'There was some imposition on the part of some of

the sick members on half pay' (TNA, FS 1/574/16). The society re-formed as Banbury 80.

80.   Reformers United Friendly Society

Status: Registered, OXF 287   **Type:** Permanent friendly society
Established: June 1867   **Registered:** 13 August 1867   **Dissolved:**1876
Headquarters: Plough Inn, Cornhill (1867-1876)
Anniversary/feast day: First Tuesday in July
Minimum age at entry: 17 Maximum age at entry: 35
Membership: 31 members in 1868, 27 in 1874, 20 in 1876
Primary Sources: Rulebook of 1868, TNA, FS 1/582/287; TNA, FS 4/42/287; BPP 1874, XXIII, (c.997), pp.106-107
Notes: Re-formed from Banbury 79. In 1872 the secretary, Mr J. Ward reported to the Assistant Commissioner that all the members were old men and young ones would not join them (BPP 1874, XXIII, (c.997), p.107). The society dissolved on 5 September 1876 with 20 members and £145 11s 10d.

81.   Sampson Tent

Status: Branch of an affiliated order, OXF 94   **Type:** IOORSU **Branch no.** 732
Established: 1844   **Registered:** 25 March 1845   **Dissolved**: Last known 1847
Headquarters: Temperance Lecture Room (1847)
Anniversary/feast day: First Tuesday in July
Minimum age at entry: 16 **Maximum age at entry**: 45
Primary Sources: Rulebook of 1845, TNA, FS 1/578/94; TNA, FS 4/42/94
Notes: A pledge of abstinence had to be signed by members and they were expelled if they broke it.

82.   Tradesmen's Benefit Society

Status: Enrolled, OXF 55   **Type**: Permanent friendly society
Established: 28 June 1839   **Registered:** 3 April 1840   **Dissolved**: 1871
Headquarters: Bear Inn (1839-1871), Star Inn (1844)
Anniversary/feast day: First Tuesday in August
Maximum age at entry: 35
Membership: 14 members in 1846, 16 in 1850, 13 in 1865 and 10 in 1871
Primary Sources: Rulebook of 1840, TNA FS 1/576/55 and Bodl. G.A. 8° 635(11); TNA FS 4/42/55; BPP 1874, XXIII, (c.997), p.106-7

Notes: There was a maximum of 100 members and membership required wages of at least £1 a week (TNA FS 1/576/55). The Assistant Commissioner reported that in 1871 there were just ten members and that £200 was divided between members in c.1859 (BPP 1874, XXIII, (c.997), p.106). A letter of 8 October 1878 states there was no such society at the Bear Hotel and had not been for the seven years the writer had been there (TNA, FS 4/42/55).

83.   United Britons Friendly Society

Status: Enrolled, OXF 140   **Type**: Permanent friendly society
Established: 1852   **Registered:** 1853 **Dissolved**: Last known 1910
Headquarters: Co-operative Stores Inn, Butchers Row (1855), Chapel Schoolroom, Bridge Street [1875-1910)
Anniversary/feast day: Second Tuesday in July
Membership: 50 members in 1855, 115 in 1865, 200 in 1875, 224 in 1885, 159 in 1902, 91 in 1905, 68 in 1910
Primary Sources: (BPP 1874, XXIII, [c.997], pp.107-112)
Notes: This society was established from an old co-operative movement and was possibly formed from the Banbury Working Man's Co-operative Friendly society (Banbury 53). Many of the original members had shares in Feargus O'Connor's land scheme. The decision on entry rested with the committee but seldom did it take on any new member over 30 years of age (BPP 1874, XXIII, (c.997), p.107). The society previously had dinner at the schoolroom but in 1867 moved to the Bear Inn (BG, 4 July 1867).

84.   United Christian Benefit Society

Status: Enrolled, OXF 51   **Type:** Permanent friendly society
Established: 1836   **Registered:** 1842   **Dissolved:** 16 May 1912
Headquarters: Wesleyan School [1840-1877], Temperance Hall, Bridge St [1880-1912)
Anniversary/feast day: Whit Monday
Minimum age at entry: 15, then 16 from 1889 Maximum age at entry: 43, reduced to 35 from 1889
Membership: 30 members in 1841, 67 in 1842, 80 in 1843, 123 in 1850,155 in 1857, 34 in 1863, 140 in 1872, 125 in 1885, 67 in 1899, 49 in 1905, 34 in 1912
Primary Sources: Rulebooks of 1840 and 1889, TNA, FS 3/319/51; Rulebook of 1841, Bodl. G.A. 8° 635(7); Some records at TNA are misfiled with TNA, FS 1/576/53; BPP 1874, XXIII, (c.997), pp. 15, 104-112
Notes: The society was for 'religious and conscientious people of all denominations'. It did not have any honorary members and although open

to all denominations, many of the Wesleyan chapel congregation belonged. The occupation of most members was mercantile and artisans. Members were not permitted to belong to another friendly society and the society could not meet at Inns or public houses. It had three bands of contribution, with benefits graded accordingly. The society was established in 1836 but re-founded in 1840 (BPP 1874, XXIII, (c.997), p.15). The annual celebration was a public tea. 1841 rules permitted the division of funds when they became too large and three-quarters of members agreed. (Bodl. G.A. 8° 635(7)). The society was dissolved with 34 members and £753 10s. 3d.

United Order of Smiths – see Whitesmiths Club, Banbury 86

85.   **The Weavers Arms Friendly Society, also Old Friendly Society**

Status: Unregistered   **Type**: Annual dividing friendly society
Established: 1816 **Dissolved**: Last known 1878
Headquarters: Weavers Arms [1832-1856], later known as The Case is altered [1860-1878]
Anniversary/feast day: First Tuesday in July
Membership: 44 members in 1844, 61 in 1854, 72 in 1860, 50 in 1866, 22 in 1871
Primary Sources: (BPP 1874, XXIII, (c.997), pp.105-106)
Notes: The society was one of the three principle clubs in Banbury in 1843 (JOJ, 8 July 1843), and in 1855 it was described as the oldest surviving club in the town (BG, 5 July 1855). The society had a new flag in 1863 which depicted figures representing virtue, commerce, music, and orphans (BG, 9 July 1863). In 1870 the society ceased attending church as part of club day (BG, 7 July 1870). In 1872 the Assistant Commissioner reported that the club was 'almost worn out'. Two years before, 25 young members left the society in one go due to the ageing membership and it needed to increase payments and make levies. There was a division by agreement and old members were 'balloted out'. It was an annual dividing society but division was abandoned at an unknown date. The Fountain of Liberty Lodge (Banbury 70) met at the Weavers Arms but dissolved in 1846 and joined this society.

86.   **Whitesmiths Club, also Derby United Smiths Society (in 1844) and United Order of Smiths (1860-1862)**

Status: Unregistered   **Type**: Permanent friendly society
Established: First known 1840   **Dissolved**: Last known 1862

Headquarters: Butcher's Arms (1840), Whitesmiths Arms (1844), Wheatsheaf Inn (1856), Old George [1860-1862)
Anniversary/feast day: First Tuesday in July
Notes: A society of smiths was in existence in Banbury from at least 1840. The continuity of the various names of this society is unclear. A friendly society named the United Order of Smiths were registered in Lancashire in 1857 (LAN 3220) and was also a trade society but there is no evidence of any link. The Banbury society was independent and closely linked to the Britannia Works where several members of the society worked. In 1861 the society did not meet on Banbury club day for dinner as those at the Britannia works could not afford the day off (BG, 4 July 1861). Although described as a small society, the funds were said to be abundant and the club flourishing (BG, 5 July 1860 and 3 July 1862).

Barton – see Westcote Barton

Beckley

No. of friendly societies and members 1802/3 – 1, 51
No. of members of a friendly society 1813/14/15 – 110, 118, 118

> **Beckley Friendly Society** – see Stowood 628

87.   Loyal Farmers' Home Lodge

Status: Branch of an affiliated order, OXF 236 **Type**: IOOFMU **Branch no.** 3138
Established: 1845   **Registered:** 1845   **Dissolved**: Post 1918
Headquarters: Abingdon Arms Inn (1845-1918)
Anniversary/feast day: Last Thursday in July
Membership: 19 members in 1846, 27 in 1850, 37 in 1858, 75 in 1863, 95 in 1868, 130 in 1877, 176 in 1887, 186 in 1892, 182 in 1901, 153 in 1910, 156 in 1914
Notes: Oxford District of IOOFMU. In 1889, the club dinner was held in a barn opposite the Abingdon Arms (JOJ, 3 August 1889). (See also appendix 2, Crimes 10).

88.   (United) Beckley Friendly Society

Status: Registered, OXF 263   **Type:** Friendly society

Established: 1865   **Registered:** 20 May 1865   **Dissolved:** 30 September 1872
Headquarters: Abingdon Arms (1865-1872)
Minimum age at entry: 12 Maximum age at entry: 45
Membership: 34 members in 1872
Primary Sources: Rulebook of 1865, TNA, FS 1/582/263; TNA, FS 4/42/263;
Notes: Members were required to be from Elsfield, Horton, Murcott, Noke, and Otmoor at their time of admission. Dissolved with 34 members and £63 5s 7d. (See also appendix 2, Crimes 9).

Benson

No. of friendly societies and members 1802/3 – None
No. of members of a friendly society 1813/14/15 – None

> **The Acorn Friendly Society** – see Bensington Friendly Society, Benson 89

89.   Bensington Friendly Society

Status: Registered, OXF 12   **Type:** 5-year dividing friendly society
Established: 1831   **Registered:** 18 May 1831   **Dissolved:** 1892
Headquarters: Three Horseshoes Inn (1831-1839], Crown Inn [1851-1892)
Anniversary/feast day: Whit Tuesday
Minimum age at entry: 14 Maximum age at entry: 45
Membership: 114 members in 1861, 112 in 1882, 127 in 1886, 119 in 1890
Primary Sources: Rulebook of 1831 and 1841, TNA, FS 3/319/12; TNA, FS 4/42/12
Notes: This was a society for labourers, servants, mechanics, manufacturers, tradesmen, and other industrious classes resident in Benson or adjacent hamlets, parishes or places in Oxfordshire and Berkshire. The society had strong support from honorary members with 13 in 1884. However, there was pressure from them for the club to change to a permanent society at its quinquennial division in 1885 (WT, 29 May 1885). An effort had been made to form another society called 'The Acorn' but working men were unable to afford the additional subscription to pay for superannuation that was a mandatory part of the rules. In 1889 the Board of Guardians of the Wallingford Union stated that dividing societies were 'a social evil' and the board would refuse to recognize membership of dividing societies as a qualification for outdoor relief (BOA, 14 June 1889). At the time of division a year later the honorary members again pressed to make the society permanent but there was a vote

to retain the existing status (JOJ, 3 May 1890). This precipitated an exit of honorary members who questioned their continuing honorary subscriptions when members themselves spent £24 12s 10d on club day festivities (BOA, 22 May 1891). This led to the demise of the society the following year. A letter of 1 November 1894 stated the society was declared insolvent at end of 1891 or early 1892 with 15 to 20 old members being supported solely by honorary members' subscriptions (FS 4/42/12). On Club day in 1892, at the formation of a new club (Benson 90) a black flag was hoisted from a window of the Crown Inn, the headquarters of the former society. A man was dressed up in crepe and sent around the village ringing a bell to invite people to the funeral of the old club at 8.00 p.m. at the Crown Inn (BOA, 10 June 1892). (See also appendix 2, Crimes 11).

90.   Benson Benefit Society

Status: Unclear   **Type**: Friendly society
Established: 1892   **Dissolved**: 1895
Headquarters: National schoolroom (1892-1895)
Anniversary/feast day: Whit Tuesday
Primary Sources: TNA, FS 3/319/12
Notes: This society was formed after the dissolution of the dividing society (Benson 89). The registration status is unclear and the club may have retained the registered number OXF 12 but no change of registered office was notified to the Registrar. There was no dinner, feasting or merry-making to celebrate the new club (BOA, 10 June 1892). It appears it was to be a permanent society and honorary members were to raise £25 a year for the club. An envelope from the Registrar was returned on 26 March 1897 stating the society had been dissolved two or three years previously (TNA, FS 3/319/12).

Bicester

No. of friendly societies and members 1802/3 – 2, 119
No. of members of a friendly society 1813/14/15 – 150, 150, 150
Notes: Bicester was unusual in that it supported two very successful branches of London friendly societies in the United Provident and London Friendly Institution, as well the only branches of the Nottingham Ancient Imperial United Order of Oddfellows and Derby Midland United Order of Oddfellows in the county. Bicester hosted a conference on 9 June 1911 by Mr Alfred Hamersley, MP for Mid Oxfordshire. The meeting was held to ascertain the feelings and concerns of the societies in this part of his constituency. He was not so concerned with the affiliated orders as they had their own voice in the

form of their national association that spoke on their behalf and held significant influence. Eighteen societies and branches from the Bicester area attended (BicA, 16 June 1911). (See also appendix 2, Crimes 15).

91.   Bicester Brewery Sick Club

Status: Unregistered   **Type**: Shop club
Established: First known 1887   **Dissolved**: Last known 1888
Headquarters: Dog Inn (1887-1888)
Membership: 36 members in 1888
Notes: £9 6s in hand in 1888 (JOJ, 7 January 1888). The brewery was operated by Charles Shillingford, who was bought out by Hanleys of Oxford in 1891.

92.   Bicester Friendly Society

Status: Enrolled, OXF 173   **Type**: 7-year dividing friendly society
Established: Earliest known 1802   **Registered:** 1802   **Dissolved**: Last known 1859
Headquarters: Kings Head (1802-1859)
Anniversary/feast day: Whit Monday
Maximum age at entry: 40
Primary Sources: Undated rules, TNA, FS 1/580/173; TNA, FS 4/42/173

93.   Bicester Friendly Society

Status: Unregistered   **Type**: Permanent friendly society
Established: 1884   **Dissolved**: Last known 1911
Headquarters: Dog Inn (1885-1893), Red Lion (1894), Nag's Head Inn (1900)
Membership: 46 members in 1889, 41 in 1890

94.   Bicester Juvenile Foresters Friendly Society

Status: Juvenile branch of an affiliated order, OXF 371 **Type:** AOF Branch no. 5497
Established: 1890   **Registered:** 10 September 1890   **Dissolved:** 1903
Headquarters: The Rookery, Sheep Street (1890-1903)
Anniversary/feast day: Unspecified date in January
Minimum age at entry: 4 Maximum age at entry: 16
Membership: 19 members in 1892, 17 in 1900
Primary Sources: Rulebook of 1890, TNA, FS 3/322/371; TNA, FS 4/42/371

Notes: Registration cancelled on 14 February 1903 on amalgamation with Court Loyal Oxonian (Bicester 99).

95.   Bicester Provident Society

Status: Unregistered   **Type**: Permanent friendly society
Established: 1874   **Dissolved**: 1883
Notes: The society ceased to exist after nine years when the cash box was robbed of £30. The Bicester Medical Aid Club, a subscription society to provide medical attendance only, took it under its wing (JOJ, 1 June 1883). (See also appendix 2, Crimes 17).

96.   Bicester Subordinate Division

Status: Branch of an affiliated order **Type**: OSOT **Branch no.** 711
Established: 1889 **Dissolved**: Last known 1913
Headquarters: St Eadburge's Hall (1890), Congregational Schoolroom, Chapel St [1905-1913]
Membership: 84 members in 1905, 230 in 1910

97.   Britain's Glory Lodge

Status: Branch of an affiliated order **Type**: AOD **Branch no.** 367
Established: August 1845 **Dissolved**: Last known 1861
Headquarters: Cross Keys Inn (1845-1861)
Notes: This was not a friendly society within the meaning of this calendar in that it was not a mutual association for insurance against sickness or death for its members, but is included for completeness. It was a mixture of a fraternal organization, a philanthropic organization and a spiritual one akin to a Masonic Lodge.

98.   Coker Lodge

Status: Branch of an affiliated order **Type**: IOOFMU **Branch no.** 3651
Established: 1843 **Dissolved**: 1850
Headquarters: Fox Inn, King's End (1843-1850)
Membership: 41 members in 1844, 54 in 1846, 44 in 1850
Notes: Oxford District of IOOFMU (1844-1850). The branch was 'out of compliance' with the district resolutions in 1850 and was suspended from the order. The Lodge reformed as the Loyal Coker Friendly society (Bicester 102).

99.   Court Loyal Oxonian

Status: Branch of an affiliated order, OXF 324   **Type:** AOF **Branch no.** 5947
Established: 1874 **Dissolved:** Post 1918
Headquarters: Red Lion Inn, Market Place (1874-1918)
Anniversary/feast day: 25 February
Membership: 35 members in 1874, 68 in 1876, 93 in 1880, 169 in 1890, 263 in 1900, 302 in 1910
Notes: London United District of AOF. Bicester Juvenile Foresters Friendly Society (Bicester 94) amalgamated with the main court when the juvenile branch dissolved in 1903.

100.   Friendly Society of Tradesmen

Status: Enrolled, OXF 7   **Type:** Permanent friendly society
Established: 1828   **Registered:** 3 January 1831   **Dissolved:** 21 August 1886
Headquarters: Cross Keys [1831-1866], Red Lion Inn [1873-1886)
Anniversary/feast day: Last Wednesday in June
Minimum age at entry: 18 Maximum age at entry: 35
Membership: 53 members in 1846, 52 in 1850, 48 in 1862, 30 in 1872, 20 in 1875, 18 in 1880, 14 in 1886
Primary Sources: Rulebook of 1841, TNA, FS 1/574/7; TNA, FS 4/42/173
Notes: The society was required to have a minimum 13 members and maximum 150 members. It was dissolved by Instrument with 14 members and £64. (See also appendix 2, Crimes 13, 14 and 16).

Kirtland's Club – see United Provident Institution, Bicester 107

101.   London Friendly Institution, Bicester Branch

Status: A branch of an enrolled society, LND 57   **Type:** Permanent friendly society
Established: 1839   **Dissolved:** Last known 1900
Headquarters: Black Boy Inn [1843-1852], Nags Head (1859), Kings Head (1860)
Membership: 135 members in 1844, 146 in 1859, 125 in 1871
Primary Sources: TNA, FS 15/1662; BPP 1874, XXIII, (c.997), pp.92-93
Notes: A medical attendant for the LFI was present at Bicester in 1841, 1869, 1882, and 1900 indicating the continuing presence of presence of a branch

(TNA, FS 15/1662). The Assistant Commission also notes the presence of the society in 1872 (BPP 1874, XXIII, [c.997], p.92). A sub-district of the Bicester branch existed at Fringford from at least 1854 (Fringford 294).

102.   Loyal Coker Friendly Society

Status: Enrolled, OXF 149   **Type:** Permanent friendly society
Established: 1851   **Registered:** 26 June 1851   **Dissolved:** Last known 1876
Headquarters: Fox Inn (1851-1876)
Anniversary/feast day: Annual dinner held at the end of January
Minimum age at entry: 18 Maximum age at entry: 45
Membership: 29 members in 1860, 27 in 1865
Primary Sources: Rulebook of 1851, TNA, FS 1/579/149; TNA, FS 4/42/149
Notes: The society was formed after the Loyal Coker Lodge of IOOFMU (Bicester 98) was suspended from that order.

> **The Loyal Drake Benevolent Sick Society** – see Loyal Drake Lodge, Bicester 103

103.   Loyal Drake Lodge, later The Loyal Drake Benevolent Sick Society.

Status: Branch of an affiliated order, OXF 125 **Type**: NAIUOOF
Established: 1846   **Registered:** 18 November 1847 **Dissolved**: Last known 1885
Headquarters: Rose and Crown Inn [1847], White Hart [1849], Nags Head Inn [1852-1856], Rose and Crown [1876- 1885)
Primary Sources: TNA, FS 4/42/125
Notes: This society was formed as a Lodge of the NAIUOOF in 1846 but no record of the lodge can be found after a report of its eleventh anniversary in 1856 (JOJ, 12 July 1856). The Loyal Drake Lodge was registered as OXF 125, and some time after 1856 the lodge appears to have de-affiliated from the NAIUOOF and become the independent Loyal Drake Benevolent Sick Society, which is reported as using registration number OXF 125 between 1876 and 1885 in reports of the Registrar of Friendly Societies. A letter of 5 January 1891 was returned to the Registrar marked 'no club at Rose and Crown, Bicester' (TNA, FS 4/42/125). There are no records at TNA in relation to OXF 125.

104.   National Deposit Friendly Society, Bicester branch

Status: Branch of a national society **Type**: Collecting society
Established: First known 1911 **Dissolved**: Last known 1911
Notes: Attended conference on 9 June 1911 of friendly societies in the Bicester
district to consider the changes proposed by parliament (BicA, 16 June 1911).

105.   Old Friendly Society

Status: Enrolled, OXF 25   **Type**: Permanent friendly society
Established: 1831   **Registered:** 5 December 1831   **Dissolved**: Last known
1845
Headquarters: (Blackwell) Dog Inn (1831-1845)
Primary Sources: TNA, FS 4/42/25
Notes: On 11 June 1835 the clubhouse was broken into and £10 stolen
(appendix 2, Crimes 12).

106.   The Star of Hope Lodge

Status: Branch of an affiliated order **Type**: DMUOOF **Branch no.** 47
Established: 14 September 1889 **Dissolved**: 1891
Headquarters: Cross Keys Inn (1899)
Membership: 15 members in 1889, 18 members in 1891
Notes: Dissolved by instrument in 1891 with 18 members and £4 funds.

107.   United Provident Institution, Bicester Branch

Status: Branch of an enrolled society, MDX 3103   **Type**: Permanent friendly
society
Established: 1847 **Dissolved**: Post 1915
Headquarters: Finchley, Middlesex
Membership: 130 in 1906, 122 in 1913.
Primary Sources: UPI papers, TNA, FS 15/1916
Notes: The UPI was a London Friendly society with branches, established in
1847 with its head office at Finchley. It was a patronized society supported by
the gentry, similar to a County society. The Bicester branch was established the
same year and was the largest of the 26 branches of the UPI in 1880. It had a
sub-branch at Chesterton and continued to hold a joint club day there with the
Chesterton Sick Club (Chesterton 185) until 1913. In 1906 the UPI had 360
members, of which 130 were in the Bicester branch (including Chesterton) and

was the only branch outside London. It was known as Kirtland's club locally (BicA, 14 June 1895), named after the club secretary who served for over 30 years.

Blackthorn

No. of friendly societies and members 1802/3 – None
No. of members of a friendly society 1813/14/15 – None

108.   Blackthorn Friendly Society

Status: Unregistered   **Type**: Friendly society
Established: First known 1911   **Dissolved**: Last known 1911
Notes: A representative of the society attended a conference of friendly societies on 9 June 1911 in the Bicester district to consider the changes proposed by parliament (BicA, 16 June 1911).

Bladon

No. of friendly societies and members 1802/3 – None
No. of members of a friendly society 1813/14/15 – None

109.   Bladon Friendly Society

Status: Registered, OXF 217   **Type**: 5-year dividing friendly society
Established: First known 1859   **Registered:** 7 May 1859   **Dissolved**: Last known 1867
Headquarters: Lamb Inn (1859-1867)
Anniversary/feast day: Second Monday in July
Minimum age at entry: 12 **Maximum age at entry**: 40
Primary Sources: Rulebook of 1859, TNA, FS 1/581/217; TNA, FS 4/42/217
Notes: An undated note from Edwin Savage stated the society broke up two years before he became tenant of the Lamb Inn (TNA, FS 4/42/217).

110.   New Bladon Friendly Society

Status: Registered, OXF 327   **Type:** Permanent friendly society
Established: 1875   **Registered:** 5 January 1875   **Dissolved:** 1877
Headquarters: Lamb Inn (1875)
Anniversary/feast day: First Monday in July
Minimum age at entry: 14 Maximum age at entry: 45

Membership: 15 members in 1877
Primary Sources: Rulebook of 1875, TNA, FS 1/582/327; TNA, FS 4/42/327
Notes: The society dissolved in 1877 with 15 members and £20 funds.

Bletchingdon

No. of friendly societies and members 1802/3 – 1, not stated
No. of members of a friendly society 1813/14/15 – 137, 137, 135

111.   Bletchingdon Friendly Society

Status: Registered, OXF 167   **Type:** Friendly society, then 7-year dividing friendly society from 1862
Established: 7 July 1783   **Registered:** 1 September 1794   **Dissolved:** 1888
Headquarters: Black Moor's Head Inn (1783), Green Man and Black Moor's Head (1794), Black Moor's Head Inn (Blacks Head Inn) [1845-1885], Red Lion (1888)
Anniversary/feast day: Whit Monday
Maximum age at entry: 40, 45 (from 1865)
Membership: 94 members in 1872, 100 in 1880, 72 in 1882
Primary Sources: Manuscript rules of 1794, TNA, FS 3/320/167; TNA, FS 4/42/167; Rulebook of 1865 and 1879, Bodl. G.A. OXF 8° 1307
Notes: Black and white balls were used to determine the selection of new members. Ten black balls meant a rejection. The society was declining due to the level of long-term sickness in 1845 (JOJ, 17 May 1845). The society was converted to 7-year club about 1862 (VCH, Parishes: Bletchingdon, *A History of the County of Oxford: Volume 6* [1959], pp. 56-71). The last known division of funds was in 1882 (BicA, 8 June 1882). The society appears to have reformed as an unregistered society, Bletchingdon 112.

112.   Bletchingdon Friendly Society

Status: Unregistered   **Type:** Permanent friendly society
Established: 1889 **Dissolved:** Last known 1910
Headquarters: Red Lion (1889-1910)
Anniversary/feast day: Whit Monday
Membership: 69 members in 1892, 61 in 1901 and 37 in 1910
Primary Sources: TNA, FS 4/42/162
Notes: In response to an enquiry from the Registrar concerning the Bletchingdon Friendly Society (Bletchingdon 111), a note from A.E. Kirtland, dated 20 March 1894 stated, 'This club is not a registered society, nor never

has been' (TNA, FS 4/42/162). A blue banner with gold lettering and orange frill, displaying the words, 'Bletchington Friendly society, Estb. 1855, Jubilee 1897' is in private hands in Bletchingdon. This indicates the society was seen as a continuation of Bletchingdon 111. The rules were revised in 1905.

> **Loyal Valentia Lodge** – see Loyal Valentia Lodge, Kirtlington 405

113.   **Valentia Club**

Status: Registered, OXF 154   **Type**: 7-year dividing friendly society
Established: 1855   **Registered:** 8 April 1856   **Dissolved**: 1889
Headquarters: Red Lion Inn [1855-1862], National School House [1872-1885]
Anniversary/feast day: Whit Monday
Maximum age at entry: 45
Membership: 92 members in 1863, 116 in 1866, 107 in 1872, 80 in 1880, 60 in 1888
Primary Sources: Rulebooks of 1856 and 1872 Bodl. G.A. 8° 1296; TNA, FS 4/42/154
Notes: Black and white balls were used to determine the selection of new members. Ten black balls meant a rejection. On division, two years' subscriptions per member were retained in the club (Bodl. G.A. 8° 1296). A new banner was presented to the society by Lord Valentia in 1862 (JOJ, 21 June 1862). The society was in a 'parlous state' in 1866 and villagers were asked to give up one-fiftieth of their Poor Law rateable value to support the club (JOJ, 26 May 1866). The club was suspended for three months by the Registrar on 13 February 1884, and for a further three months on 13 May 1884, and again on 29 August 1888 for failing to make a valuation of its assets. A letter to Registrar dated 17 July 1889 from William Kirkland, secretary of the club, stated the society was insolvent and had been broken up (TNA, FS 4/42/154). (See also appendix 2, Crimes 18 and 19).

Bloxham

No. of friendly societies and members 1802/3 – 2, 140
No. of members of a friendly society 1813/14/15 – 205, 195, 196
Notes: A traditional club day continued in Bloxham until at least 1902. (See also appendix 2, Crimes 20, 22 23, 24 and 25).

114.   **Bloxham Amicable Society, also Old Club also Joiners Arms Club**

Status: Enrolled, OXF 182   **Type**: Permanent friendly society, 3-year dividing friendly society after 1848, returning to a permanent friendly society in 1857
Established: 30 April 1804   **Registered:** 24 October 1815   **Dissolved**: 1889
Headquarters: Horse and Groom (1804), Joiners Arms [1871-1889)
Membership: 84 members in 1871
Primary Sources: Rules of 1804, TNA, FS 1/580/182; TNA, FS 4/42/182; BPP 1874, XXIII, (c.997), p.116)
Notes: The society had no maximum or minimum ages in their rules of 1804. The Assistant Commissioner reported in 1872 that the club accumulated money after its formation and in 1848 members voted for a division of funds every three years. On the third division in 1857 there was little to distribute and so the club returned to its former position. He noted that feast beer was bought out of the fund. The secretary, Mr Gascoigne was father of the secretary of Court British Lion, Bloxham 119.

115.   **(Bloxham Friendly Society)**

Status: Enrolled   **Type**: Friendly society
Established: 1769   **Registered:** 1804   **Dissolved**: Last known 1804
Headquarters: Red Lion (1804)
Primary Sources: Cal. QS iii, p.615
Notes: The rules of the society were enrolled at 1804 Quarter Sessions.

116.   **Bloxham Friendly Society**

Status: Enrolled, OXF 150   **Type**: Permanent friendly society
Established: 1850   **Registered:** 6 June 1851   **Dissolved**: Last known 1858
Headquarters: The Court House (1851-1855]
Anniversary/feast day: Whit Monday
Minimum age at entry: 10
Primary Sources: Rulebook of 1851, TNA, FS 1/579/150; TNA, FS 4/42/150
Notes: Open to male and female members. Membership was for residents of Bloxham and its neighbourhood. Married women were excluded unless the written permission of their husband was given. Minors also required the consent of a parent, master or guardian. Only male members could vote. Honorary members had a general meeting on the first Tuesday in May. There

was no indication of a maximum age of entry but graded benefits according to age were in place. Superannuation was payable at 65. If a member was in the workhouse, no payments were required to the club by the member but no benefit was received either. The rules were amended in 1858.

117. Bloxham Lodge of IMBFS

Status: A branch of a registered society, MIDDX 4889 **Type**: Permanent friendly society **Branch no. 201**
Established: First known 1884 **Dissolved**: Last known 1885
Headquarters: Hawk and Partridge (1884-1885)
Anniversary/feast day: Whit Monday
Membership: 39 members in 1885
Notes: In 1885 it was reported that the branch did not meet as it had done in previous years (BG, 28 May 1885).

118. Bloxham Old Friendly Society

Status: Registered, OXF 368 **Type:** Permanent friendly society
Established: 1889 **Registered:** 19 October 1889 **Dissolved:** 11 December1897
Headquarters: Joiners Arms (1889-1897)
Anniversary/feast day: Whit Monday
Minimum age at entry: 16 Maximum age at entry: 40
Membership: 69 members in 1891
Primary Sources: Rulebook of 1889, TNA, FS 3/322/368; TNA, FS 4/42/368
Notes: This society was formed after the Bloxham Amicable Friendly society dissolved (Bloxham 114). It claimed continuity from 1804. The registration was cancelled when the society was taken over as Loyal Old Friendly Lodge of the IOOFMU, 7421 (Bloxham 122).

119. Court British Lion

Status: Branch of an affiliated order, OXF 285 **Type:** AOF **Branch no.** 3167
Established: 1859 **Registered:** 1868 **Dissolved**: Post 1918
Headquarters: Red Lion (1859-1864), Hawk and Partridge Inn (1864-1882), Red Lion Inn (1883-1918)
Anniversary/feast day: Whit Monday
Membership: 40 members in 1866, 58 in 1871, 76 in 1874, 96 in 1875, 112 in 1880, 152 in 1885, 178 in 1895, 199 in 1900, 203 in 1905, 197 in 1910
Primary Sources: BPP 1874, XXIII, (c.997), p.117

Notes: Initially not associated with a district, the lodge became part of Warwickshire Central District (1864-1876) and then Banbury District (1876-post 1918). The society comprised many agricultural labourers. The secretary of the club, Mr Gascoigne was the son of the secretary of the Joiners Arms club (Bloxham 114) (BPP 1874, XXIII, (c.997), p.117). In 1867, three officers of the lodge were prosecuted theft of £67 (JOJ, 11 May 1867) (see also appendix 2, Crimes 21). A year later the society registered with the Registrar as an Oxfordshire branch. The society had a juvenile branch (Bloxham 120).

120.   Court British Lion Juvenile Branch

Status: Juvenile branch of an affiliated order, OXF 333 **Type:** AOF
Established: 1875   **Registered:** 1875   **Dissolved:** Post 1927
Headquarters: Court House (1876-post 1918)
Minimum age at entry: 8 Maximum age at entry: 18
Membership: 23 members in 1877, 28 in 1885, 15 in 1895, 21 in 1905, and 16 in 1910
Primary Sources: Rulebook of 1875, TNA, FS 15/578
Notes: Registration was cancelled when the society amalgamated with Court British Lion, AOF, 3167 (Bloxham 119).

121.   (Elephant and Castle Club)

Status: Unregistered   **Type:** Friendly society
Established: First known 1864 **Dissolved:** Last known 1864
Headquarters: Elephant and Castle (1864)
Anniversary/feast day: Whit Monday
Notes: Described as a 'minor club' (BG, 19 May 1864).

> **Joiners Arms Club** – see Bloxham Amicable Society, Bloxham 114

122.   Loyal Old Friendly Lodge

Status: Affiliated Order **Type:** IOOFMU **Branch no.** 7421
Established: 1897 **Dissolved:** Post 1918
Headquarters: Joiner's Arms (1897 – post 1918)
Notes: Banbury District of IOOFMU. Members of the Bloxham Old Friendly society (Bloxham 118) formed this branch when that society dissolved in 1897.

123.   Loyal Union Friendly Society

Status: Enrolled, OXF 95   **Type**: Permanent friendly society
Established: 4 April 1831 **Registered:** 21 April 1845   **Dissolved**: 1877
Headquarters: Red Lion [1846-1847], Unicorn Inn [1855-1877)
Anniversary/feast day: Whit Monday
Maximum age at entry: 35
Membership: 53 members in 1846, 63 in 1847, and 30 in 1872
Primary Sources: Rulebook of 1845, TNA, FS 3/319/95; TNA, FS 4/42/95;
BPP 1874, XXIII, (c.997), p.116
Notes: The Assistant Commissioner described the society in 1872 as a small
club supported by a small local farmer, Mr Hickman. It had 30 members and
was an accumulating society. A letter to the Registrar, dated 26 February 1892
from Mr Robinson stated the society was broken up 15 years before (TNA, FS
4/42/95).

Old Club – see Bloxham Amicable Society, Bloxham 114

124.   (Red Lion Club)

Status: Unregistered   **Type**: Friendly society
Established: First known 1864 **Dissolved**: Last known 1864
Headquarters: Red Lion (1864)
Anniversary/feast day: Whit Monday
Notes: Described as a 'minor club' (BG, 19 May 1864).

125.   Tradesmen's Beneficial Friendly Society

Status: Enrolled, OXF 199   **Type**: Permanent friendly society
Established: 1852   **Registered:** 29 April 1852   **Dissolved**: Last known
1876
Headquarters: White Lion Inn (1852-1876), Horse and Groom (1866),
Elephant & Castle Inn (1876)
Anniversary/feast day: Whit Monday
Maximum age at entry: 30
Membership: 39 members in 1862, 34 in 1866, 35 in 1871, 35 in 1874
Primary Sources: Rulebook of 1852, TNA, 1/581/199; TNA, 1/581/197;
TNA, FS 4/42/199; BPP 1874, XXIII, (c.997), p.117

Notes: The rules had no occupational exclusions as with many tradesmen's societies. It was described by the Assistant Commissioner in 1872 as a small club.

Bodicote

No. of friendly societies and members 1802/3 – None
No. of members of a friendly society 1813/14/15 – 48, 50, 51
Notes: In c.1824 a serious riot took place in Bodicote and many inhabitants were attacked and beaten by a body of strangers on club day. A similar occurrence took place at club day on Whit Friday 1844. In the late evening 30-50 men from Northamptonshire, Banbury and other parts appeared at Bodicote and were most boisterous with the riot continuing for two to three hours (BG, 13 June 1844) (see appendix 2, Crimes 26) The Bodicote club day continued to attract large numbers of visitors from Banbury for many years. (See also appendix 2, Crimes 27 and 29).

The Amicable – see Bodicote Friendly Society, Bodicote 126

Bakers Arms club – see Bodicote Old Friendly Society, Bodicote 129

126.   Bodicote Friendly Society, also The Amicable and Bodicote Old Friendly Society

Status: Registered, OXF 282   **Type**: Permanent friendly society
Established: 3 June 1803   **Registered:** 2 October 1867 **Dissolved**: 1870
Headquarters: White Hart Inn (1803), Horse and Jockey Inn [1857-1869]
Anniversary/feast day: Whit Friday
Maximum age at entry: 35
Membership: 92 members in 1865, and 100 in 1870
Primary Sources: Rulebooks of 1821 and 1867, TNA, FS 1/582/282; TNA, FS 4/42/282; BPP 1874, XXIII, (c.997), p.115
Notes: In 1865 two honorary members offered to bear the cost of becoming registered and the following year the vicar offered £50 for the same purpose but both were rejected (BG, 15 June 1865 and 31 May 1866). The society owned land to the amount of 5 acres 3 roods 25 perches and rented it to club members at a total income of £25 12s (JOJ, 17 April 1869). The club broke up soon after registering in 1870. It had considerable funds but most were invested in a local field which upon registration they had to sell. They received the income from the sale of the field but members decided to divide the funds and dissolve the

club. The Assistant Commissioner, reporting in 1872, found the field to be mortgaged to almost its full value due to the 'extravagant' nature of benefits. An offer for the field from the local clergyman of £610 was £112 above the mortgaged amount. However, the landlord of the Horse and Jockey, who was also the club treasurer, insisted on a reserve price of £800. This frightened off all purchasers. The land was subsequently sold for £560 by private contract. (See also appendix 2, Crimes 28 and 30).

Bodicote Old Club – see Royal Albert Union Friendly Society, Bodicote 129

Bodicote Old Friendly Society – see Bodicote Friendly Society, Bodicote 126

127.   Court Hand in Hand

Status: Branch of an affiliated order **Type**: AOF **Branch no.** 6277
Established: 1876 **Dissolved**: Post 1918
Headquarters: Plough Inn [1878-1898], Church House, Main St [1905-1918]
Anniversary/feast day: Whit Monday
Membership: 43 members in 1878, 61 in 1881, 73 in 1885, 53 in 1890, 68 in 1900, 85 in 1910
Notes: Banbury district of AOF. A new banner was purchased in 1883 from subscriptions raised (BG, 24 May 1883). In 1899 the Court suffered the theft of over £61 by its secretary, George Bailey (BG, 2 November 1899). (See also appendix 2, Crimes 31). The Court had a juvenile branch (Bodicote 128)

128.   Court Hand in Hand, Juvenile branch

Status: Juvenile branch of an affiliated order **Type**: AOF
Established: 1890 **Dissolved**: Post 1918
Headquarters: Schoolroom (1890)
Membership: 5 members in 1890, 5 in 1895, 3 in 1900
Notes: Juvenile branch of Bodicote 127

129.   Royal Albert Union Friendly Society, also Bakers Arms club and Bodicote Old Club

Status: Unregistered   **Type**: 3-year dividing friendly society
Established: 1851 **Dissolved**: Last known 1895

Headquarters: Plough Inn (1859), Bakers Arms [1861-1895]
Anniversary/feast day: Whit Friday
Membership: 40 members in 1865, 31 in 1872 and 15 in 1883
Primary Sources: BPP 1874, XXIII, (c.997), p.115
Notes: The Assistant Commissioner reported this to be a small unregistered dividing club that had been going for 20 years. In 1895 the society abandoned its annual dinner (BG, 13 June 1895).

Bourton (Great and Little)

No. of friendly societies and members 1802/3 – None
No. of members of a friendly society 1813/14/15 – None
Notes: Traditional club day continued until at least 1900. (See also appendix 2, Crimes 32).

130.   (Bourton Friendly Society)

Status: Unregistered   **Type**: Friendly society
Established: First known 1857 **Dissolved**: 1864
Anniversary/feast day: Friday before Whit Sunday
Primary Sources: BPP 1874, XXIII, (c.997), p.115
Notes: The Assistant Commissioner reported that there was an old, unregistered club that had divided in about 1864, and a new registered one formed (Bourton 131).

131.   Great Bourton Friendly Society

Status: Registered, OXF 264   **Type**: Permanent friendly society
Established: 1865   **Registered:** 4 September 1865   **Dissolved**: 1903
Headquarters: Bell Inn, Great Bourton (1865-1903)
Anniversary/feast day: Friday before Whit Sunday
Maximum age at entry: 35
Membership: 45 members in 1866, 65 in 1876, 79 in 1880, 61 in 1889, 41 in 1899, 16 in 1903.
Primary Sources: Rulebook of 1865, TNA, FS 3/321/264; TNA, FS 4/42/264; BPP 1874, XXIII, (c.997), p.115
Notes: It was reported by the Assistant Commissioner that when the society was formed the vicar intervened and insisted members of the old club (Bourton 130) be admitted. Many were aged and this affected the viability of the new club. It was also reported that the late secretary, Mr Lewis was obliged to resign as the members were quarrelsome and used bad language. The members

did not like the restrictions of enrolment, especially that club funds could not be used for the feast. Lewis belonged to the Welshpool First Friendly society. The financial state of the club was reported as 'not promising' in 1899 (DDM, June 1899). When the society dissolved there were 16 members and £11 funds.

Brightwell Baldwin

No. of friendly societies and members 1802/3 – None
No. of members of a friendly society 1813/14/15 – None

132.   Berkshire Friendly Society, Brightwell Branch

Status: Branch of a registered friendly society, BRK 299   **Type**: Permanent friendly society
Established: First known 1895 **Dissolved**: Post 1914
Anniversary/feast day: Whit Monday
Membership: 14 members in 1895, 34 in 1901, 43 in 1911
Notes: The annual dinner was held in the parish room. The membership figures include benefit and honorary members. In 1911 here were 21 benefit and 22 honorary members (TG, 13 June 1911).

Britwell Salome

No. of friendly societies and members 1802/3 – None
No. of members of a friendly society 1813/14/15 – None

133.   Britwell Provident Society

Status: Unregistered   **Type**: 5-year dividing friendly society
Established: First known 1839 **Dissolved**: Last known 1844
Headquarters: Red Lion (1844)
Anniversary/feast day: First Thursday in June
Notes: On club day, there was 'No useless band or flag, just songs and jest' (JOJ, 15 June 1844). The society divided its funds after five years in December 1844 (7 December 1844).

Brize Norton

No. of friendly societies and members 1802/3 – 1, 44
No. of members of a friendly society 1813/14/15 – None
Notes: (See also appendix 2, Crimes 33).

134.   Brize Norton Friendly Society

Status: Enrolled   **Type**: Permanent friendly society
Established: First known 1809 **Registered:** 1809   **Dissolved**: Last known 1809
Anniversary/feast day: Whit Monday
Maximum age at entry: 35
Primary Sources: Manuscript rules, undated, OHC, QSD/R/6

135.   Brize Norton Friendly Society

Status: Enrolled, OXF 90   **Type**: 7-year dividing friendly society
Established: 1846 **Registered:** 28 January 1846   **Dissolved**: 1853
Headquarters: Carpenters Arms (1846-1853)
Anniversary/feast day: Whit Monday
Maximum age at entry: 45
Primary Sources: Rules of 1846, TNA, FS 1/578/90; TNA, FS 4/42/90
Notes: The society divided in 1853 and a new society was formed (Brize Norton 139).

136.   Brize Norton Provident Club

Status: Unregistered   **Type**: Friendly society
Established: First known 1876 **Dissolved**: Last known 1895
Headquarters: National schoolroom (1876-1890]
Anniversary/feast day: Whit Monday, Whit Tuesday in 1895
Membership: 167 members in 1885, 175 in 1890
Notes: Benefits included a provident medical dispensary as well as sickness and burial money (WG, 23 May 1885). It was formed at the dissolution of the Royal Albert Friendly Society (Brize Norton 139).

137.   Loyal Friendly Society

Status: Unregistered   **Type**: Friendly society
Established: First known 1895 **Dissolved**: Last known 1906
Headquarters: Chequers Inn (1895-1906)
Anniversary/feast day: Whit Tuesday

138.   (Mason's Arms club)

Status: Unregistered   **Type:** Friendly society
Established: First known 1865 **Dissolved**: Last known 1866
Headquarters: Mason's Arms (1865-1866)
Notes: Accounts of the society were published in JOJ, 6 April 1867.

139.   Royal Albert Friendly Society

Status: Enrolled, OXF 142   **Type:** Friendly society
Established: 1853 **Registered:** 23 February 1854   **Dissolved**: Last known 1876
Headquarters: Carpenters Arms (1853-1875), Chequers Inn (1876)
Anniversary/feast day: Whit Monday
Maximum age at entry: 35
Primary Sources: Rulebook of 1854, TNA, FS 1/579/142; TNA, FS 4/42/142
Notes: The society was established at the dissolution of the Brize Norton Friendly Society (Brize Norton 135).The maximum age at joining was 35 except those who were members of the previous friendly society held at the Carpenters Arms. Brize Norton Provident Club (Brize Norton 136) was formed at its dissolution.

Broadwell

No. of friendly societies and members 1802/3 – None
No. of members of a friendly society 1813/14/15 – None

140.   Friendly Society

Status: Enrolled, OXF 126   **Type:** Friendly society
Established: 1847 **Registered:** 30 December 1847   **Dissolved:** 22 November 1878
Headquarters: Five Bells Inn, Broadwell (1847-1878)
Anniversary/feast day: Whit Tuesday
Minimum age at entry: 15 Maximum age at entry: 56
Membership: 57 members in 1862, 31 in 1865, 22 in 1878
Primary Sources: Rulebook of 1847, TNA, FS 1/579/126; TNA, FS 4/42/126
Notes: The society was for the villages of Alvescot, Broadwell, Broughton, Clanfield, Kencot, Langford, and Shilton. New members had to live in one of the parishes at time of joining and each village had a steward. The treasurer

and president was William Hervey of Broadwell Grove. The management committee consisted of seven honorary and six benefit members plus the president, giving a majority vote to honorary members. There was exclusion of sickness payment for 'idiotcy and insanity'. (TNA, FS 1/579/126). Club day was rotated between the villages until 1854 when it settled at Broadwell (JOJ, 17 June 1854). The society dined at Broadwell National School on club day in 1872, with food provided by the Five Bells Inn, but otherwise club day was held at the Five Bells. The society dissolved with 22 members and £511 7s 2d capital.

Brookhampton – see Stadhampton

Broughton – see North Newington

Bucknell

No. of friendly societies and members 1802/3 – None
No. of members of a friendly society 1813/14/15 – None

141.   National Deposit Friendly Society, Bucknell Branch

Status: Branch of a registered society **Type**: Friendly society
Established: First known 1899 **Dissolved**: Last known 1901
Anniversary/feast day: Whit Monday
Minimum age at entry: 7 Maximum age at entry: 55
Membership: 57 members in 1862, 31 in 1865, 22 in 1878
Notes: Open for male and female members.

Burford

No. of friendly societies and members 1802/3 – 2, 159
No. of members of a friendly society 1813/14/15 – 239, 235, 231
Notes: The first recorded use of a band to lead a club day parade in Oxfordshire was at Burford in 1836 when the Burford Band playted for the Burford Friendly Society (Burford 143). Club day continued to be held in Burford until at least 1902.

142.   Burford Friendly Institution

Status: Enrolled, OXF 164   **Type**: Permanent friendly society
Established: 1826   **Registered:** 1827 **Dissolved**: 1847
Headquarters: Free Schoolroom (1826), George Inn (1827-1847)
Minimum age at entry: 10 **Maximum age at entry**: 50
Primary Sources: Oxon. Cal. QS iii, p. 677; rulebooks of 1826, TNA, FS 1/580/164, Bodl. G.A. OXF. 8° 438 and OHC COS P/BURF 334.7; TNA, FS 4/42/164
Notes: Open for male and female members. A table of payments and allowances was registered with the Epiphany sessions, 1827 for (Cal. QS iii, p. 677). The society had a range of payments with ten classes. The lowest payment was 5d a month and another had an annuity at age 60, 65 or 70. There was to be 'no waste of money in forcing members to spend on any drinking or feasting'. New members had to reside within 12 miles of Burford, and this specifically included Witney, Charlbury, Bampton, Lechlade, Stow on the Wold, Northleach, Fairford, Chipping Norton, and Faringdon. The rules permitted that the society could appoint local agents. The society was under the management of twelve trustees, elected from honorary members, with the majority to be 'substantial householders' and minimum assessment under the Poor Law of £50. Eight Stewards paid 12s per annum (TNA, FS 1/580/164). A letter dated January 1882 was returned to Registrar stating the society had been broken up thirty-five years before, and the named contact held by the Registrar (Mr W. Ward) died 22 years before (TNA, FS 4/42/164).

143.   Burford (Old) Friendly Society

Status: Enrolled, OXF 69   **Type:** Permanent friendly society
Established: 1769   **Registered:** 1799 **Dissolved:** 1859
Headquarters: White House (1810), King's Arms Inn [1833-1843], Bear Inn (1846-1859)
Anniversary/feast day: Whit Monday, Whit Tuesday from 1857
Minimum age at entry: 15 from 1843 Maximum age at entry: 35 from 1799, 30 (1810), 55 (1843), 50 (1846)
Membership: 84 members in 1846, 73 in 1850
Primary Sources: Manuscript rules of 1799, printed rules of 1810 and 1843, TNA, FS 1/577/69; TNA, FS 4/42/69
Notes: Open to male and female members. A hat-band and gloves had to be worn to the funeral of a member. A rule amendment of 1843 listed local stewards for the areas outside Burford from which members were drawn as

1. Burford and Fulbrook, 2. Swinbrook and Shilton, 3. Signett, Holwell and Westwell, 4. Upton and Taynton. The society had £800 funds in 1833 (JOJ, 1 June 1833). An emergency meeting of the society was held on 22 November 1849 as a rumour of imminent insolvency had spread. The treasurer reassured the members this was not the case and that there was no cause for alarm (JOJ, 1 December 1849). However, in 1852 it was reported the society was on the wane (BG, 3 June 1852) and few members attended club day due to the insolvent nature of the society (JOJ, 5 June 1852). (See also appendix 2, Crimes 34).

144.   Burford Mutual Benefit Society, also Lamb Benefit Society

Status: Enrolled society, OXF 144   **Type**: 7-year dividing friendly society
Established: 1854   **Registered:** 27 October 1854   **Dissolved**: 21 May 1861
Headquarters: Royal Oak Inn (1854-1855), Lamb Inn (1856-1861)
Anniversary/feast day: Whit Monday, Whit Tuesday in 1861
Maximum age at entry: 55
Membership: 80 members in 1861
Primary Sources: Rulebook of 1854, TNA, FS 1/579/144; FS 4/42/144
Notes: On dissolution 80 members received £3 10s each. The society reformed as Burford 145.

145.   Burford Mutual Benefit Society

Status: Enrolled, OXF 239   **Type**: 7-year dividing friendly society
Established: 5 June 1861   **Registered:** 13 September 1861   **Dissolved**: 1868
Headquarters: Lamb Inn (1861 - 1868)
Anniversary/feast day: Whit Tuesday
Maximum age at entry: 50
Membership: 48 in 1861, 76 in 1864
Primary Sources: Rulebook of 1861, TNA, FS 1/581/239; TNA, FS 4/42/239
Notes: The society followed on from Burford 144. It commenced with 48 benefit and eight honorary members. The Burford Band was engaged to perform at club day for the seven Whit Tuesdays. A letter of 15 January 1870 explained that the two registered societies, OXF 144 (Burford 144) and this society were dissolved (TNA, FS 1/581/239).

146.   Burford Mutual Benefit Society

Status: Unregistered   **Type**: 5-year dividing friendly society
Established: 1868 **Dissolved**: Last known 1902

Headquarters: Lamb Inn [1880-1902)
Anniversary/feast day: Varied between Whit Tuesday and Whit Thursday
Notes: In 1888 and 1892 there was discussion on becoming a permanent society (JOJ, 2 June 1888 and 18 June 1892). On division in 1899 the fully paid up members received £3 5s of the £282 4s 7d available for division (WG, 27 May 1899). Newspaper reports claimed the society was formed in 1874, although a society of the same name had existed between 1868 and 1874 with apparent continuity to this society indicating a longer lineage. The society received a bequest of £500 in the will of Lord Northwick in 1887 (JOJ, 10 December 1887). Division of funds on a 5-year basis took place in 1889.

147.   Court Loyal Priory

Status: Branch of an affiliated order **Type**: AOF **Branch no.** 7226
Established: 1884 **Dissolved**: Post 1918
Headquarters: Three Pigeons Inn (1884-1885], Bear Inn (1892), Bull Hotel [1899-1918)
Membership: 22 members in 1885, 37 in 1895, 53 in 1900, 47 in 1910
Notes: London United District of AOF.

148.   Friend in Need Society

Status: Unregistered   **Type**: Friendly society
Established: First known 1860 **Dissolved**: Last known 1860
Headquarters: Town Hall (1860)
Membership: 120 members in 1860
Notes: The society held an annual tea meeting at the Town Hall (JOJ, 28 July 1860).

> **Lamb Benefit Society** – see Burford Mutual Benefit Society, Burford 144

149.   Loyal Tree of Friendship Lodge

Status: Branch of an affiliated order, OXF 139   **Type**: IOOFMU **Branch no.** 3471
Established: 21 April 1843   **Registered:** 14 September 1852   **Dissolved**: 1852
Headquarters: White Horse Inn, Market Square (1843-1855)
Anniversary/feast day: Easter Monday
Membership: 50 members in 1844, 27 in 1850

Primary Sources: TNA, FS 4/42/139
Notes: Oxford District of IOOFMU (1844-46), Witney District (1850).

Caversham

No. of friendly societies and members 1802/3 – None
No. of members of a friendly society 1813/14/15 – None

150. Caversham Friendly Society

Status: Enrolled, OXF 99   **Type:** Permanent friendly society
Established: 21 May 1832   **Registered:** 24 November 1843   **Dissolved:** 28 April 1858
Headquarters: Black Horse Inn (1832-1858)
Anniversary/feast day: Whit Monday
Minimum age at entry: 18 Maximum age at entry: 30
Membership: 51 in 1858
Primary Sources: Rulebook of 1843, TNA, FS 1/578/99; TNA, FS 4/42/99; rulebook of 1844, BRO D/EX 1044/7/2
Notes: The society permitted a maximum of 101 members with new members required to reside within four miles of the club house at the Black Horse Inn. New members decided by ballot using black and white balls. A blue and white bow had to be worn on members' hats on each club day by members. Eleven governors and honorary members held control over the society.

151. Caversham Subordinate Division

Status: Branch of an affiliated order **Type:** OSOT **Branch no.** 1484
Established: 1910 **Dissolved:** Last known 1910
Headquarters: Wesleyan Schoolroom, Gosbrook Rd (1910)
Membership: 23 members in 1910

152. Court Noble

Status: Branch of an affiliated order, OXF 307   **Type:** AOF **Branch no.** 5534
Established: 1870   **Registered:** 1871   **Dissolved:** Post 1918
Headquarters: Clifton Arms (1871-1875), British Schoolroom (1876-1880), Fox and Hounds [1890], Clifton Arms [1905-post 1918)
Membership: 22 members in 1885, 37 in 1895, 53 in 1900, 47 in 1910
Primary Sources: BRO D/EX 1793/1

Notes: London United District of AOF. A joint testimony with Court Saunders (Caversham 153) was presented to Reverend William Sully Unwin, dated 5 January 1893 for his services to the inauguration and development of the annual Hospital Sunday parade (BRO D/EX 1793/1).

153.   Court Saunders

Status: Branch of an affiliated order **Type**: AOF **Branch no.** 6772
Established: 1881 **Dissolved**: Post 1918
Headquarters: Black Horse Inn, Emmer Green (1881-post 1918)
Membership: 25 members in 1881, 63 in 1885, 120 in 1890, 170 in 1895, 204 in 1900, 242 in 1905, 313 in 1910
Primary Sources: BRO D/EX 1793/1
Notes: Reading District of AOF. Merged with Emmer Green Juvenile Foresters Friendly society (Caversham 154) on its dissolution in 1907. A joint testimony with Court Noble (Caversham 152) was presented to Reverend William Sully Unwin, dated 5 January 1893 for his services to the inauguration and development of the annual Hospital Sunday parade.

154.   Emmer Green Juvenile Foresters Friendly Society

Status: Juvenile branch of an affiliated order, OXF 362   **Type:** AOF
Established: 1885   **Registered:** 29 September 1888   **Dissolved:** 7 March 1907
Headquarters: Reading Room, Emmer Green (1885-1907)
Anniversary/feast day: January
Minimum age at entry: 6 Maximum age at entry: 17
Membership: 51 members in 1890, 62 in 1891, 52 in 1899, 49 in 1905
Primary Sources: Rulebooks of 1888 and 1903, TNA, FS 3/322/362; TNA, FS 4/42/361
Notes: The registration was cancelled on amalgamation with Court Saunders (Caversham 153).

155.   Loyal St Peter's Lodge

Status: Branch of an affiliated order, OXF 322   **Type:** IOOFMU **Branch no.** 5595
Established: 1873   **Registered:** 1874   **Dissolved**: Post 1918
Headquarters: Griffin Inn (1873-1876), Duke of Edinburgh, Caversham Road, Reading (1877), Blagrave Arms, Blagrave Street, Reading (1878-1894], Lower Ship Hotel, Reading [1901-post 1918)

Membership: 21 members in 1874
Notes: Reading District of IOOFMU. Society was initially based in Caversham but moved to Reading, Berkshire in 1877.

156.   Loyal Stephen Bristow Lodge

Status: Branch of an affiliated order **Type**: IOOFMU **Branch no.** 7757
Established: 1903 **Dissolved**: Last known 1910
Headquarters: Prince of Wales Inn, Prospect Street (1905), Weston Mead, Church St (1910)
Membership: 68 members in 1905, 62 in 1910
Notes: Reading District of IOOFMU.

157.   Noble Juvenile Foresters Friendly Society

Status: Juvenile branch of an affiliated order, OXF 391 **Type**: AOF
Established: 1886   **Registered:** 1903 or 1904 **Dissolved**: Post 1914
Headquarters: Fox and Hounds (1886), Clifton Arms [1895-1914]
Minimum age at entry: 3 **Maximum age at entry**: 16
Membership: 23 members in 1886, 27 in 1895, 37 in 1900, 99 in 1905, 73 in 1910

158.   Sanctuary Noble

Status: Branch of an affiliated order, OXF 326   **Type**: AOS
Established: 1874   **Registered:** 1875   **Dissolved**: Last known 1880
Headquarters: Clifton Arms (1874), White Horse Inn [1876-1878], Fox and Hounds Inn (1880)
Membership: 10 members in 1876, 17 in 1880

Chadlington

No. of friendly societies and members 1802/3 – 1, 80
No. of members of a friendly society 1813/14/15 – 75, 78, 76
Notes: (See also appendix 2, Crimes 35).

159.   Chadlington Friendly Society

Status: Enrolled   **Type**: Friendly society
Established: 1766   **Registered:** 1794   **Dissolved**: Last known 1794
Headquarters: Horseshoe Inn (1766-1794)

Anniversary/feast day: Easter Monday
Maximum age at entry: under 35
Primary Sources: Rules, dated 1 January 1776, OHC, QSD/R/7
Notes: The society is not known in records after enrolment in 1794 but is probably the one in existence in 1802/3 and 1813-1815.

160.   Chadlington Friendly Society

Status: Registered, number OXF 230   **Type:** Friendly society
Established: 1860   **Registered:** 20 September 1860   **Dissolved:** 11 January 1866
Headquarters: Horseshoe Inn (1860-1864), Reading Room (1864-1866)
Anniversary/feast day: Easter Monday
Minimum age at entry: 15 Maximum age at entry: under 40
Membership: 26 members in 1862, 19 in 1866
Primary Sources: Rulebook 1860, Agreement for dissolution 1866, NA, FS1/581/230; NA, FS4/42/230
Notes: The society dissolved with 19 benefit members, three honorary members and £90.

161.   Chadlington New Friendly Society

Status: Registered, number OXF 276   **Type:** Friendly society
Established: 1866   **Registered:** 16 February 1867   **Dissolved:** 1892
Headquarters: Reading-room [1876-1885), Sandy Arms Inn (1885-1892)
Anniversary/feast day: Easter Monday
Minimum age at entry: 15 Maximum age at entry: 45
Membership: 40 in 1872, 22 in 1875, 32 in 1878, 30 in 1885
Primary Sources: Rulebook 1866, NA, FS 3/321/276; NA, FS 4/42/276
Notes: Registration was cancelled by the Registrar as the society had ceased to exist, date not stated. A letter of 6 March 1894 explained the demise of the club was due to high mortality and lack of funds.

162.   (Horseshoe Club)

Status: Unregistered   **Type:** Friendly society
Established: 1857   **Dissolved:** Last known 1857
Headquarters: Horseshoe Inn (1857)
Anniversary/feast day: Easter Monday
Notes: The society held a joint club day in 1857 with the New Union Friendly Society (Chadlington 164) (JOJ, 18 April 1857).

163.   Loyal Pride of Chadlington Lodge

Status: Branch of an affiliated order **Type**: IOOFMU **Branch no.** 7372
Established: 1896   **Dissolved**: After 1914
Headquarters: Sandys Arms (1896-1901), Parish Room (1905-1912)
Membership: 25 in 1897, 168 in 1905, 196 in 1913.
Notes: Banbury District of IOOFMU.

164.   New Union Friendly Society

Status: Unregistered   **Type**: Friendly society
Established: 1840   **Dissolved**: Last known 1857
Headquarters: Sandy's Arms (1852-1857)
Anniversary/feast day: Easter Monday
Maximum age at entry: under 35
Notes: In 1855 this was the only club in the village. *Jackson's Oxford Journal* reported in 1852 that on club day an old practice was undertaken with people tied in their houses, gates lifted off their hinges and thrown in the brook, and knockers and bells in the village pulled off or spoilt. 'With the exception of these mischievous proceedings all passed off very quietly' (JOJ, 17 April 1852). The society held a joint club day in 1857 with the Horseshoe Club (Chadlington 162) (JOJ, 18 April 1857).

165.   Sandys Arms Club

Status: Unregistered   **Type**: Friendly society
Established: First known 1899 **Dissolved**: Last known 1899
Headquarters: Sandys Arms (1899)
Anniversary/feast day: Easter Monday
Notes: An application for an extension of licensing hours for club day was heard at Chadlington PSD (JOJ, 25 March 1899).

Chalgrove

No. of societies and members 1802/3 – None
No. of members of a friendly society 1813/14/15 – None
Notes: A restored banner of the Chalgrove Friendly Society is on display at St Mary's Church, Chalgrove. It is royal blue with a red border and has two scrolls with wording 'Chalgrove Friendly Society' and 'Established July 6th 1840'. The centre of the banner contains a laurel and oak wreath with two

clasped hands in the centre. The hands represent mutual help, responsibility and reciprocal friendship (Victoria Solt Dennis, *Discovering Friendly and Fraternal Societies: Their badges and* regalia [Oxford 2005], p.53). The reverse is identical. The age of the banner is unknown. Club day was still celebrated until at least 1911.

166.   Chalgrove Friendly Society

Status: Enrolled, OXF 58   **Type**: Permanent friendly society
Established: 6 July 1840   **Registered:** 2 November 1840   **Dissolved**: 1853
Headquarters: Red Lion Inn (1840-1845]
Anniversary/feast day: Whit Wednesday
Minimum age at entry: 14 **Maximum age at entry**: 45
Primary Sources: Rulebook of 1845, TNA, FS 1/579/141; TNA, FS 4/42/58
Notes: Two sets of rules of different clubs appear under TNA, FS 1/579/141. The first is dated 1845 and refers to this society. They indicate that there was a break in the society, probably a division of funds, in 1845 and all members were admitted to the re-formed society 'without limitation' which continued until 1853. A second rule book, dated 1853 is substantially the same, but it appears the society divided again and re-formed anew that year with new registration number OXF 141 (Chalgrove 167). There was confusion at the Registrar's Office between the two societies. No separate records for OXF 58 (this society) appear in the Registrar's records under that reference in the TNA.

167.   Chalgrove Friendly Society

Status: Enrolled, OXF 141   **Type:** Permanent friendly society
Established: 1853   **Registered:** 1854   **Dissolved:** Last known 1880
Headquarters: Red Lion Inn (1853-1880)
Anniversary/feast day: Whit Wednesday
Minimum age at entry: 14 Maximum age at entry: 45
Membership: 71 members in 1855, 106 in 1865, 92 in 1872, 71 in 1875, 90 in 1876 and 99 in 1880
Primary Sources: Rulebook of 1853, TNA, FS 1/579/141; TNA, FS 4/42/58
Notes: In later reports to the Registrar, the reference OXF 58 was predominantly used as the reference although it had been re-registered under the new number OXF 141. Similar confusion existed at the Registrar's office in the Index to Rules and Amendments, Series II (TNA, FS 4/42/58) between OXF 58 and OXF 141 (Chalgrove 166 and 167). A letter dated 13 January 1881 from an unnamed person to the Registrar stated, 'There is no Registered club at Red Lion Chalgrove now, there used to be a few years back' (TNA, FS 4/42/58).

The society still met at the Red Lion in 1878 (TG, 25 June 1878) and the Report of the Chief Registrar for the year ending 31 December 1880 showed the society had made a return for that year reporting 99 members and no change in registered office (BPP 1883, LXVII (212), pp.662-663). (See also appendix 2, Crimes 36).

168.   Chalgrove Friendly Society

Status: Registered, OXF 382   **Type:** Permanent friendly society
Established: 1892   **Registered:** 24 February 1893   **Dissolved:** 23 June 1913
Headquarters: Red Lion Inn (1892-1913)
Anniversary/feast day: Whit Wednesday
Minimum age at entry: 16 Maximum age at entry: 40
Membership: 99 members in 1899, 92 in 1905, 82 in 1911
Primary Sources: Rulebook of 1893, TNA, FS 3/322/382; TNA, FS 4/42/382
Notes: In 1900 William Phelps was charged with stealing £4 4s from the society (see appendix 2, Crimes 37). The society dissolved with 74 members and £275 17s 9d.

Charlbury

No. of societies and members 1802/3 – 4, 296
No. of members of a friendly society 1813/14/15 – 153, 157, 159
Notes: Charlbury had the second highest number of societies in Oxfordshire in 1803 alongside Witney and Woodstock, with Oxford having most. The club feast continued until at least 1899. (See also appendix 2, Crimes 39, 40, and 41).

The Bell Club – see Charlbury Old Club, Charlbury 171

169.   Bull Club (1809), then Charlbury Friendly Provident Society (1843)

Status: Enrolled, OXF 68   **Type:** Permanent friendly society
Established: 14 June 1806   **Registered:** 1809   **Dissolved:** 1843
Headquarters: Bull (1809), Grammar School (1843)
Anniversary/feast day: 29 May
Minimum age at entry: 14 **Maximum age at entry:** 40, then 50 (1843)
Primary Sources: Rules of 1809, TNA, FS 1/578/89; rulebook of 1843, TNA, FS 1/578/68; TNA, FS 1/577/68

Notes: The society was for male and female members. Some papers for this society were misfiled by the Registrar under TNA, FS 1/578/89. The club permitted a maximum of 101 members. The revised rules of 1843 stated residents from Charlbury or any village within four miles could be admitted as members. The society was controlled by its honorary members. Benefits were payable up to 65, and included the life assurance of members' children. A letter of 28 March 1856 from W.S. Allen explained that the society was dissolved in 1843 when only two members joined under new rules.

Charlbury Friendly Provident Society – see Bull Club, Charlbury 169

170.   Charlbury New Friendly Benefit Society

Status: Registered, OXF 210   **Type:** Permanent friendly society
Established: January 1858   **Registered:** 21 December 1858   **Dissolved:** 1906
Headquarters: The registered office is unclear at certain times and the following includes all possibilities identified by the sources. Oxford House (1858-68], Rose and Crown Inn [1875-1882), White Hart [1889], White Hart [1893], Bell Inn (1889 -1899), White Hart Inn (1899-1906)
Anniversary/feast day: Second Tuesday in July; then either first or second Friday in July; then from 1893 first Monday in December
Minimum age at entry: 18 Maximum age at entry: 40
Membership: 47 members in 1858, 76 in 1862, 91 in 1866, 118 in 1871, 126 in 1878, 165 in 1885, 159 in 1895, 151 in 1902, 60 in 1905
Primary Sources: Rulebook of 1858, TNA, FS 3/320/210; FS 4/42/210
Notes: In 1899 it was described as the oldest club in Charlbury (JOJ, 24 June 1899). A letter dated 18 November 1907 to the Registrar stated that no money had been received from members since 1906. Further correspondence ensued and legal action was threatened by the Registrar on 5 December 1907 unless the Trustees filed the appropriate papers of dissolution. The registration of the society was eventually cancelled on 3 January 1908. (TNA, FS 3/320/210).

171.   Charlbury Old Club, also The Bell Club

Status: Enrolled, OXF 174   **Type**: Permanent friendly society
Established: 8 February 1762   **Registered:** 13 January 1794   **Dissolved**: 7 January 1870
Headquarters: Bell Inn [1840-1870)
Anniversary/feast day: 29 May

Maximum age at entry: 40
Membership: 35 members in 1862
Primary Sources: Oxon. Cal. QS iii, p.594; undated manuscript rules
(probably 1794), and rulebook of 1858, TNA, FS 1/580/174; George Jennings
Davies, *A farewell letter to the parishioners of Charlbury, Oxon* (1857), p.29,
OHC, P CHARa/283/(DAV)
Notes: The Charlbury Old Club was the first in Oxfordshire to achieve 100
years continued existence. The rules were confirmed at the Epiphany Quarter
Sessions, 1794 (Oxon. Cal. QS iii, p.594) and it changed its name to Old Club
at this time. Its previous name is unknown. In 1852, the railway labourers
building the new Oxford, Worcester, and Wolverhampton line participated
in club day (BG, 10 June 1852). In 1857, the former curate of St Mary's,
Charlbury, George Jennings Davies stated the Bell club had a 'bad system' in
relation to how it calculated its subscriptions to meet benefit payments which
were not in accordance with actuarial principles. On Saturday 8 February 1862
a large flag flew from the window of the Bell Hotel, together with a smaller
flag containing the inscription 'Braved 100 years' (JOJ, 15 February 1862). A
letter to the Registrar dated 8 January 1880 stated the society had dissolved on
7 January 1870 on a unanimous vote of members (TNA, FS 1/580/174). (See
also appendix 2, Crimes 38).

172.   Court Wychwood Forest

Status: Branch of an affiliated order **Type:** AOF **Branch No.** 7148
Established: 1883   **Dissolved:** Post 1918
Headquarters: Bell Inn (1884-post 1918)
Membership: 19 members in 1884, 57 in 1885, 106 in 1886, 97 in 1890, 127
in 1895, 133 in 1900, 181 in 1905, 218 in 1910
Notes: Oxford District of AOF.

> **The Crown Club** – see Elder Brothers Friendly Society, Charl-
> bury 173

173.   Elder Brothers Friendly Society, also The Crown Club

Status: Enrolled, OXF 218   **Type:** Permanent friendly society
Established: 8 May 1769   **Registered:** 21 May 1859   **Dissolved:** Last
known 1863
Headquarters: Rose & Crown [1846-1863)
Anniversary/feast day: 29 May
Minimum age at entry: 15 Maximum age at entry: 40

Membership: 34 members in 1862
Primary Sources: Manuscript rule of 8 May 1769, OHC, QSD/R/8; manuscript rules of 2 October 1810, and rulebook of 1859, TNA, FS 1/581/218; TNA, FS 4/42/218; George Jennings Davies, *A farewell letter to the parishioners of Charlbury, Oxon* (1857), p.29-30, OHC, P CHARa/283/(DAV)
Notes: The society permitted a maximum of 101 members. George Jennings Davies expressed a similar view of this society as the Charlbury Old Club (Charlbury 171). He stated that beyond a 'good dinner' at club day, the Crown Club finances were in a hopeless state. He suggested they joined the Oxfordshire Friendly and Medical Society (Charlbury 178), but the advice was not followed.

174.   (Glovers' club)

Status: Unregistered   **Type**: Annual dividing friendly society
Established: First known 1857 **Dissolved**: Last known 1857
Notes: George Davies, curate described a glovers' club that was in existence in 1857. It was an annual dividing society, 'so that a man migrating to another glove factory can get his money returned' (George Jennings Davies, *A farewell letter to the parishioners of Charlbury, Oxon* [1857], p.29, OHC, P CHARa/283/[DAV]). In 1851, 77 men and boys were employed at Samuel Pritchett's glove factory in Charlbury.

175.   Loyal Amicable Foresters Benefit Society

Status: Enrolled, OXF 137   **Type:** 5-year dividing friendly society
Established: 27 June 1848   **Registered:** June 1848   **Dissolved:** 1893
Headquarters: White Hart Inn (1848 -1887]
Anniversary/feast day: 27 June until 1867, then the Friday after first Tuesday in July
Minimum age at entry: 18 (17 from 1884) Maximum age at entry: 36 (41 from 1884)
Membership: 66 members in 1877, 70 in 1880, 63 in 1885
Primary Sources: Rulebooks of 1848 and 1869 with substantial amendments in 1884, TNA, FS 3/320/137; TNA, FS 4/42/137
Notes: The society was formed after the cessation of the Loyal Churchill Lodge, IOOFMU (Charlbury 176) and after Lord Churchill had turned his attention to the Oxfordshire Friendly and Medical Society (Charlbury 178). In 1869 the rules stated new members must earn at least 15s a week. The division of funds was to take place for the amount exceeding £500. Registration of the society was cancelled on 24 March 1897 as it had ceased to exist, but a letter

to the Registrar dated 2 May 1894 explained the society broke up 'more than a year ago' (TNA, FS 4/42/137).

176.   Loyal Churchill Lodge

Status: Branch of an affiliated order **Type**: IOOFMU **Branch No.** 3522
Established: 27 June 1843   **Dissolved**: 1848
Headquarters: White Hart Inn, Ship Street (1843-1848)
Membership: 25 members in 1844, 53 in 1846
Notes: Oxford District of IOOFMU. The society was dissolved on the formation of the Loyal Amicable Foresters Benefit Society (Charlbury 175) (JOJ, 17 June 1848).

177.   Loyal Evenlode Lodge

Status: Branch of an affiliated order **Type**: IOOFMU **Branch No.** 8015
Established: 1907   **Dissolved**: Post 1918
Headquarters: Rose and Crown (1907-10], Vicarage Room (1913)
Membership: 52 members in 1910, 55 in 1914
Notes: Banbury District of IOOFMU

178.   Oxfordshire Friendly and Medical Society

Status: Enrolled, OXF 110   **Type:** Permanent friendly society
Established: 1847   **Registered:** 14 April 1847   **Dissolved:** 1876
Headquarters: Cornbury Park, Charlbury (1847), Savings Bank, Oxford (1875), Cornbury Park, Charlbury (1877)
Anniversary/feast day: 19 May; Ascension Day from 1867
Minimum age at entry: 15 Maximum age at entry: 55
Membership: 20 members in 1855, 39 in 1860, 95 in 1863, 79 in 1866, 31 in 1870, 22 in 1875
Primary Sources: Rulebook of 1847, TNA, FS 1/578/110; TNA, FS 4/42/110
Notes: The aim of the Oxfordshire Friendly and Medical Society was to be a county society. It was initially established for three years and if at end of that period membership was greater than 50 it was to become a permanent society. If there were fewer than 50 members, the club was to be dissolved. It was open to male and female members in Oxfordshire and adjacent parishes. The society was to consist of branch clubs to be formed where there were at least ten benefit members and one honorary member. Rules permit the incorporation of other clubs subject to agreement of the committee. Branch clubs could have

an annual feast at a place fixed by the committee, but not at a public house. (TNA, FS 1/578/110)

The society did not achieve its aims and consisted of just two branches, initially at Finstock and then Charlbury, and never exceeded 95 benefit members in total. It had ten trustees including Duke of Marlborough, Earl of Macclesfield, Sir George Dashwood, Lord Norreys, Viscount Villiers, and Lord Churchill of Cornbury Park. The latter was also President of the managing committee that consisted of ten honorary members and control of the club rested with them (JOJ, 20 May 1854). George Davies, curate at Charlbury described The Oxfordshire as being better known as 'Lord Churchill's Club', and stated it was flourishing. He also reported, 'It has the advantage of having a branch in most parishes in the county of Oxford, so that any member may transfer his account if he moves to another village' (George Jennings Davies, *A farewell letter to the parishioners of Charlbury, Oxon* (1857), p.29, OHC, P CHARa/283/ [DAV]). This was incorrect. The society advertised widely and published its full accounts annually in *Jackson's Oxford Journal* (e.g. 20 May 1854). Lord Churchill managed the Finstock branch of the society whilst Benjamin Whippy of Lee Place managed the Charlbury branch. Club day was held on 19 May, Lord Churchill's wedding anniversary, but was changed to Ascension Day in 1867 to coincide with that of Finstock Independent Friendly Benefit Society (Finstock 288).

The Oxfordshire was dissolved by instrument in 1876 with 22 members and £914 19s 1½d assets, representing between 157% and 257% of contributions paid by the members. Large 'profits' accrued due to withdrawal of members who 'had been induced to leave by the attractions of dividing and other societies in the neighbourhood' (BPP 1877, LXXVII, [429], p.32). The remaining funds at dissolution were largely due to generous honorary subscriptions in the early years of the society.

The Oxfordshire was the only attempt at a whole county society although the South Oxfordshire Friendly Society (Henley on Thames 359) and Central Oxfordshire Friendly Society (Oxford 469) exhibited county society characteristics. The editorial in *Jackson's Oxford Journal* for 3 August 1889 lamented, 'The main drawback of establishing a County Society in Oxfordshire is the existence of village clubs in a dubious state'.

179. Star Friendly Society

Status: Enrolled   **Type**: Permanent friendly society
Established: 1 June 1778   **Registered:** 1794   **Dissolved**: Last known 1794
Headquarters: The Star (1794)
Anniversary/feast day: 29 May

Maximum age at entry: 40
Primary Sources: Rules of 8 November 1794 OA, QSD/R/10
Notes: The rules permitted a maximum of 101 members.

180.   White Hart Club

Status: Enrolled   **Type**: Permanent friendly society
Established: 30 June 1777   **Registered:** 1794   **Dissolved**: Last known 1805
Headquarters: White Hart Inn (1777-1805)
Anniversary/feast day: 30 May
Maximum age at entry: 40
Primary Sources: Oxon. Cal. QS iii, p.615; manuscript rules of 1794, OHC,
QSD/R/9
Notes: The rules were enrolled at Epiphany Quarter Sessions 1805.

Charlton on Otmoor

No. of societies and members 1802/3 – None
No. of members of a friendly society 1813/14/15 – None
Notes: (See also appendix 2, Crimes 42, 43 and 44)

181.   Charlton Friendly Society

Status: Enrolled, OXF 175   **Type**: Permanent friendly society
Established: 11 June 1771 **Dissolved**: Last known 1794
Headquarters: George Inn (1771-1794)
Anniversary/feast day: First Thursday in June
Maximum age at entry: 40
Primary Sources: Manuscript rules, TNA, FS 3/320/175; TNA, FS 4/42/175
Notes: If the report, *Abstract of Answers and Returns under Act for procuring
Returns relative to Expense and Maintenance of Poor in England* (BPP
1803-04, XIII) is accurate, this society ceased to exist by Easter 1802. There
was confusion in registration numbers at the Registrar's office thereafter. A
letter received by the Registrar dated 14 November 1895 and recorded under
reference TNA, FS 4/42/175 stated the society at Charlton on Otmoor had
commenced in 1863 but was not registered. This society had been registered
by the Registrar at least 44 years after it had ceased to exist, and its registration
was only formally cancelled on 24 March 1897.

182.   Charlton Friendly Society

Status: Enrolled, OXF 160   **Type**: Permanent friendly society
Established: 25 March 1825   **Registered:** 1825   **Dissolved**: Last known 1825
Headquarters: Crown Inn (1825)
Anniversary/feast day: Last Thursday in May
Maximum age at entry: 35
Primary Sources: Rulebook of 1825, TNA, FS 1/579/160; TNA, FS 4/42/160
Notes: The rules permitted a maximum of 101 members. The *Banbury Guardian* of 13 June 1844 reported the club feast and describes the club as a seven year dividing society. It is unclear if it was this society or a new one. The records of the Registrar do not reveal the date of cessation of the society and all correspondence concerns Charlton 181, registered society OXF 175.

183.   Charlton Friendly Society

Status: Unregistered   **Type:** 7-year dividing friendly society
Established: 1863 **Dissolved:** Last known 1911
Headquarters: George Inn (1863), Crown Inn (1880-1911)
Anniversary/feast day: Ascension Day
Minimum age at entry: 14 Maximum age at entry: 40
Membership: 47 members in 1880, 74 in 1896
Primary Sources: Rulebook of 1880 of Richard Fawdrey, Bodl. G.A. 8° 1255(8); TNA, FS 4/42/175
Notes: On division, one year's subscription per member was retained by the society. The George and Dragon is crossed out as club headquarters and replaced by a handwritten note, 'Crown Inn' (Bodl. G.A. 8° 1255(8)). A letter was received by the Registrar from J.S. Honour, dated 14 November 1895 regarding a previous registered society (Charlton on Otmoor 181). He stated the current society had commenced in 1863 but was not registered. An annual return to the Registrar had been made in 1887 but this was an error by the secretary of the club at is was an unregistered society (TNA, FS 4/42/175).

Checkendon

No. of societies and members 1802/3 – None
No. of members of a friendly society 1813/14/15 – None

184.   Checkendon Amicable Society

Status: Unregistered   **Type**: Permanent friendly society
Established: 5 May 1843 **Dissolved**: Last known 1898
Headquarters: Four Horseshoes (1843 and 1898)
Anniversary/feast day: Whit Wednesday
Minimum age at entry: 18 **Maximum age at entry**: 35
Primary Sources: Rulebook of 1843, BRO D/EX 1044/7/3;
Notes: The rules of 1843 permitted a maximum of 60 members. A benefit society met at the Four Horseshoes on club day, Whit Wednesday 1898. It is unclear if it was a continuation of Checkendon Amicable or a new society (HSOS, 10 June 1898). The society held an account with the Reading Savings Bank.

Chesterton

No. of societies and members 1802/3 – None
No. of members of a friendly society 1813/14/15 – None
Notes: (See also appendix 2, Crimes 45).

185.   Chesterton Sick Club

Status: Unregistered   **Type:** Annual dividing friendly society
Established: 1862 **Dissolved:** Last known 1915
Headquarters: National schoolroom (1865-1874], Reading Room [1880-1909]
Anniversary/feast day: Trinity Monday
Minimum age at entry: 14
Membership: 15 in 1882, 8 members in 1890, 7 in 1892, 4 in 1900, 3 in 1908, 2 in 1911
Primary Sources: Printed rules, undated but referring to rule amendments of 1865, 1867 and 1868, Bodl. G.A. OXF. B.185
Notes: Sickness benefit was for a maximum of six months. There were graded subscriptions of 1d weekly for ages 14 to 16 years, 1½d weekly for 16 to 18 years and 2d weekly for over 18s, providing benefit of 4s, 6s and 8s weekly. New members were required to reside within the immediate neighbourhood of the parish. Several members left in 1875 because of the activities of the Agricultural Labourers' Union, although the newspaper report was not clear whether they were honorary or benefit members (BH, 28 May 1875). By the late 1880s the club was closed to new members and had just a handful of

remaining members who were elderly. The wish of the Reverend William Fortescue (died 1889), the club founder, was that it should continue as long as one member survived. With honorary subscriber support this was achieved and in 1911 just two members survived (G. Hayward and J. Holland). From 1879 a joint club day and dinner was held with the Chesterton branch of the UPI (Chesterton 186). The club headquarters was decorated with laburnum (BicA, 7 June 1901). Club day and was abandoned in 1915 due to the Great War (BicA, 28 May 1915).

186.   United Provident Institution, Chesterton sub-branch

Status: A sub-branch of a registered society, MDX 3103   **Type**: Permanent friendly society **Branch No.** 96
Established: First known 1879 **Dissolved**: Post 1915
Headquarters: Reading Room [1880-1909]
Anniversary/feast day: Trinity Monday
Membership: Membership figures were generally included in the Bicester branch (Bicester 97). Chesterton sub-branch had 40 members in 1890 and 50 in 1913
Notes: Chesterton was a sub-branch of the Bicester branch (Bicester 107) of the UPI that had its headquarters in Finchley. From 1879 a joint club day and dinner was held with the Chesterton Sick club (Chesterton 185). In 1900 the Rev. A. Walsh decided the church would take no part in the proceedings and there was no church service or children's tea. He objected to certain conduct on club days (BicA, 15 June 1900). In 1901, the Reading Room was decorated with laburnum for club day, and two flags with mottos, 'Union is Strength' and 'And become the first fruits of themselves' (BicA, 7 June 1901). Club day and was abandoned in 1915 due to the Great War (BicA, 28 May 1915).

Chinnor

No. of societies and members 1802/3 – None
No. of members of a friendly society 1813/14/15 – None

187.   Crown Inn Benefit Society

Status: Unregistered   **Type**: Friendly society
Established: First known 1870 **Dissolved**: Last known 1905
Headquarters: Crown Inn (1870-1905)
Anniversary/feast day: Whit Monday

188.   Loyal John Hampden Lodge

Status: Branch of an affiliated order **Type:** IOOFMU **Branch No.** 7393
Established: 1896   **Dissolved:** Post 1918
Headquarters: (Old) British School [1900-1910]
Membership: 36 in 1905, 29 in 1910
Notes: Buckingham District of IOOFMU.

189.   True Britons Friendly Society, also Tradesmen's club or Royal Oak Benefit club

Status: Unregistered   **Type:** 3-year dividing friendly society, changed to annual division after 1858
Established: 1853 **Dissolved:** Last known 1894
Headquarters: Royal Oak Inn [1857-1894)
Anniversary/feast day: Whit Wednesday, then Whit Monday (1891)
Notes: The society was subject to the theft of a gold bar worth £41 from the club box in 1858 (TG, 1 June 1858) (See appendix 2, Crimes 46). Thirty people were present for club dinner on Whit Monday, 1894 (HSOS, 18 May 1894).

Chipping Norton

No. of societies and members 1802/3 – 2, 202
No. of members of a friendly society 1813/14/15 – 202, 190, 184
Notes: Club day at Chipping Norton waned in the early 1850s but recovered in 1860s, where a cherry stall, shows, shooting galleries, photographic studios, merry-go-rounds, swings, tumblers, Morris dancers, and cheap jacks were reported (JOJ, 5 July 1864). A branch line of the Oxford, Worcester, and Wolverhampton railway had been extended to Chipping Norton in 1855. In 1874 it was reported there were 2000 visitors to club day. In the late 1880s the Oddfellows' fete became pre-eminent on club day as the Old Elm Tree Lodge (Chipping Norton 198) grew to be the largest society or branch in the county. (See also appendix 2, Crimes 48).

190.   Chipping Norton Friendly Society

Status: Enrolled, OXF 168   **Type:** Permanent friendly society
Established: 25 March 1765   **Registered:** 13 December 1794   **Dissolved:** 1885
Headquarters: White Hart Inn (1765-1794), Unicorn Inn (1794-1880]

Anniversary/feast day: First Tuesday in July
Minimum age at entry: 18 (1765 rules only) Maximum age at entry: 35 (1765) 40
Membership: 65 members in 1865
Primary Sources: Manuscript rules of 6/3/1765, OHC, QSD/R/11; rules of 1794, TNA. FS 1/580/168; TNA, FS 4/42/168
Notes: The rules permitted a maximum of 151 members. A new flag was displayed at the 1771 feast, depicting faith, hope and charity supported by peace with an olive branch, and strength with a bowl. The motto was 'Charity is our guide' (Dennis Lewis, *Chipping Norton Inns* p.62 [Chipping Norton, 2004]). No returns were made to the Registrar after 1867.

191.   Chipping Norton Friendly Society

Status: Enrolled, OXF 30   **Type**: Permanent friendly society
Established: First known 1839   **Registered:** 29 August 1839   **Dissolved**: 6 July 1886
Headquarters: King's Head Inn (1839-1855], Chequers Inn [1860-1876], King's Arms Inn [1881-1886)
Membership: 49 members in 1855, 70 in 1860, 69 in 1866, 32 in 1877, 20 in 1878, 17 in 1885
Primary Sources: TNA, FS 4/42/30
Notes: A letter of 13 September 1886 from three members stated the club was broken up on 5 July and all monies divided (TNA, FS 4/42/30).

192.   Chipping Norton Tent

Status: Branch of an affiliated order, OXF 97   **Type**: IORSU **Branch No:** 230
Established: 1840 **Registered:** 6 October 1840   **Dissolved**: 1849
Headquarters: Mr William Hawkins, New St (1855)
Anniversary/feast day: First Tuesday in July
Minimum age at entry: 16 **Maximum age at entry**: 45
Primary Sources: Rulebook of 1840, TNA, FS 1/578/97
Notes: An increase in club day attendees at Chipping Norton in 1842 was credited to the presence of the Rechabites. A tent was erected in New Street for the gathering (JOJ, 9 July 1842).

> **Chipping Norton Union Benefit Society** – see Union Society of Chipping Norton, Chipping

Norton 206

193.   Chipping Norton United Provident Juvenile Society

Status: Juvenile branch of registered society, OXF 353   **Type:** Juvenile friendly society
Established: 1885   **Registered:** 29 May 1885 **Dissolved:** 20 December 1902
Headquarters: Schoolroom, Baptist Chapel (1885-1902)
Minimum age at entry: 10 Maximum age at entry: 16
Membership: 16 in 1885, 20 in 1991, 3 in 1899
Primary Sources: Rulebook of 1885, TNA, FS 3/322/353
Notes: The society amalgamated with Chipping Norton United Provident Society on 20 December 1902 (Chipping Norton 194).

194.   Chipping Norton United Provident Society

Status: Enrolled, OXF 195   **Type:** Friendly society
Established: July 1851   **Registered:** 17 July 1857   **Dissolved:** 20 February 1914
Headquarters: Baptist Chapel Vestry [1857-1883], Baptist Chapel Schoolroom [1892-1914]
Anniversary/feast day: First Tuesday in July
Minimum age at entry: 18, 16 (from 1890) Maximum age at entry: 40
Membership: 90 members in 1860, 132 in 1863, 197 in 1870, 263 in 1876, 330 in 1879, 500 in 1885, 473 in 1891, 363 in 1902, 265 in 1905, 152 in 1913, 138 in 1914
Primary Sources: Rulebook of 1857 and 1890, TNA, FS 15/566;
Notes: Mowbray Jackson was surgeon in 1879 and he also served several other friendly societies in the area, namely Kingham Friendly Society (Kingham 397), Churchill and Sarsden Benefit Society (Churchill 209), United Christian Benefit Society (Chipping Norton 207), the Loyal Old Elm Tree Lodge (Chipping Norton 198) and the Old Guildhall Club (Chipping Norton 204) (JOJ, 12 July 1879). The society amalgamated with Chipping Norton United Provident Juvenile Society (Chipping Norton 193) in 1902. It was dissolved in 1914 with 138 members and £6 4s 6d funds.

195.   Chosen Lodge

Status: Branch of an affiliated order   **Type**: IOOFMU **Branch No. 3609**
Established: 1843 **Dissolved**: 1846
Headquarters: Chequers Inn (1844-1846)

Membership: 15 in 1844, 17 in 1845
Notes: Banbury District of IOOFMU (1844-1846).

196.   Four Shires Subordinate Division

Status: Branch of an affiliated order **Type:** OSOT **Branch No.** 618
Established: 1884 **Dissolved**: Last known 1910
Headquarters: British Schoolroom [1905-1910)
Membership: 211 members in 1905, 244 in 1910

197.   Friend in Need Benefit and Sick Fund Society, Chipping Norton Branch

Status: A branch of an enrolled society   **Type**: Permanent friendly society
Established: First known 1863 **Dissolved**: Last known 1863
Anniversary/feast day: 29 May
Notes: The Chipping Norton branch of a London based society, open to male and female members. Club day in 1863 was at a marquee in a field at Turnpike Road, Salford. This was a public tea meeting, costing 6d, and the first meeting of the branch. Rules stated that no meetings should take place at a public house, no beer money should be collected and that there should be 'no inducements to squander hard earned money' (JOJ, 13 June 1863). There were 150 people present at the tea.

198.   Loyal Old Elm Tree Lodge

Status: Branch of an affiliated order, OXF 315   **Type**: IOOFMU **Branch No.** 5964
Established: 1871 **Dissolved**: Post 1918
Headquarters: Blue Boar Inn (1871-1877), Fox Inn (Hotel) (1878-1907], Oddfellows Hall (1910-post 1918)
Membership: 190 members in 1872, 252 in 1877, 330 in 1881, 459 in 1886, 607 in 1895, 756 in 1901, 855 in 1905, 912 in 1910, 1000 in 1913
Primary Sources: Lodge rulebook of 1896, Main Committee minute book 1912-1921, personal membership cards for several members, Chipping Norton Museum
Notes: Banbury District of IOOFMU. The society commenced with three honorary members. Mowbray Jackson was surgeon in 1879 and he also served several other friendly societies in the area, namely Kingham Friendly Society (Kingham 397), Churchill and Sarsden Benefit Society (Churchill 209), Chipping Norton United Provident Society (Chipping Norton 194),

United Christian Benefit Society (Chipping Norton 207), and the Old Guildhall Club (Chipping Norton 204) (JOJ, 12 July 1879). It was the largest branch or society in the county and as it grew in size and influence within the Banbury District, there were tensions with the district structure (JOJ, 4 August 1900). In 1910 it had 50% more members than any other society or affiliated branch in Oxfordshire. Chipping Norton Museum has a permanent display on the Old Elm Tree Lodge that includes photographs, memorabilia, membership sashes, and regalia as well as several of the primary sources listed. A history of the branch has been written by Malcolm Bee, 'Within the Shelter of the Old Elm Tree: Oddfellowship and Community in North Oxfordshire, 1871-2002', *Family and Community History*, Vol. 6:2, (Nov. 2003), pp.85-96 (See also appendix 2, Crimes 47).

199.   Loyal Old Elm Tree Lodge, Juvenile Branch

Status: Juvenile branch of an affiliated order, OXF 335   **Type**: IOOFMU
Established: 1876 **Dissolved**: 1912
Headquarters: National Schoolroom (1876-1885], Co-operative Hall, High Street [1899-1912)
Membership: 60 members in 1877, 69 in 1880, 89 in 1891, 168 in 1899, 231 in 1905, 235 in 1910
Notes: Juvenile branch of Chipping Norton 198.

200.   Loyal Pride of the Old Elm Tree Female Lodge

Status: Branch of an affiliated order **Type:** IOOFMU **Branch No.** 7512
Established: 1899 **Dissolved**: Post 1918
Headquarters: Co-Operative Hall (1899-1907], Oddfellows Hall (1910-1912)
Membership: 42 members in 1900, 105 in 1905, 153 in 1910, 168 in 1913, 106 in 1914
Notes: Banbury District of IOOFMU.

201.   New Street Friendly Benefit Society

Status: Enrolled, OXF 108   **Type:** Permanent friendly society
Established: First known 1844   **Registered:** 22 August 1844   **Dissolved:** Last known 1876
Headquarters: George Inn (1844-1869), Fox Inn (1869-1876)
Anniversary/feast day: First Tuesday in July
Minimum age at entry: 18 Maximum age at entry: 40
Membership: 63 in 1862, 64 in 1866

Primary Sources: Rulebook of 1844, TNA, FS 1/578/108; TNA, FS 4/42/108
Notes: The society rules permitted a maximum 81 members. New members were required to earn a minimum of 12s a week.

202.　New Union Friendly Society, also Tradesmen's Club

Status: Enrolled, OXF 100　　**Type**: Permanent friendly society
Established: 6 August 1822　**Registered:** 4 July 1826　**Dissolved**: Last known 1843
Headquarters: Unicorn Inn [1826-1843), Kings Arms Inn (1843)
Anniversary/feast day: First Tuesday in July
Minimum age at entry: 16 **Maximum age at entry**: 35 (1826), 40 (1840), 35 (1843)
Primary Sources: Rulebooks of 1826, 1840 and 1843, TNA, FS 1/578/100; TNA, FS 4/42/100; Oxon. Cal. QS iii, p. 676
Notes: Rules enrolled at Michaelmas Quarter Sessions 1826 (Oxon. Cal. QS iii, p. 676). The 1826 rules state the society was established on 6 August 1822 and the 1840 rules on 1 October 1839. It appears there was a division, or dissolution and reforming of the society in 1839, at the same time a separate club was established, the Tradesmen's Union Society (Chipping Norton 205).

203.　New United Friendly Society

Status: Enrolled, OXF 219　　**Type**: Permanent friendly society
Established: First known 1859　**Registered:** 2 August 1859　**Dissolved**: 1885
Headquarters: Unicorn Inn (1859-1880]
Anniversary/feast day: First Tuesday in July
Minimum age at entry: 16 **Maximum age at entry**: 40
Primary Sources: Rulebook of 1859, TNA, FS 1/581/219; TNA, FS 4/42/219
Notes: New members were required to be in receipt of an average wage at joining at least 12s a week.

204.　Old Guildhall Club

Status: Enrolled, OXF 242　　**Type**: Permanent friendly society
Established: First known 1862　**Registered:** 22 January 1862　**Dissolved**: Last known 1882
Headquarters: Old Guildhall (1862-1882)
Anniversary/feast day: First Tuesday in July
Membership: 66 members in 1864, 76 in 1865

Primary Sources: TNA FS 4/42/242
Notes: Mowbray Jackson was surgeon in 1879 and he also served several other friendly societies in the area, namely Kingham Friendly Society (Kingham 397), Churchill and Sarsden Benefit Society (Churchill 209), Chipping Norton United Provident Society (Chipping Norton 194), the Loyal Old Elm Tree Lodge (Chipping Norton 198) and the United Christian Benefit Society (Chipping Norton 207) (JOJ, 12 July 1879). The society was described as 'one of the oldest benefit societies of the town' (JOJ, 10 July 1880) indicating it had descent from an earlier society. An un-dated letter from the Registrar was returned, stating 'No such club now existing at Chipping Norton' (TNA FS 4/42/242), and it appears to be similar to notes sent out by Registrar in the early 1880s.

> **Tradesmen's Club** – see New Union Friendly Society, Chipping Norton 202

205.   Tradesmen's Union Society

Status: Enrolled, OXF 32   **Type:** Permanent friendly society
Established: 1839   **Registered:** 27 September 1839   **Dissolved:** 1876
Headquarters: Blue Boar Inn (1839-1864]
Anniversary/feast day: First Tuesday in July
Membership: 42 members in 1863, 40 in 1866 and 16 in 1876
Primary Sources: Undated rulebook, TNA, FS 1/575/32; TNA, FS 4/42/32
Notes: New members were required to have a minimum income of 15s a week. Contributions were 2s a month if aged up to 40 years and 2s 6d thereafter. A note on the Registrar's file states the society was dissolved without any legal forms in 1876, and with 16 members and £96 (TNA, FS 4/42/32).

206.   Union Society of Chipping Norton, also Chipping Norton Union Benefit Society

Status: Enrolled, OXF 61   **Type:** Permanent friendly society, annual dividing friendly society after 1839
Established: 1807   **Registered:** 5 November 1836   **Dissolved:** Last known 1841
Headquarters: Bell Inn (1807), Fox Inn (1836-1841), King's Arms Inn (1841)
Anniversary/feast day: First Tuesday in July
Minimum age at entry:- Maximum age at entry: 35
Primary Sources: Rulebooks of 1807, 1836 and 1839, TNA, FS 1/576/61; TNA, FS 4/42/61

Notes: Members aged 65 received superannuation of 3s a week, and at 70 received 4s 6d a week. Up to 1839, if funds were below £30 members made them up by additional subscription. After 1839 it became an annual dividing society with any amount over £50 being divided between members.

207.   United Christian Benefit Society

Status: Enrolled, OXF 204   **Type:** Permanent friendly society
Established: 1858   **Registered:** 21 August 1858   **Dissolved:** 20 April 1898
Headquarters: Wesleyan Chapel (1858-1898)
Anniversary/feast day: Whit Monday
Minimum age at entry: 18 Maximum age at entry: 45
Membership: 68 members in 1874, 63 in 1877, 43 in 1885, 24 in 1898
Primary Sources: Rulebook of 1858, TNA, FS 3/320/204; FS 4/42/204
Notes: The rules permitted the appointment of local agents to collect subscriptions in outlying communities. The medical attendant covered the area of Chipping Norton, Over Norton and Salford. Mowbray Jackson was surgeon in 1879 and he also served several other friendly societies in the area, namely Kingham Friendly Society (Kingham 397), Churchill and Sarsden Benefit Society (Churchill 209), Chipping Norton United Provident Society (Chipping Norton 194), the Loyal Old Elm Tree Lodge (Chipping Norton 198) and the Old Guildhall Club (Chipping Norton 204) (JOJ, 12 July 1879). A letter dated 16 February 1898 stated the society was to be dissolved. A note on the Registrar's file stated it was dissolved on 20 April that year with 24 members and £31 18s 8d (TNA, FS 4/42/204).

208.   (Women's Benefit Club)

Status: Unregistered **Type**: Female shop club
Established: First known 1887 **Dissolved**: Last known 1887
Notes: This was a women's benefit society in connection with the Bliss Tweed Mill, a large woollen factory in the town, and had 300 members (JOJ, 26 March 1887)

Church Hanborough – see Hanborough

Churchill

No. of societies and members 1802/3 – None
No. of members of a friendly society 1813/14/15 – None

Notes: The club feast was still held until at least 1909 when sports played a part in the day of celebration.

209.   Churchill and Sarsden Benefit Society

Status: Unregistered   **Type:** Permanent friendly society
Established: 1841 **Dissolved:** Last known 1909
Anniversary/feast day: Whit Thursday
Membership: 73 members in 1892, 77 in 1899, 50 in 1905, 39 in 1907, 33 in 1909
Notes: On club day, dinners were held at the school provided by the Chequers Inn. At the time of the annual dinner, a tea was held for wives and children in a nearby field (CNDM, July 1882). Mowbray Jackson was surgeon in 1879 and he also served several other friendly societies in the area, namely Kingham Friendly Society (Kingham 397), United Christian Benefit Society (Chipping Norton 207), Chipping Norton United Provident Society (Chipping Norton 194), the Loyal Old Elm Tree Lodge (Chipping Norton 198) and the Old Guildhall Club (Chipping Norton 204) (JOJ, 12 July 1879). The society was supported by eleven honorary members in 1892 and ten in 1909. (See also appendix 2, Crimes 49).

Clanfield

No. of societies and members 1802/3 – None
No. of members of a friendly society 1813/14/15 – None

210.   Clanfield Provident Society

Status: Registered, OXF 345   **Type:** Permanent friendly society
Established: 1881   **Registered:** 3 January 1882   **Dissolved:** 1900
Headquarters: Public Elementary School (1881-1900)
Anniversary/feast day: Ascension Day
Minimum age at entry: 16 Maximum age at entry: 45
Membership: 28 members in 1885, 13 in 1899, 15 in 1900
Primary Sources: Rulebook of 1881, TNA, FS 3/321/345
Notes: The society was dissolved in 1900 with 15 members and £13 funds.

211.   Court Prince of Wales

Status: Branch of an affiliated order, OXF 299   **Type:** AOF Branch No. 5191
Established: 1868   **Registered:** 14 May 1869   **Dissolved:** 1874

Headquarters: Mason's Arms Inn (1868-1874)
Minimum age at entry: 18 Maximum age at entry: 40
Membership: 34 members in 1874
Primary Sources: Rulebook of 1869, TNA, FS 1/582/299; TNA, FS 4/42/299
Notes: Not associated with any district of AOF. An un-dated letter from William Farmer to the Registrar states the society had been abolished four years before (TNA, FS 4/42/299).

212.   (Mason's Arms Club)

Status: Unregistered   **Type**: Friendly society
Established: First known 1860 **Dissolved**: Last known 1862
Headquarters: Mason's Arms Inn (1860-1862)
Anniversary/feast day: Whit Thursday
Membership: 63 members in 1860, almost 100 in 1861

213.   Prince of Wales Club

Status: Registered, OXF 288   **Type:** Permanent friendly society
Established: 1 January 1868   **Registered:** 14 August 1868   **Dissolved:** 1913
Headquarters: Plough Inn (1868-1871], Masons' Arms Inn [1874-1877), Plough Inn (1877-1878), Mason's Arms Inn (1878-1913)
Anniversary/feast day: Whit Thursday
Minimum age at entry: 16 Maximum age at entry: 45
Membership: 18 members in 1871, 26 in 1874, 46 in 1880, 41 in 1885, 64 in 1899, 66 in 1910, 64 in 1913
Primary Sources: Rulebook of 1868, TNA, FS 3/321/288; TNA, FS 4/42/288; rulebook of 1875, Bodl. G.A. OXF 8° 688(2)
Notes: The rulebook of 1875 states the society was established on 14 June 1875, indicating that a division of funds took place but it re-formed or continued that year under the same registration number. Later reports acknowledge 1868 as the year of establishment. The rules unusually permitted members of this society to be a member of another friendly society. Most friendly societies excluded dual membership. The clubroom at the Masons' Arms was refurbished in 1899 (WG, 27 May 1899). The flag of the society was a Union Flag with a Fleur de Lis contained in a circle in the centre. It dissolved on 24 June 1913 with 64 members and £385 funds.

Claydon

No. of societies and members 1802/3 – None
No. of members of a friendly society 1813/14/15 – 5, 5, 5

214.   Claydon Friendly Society

Status: Unregistered   **Type:** Annual dividing friendly society
Established: 1863 **Dissolved:** Last known 1896
Headquarters: Sun Rising Inn [1881-1882], Old Malthouse [1895-1896]
Anniversary/feast day: Club day held various days including Friday before
Whitsun and Whit Tuesday.
Membership: 33 members in 1872, 46 in 1881
Primary Sources: BPP 1874, XXIII, (c.997), p.114-5
Notes: Club day was not held from 1896 (DDM, June 1896). The secretary,
Henry Perry was an agricultural labourer. The society discussed registration
but decided against as they wished to continue the annual division of funds. At
the time of the Assistant Commissioner's investigation in early 1872 the club
was eight years old (BPP 1874, XXIII, (c.997), p.114-5).

Cogges

No. of societies and members 1802/3 – None
No. of members of a friendly society 1813/14/15 – None

> **Carpenters Arms Friendly Society** – see Newland Friendly
> Society, Cogges 216

215.   Griffin Club

Status: Unregistered   **Type:** Friendly society
Established: First known 1872   **Dissolved:** 1884
Headquarters: The Griffin, Newland [1872-1881]
Anniversary/feast day: Whit Tuesday

216.   Newland Friendly Society, also Carpenters Arms Friendly
Society

Status: Unregistered   **Type:** Friendly society
Established: First known 1870   **Dissolved:** Last known 1901
Headquarters: Carpenters Arms, Newland (1870-1901)

Anniversary/feast day: Whit Tuesday.
Membership: 26 in 1901
Notes: A fair was held in the road on club day (WE, 8 June 1876). The society was the only one at Witney that continued to engage a band for club day from 1888 (JOJ, 26 May 1888) but they eventually dispensed with them in 1901 (JOJ, 1 June 1901).

Combe

No. of societies and members 1802/3 – 1, 101
No. of members of a friendly society 1813/14/15 – 99, 78, 85
Notes: The final club feast in Combe appears to have been in 1889 before the collapse of the last society.

217.   Combe Friendly Society

Status: Enrolled   **Type**: Friendly society
Established: 19 May 1780   **Registered:** 1794   **Dissolved**: Last known 1794
Headquarters: Cock Inn (1794)
Anniversary/feast day: Ascension Day
Maximum age at entry: 35
Primary Sources: Manuscript rules of 1794, OHC, QSD/R/12
Notes: Rules permitted a maximum of 121 members.

218.   Combe Friendly Society

Status: Enrolled, OXF 66   **Type**: Friendly society
Established: 1839   **Registered:** 10 December 1841   **Dissolved**: 1862
Headquarters: Blandford Arms Inn (1839-1855]
Anniversary/feast day: Ascension Day
Maximum age at entry: 30
Membership: 11 members in 1846, 32 in 1850, 70 in 1862
Primary Sources: Rulebook of 1842, TNA, FS 1/578/99; TNA, FS 1/576/66
Notes: Registrar's records for this society are misfiled under TNA, FS 1/578/99. The society was dissolved in 1862 with 70 members and £340 funds. Two new societies were formed on its dissolution, Combe Friendly Society (Combe 219) and Combe New Friendly Society (Combe 222).

219.   Combe Friendly Society

Status: Registered, OXF 255   **Type**: Friendly society

Established: 1863   **Registered:** 9 December 1863   **Dissolved**: 28 June 1879
Headquarters: Blandford Arms Inn (1863-1875), Royal Oak (1875-1879)
Anniversary/feast day: Ascension Day
Maximum age at entry: 30
Membership: 104 members in 1879
Primary Sources: Rulebook of 1863, TNA, FS 1/582/255; TNA, FS 4/42/255
Notes: One of two societies established on the dissolution of Combe 218. In 1879 Dr F. Stockwell was surgeon to the club as well as to societies at Stonesfield (626), Woodstock (727), and Tackley (632).The society dissolved with 104 members and £395 11s 10d funds and continued as Combe 220.

220.   Combe Friendly Society

Status: Registered, OXF 342   **Type:** Friendly society
Established: 1880   **Registered:** 17 December 1880   **Dissolved:** 1885
Headquarters: Royal Oak Inn (1880-1885)
Anniversary/feast day: Ascension Day
Minimum age at entry: 16 Maximum age at entry: 30
Membership: 104 members in 1879, 96 members in 1885
Primary Sources: Rulebook of 1880, TNA, FS 3/321/342; TNA, FS 4/42/342
Notes: This was a continuation of Combe 219. A division of funds was to take place when it reached £400, with one year's membership being retained. A letter of 29 May 1894 from H. Martin, late secretary, to the Registrar stated the society ceased to exist in 1885. 'The funds were entirely exhausted, and the last shilling paid to sick members' (TNA, FS 4/42/342). The registration was cancelled on 24 March 1897, and the society re-established as Combe 221. (See also appendix 2, Crimes 50)

221.   Combe Friendly Society

Status: Unregistered   **Type**: Friendly society
Established: 1885 **Dissolved**: Last known 1890
Headquarters: Royal Oak (1885-1890)
Anniversary/feast day: Ascension Day
Membership: 99 members in 1886, 20 in 1890
Notes: Reports in *Jackson's Oxford Journal* state the society was formed in 1839 showing lineage from societies Combe 218, Combe 219, and Combe 220. All previous clubs were registered. There was a complete collapse of the society in 1890 and the holiday on Ascension Day was 'completely blank' (JOJ, 24 May 1890). It was unable to meet its sickness payments as there had

been a division of funds some years earlier (it is unclear if the division took place during the term of this society or a previous incarnation).

222.   Combe New Friendly Society

Status: Registered, OXF 247   **Type**: 5-year dividing friendly society
Established: 1862   **Registered:** 17 November 1862   **Dissolved:** 4 January 1873
Headquarters: Royal Oak (1862-1873)
Anniversary/feast day: Second Friday in July
Minimum age at entry: 12 Maximum age at entry: 40
Membership: 63 members in 1863, 79 in 1866, 26 in 1873
Primary Sources: Rulebook of 1862, TNA, FS 1/581/247; TNA, FS 4/42/247
Notes: One of two societies established on the dissolution of Combe 218. On 3 October 1863, the Hand in Hand Benefit Society (Combe 223) amalgamated with this club. The society dissolved with 26 members and £32 4s 7d funds.

223.   Hand in Hand Benefit Society

Status: Registered, OXF 202   **Type**: 5-year dividing friendly society
Established: 1857   **Registered:** 17 March 1858   **Dissolved**: 3 October 1863
Headquarters: Marlborough Arms Inn (1858-1863), Mr T Collet's (1863)
Anniversary/feast day: 1 July
Minimum age at entry: 12 **Maximum age at entry**: 40
Primary Sources: Rulebook of 1857, TNA, FS 1/581/202; TNA, FS 4/42/202
Notes: A letter to the Registrar dated 5 August 1863 stated that due to the treatment of one of the members by the landlord of the Marlborough Arms, the society had removed to the house of Mr Collett at Long Combe. A further letter of 20 December 1864 stating the Hand in Hand society had amalgamated with the New Friendly Society held at the Royal Oak (Combe 222).

Cowley

No. of societies and members 1802/3 – None
No. of members of a friendly society 1813/14/15 – None

224.   Court Knight of the Temple

Status: Branch of an affiliated order **Type**: AOF **Branch No.** 7724
Established: 1889   **Dissolved**: Post 1918
Headquarters: The Exeter Hall (1890), Nelson Inn [1905-post 1918]

Membership: 33 members in 1883, 53 in 1886, 101 in 1891, 122 in 1901, 148 in 1910, 194 in 1913
Notes: Oxford District of AOF. In 1899 William Churchill was charged with withholding £30 of club money (see appendix 2, Crimes 51).

225.   Cowley Benefit Society

Status: Registered, OXF 375   **Type:** Permanent friendly society
Established: 1892   **Registered:** 5 April 1892   **Dissolved:** 17 November 1894
Headquarters: Nelson Inn (1892-1894)
Anniversary/feast day: First Monday after 26 December
Minimum age at entry: 16 Maximum age at entry: 38
Membership: 42 members in 1894
Primary Sources: Rulebook of 1892, TNA, FS 3/322/375; TNA, FS 4/42/375
Notes: There were 42 members and £107 funds when the society dissolved in 1894 (TNA, FS 4/42/375).

226.   Cowley Excelsior Subordinate Division

Status: Branch of an affiliated order **Type**: OSOT **Branch No.** 829
Established: 1896   **Dissolved**: Last known 1910
Headquarters: Primitive Methodist Mission Room [1905-1910)

227.   Cowley United Benefit Society

Status: Unregistered   **Type**: Friendly society
Established: 1831 **Dissolved**: Last known 1894
Headquarters: Carpenters Arms (1860-1870), Nelson Inn [1873], Carpenters Arms [1883-1890), Nelson Inn (1894)
Anniversary/feast day: Whit Tuesday
Membership: 100 members in 1883, 94 in 1885

Cropredy

No. of societies and members 1802/3 – 1, 84
No. of members of a friendly society 1813/14/15 – 100, 102, 105

228.   Advance Tent

Status: Branch of an affiliated order **Type**: IORSU **Branch No.** 4198

Established: 1912   **Dissolved**: Post 1914
Primary Sources: TNA, FS 3/322/367
Notes: The society was formed from Cropredy United Temperance Friendly society (Cropredy 231) in 1912.

229.   Cropredy Benefit Society

Status: Enrolled, OXF 171   **Type**: Permanent friendly society
Established: 23 September 1783   **Registered:** 1818   **Dissolved**: 1830
Headquarters: Red Lion Inn (1783 -1830)
Anniversary/feast day: Whit Tuesday
Maximum age at entry: 40
Membership: 102 members in 1783
Primary Sources: Manuscript rules of 1783, TNA, FS 3/320/171; Oxon. Cal. QS iii, p.663
Notes: The society was founded at the Red Lion on 23 September 1783 when 102 members signed the rules (TNA, FS 3/320/171). The rules were amended on 16 June 1823 and approved at Trinity Session 1823 (Oxon. Cal. QS iii, p.663). A letter dated 8 March 1894 stated the society established at Cropredy in 1783 broke up about 1830. It explained a new, unregistered society commenced in Cropredy in 1838 and continued at time of writing (Cropredy 230) (TNA, FS 4/42/171). Registration of the society was not cancelled until 24 March 1897 although it had ceased to exist 64 years earlier.

230.   Cropredy Benefit Society

Status: Unregistered   **Type**: Permanent friendly society
Established: 18 June 1838   **Dissolved**: Last known 1908
Headquarters: Red Lion Inn and Brasenose, alternate years (1838-1908)
Anniversary/feast day: Whit Tuesday
Membership: 144 members in 1882
Primary Sources: TNA, FS 4/42/171; BPP 1874, XXIII, (c.997), p.115
Notes: A letter to the Registrar dated 8 March 1894 concerning the enrolled society, Cropredy 229, stated a new, unregistered society commenced in 1838. The writer had been an honorary member since 1857 and the society was still in existence when he wrote (TNA, FS 4/42/171). The Assistant Commissioner noted in 1872 that the society met alternately at two Inns in the village. It had 118 members and some 'very rich men' among the eleven honorary members. The funds were invested at 6½% or 7% in trade stocks and shares. The society remained unregistered so there were no restrictions on investment as with registered societies, and so gained a higher interest rate on their funds with

higher risk investments. Subscription was 3s 3d a quarter but only 9s 9d a year as it appeared the further amount was paid back in beer in the club room. Benefit for burial was £2 plus 1s levy on each member. The Cropredy club day was still well attended by Banbury residents in 1908 (JOJ, 20 June 1908).

231.   Cropredy United Temperance Friendly Society

Status: Registered, OXF 367   **Type**: Permanent friendly society
Established: 1888   **Registered:** 12 August 1889   **Dissolved**: 9 March 1912
Headquarters: Wesleyan schoolroom (1889-1912)
Anniversary/feast day: Second Tuesday in June
Primary Sources: Rulebook of 1889, TNA, FS 3/322/367; TNA, FS 4/42/367
Notes: Registration was cancelled in 1912 to become the 'Advance Tent' of the IORSU (Cropredy 228).

Crowmarsh Gifford

No. of societies and members 1802/3 – None
No. of members of a friendly society 1813/14/15 – None

232.   Crowmarsh Friendly Society, also Crowmarsh and Newnham Murren Benefit Society

Status: Registered, OXF 331   **Type**: Permanent friendly society
Established: Earliest known 1875   **Registered:** 21 August 1875   **Dissolved**: 12 February 1886
Headquarters: Queens Head Inn (1876-1880), National schoolroom (1880-1886)
Anniversary/feast day: Whit Tuesday
Membership: 40 members in 1875, 75 in 1880, 73 in 1885, 26 in 1886
Primary Sources: The Registrar's records at TNA are misfiled under reference FS 1/575/31; TNA, FS 4/42/331
Notes: Club day involved activities at Newnham Park (WT, 2 June 1882). It was described as a 'small society' in 1883 (WT, 18 May 1883) and was dissolved by instrument with £43 19 s 5d funds and 26 members.

> **Crowmarsh and Newnham Murren Benefit Society** – see
> Crowmarsh Friendly Society,
>
> Crowmarsh Gifford 232

233.   Hand in Hand Benefit Society

Status: Enrolled, OXF 85   **Type:** Annual dividing friendly society
Established: Earliest known 1843   **Registered:** 12 August 1843   **Dissolved:** 6 June 1867
Headquarters: Bell Inn (1843-1865]
Anniversary/feast day: Whit Wednesday
Minimum age at entry: 16 Maximum age at entry: 35
Membership: 55 members in 1846, 56 in 1847, 52 in 1850, 33 in 1867
Primary Sources: Rulebook of 1843, TNA, FS 1/577/85; TNA, FS 4/42/85
Notes: At the annual division of funds, twelve months' contribution of each continuing member was carried over, together with all contributions from honorary members.

Curbridge

No. of societies and members 1802/3 – None
No. of members of a friendly society 1813/14/15 – None

234.   Curbridge Friendly or Savings Club

Status: Enrolled, OXF 64   **Type:** 7-year dividing friendly society
Established: 3 July 1840   **Registered:** 23 September 1842   **Dissolved**: Last known 1842
Anniversary/feast day: Whit Tuesday
Maximum age at entry: 40 on establishment, then 30 (from 1844)
Primary Sources: Rules of 1842, TNA, FS 1/576/64; TNA, FS 4/42/64
Notes: A friendly society providing sickness and death benefit. A hatband and gloves was to be worn at the funeral of a member.

Cuxham

No. of societies and members 1802/3 – None
No. of members of a friendly society 1813/14/15 – None

235.   Cuxham United Friendly Society

Status: Registered, OXF 96   **Type**: 7-year dividing friendly society
Established: 1845   **Registered:** 7 August 1845   **Dissolved**: Last known 1845

Headquarters: Half Moon Inn (1845)
Anniversary/feast day: Whit Tuesday
Minimum age at entry: 16 **Maximum age at entry**: 35
Primary Sources: Rules of 1845, TNA, FS 1/578/96; TNA, FS 4/42/96

Deddington

No. of societies and members 1802/3 – 2, 196
No. of members of a friendly society 1813/14/15 – 320, 319, 325
Notes: (See also appendix 2, Crimes 54, 55, 58 and 59)

> **Butcher's Arms Club** – see Plough Inn Friendly Society, Deddington 246

> **Crown and Tuns Club** – see Plough Inn Friendly Society, Deddington 246

236.   Court Robin Hood

Status: Branch of an affiliated order, OXF 311   **Type**: AOF **Branch No.** 5490
Established: 1870 **Registered:** 1871   **Dissolved**: Post 1918
Headquarters: Red Lion Inn, Market Place (1870-1878], Unicorn Hotel [1880-post 1918)
Anniversary/feast day: Whit Wednesday
Membership: 12 members in 1872, 17 in 1875, 33 in 1876, 57 in 1881, 75 in 1883, 100 in 1886, 155 in 1895, 189 in 1900, 220 in 1910
Notes: Warwickshire Central District of AOF (1870-1878) and Banbury District (1878-post 1918).

237.   Court Robin Hood Juvenile Foresters

Status: Juvenile branch of Affiliated   **Type**: AOF
Established: 1885 **Dissolved**: Post 1918
Headquarters: Unicorn Hotel [1905]
Anniversary/feast day: Whit Wednesday
Minimum age at entry: 5 **Maximum age at entry**: 15
Membership: 57 members in 1891

> **Deddington Friendly Society** – see Plough Inn Friendly Society, Deddington 246

238.   Deddington Friendly Society

Status: Enrolled, OXF 172   **Type**: Permanent friendly society
Established: Earliest known 1795 **Registered:** 1795   **Dissolved**: Last known 1795
Headquarters: Unicorn Inn (1795)
Maximum age at entry: 31
Primary Sources: TNA, FS 4/42/172
Notes: There is no file on this society in the Registrar's records. It is possible this was a double registration of Deddington 241.

239.   Deddington Friendly Society, also Plough Inn Friendly Society (1862-1872)

Status: Enrolled, OXF 3   **Type:** Permanent friendly society
Established: 1829 **Registered:** 18 October 1830   **Dissolved:** 1872
Headquarters: Red Lion (1829-1846), Plough Inn (1846-1872)
Anniversary/feast day: Whit Wednesday
Minimum age at entry: 7 Maximum age at entry: 30
Membership: 27 members in 1846, 33 in 1850, 77 in 1856, 72 in 1866, 48 in 1872
Primary Sources: Rulebook of 1830, TNA, FS 1/574/3; FS 4/42/3
Notes: The club colours were red, white, and blue (JOJ, 17 May 1856). The society was dissolved 1872 with 48 members and approximately £200 funds (TNA, FS 1/574/3). The Plough Inn Friendly Society (Deddington 246) was formed on its dissolution.

240.   Deddington General Friendly Institution, also Exhibition Club and Exhibition Friendly Institution

Status: Registered, OXF 155   **Type**: Permanent friendly society
Established: 22 May 1841   **Registered:** 16 July 1856   **Dissolved**: 4 March 1905
Headquarters: Town Hall (1843-1857), Red Lion (1857-1858), Exhibition Inn (1858-1871), Crown and Tuns Inn (Three Tuns, Tuns Inn) (1871-1879), Exhibition Inn (1879-90), Town Hall (1890), Exhibition Inn [1892-1896], Town Hall (1899) (1902)
Anniversary/feast day: Whit Monday (to 1855), then Whit Wednesday
Minimum age at entry: 10 **Maximum age at entry**: 50 (1846), 35 (from 1856), 40 (from 1879)

Membership: 42 members in 1846, 44 in 1850
Primary Sources: Rulebook of 1856, TNA, FS 3/320/155; rulebook of 1856, Bodl. G.A. OXF 8° 1308(3); TNA, FS 4/42/155;
Notes: The society was open to male and female members and was a society for the town of Deddington and its vicinity. There were many rule changes recorded with the Registrar during the lifetime of the society. A letter to the editor of *Jackson's Oxford Journal* dated 14 July 1858 expressed dismay at the state of the dilapidated Town Hall and the need to move the society from those premises to the Red Lion the previous year (JOJ, 17 July 1858). In 1879, John Wheeler of the Crown and Tuns public house was charged with holding onto the club box when it moved to the Exhibition Inn (see appendix 2, Crimes 56). The society was strongly supported initially by honorary members with 18 in 1858, but that support decreased to twelve in 1878 and seven in 1883. It was dissolved on 4 March 1905 with 31 members. There were insufficient contributors remaining due to the loss of young members who left the society in a 'body' and founded an oddfellows' lodge (Ye Old Castle Lodge, Deddington 249).

241.   Deddington New Friendly Society, also Unicorn Friendly Society

Status: Enrolled, OXF 166   **Type:** Permanent friendly society
Established: 1 July 1795   **Registered:** 1796   **Dissolved:** Last known 1824
Headquarters: Unicorn Inn (1795-1824)
Anniversary/feast day: Whit Wednesday
Maximum age at entry: 31
Primary Sources: Rules 1 June 1795 and 9 June 1824, OHC, QSD/R/16; Rules of 1824, TNA, FS 1/580/166; TNA, FS 4/42/166
Notes: The rules of the society permitted a maximum 121 members. This was one of the two societies in existence in Deddington in 1803.

242.   Deddington Union Beneficial Society, also Plough Club, also Tradesmen's Club

Status: Enrolled, OXF 34   **Type:** Permanent friendly society
Established: 1 July 1816   **Registered:** 16 October 1816   **Dissolved:** 9 September 1879
Headquarters: Plough Inn (1816-1837), Crown and Tuns Inn (1837-1855), Unicorn Inn (1856-1879) Anniversary/feast day: Whit Wednesday
Minimum age at entry: 18 Maximum age at entry: 30, changed to 35 in 1866

Membership: 92 members in 1846, 103 in 1852, 109 in 1861, 93 in 1871, reducing steadily to 53 in 1879
Primary Sources: Oxon. Cal. QS iii, p.662; Treasurer's Bond (1837) and memorandum, OHC, QSD/R/15; rules for 1821 and Treasurer's Bond and correspondence dated 28 February 1834, 1829 and 1837, OHC, QSD/R/17; a letter concerning the approval of rules of June 1821 misfiled in Registrar's papers at TNA, FS 1/580/163; rules of 1825, 1834, 1850, and 1866, TNA, FS 1/575/34; rules for 1873, Bodl. G.A. OXF 8° 1308(12); TNA, FS 4/42/34
Notes: The rules were enrolled at the Trinity Quarter Sessions, 1823. A memorandum of 13 June 1821, amending a rule that stated the 'box' was closed for two years indicating benefits were not payable until after that time (OHC, QSD/R/15). In 1837, William Austin, landlord of the Plough Inn refused to give up the books of the club when it removed to the Crown and Tuns, but was advised to do so (see appendix 2, Crimes 52). The society comprised mostly farmers and tradesmen in its early years (BG, 11 June 1846) and in 1847 was described as, 'the most populous and wealthy for miles around' (JOJ, 5 June 1847). At a meeting at the Unicorn Inn on 7 February 1873 the rules were revised and the funds were reduced to £1,000. It appears a division of the funds above this amount took place. The rules permitted members to emigrate or travel abroad but sickness benefit was not payable, just death benefit. The wife of a member may be registered for benefit after six months of membership with a payment of 10s 6d. Death benefit of £5 was payable on her death with each member contributing 1s. In 1876 the society was described as the oldest club in the neighbourhood (BG, 5 June 1876). The society was dissolved on 9 September 1879 with 53 members and £986 funds. (See also appendix 2, Crimes 53).

> **Exhibition Club** – see Deddington General Friendly Institution, Deddington 240

> **Exhibition Friendly Institution** – see Deddington General Friendly Institution, Deddington 240

243.   Exhibition Friendly Society

Status: Unregistered   **Type**: Friendly society
Established: First known 1854 **Dissolved**: Last known 1854
Headquarters: Exhibition (1854)
Anniversary/feast day: Whit Wednesday
Notes: Held their annual club day in 1854 (JOJ, 27 May 1854).

244.   King's Arms Friendly Society

Status: Enrolled   **Type**: Permanent friendly society
Established: 7 December 1768   **Registered:** 1794   **Dissolved**: Last known 1794
Headquarters: Kings Arms Inn (1768-1794)
Anniversary/feast day: Whit Wednesday
Maximum age at entry: 25
Primary Sources: Manuscript rules of 11 June 1794, OHC, QSD/R/13
Notes: The rules of the society permitted a maximum 121 members. They further ordered that on the death of a member, if the family of the deceased provided refreshments, there was no charge deducted from the benefit, but if they did not each member was entitled to a pint of beer to be paid from the £2 benefit due to the widow or other nominated person.

245.   Mission Hall Benefit Society

Status: Unregistered   **Type**: Friendly society
Established: First known 1854 **Dissolved**: Last known 1854
Headquarters: Mission Hall (1854)
Anniversary/feast day: Whit Wednesday
Notes: Held their annual club day in 1854 (JOJ, 27 May 1854).

Old Plough Club – see Plough Inn Friendly Society, Deddington 246

Plough Club – see Deddington Union Beneficial Society, Deddington 242

Plough Inn Friendly Society – see Deddington Friendly Society, Deddington 239

246.   Plough Inn Friendly Society, also Deddington Friendly Society, Old Plough Club (1884 onwards), Butcher's Arms Club (1889), Crown and Tuns Club

Status: Unregistered   **Type**: 2-year dividing friendly society
Established: 1872 **Dissolved**: 1896
Headquarters: Plough Inn (1872-1883], Town Hall (1883-1884), Butcher's Arms (1885-1889), Crown and Tuns (1890-1896)

Anniversary/feast day: Whit Wednesday
Membership: 50 members in 1885, 40 in 1890
Notes: The society was formed on the dissolution of Deddington Friendly Society (Deddington 239), and continued as a 2-year dividing society when that permanent society dissolved in 1872. In 1879, two stewards were charged with misappropriating £30 of club funds (see appendix 2, Crimes 57). The club divided its small amount of remaining funds and dissolved in 1896. There had been a large amount of sickness (BG, 4/6/1896).

247.   Red Lion Friendly Society

Status: Enrolled   **Type:** Permanent friendly society
Established: 3 June 1786   **Registered:** 1794   **Dissolved:** Last known 1794
Headquarters: Red Lion Inn (1786-1794)
Anniversary/feast day: Whit Wednesday
Maximum age at entry: 31
Primary Sources: Manuscript rules of 11 June 1794, OHC, QSD/R/14
Notes: The rules of the society permitted a maximum 121 members.

> **Tradesmen's Club** – see Deddington Union Beneficial Society, Deddington 242

> **Unicorn Friendly Society** – see Deddington New Friendly Society, Deddington 241

248.   Widows Hope Lodge

Status: Branch of an affiliated order **Type:** IOOFMU **Branch No.** 3473
Established: 1843 **Dissolved:** 1850
Headquarters: Unicorn Inn, Market Street (1844-1846)
Anniversary/feast day: Whit Wednesday
Membership: 51 members in 1844, 47 in 1846
Notes: Oxford District of IOOFMU. The branch had ceased to exist by 1850, and possibly as early as 1846. It was reported there was trouble in the management of the society and that it may have affected the successful presence of Oddfellows in the town by discrediting the organization (BG, 11 June 1846).

249.   Ye Old Castle Lodge

Status: Branch of an affiliated order **Type:** IOOFMU **Branch No.** 7474

Established: 1898 **Dissolved**: Post 1918
Headquarters: Crown and Tuns Inn (1898-post 1918)
Notes: Banbury District of AOF. The General Friendly Institution (Deddington 240) dissolved in 1905 having suffered a reduction in membership due to the loss of young members in 1898 who left the society and founded Ye Old Castle Lodge.

Dorchester

No. of societies and members 1802/3 – None
No. of members of a friendly society 1813/14/15 – 84, 89, 91
Notes: The effect of the National Insurance Act 1911 was felt in Dorchester the following year as the *Berkshire and Oxfordshire Advertiser* reported 'Chiefly due to the National Insurance Act the village clubs did not hold their usual dinner and parades. Consequently Dorchester was somewhat shorn of festive appearance' (BOA, 31 May 1912).

250.   Bath and Bristol Friendly Society, Royal Oxonian branch

Status: A branch of a registered society **Type**: Permanent friendly society
Established: First known 1888 **Dissolved**: Last known 1888
Notes: Vincent Cobb was charged with embezzlement from the society in 1888 (see appendix 2, Crimes 60).

251.   Court Royal Oxonians

Status: Branch of an affiliated order, OXF 312 **Type**: AOF **Branch No.** 5546
Established: 1870   **Registered:** 13 December 1871   **Dissolved**: Post 1918
Headquarters: White Hart (Star) Inn (1870-post 1918)
Anniversary/feast day: Whit Wednesday (1882) Whit Monday (1890)
Membership: 62 members in 1880, 67 in 1885, 74 in 1890, 110 in 1895, 102 in 1900, 100 in 1905, 75 in 1910
Primary Sources: TNA, FS 4/42/312;
Notes: Bristol United District of AOF. The society was suspended for three months on 27 May 1885 and there were further three month suspensions on 29 August 1885 and 27 November 1885. The Registrar was due to cancel the society's registration on 29 January 1886 but it did not happen until 13 August 1886 due to the failure to submit a valuation. The court was suspended by the AOF in 1884, and reinstated in 1885. Court Royal Oxonians continued to be a branch of the AOF (TNA, FS 4/42/312). In 1908 it was reported that the banner of the society was worn out after 26 years use (BOA, 12 June 1908).

252.   Dorchester Friendly and Beneficial Society

Status: Enrolled, OXF 179 **Type**: Permanent friendly society
Established:1793 **Dissolved**: Last known 1855
Headquarters: White Hart (1850-1855)
Anniversary/feast day: Second Saturday in May, Whit Tuesday (1850-1854), Whit Monday (1855)
Membership: 180 members in 1850
Primary Sources: Rules of 1821, TNA, FS 1/580/179; TNA, FS 4/42/179
Notes: No age limits for new members were specified in the rules. They state the club day to be the second Saturday in May but newspaper reports show that it was celebrated during Whitsun in the 1850s. An enquiry concerning the society was forwarded to the assistant secretary of the Central Oxfordshire Friendly society by the Dorchester branch agent. He replied in a letter to the Registrar dated 12 May 1882 and informed him that there had been no such club at Dorchester 'for some years' (TNA, FS 4/42/179).

253.   Dorchester Friendly Society, also The George Inn Club

Status: Registered, OXF 207 **Type:** 7-year dividing friendly society, permanent from 1907
Established: 31 May 1858   **Registered:** 23 September 1858   **Dissolved:** 14 February 1913
Headquarters: George Inn (1858-1913)
Anniversary/feast day: Whit Tuesday
Minimum age at entry: 14 (16 from 1900) Maximum age at entry: 45 (40 from 1900)
Membership: 42 members in 1860, 54 in 1865, 59 in 1870, 66 in 1886
Primary Sources: Rulebooks of 1858 and 1900, TNA, FS 3/320/207; rulebook of 1858, OHC, O119/A/1
Notes: Any person emigrating was excluded from the society. A new Banner was purchase by subscription for the society in 1888 (WT, 25 May 1888). The society was prosecuted by the Registrar in 1895 for failing to make annual returns. The Registrar's records also contain a draft notice of a summons to the Petty Sessions in 1898 for failing to complete annual return for three years. The defence of the society was the records had not been completed due to the ill health of the secretary. It was fined £6 14s. The society was dissolved 14 February 1913 with 35 members and £84 2 0½ funds. (See also appendix 2, Crimes 61).

The George Inn Club – see Dorchester Friendly Society, Dorchester 253

254. Hand-in-Hand Benefit Society

Status: Enrolled, OXF 87 **Type**: Annual dividing friendly society
Established: 1842 **Registered:** 22 August 1842 **Dissolved**: Last known 1863
Headquarters: Castle Inn (1842-1855]
Anniversary/feast day: Whit Monday
Membership: 51 members in 1852, 77 in 1863
Primary Sources: TNA, FS 4/42/87
Notes: A letter from the Registrar to the society was returned on 11 May 1882 stating 'society abolished' (TNA, FS 4/42/87). In 1850 it was reported that the Poor Law Guardians would pay half-amount for members of the society (JOJ, 25 May 1850). No individual file relating to the society exists in the Registrar's records.

255. Hand-in-Hand Benefit Society

Status: Registered, OXF 269 **Type:** Permanent friendly society
Established: 5 June 1865 **Registered:** 9 March 1866 **Dissolved:** 1877
Headquarters: Castle Inn (1865-1877)
Anniversary/feast day: Whit Monday
Minimum age at entry: 14 Maximum age at entry: 45
Membership: 22 members in 1866
Primary Sources: Rulebook of 1866, TNA, FS 1/582/269; TNA, FS 4/42/269
Notes: A letter to the Registrar dated 13 March 1866 states that the present society had no connection with the Hand-in-Hand society established in 1842 (Dorchester 254). Another letter of 14 May 1877 stated the club had 'broken up' (TNA, FS 4/42/269).

256. Juvenile Court Royal Oxonian

Status: A juvenile branch of an affiliated order **Type**: Juvenile friendly society
Established: First known 1907 **Dissolved**: Last known 1907
Membership: 18 members in 1907

257. United Burial Friendly Society

Status: Enrolled, OXF 148 **Type**: Friendly society

Established: 1844   **Registered:** 28 November 1851   **Dissolved**: 1871
Headquarters: Fleur-de-Lis Inn (1849-1853]
Membership: 174 members in 1853, 31 in 1871
Primary Sources: TNA, FS 4/42/148
Notes: The society was dissolved by the Registrar in 1871. No individual file relating to the society exists in the Registrar's records.

Drayton

No. of societies and members 1802/3 – 1, 42
No. of members of a friendly society 1813/14/15 – 41, 42, 42

258.   Drayton Friendly Society

Status: Enrolled   **Type**: Permanent friendly society
Established: 9 June 1789   **Registered:** 1815   **Dissolved**: Last known 1815
Headquarters: Buck Inn (1789-1794]
Anniversary/feast day: Whit Friday
Maximum age at entry: 40
Primary Sources: Manuscript rules of 9 June 1789, OHC, QSD/R/18

259.   Drayton Friendly Society

Status: Registered, OXF 191   **Type**: Permanent friendly society
Established: First known 1857   **Registered:** 5 May 1857   **Dissolved**: 1875
Headquarters: Roebuck Inn (1857-1875)
Anniversary/feast day: Whit Friday
Maximum age at entry: 40
Membership: 40 in 1871
Primary Sources: TNA, FS 4/42/191; BPP 1874, XXIII, (c.997), p.119
Notes: The Assistant Commissioner described the society in 1872 as a club mostly of agricultural labourers, although the secretary, Mr Webb worked at Samuelson's foundry in Banbury. He reported the landlady of the Roebuck found some of the members 'very disagreeable' and although the doctor, farmer and parson attended the feast they found the members very noisy. Funds of the society were invested with Messrs Harman, brewers and owners of the pub. In 1875 the officers of the club were summoned to court over the way they had dissolved the club. (See also appendix 2, Crimes 62 and 63.)

Drayton St Leonard

No. of societies and members 1802/3 – None
No. of members of a friendly society 1813/14/15 – None

260.   Central Oxfordshire Friendly Society, Drayton branch

Status: A branch of a registered society, OXF 500   **Type:** Permanent friendly society
Established: First known 1890 **Dissolved**: Last known 1893
Headquarters: Schoolroom (1890)
Anniversary/feast day: Whit Wednesday
Notes: A branch of Central Oxfordshire Friendly Society (Oxford 469).

Ducklington

No. of societies and members 1802/3 – None
No. of members of a friendly society 1813/14/15 – None

261.   Ducklington Friendly Society

Status: Registered, OXF 258   **Type:** Permanent friendly society
Established: 1864   **Registered:** 1864   **Dissolved**: May 1864
Headquarters: Strickland Arms (1864)
Anniversary/feast day: Whit Friday
Minimum age at entry: 18 **Maximum age at entry**: 50
Primary Sources: Rulebook of 1864, TNA, FS 1/582/258; TNA, FS 4/42/258
Notes: The club was for residents of Ducklington and the hamlet of Hardwick, and members had to be resident at joining. The society was dissolved and the annual return of 1866 stated 'No subscriptions have been paid and no business transacted since May 1864.' There was £14 in hand, and as no members had paid, all were considered excluded (TNA, FS 1/582/258).

Duns Tew

No. of societies and members 1802/3 – None
No. of members of a friendly society 1813/14/15 – None
Notes: Club day continued at Duns Tew until at least 1901.

262.   Duns Tew Friendly Society

Status: Enrolled, OXF 245   **Type:** Permanent friendly society
Established: 1847   **Registered:** 1848   **Dissolved:** 13 April 1914
Headquarters: White Horse Inn (1847-1914)
Anniversary/feast day: First Tuesday in May
Minimum age at entry: 16 (from 1894) Maximum age at entry: 35
Membership: 56 members in 1855, 76 in 1860, 93 in 1865, 107 in 1870, 112
in 1875, 120 in 1880, 128 in 1885, 156 in 1892, 110 in 1901, 88 in 1905, 63 in
1910, 39 in 1913
Primary Sources: Rulebook of 1847 and 1869, TNA, FS 15/565;
Notes: The society donated 13s to Indian famine relief in 1861 (JOJ, 18 May
1851). In 1873 the society held two acres and three roods of land (BPP 1874,
LXXII, (c.1097), Oxford, p.8). The society dissolved with 46 members and
£638 19s 1d funds. (See also appendix 2, Crimes 64 and 65).

Enstone

No. of societies and members 1802/3 – 1, 74
No. of members of a friendly society 1813/14/15 – 94, 90, 84
Notes: (See appendix 2, Crimes 67).

263.   Church of England Temperance Sick and Burial Society, Enstone Branch

Status: A branch of a registered society, MDX 5056   **Type:** Permanent
friendly society
Established: First known 1885 **Dissolved**: Last known 1885
Anniversary/feast day: Ascension Day
Notes: The object of the society was to provide for a weekly payment during
the sickness of a member, and the payment of a sum of money on the death of
a member or member's wife (Charles Dickens, Jr., 'Dickens's Dictionary of
London', *Friendly and Benevolent Societies* [London, 1879]). A tea was held
on the vicarage lawn for club day (JOJ, 6 June 1885).

264.   Court Victoria

Status: Branch of an affiliated order **Type**: AOF **Branch No.** 7451
Established: 1886 **Dissolved**: Post 1918
Headquarters: Swan Inn (1887), Schoolroom [1905-post 1918)

Anniversary/feast day: Whit Thursday
Membership: 21 members in 1887, 34 in 1890, 49 in 1895, 76 in 1900, 121 in 1905, 129 in 1910
Notes: Oxford District of AOF.

265.   Enstone Friendly Society

Status: Enrolled, OXF 36   **Type:** Permanent friendly society
Established: 16 March 1786   **Registered:** 1818   **Dissolved:** Last known 1864
Headquarters: Talbot Inn (1786-1864)
Anniversary/feast day: 29 May
Maximum age at entry: 34
Membership: 175 in 1846, 142 in 1850, 133 in 1860, 112 in 1866
Primary Sources: Rulebook 1820, OHC, QSD/R/34; Oxon. Cal. QS iii, p.647; TNA, FS 4/42/36
Notes: The rules of the society were enrolled at the Easter Quarter Session, 1818 and were amended on 29 May 1834. The rules permitted a maximum of 100 members. The society marched to Heythrop Roman Catholic chapel on club day (BG, 11 June 1846 and other years). No file is present in the Registrar's records at TNA although one is indicated in the index at FS 1/575/36. (See also appendix 2, Crimes 66.)

266.   New Friendly Medical and Benefit Society

Status: Registered, OXF 300   **Type:** Permanent friendly society
Established: 1869   **Registered:** 17 June 1869   **Dissolved:** 8 September 1874
Headquarters: Old Swan Inn (1869-1874)
Anniversary/feast day: Ascension Day
Maximum age at entry: 40
Membership: 54 in 1874
Primary Sources: Rulebook 1879, TNA, FS 1/582/300;
Notes: New members were required to earn a minimum of 12s a week. The club was dissolved with 54 members but 10s was retained for each members to form a new club (Enstone 267).

267.   New Friendly Medical and Benefit Society

Status: Registered, OXF 332   **Type:** Permanent friendly society
Established: 1875   **Registered:** 23 September 1875   **Dissolved:** 1888

Headquarters: No. 2 National Schoolrooms (1876-1885), Crown Inn, Church Enstone (1885-1888)
Anniversary/feast day: Ascension Day
Membership: 32 members in 1885, 24 in 1888
Primary Sources: TNA, FS 1/582/332
Notes: The society was formed of members from Enstone 265. Dinner was held in Mr Hawtin's barn in 1885 (CNDM, May 1885). It dissolved with 24 members and £95 2s funds.

Ewelme

No. of societies and members 1802/3 – None
No. of members of a friendly society 1813/14/15 – None

268.   [Ewelme Friendly Society]

Status: Unregistered   **Type**: Annual dividing friendly society
Established: First known 1869 **Dissolved**: Last known 1869
Headquarters: Greyhound Inn (1869)
Anniversary/feast day: Trinity Monday
Notes: Described as a 'flourishing club' in 1869 (TG, 1 June 1869).

Eye and Dunsden

No. of societies and members 1802/3 – None
No. of members of a friendly society 1813/14/15 – None

> **Sonning Friendly Society** – see United Brethren Benefit Society, Eye and Dunsden 269

269.   United Brethren Benefit Society, also Sonning Friendly Society

Status: Enrolled, OXF 83   **Type**: Permanent friendly society
Established: 1 January 1824   **Registered:** 1826   **Dissolved**: Last known 1844
Headquarters: (French) Horn Inn, Sonning Eye (1824-1844)
Anniversary/feast day: Whit Monday
Primary Sources: Oxon. Cal. QS iii, p. 676; rulebook of 1839, BRO, D/EX 1044/6/41; rulebook of 1844, TNA, FS 1/577/83; TNA, FS 4/42/83

Notes: Enrolled at Michaelmas Quarter Session 1824. At the funeral of a member, a hat band and gloves provided by society had to be worn by those attending, to be returned on the next Monday monthly meeting. The rules catered for a militia substitute, a benefit where if a member were selected for Militia service, they were given up to £5 towards the cost of paying for a substitute to serve in their place. New members were required to reside within five miles of Sonning at the time of admission.

Eynsham

No. of societies and members 1802/3 – None
No. of members of a friendly society 1813/14/15 – 69, 68, 87

270.   Court The Abbey

Status: Branch of an affiliated order, OXF 325 **Type:** AOF **Branch No.** 7753
Established: 1889 **Dissolved**: Post 1918
Headquarters: Red Lion Inn (1890-post 1918)
Anniversary/feast day: Whit Monday
Membership: 24 members in 1890, 51 in 1892, 75 in 1895, 74 in 1900, 78 in 1905, 56 in 1910
Notes: Oxford District of AOF. Played a cricket match against East Oxford Slate Club (Oxford 483) in 1899 (JOJ, 27 May 1899).

271.   Eynsham Friendly Society

Status: Enrolled, OXF 60   **Type**: Friendly society
Established: 6 August 1807   **Registered:** 1809   **Dissolved**: Last known 1861
Headquarters: Red Lion Inn (1807-1823], Maltster and Shovel (1834-1855]
Anniversary/feast day: Whit Friday
Maximum age at entry: 35
Primary Sources: Rulebook of 6 August 1807, OHC, QSD/R/19; Rules of 1823 and 1830, TNA, FS 1/576/60; TNA, FS 4/42/56
Notes: The rules of 1823 permitted a maximum of 131 members. Monthly contributions of 10d were required and members had to spend 2d in the Public House on club nights. The 1836 rules show the club commenced 1 September 1834 at the Maltster and Shovel, indicating it was a dividing society or had divided and removed at that time (TNA, FS 1/576/60). (See also appendix 2, Crimes 68.)

272.   Eynsham Friendly Society

Status: Registered, OXF 292 **Type:** Permanent friendly society
Established: 1868   **Registered:** 22 October 1868   **Dissolved:** 25 February 1879
Headquarters: White Hart Inn (1868-1879)
Anniversary/feast day: Whit Tuesday
Minimum age at entry: 12 Maximum age at entry: 50
Membership: 15 in 1870, 14 in 1875, 10 in 1879
Primary Sources: Rulebook of 1868, TNA, FS 1/582/292; TNA, FS 4/42/292
Notes: The society dissolved with ten members and £80 8s 9d funds.

273.   Eynsham Permanent Benefit Society

Status: Registered, OXF 377 **Type:** Permanent friendly society
Established: July 1891   **Registered:** 4 June 1892   **Dissolved:** 29 August 1913
Headquarters: Swan Hotel (1892-1910]
Anniversary/feast day: Whit Monday
Minimum age at entry: 16 Maximum age at entry: 45
Membership: 40 members in 1899, 32 in 1902, 69 in 1905, 67 in 1910, 59 in 1913
Primary Sources: Rulebook of 1892TNA, FS 3/322/377; TNA, FS 4/42/377
Notes: At the 1907 club day, the society unfurled a new flag of blue silk, displaying clasped hands in the centre and an inscription in blue and gold lettering, 'Eynsham Permanent Benefit Society 1891' (WG, 25 May 1907). The society dissolved with 59 members and £476 funds.

274.   Eynsham Savings Club

Status: Enrolled   **Type**: Friendly society
Established: 3 June 1828 **Dissolved**: Last known 1845
Headquarters: Swan Inn (1828)
Anniversary/feast day: Easter Monday
Primary Sources: Rules of 1828, OHC, QSD/R/20
Notes: The society was for male and female members. It paid death benefit only, and was primarily a savings club for members as an alternative to a savings bank.

275.   Eynsham Seven Years Benefit Society

Status: Registered, OXF 277 **Type:** 7-year dividing friendly society
Established: 1867   **Registered:** 18 March 1867   **Dissolved:** 1893
Headquarters: New Inn (1867 -1893)
Anniversary/feast day: Whit Tuesday
Minimum age at entry: 12 Maximum age at entry: 45
Membership: 90 members in 1874, 110 in 1878, 103 in 1885, 124 in 1891,
56 in 1893
Primary Sources: Rulebook of 1867, TNA, FS 3/321/277; TNA, FS 4/42/277
Notes: At the end of each division, £20 was kept back for the next club. The
society was dissolved with 56 members and £29 6s. Of these, 46 members had
a seven-year portion, three a four-year portion and seven a two-year portion.

276.   Hand-in-Hand Friendly Society

Status: Enrolled, OXF 193 **Type**: Permanent friendly society
Established: 6 June 1853 **Registered:** 27 May 1857 **Dissolved**: 22
December 1870
Headquarters: Swan Inn (1853-1870)
Anniversary/feast day: Whit Tuesday
Membership: 87 members in 1864, 72 in 1870
Primary Sources: Rulebook of 1857, TNA, FS 1/580/193; TNA, FS 4/42/193
Notes: Dissolved with 72 members and £320 funds.

277.   London Friendly Institution, Eynsham Branch

Status: A branch of an enrolled society, LND 57   **Type**: Friendly society
Established: First known 1841 **Dissolved**: Last known 1882
Primary Sources: BPP 1874, XXIII, (c.997), p.93; TNA, FS 15/1662
Notes: A branch of the LFI was recorded by the Assistant Commissioner
in 1872 at Eynsham (BPP 1874, XXIII, [c.997], p.93). A medical attendant
is recorded at Eynsham in 1841, 1869, and 1882 rulebooks of the LFI for
treatment of its members, indicating the presence of a branch in these years
(TNA, FS 15/1662).

278.   Macclesfield Lodge

Status: Branch of an affiliated order **Type:** IOOFMU **Branch No:** 3201
Established: 1846 **Dissolved**: 1846

Headquarters: Swan Inn (1846)
Notes: Oxford District of IOOFMU. The 1846/47 IOOFMU directory lists this branch but does not indicate the level of membership. There is no trace of this society after this date in the Oddfellows records.

279.   New Inn Permanent Benefit Society

Status: Registered, OXF 385 **Type:** Permanent friendly society
Established: First known 1894   **Registered:** 1894   **Dissolved:** Post 1918
Headquarters: New Inn (1894-post 1918)
Minimum age at entry: 16 Maximum age at entry: 45
Membership: 33 members in 1899, 36 in 1902, 28 in 1905, 27 in 1910
Primary Sources: BPP 1921, XXVII (140), p.70
Notes: On the schedule of proceedings taken by Registrar in 1920, the society was summonsed to Witney court on 10 June 1920 for failure to submit the 1918 annual return but the case was withdrawn and the society paid costs of 10s 6d.

280.   Queen of England Lodge

Status: Branch of an affiliated order, OXF 325 **Type**: IOOFMU **Branch No.** 5994
Established: 1873   **Registered:** 1874   **Dissolved**: Post 1918
Headquarters: Railway Inn (1873-1876), Druid's Head (1877), Railway Inn (1878-1890), Swan Inn (1890-post 1918)
Membership: 25 members in 1873, 24 in 1878, 31 in 1886, 52 in 1892, 36 in 1901, 37 in 1910, 41 in 1914
Notes: Oxford District of IOOFMU

Fencott and Murcott

No. of societies and members 1802/3 – None
No. of members of a friendly society 1813/14/15 – None

281.   Murcott and Fencott Friendly Society

Status: Unregistered   **Type:** 7-year dividing friendly society
Established: First known 1854 **Dissolved**: Last known 1873
Headquarters: The Marlake House, Murcott (1854) (1872)
Minimum age at entry: 12 **Maximum age at entry**: 45
Primary Sources: Rulebook of 1872, Bodl. G.A. OXF 8° 1308(11)

Notes: On division, two years' membership fees were retained in the society. In 1854 club day comprised 'rural games and rustic amusements' (BG, 8 June 1854). In 1873, the landlord of the Marlake House was charged with stealing £10 from the club (see appendix 2, Crimes 69).

Fifield

No. of societies and members 1802/3 – None
No. of members of a friendly society 1813/14/15 – None
Notes: In 1885, club day was changed from Whit Monday to Trinity Monday.

282.   Fifield Benefit Club

Status: Unregistered   **Type:** Friendly society
Established: First known 1884 **Dissolved**: Last known 1892
Anniversary/feast day: Whit Monday, changed to Trinity Monday (1885)
Notes: The club paid sick benefit only (CNDM, August 1899). Annual club days were held in a barn in the village (CNDM, July 1884).

283.   Fifield Friendly Society

Status: Registered, OXF 380   **Type:** 7-year dividing friendly society
Established: 1892   **Registered:** 23 May 1893   **Dissolved**: 3 May 1913
Anniversary/feast day: Trinity Monday
Minimum age at entry: 16, 12 (from 1895) **Maximum age at entry**: 40
Membership: 44 members in 1899, 43 in 1905, 35 in 1913
Primary Sources: Rulebooks of 1892 and 1895, TNA, FS 3/322/380; TNA, FS 4/42/380; (BPP 1923, XIX (133), pp.120-121).
Notes: Club dinners were held in Mr Matthews' barn. The society was dissolved with 35 members and £321 funds. The society continued as an unregistered club and the funds of the society transferred to the new one, Fifield 284. (See also appendix 2, Crimes 70).

284.   Fifield Friendly Society

Status: Unregistered   **Type: Friendly Society**
Established: 1913 **Dissolved**: Last known 1922
Notes: The society was a continuation of Fifield 283. A Savings Bank dispute hearing was held on 12 April 1922 (BPP 1923, XIX (133), pp.120-121). At the dissolution of the previous society there was £113 7s 8d in the Post Office Savings Bank and according to the agreement made, this should have been

divided amongst the members. However, they formed a new, unregistered society which they considered a continuation and left the money in the bank as a nucleus fund for the new society. The money was awarded to this society after the consent of all members of this dissolved registered society was obtained that the funds be placed in a new account in the name of the Trustees of the Fifield Friendly society.

285.   Fifield Loyal United Benefit Society

Status: Enrolled, OXF 138   **Type:** 5-year dividing friendly society
Established: 1852   **Registered:** 11 August 1852   **Dissolved:** 1862
Headquarters: Merrymouth Inn (1852-1862)
Anniversary/feast day: Whit Monday
Minimum age at entry: 14 Maximum age at entry: 35
Membership: 54 members in 1862
Primary Sources: Rulebook of 1852, TNA, FS 1/579/138; TNA, FS 4/42/138
Notes: The rules stipulated that gloves and hat band had to be worn at the funeral of member.

Filkins

No. of societies and members 1802/3 – None
No. of members of a friendly society 1813/14/15 – None

286.   The Red, White and Blue Club

Status: Unregistered   **Type:** 5-year dividing friendly society, then permanent society from 1907
Established: 19 May 1879 **Dissolved:** 1953
Headquarters: Lamb Inn (1879 1894), The Bull Inn (1895-post 1912)
Anniversary/feast day: Whit Tuesday
Minimum age at entry: 16 Maximum age at entry: 45
Membership: 73 members in 1903
Primary Sources: Rulebook of 1907, OHC, P115/A/1 and Bodl. G.A. OXF 8° 744(25); The Swinford Museum, Filkins has deposited a substantial amount of administrative and financial records of the society at OHC under accession number 5658, R8.9-52. These were waiting to be catalogued at the time of publication, and include rulebooks (1879, 1894, 1895, and 1907), sick notes (1880-1904), doctors' receipted accounts (1881-1910), society accounts (1880-1901), miscellaneous administrative and financial records.

Notes: Red, white, and blue rosettes were worn on club day. This society left some of the widest ranging primary source material of any in the county for the late-nineteenth and early-twentieth century.

Finmere

No. of societies and members 1802/3 – None
No. of members of a friendly society 1813/14/15 – None
Notes: Finmere was the scene of an unusual event on club day in 1887. The club were parading the village when the Salvation Army appeared and demonstrated as part of a temperance drive. They were met by a march of the Skeleton Army, an informal anti-temperance movement. The intervention of the Police prevented any confrontation and the Salvation Army dispensed with their march (BicA, 3 June 1887), (see appendix 2, Crimes 71).

287.   Finmere Friendly Society

Status: Registered, OXF 344   **Type:** Permanent friendly society
Established: 1880   **Registered:** 3 June 1881   **Dissolved:** 22 February 1905
Headquarters: King's Head Inn (1880-1902]
Anniversary/feast day: Whit Tuesday
Minimum age at entry: 16 Maximum age at entry: 35
Membership: 50 members in 1885, 54 in 1891, 23 in 1899, 24 in 1902, 9 in 1905
Primary Sources: Rulebook of 1880, TNA, FS 3/321/344
Notes: New members were required to reside within four miles of Finmere on admission. The society dissolved with nine members and £13 funds.

Finstock

No. of societies and members 1802/3 – None
No. of members of a friendly society 1813/14/15 – 2, 2, 2
Notes: The village feast and club day was celebrated on Ascension Day, the traditional day of the Finstock Youth Ale that died out in the early- to mid-nineteenth century. Club day was last celebrated in 1908. (See also appendix 2, Crimes 74).

288.   Finstock Independent Friendly Society

Status: Registered, number OXF 260   **Type:** 5-year dividing friendly society until 1893, then permanent

Established: 1863   **Registered:** 1864   **Dissolved**: 31 October 1911
Headquarters: Crown Inn (1863-1876), Plough Inn (1876-1885), Crown Inn (1886-1898), Mr Henry Dore's (1898–1911)
Anniversary/feast day: Ascension Day
Maximum age at entry: 35
Membership: 41 members in 1865, 50 in 1872, 72 in 1874, 84 in 1876, 78 in 1878, 52 in 1880, 64 in 1885, 47 in 1891, 47 in 1899, 53 in 1905, 45 in 1910
Primary Sources: Rulebook, TNA, FS3/321/260; TNA, FS4/42/260
Notes: The club colours were blue and gold and the clubhouse was decorated with horse chestnut on club day. In 1886 it was reported that no-one attended the evening church service on club day for the first time in 22 years (CNDM, July 1886). In 1890, the head teacher of Finstock school changed the school holiday arrangements so only the club day, Ascension day, was allowed off instead of the whole week. So few children attended school on Friday that in following years the two days were allowed as holidays (OHC, T/SL 26). The society dissolved with 42 members and £1, the remainder having been distributed. The blue and gold silk flag of the society is in the possession of the Finstock Local History Society, together with the 17' flag pole and four 7' staves. (See also appendix 2, Crimes 72 and 73).

289.   **Finstock United Benefit Society**

Status: Registered, number OXF 350   **Type**: 5-year dividing friendly society
Established: 1883   **Registered:** 1883   **Dissolved**: 1903
Headquarters: Mr Bolton's House, Manor Farm (1883-1905)
Maximum age at entry: 35
Membership: 50 members in 1885, 51 in 1891, 58 in 1899
Primary Sources: Rulebook of 1883, TNA, FS3/322/350; TNA, FS 4/42/350
Notes: A letter of 20 April 1905 stated the society had collapsed and no contributions had been paid since 1903. Bolton was a prominent Wesleyan Methodist and this was likely to be a temperance society. The registration was cancelled by request on 30 March 1906 (TNA, FS3/322/350).

Fordwells

No. of societies and members 1802/3 – None
No. of members of a friendly society 1813/14/15 – None

290.   Fordwells Benefit Society

Status: Unregistered   **Type:** 5-year dividing friendly society (until 1893), then 10-year dividing friendly society (until 1903), then permanent friendly society
Established: 1858 **Dissolved**: Last known 1908
Headquarters: Methodist Chapel (1908)
Anniversary/feast day: First Friday in June
Membership: 46 members in 1908
Notes: The society had been in existence for 50 years in 1908, and had a balance of funds of £151 7s 2d (WG, 13 June 1908). The VCH states the first buildings in Fordwells were erected in 1861 and so the society probably had its origins in residents of Asthall, Fulbrook, and Wychwood (Leafield) parishes which the hamlet of Fordwells straddled.

Forest Hill

No. of societies and members 1802/3 – None
No. of members of a friendly society 1813/14/15 – None

291.   Forest Hill Benefit Club Society

Status: Registered, OXF 98   **Type:** Permanent friendly society
Established: 1845   **Registered:** 18 November 1845   **Dissolved**: 1864
Headquarters: King's Arms Inn, Cuddesdon (1845-1864)
Anniversary/feast day: Whit Monday
Membership: 40 members in 1864
Primary Sources: Rulebook of 1845, TNA, FS 3/321/259; TNA, FS 4/42/259
Notes: No file exists in the Registrar's papers in TNA for OXF 98 and those papers relating to this society are filed under FS 3/321/259.

292.   Forest Hill (with Shotover) Benefit Society

Status: Registered, OXF 259   **Type:** Permanent friendly society
Established: 1864   **Registered:** 1 July 1864   **Dissolved:** 2 November 1908
Headquarters: King's Arms Inn, Cuddesdon (1864 -1908)
Anniversary/feast day: Whit Monday
Minimum age at entry: 15 Maximum age at entry: 45
Membership: 42 members in 1865, 47 in 1871, 55 in 1899, 52 in 1905, 46 in 1908

Primary Sources: Rulebook of 1864, TNA, FS 3/321/259; TNA, FS 4/42/259
Notes: A new banner was introduced in 1899 and the old one placed in the church (JOJ, 27 May 1899). The society dissolved with 46 members and £728 12s 6d funds. (See also appendix 2, Crimes 75).

Fringford

No. of societies and members 1802/3 – None
No. of members of a friendly society 1813/14/15 – None

293.   Fringford Benefit Friendly Society

Status: Registered, OXF 392   **Type:** Permanent friendly society
Established: 1871   **Registered:** 1871 **Dissolved**: 1914
Headquarters: Schoolroom [1905-1914)
Anniversary/feast day: Whit Tuesday
Membership: 48 members in 1914
Notes: The society dissolved with 48 members and £171. No file relating to this society can be located in the papers of the Registrar at TNA.

294.   London Friendly Institution, Fringford District of Bicester Branch

Status: Branch of a registered society, LND 57   **Type:** Permanent friendly society
Established: First known 1854 **Dissolved**: Last known 1860
Headquarters: Butcher's Arms (1854-1860)
Anniversary/feast day: First Wednesday in May
Notes: A sub-branch of the Bicester branch of this society (Bicester 101).

295.   Loyal Mansfield Lodge

Status: Affiliated Order, OXF 317   **Type:** IOOFMU **Branch No.** 5904
Established: 1872   **Registered:** 1873   **Dissolved**: Post 1918
Headquarters: Butcher's Arms Inn (1873-1877], Schoolroom [1886-1910]
Anniversary/feast day: Whit Tuesday
Membership: 17 members in 1873, 22 in 1876, 28 in 1885, 34 in 1895, 48 in 1905, 71 in 1910, 65 in 1913
Primary Sources: Record Book 1889-1936, OHC, O23/1/2/A2/1
Notes: Banbury District of IOOFMU. The lodge was named after the Mansfield family, farmers of Hall Farm, Fringford. The banner for the Loyal Mansfield

Lodge is retained in the village hall and is gold with a blue surround. 'All Men are Brethren' is printed on one side with a winged character, a raised sword in one hand and chain in another, looking over a grotesque body with one foot on its head. This may be representative of George slaying a dragon, or the taming of evil representing the virtue of fortitude. On the reverse are the words 'United We Stand Divided We Fall' and 'Unity is Strength' with a winged female overlooking a male attempting to break a bundle of sticks, representing unity whereby one stick could be broken but a bundle could not (Victoria Solt Dennis, *Discovering Friendly and Fraternal Societies: Their badges and regalia* [Oxford, 2005], p.53). The banner was manufactured by George Tuthill of London.

Fritwell

No. of societies and members 1802/3 – None
No. of members of a friendly society 1813/14/15 – None

296.   Fritwell District Benefit Society

Status: Enrolled, OXF 63   **Type:** Permanent friendly society
Established: 8 August 1796   **Registered:** 1796   **Dissolved:** 4 June 1866
Headquarters: The George (1796), George & Dragon Inn [1849-1866)
Anniversary/feast day: Whit Tuesday
Minimum age at entry: 10 (1849) Maximum age at entry: 45 (1796) 40 (1849)
Membership: 38 members in 1846, 40 in 1850, 21 in 1866
Primary Sources: Manuscript rules of 1796, rulebook of 1849, TNA, FS 3/319/63; TNA, FS 4/42/63
Notes: The records of the Registrar show a change of rules 18 August 1835 (TNA, FS 4/42/63). The society had no honorary members. It was dissolved in 1866 with 21 members and £52 10s funds.

297.   Fritwell Friendly Society

Status: Unregistered   **Type:** Permanent friendly society
Established: 31 August 1835 **Dissolved:** 1912
Headquarters: Kings Head (1836-1912)
Anniversary/feast day: Whit Tuesday
Minimum age at entry: 15 Maximum age at entry: 56, 30 from 1888
Membership: 147 members in 1881, 202 in 1891, 156 in 1901, 155 in 1911

Primary Sources: Minute Book of annual meetings 1835-1913, OHC, O23/1/11/A1/1; rulebook dated 1876, Bodl. G.A. 8° 1308(13); published accounts for year ending 31 December 1892, OHC, FRIT.334.7;

Notes: Initially, a society for male and female members, but a rule change in 1843 excluded women from being benefit members. New members were required to reside in Fritwell or adjacent parishes until rule changes in 1885 and 1888 included those resident in the parishes of Middleton Stoney, Upper Heyford, and Bucknell. On 5 May 1890, the medical officer, Mr Drinkwater was called upon to resign as many members had been neglected in their illness. On 25 July 1910 it was acknowledged the fund was in deficit and a change of payments was proposed and accepted. At a meeting on 10 July 1912 it was resolved to join the IOOFMU as a Lodge of that society. (OHC, O23/1/11/A1/1).

There was confusion at the offices of the Registrar concerning this unregistered society. The Fritwell District Benefit Society, Fritwell 296, was dissolved in 1866 and no mention of any registered society exists in the Registrar's records after that date until the report concerning 1910 (BPP 1812-13, XII [123], p.533) when it reports upon this society as registration number OXF 63A and is repeated for 1915 (BPP 1916, XXIV [30], p.28). However, the society joined the IOOFMU in 1912 (OHC, O23/1/11/A1/1) as Fritwell Lodge (Fritwell 298). (See also appendix 2, Crimes 76).

298.   Fritwell Lodge

Status: Branch of an affiliated order   **Type:** IOOFMU **Branch No.** 9007
Established: 2 October 1912 **Dissolved:** Post 1918
Headquarters: Kings Head (1912-post 1918)
Membership: 118 members in 1912
Notes: The lodge was formed from the members of the Fritwell Friendly Society (Fritwell 297).

299.   Fritwell Provident Society

Status: Registered, OXF 346   **Type:** Permanent friendly society
Established: 1882   **Registered:** 7 July 1882   **Dissolved:** 31 December 1895
Headquarters: Wesleyan Reform Chapel (1882-1895)
Minimum age at entry: 16 Maximum age at entry: 35
Membership: 26 members in 1885, 21 in 1891, 14 in 1892, 14 in 1895
Primary Sources: Rulebook of 1882, 13th annual report (1895), TNA, FS 3/321/346; TNA, FS 4/42/346

Notes: A letter of 4 February 1896 stated the society was dissolved on 31 December 1895 with 14 members and £198 funds. No members had joined the club for some time (TNA, FS 4/42/346).

300.   Fritwell Subordinate Division

Status: Branch of an Affiliated Order   **Type:** OSOT **Branch No.** 865
Established: 1898 **Dissolved**: Last known 1910
Headquarters: Wesleyan Reform Schoolroom [1905-1910)
Membership: 51 members in 1905, 78 in 1910

Fulbrook

No. of societies and members 1802/3 – None
No. of members of a friendly society 1813/14/15 – 19, 19, 17
No known societies

Garsington

No. of societies and members 1802/3 – 1, 64
No. of members of a friendly society 1813/14/15 – None

301.   Court Ivanhoe

Status: Branch of an affiliated order   **Type:** AOF **Branch No.** 9438
Established: 1912 **Dissolved**: Post 1918
Headquarters: Red Horse (1912-post 1918)
Notes: Oxford District of AOF.

302.   Garsington Benefit Society

Status: Enrolled, OXF 6   **Type:** 7-year Dividing friendly society
Established: First known 1830   **Registered:** 9 June 1830   **Dissolved:** 1876
Headquarters: Three Horseshoes Inn (1830-1876]
Minimum age at entry: 14 Maximum age at entry: 45
Membership: 48 members in 1846, 70 in 1848, 77 in 1850, 99 in 1855, 104 in 1860
Primary Sources: Rulebook of 1830 and 1845, TNA, FS 1/574/6; TNA, FS 4/42/6
Notes: The rules permitted a maximum of 80 members, amended to 100 members in 1845, of men from Garsington and adjacent parishes. The club

was celebrating club day on Whit Monday 1866 when news came of a large fire at Marsh Baldon and club members left to go to the village to help quell the fire (JOJ, 26 May 1866). On four occasions between 1872 and 1876 the stewards of the society were taken to court by members for failing to pay sick benefit (see appendix 2, Crimes 77, 78, 79, and 80). A letter to the Registrar dated 1879 stated the society had broken up. The society dissolved in 1876 and two new ones commenced (Garsington 303 and 304).

303.   Garsington New Benefit Society, also Old Club

Status: Enrolled, OXF 338   **Type:** Friendly society
Established: 1877   **Registered:** 19 June 1878   **Dissolved:** 26 June 1894
Headquarters: School House (1878-1894)
Minimum age at entry: 16 Maximum age at entry: 40
Membership: 41 members in 1878, 51 in 1882, 63 in 1883, 33 in 1885, 25 in 1897
Primary Sources: Rulebook of 1878, TNA, FS 3/321/338;
Notes: This was one of two societies formed at the dissolution of Garsington 302. There were eleven honorary members in 1878. The annual meeting was held at the Three Horseshoes Inn but all other business was conducted at the schoolroom (JOJ, 18 June 1881). The society dissolved with 25 members and £247 18s 8d funds.

304.   Garsington New Independent Friendly Society

Status: Enrolled, OXF 337   **Type:** Dividing friendly society
Established: 1876   **Registered:** 1877   **Dissolved**: Last known 1910
Headquarters: Red Lion Inn (1876-1910)
Membership: 27 members in 1883, 52 in 1883, 69 in 1885, 81 in 1891, 120 in 1904
Notes: This was one of two societies formed at the dissolution of Garsington 302. No file in relation to this society can be located in the Registrar's records at TNA.

Goring

No. of societies and members 1802/3 – None
No. of members of a friendly society 1813/14/15 – None

305.   Compton Pilgrims Friendly Society, Goring Branch

Status: Branch of a registered society, BRK 86   **Type:** Permanent friendly society
Established: 1910 **Dissolved**: Post 1914
Headquarters: Compton, Berkshire
Membership: 14 members in 1911, 27 in 1913

306.   Court Allnut

Status: Branch of an Affiliated Order, OXF 323   **Type:** AOF **Branch No.** 5726
Established: 1872   **Registered:** 1874   **Dissolved**: Post 1918
Headquarters: King Charles's Head Inn, Goring Heath (1874-post 1918)
Membership: 20 members in 1876, 22 in 1880, 44 in 1885, 77 in 1890, 122 in 1895, 141 in 1900, 170 in 1905, 176 in 1910
Notes: London United District of AOF. The Court left the order in 1874 by suspension (1875 AOF Directory, p.278) but was reinstated in 1877. The Pride of Whitchurch Lodge (Whitchurch 696) merged with this society in 1892.

307.   Court Allnut Juvenile Branch

Status: Juvenile branch of an affiliated order   **Type:** AOF
Established: 1889 **Dissolved**: Post 1918
Headquarters: King Charles's Head Inn, Goring Heath (1889-post 1918)
Minimum age at entry: 6 **Maximum age at entry**: 17
Membership: 25 members in 1889, 61 in 1895, 37 in 1900

308.   Garibaldian Benefit Society

Status: Registered, OXF 244   **Type:** 5-year dividing friendly society
Established: 7 January 1861   **Registered:** 25 April 1862   **Dissolved:** 1867
Headquarters: Lethern Bottle (1861), Spring House (1863)
Anniversary/feast day: Whit Monday
Minimum age at entry: 14 Maximum age at entry: 40
Membership: 23 members in 1863
Primary Sources: Rulebook of 1861, TNA, FS 1/581/244; TNA, FS 4/42/244
Notes: A letter to the Registrar dated 14 December 1867 stated the society ceased to exist in 1867 with the death of the secretary (TNA, FS 1/581/244).

309.   Loyal Volunteer Lodge

Status: Branch of an affiliated order, OXF 290   **Type:** IOOFMU **Branch No.** 5527
Established: 1867   **Registered:** 1868   **Dissolved**: Post 1918
Headquarters: Schoolroom (1867-post 1918)
Membership: 21 members in 1869, 44 in 1870, 60 in 1872, 92 in 1875, 101 in 1880, 147 in 1887, 185 in 1890, 231 in 1897, 266 in 1905, 260 in 1910, 312 in 1914
Notes: Oxford District of IOOFMU (1868-post 1918).

310.   Spring House Impartial Society

Status: Unregistered   **Type:** Friendly society
Established: 2 August 1836 **Dissolved**: Last known 1838
Headquarters: Spring House (1836)
Anniversary/feast day: Whit Monday
Minimum age at entry: 16 **Maximum age at entry**: 40
Primary Sources: Rulebook of 1836, BRO, D/EX 1044/7/4
Notes: A militia substitute was included in the benefits, enabling any member who was selected to serve in the militia to pay for a substitute. The stewards were required to organize the feast including providing 1½ lbs of meat and two quarts of beer for club day with members paying 2s each. Handwriting on the cover of the rulebook states it was enrolled with Oxfordshire Clerk of the Peace but no confirmation of this can be found.

311.   The Stag and Hounds Friendly Society

Status: Unregistered   **Type:** Friendly society
Established: 1 March 1841 **Dissolved**: Last known 1845
Headquarters: Stag and Hounds, Goring Heath (1841-1845)
Anniversary/feast day: Whit Monday
Minimum age at entry: 16 **Maximum age at entry**: 40
Primary Sources: Rulebook of 1841, BRO, D/EX 1044/7/5
Notes: The copy of the rulebook in BRO shows the holder as Thomas Allwright who entered the society on 12 May 1845. The rules contain the benefit of a militia substitute enabling any member who was selected to serve in the militia to pay up to £5 for a substitute.

Great Bourton – see Bourton

Great Haseley

No. of societies and members 1802/3 – None
No. of members of a friendly society 1813/14/15 – None

312.   Great Haseley Friendly Society

Status: Registered, OXF 378   **Type:** Permanent friendly society
Established: 1893   **Registered:** 11 May 1893   **Dissolved:** 5 December 1912
Headquarters: The Institute (1893-1910)
Anniversary/feast day: Whit Monday
Minimum age at entry: 16, amended to 5 (1901) Maximum age at entry: 35
Membership: 39 members in 1899, 42 in 1903 (plus 11 juvenile members), 59 in 1907, 54 members in 1912
Primary Sources: Rulebook of 1893, TNA, FS 3/322/378; TNA, FS 4/42/378
Notes: The application to register was made on 14 January 1893. A concert was held on Wednesday 1 February 1899 to raise money for a new flag (JOJ, 4 February 1899). The society joined the provisional scheme under S.72 National Insurance Act on 16 August 1912. It dissolved with 54 members and £673 funds.

313.   Heart and Hand Benefit Society

Status: Registered, OXF 214   **Type:** Annual dividing friendly society
Established: 1858   **Registered:** 8 February 1859   **Dissolved:** 1892
Headquarters: Plough Inn (1858-1892)
Anniversary/feast day: Whit Monday
Minimum age at entry: 14 Maximum age at entry: 45
Membership: 60 members in 1862, 82 in 1864, 54 in 1875, 78 in 1878, 90 in 1880, 87 in 1885
Primary Sources: Rulebook of 1859, TNA, FS 3/321/214; TNA, FS 4/42/214
Notes: A note on the Registrar's file states the society was illegally dissolved in 1892 (TNA, FS 4/42/214).

Great Milton

No. of societies and members 1802/3 – None

No. of members of a friendly society 1813/14/15 – None

314. Central Oxfordshire Friendly Society, Great Milton Branch

Status: Branch of registered society, OXF 500 **Type:** Permanent friendly society
Established: First known 1875 **Dissolved**: 1894
Headquarters: National schoolroom (1882-1894)
Anniversary/feast day: Whit Monday, Whit Wednesday (1882, 1893)
Membership: 60 members in 1888. A branch of Central Oxfordshire Friendly Society, Oxford 469.

315. Court Admiral Massingberd (and from 1893) Court Ashurst

Status: Branch of an Affiliated Order **Type:** AOF **Branch No.** 6961
Established: 1882 **Dissolved**: Post 1918
Headquarters: Bull Inn (1882-post 1918)
Membership: 25 members in 1883, 48 in 1885, 82 in 1886, 117 in 1890, 145 in 1895, 151 in 1900, 183 in 1905, 187 in 1910
Notes: Oxford District of AOF. The court was initially named after Vice-Admiral Vincent Amcotts Massingberd who lived in Great Milton at the Priory. He was made Admiral after his retirement in 1884. The society changed its name after Massingberd's death to that of the county MP, William Ashurst after the Executive council of the AOF gave authorization in late 1892 (The Foresters' Heritage Trust website, *http://www.aoforestersheritage.com/recentlyadded.html*, accessed 24 January 2011). Great Milton Friendly Society, (Great Milton 316) amalgamated with Court Ashurst on 11 June 1912. The banner for the society is retained in the Neighbour's Hall, Great Milton. It is green in colour, with images of two hunting men, one dressed in green and the other red. The wording is 'Ancient Order of Foresters, Court Ashurst No. 696', 'Great Milton', and 'Unitas Benevolentia et Concordia'. The reverse of the banner repeats the title of the court and has the additional words 'Unity is Strength'. It depicts a child snapping one stick and a youth attempting to break a bundle of sticks with two onlookers, representing unity – one stick could be broken but a bundle tied together could not (Victoria Solt Dennis, *Discovering Friendly and Fraternal Societies: their badges and regalia* [Oxford, 2005], p.53).

316.   Great Milton Friendly Society

Status: Registered, OXF 386 **Type:** 5-year dividing friendly society
Established: 1894   **Registered:** 24 July 1894   **Dissolved:** 11 June 1912
Headquarters: National School (1894-1912)
Anniversary/feast day: Whit Wednesday
Minimum age at entry: 16 Maximum age at entry: 40
Membership: 66 members in 1899, 58 in 1905, 46 in 1910
Primary Sources: Rulebook of 1894, TNA, FS 3/322/386; TNA, FS 4/42/386
Notes: The society was formed when the Central Oxfordshire Friendly Society
collapsed (Oxford 469) and application to register was made on 27 February
1894. It was claimed the society was first established in 1845 (TG, 15 June
1909), although there was clearly no continuity between the earlier society,
the Heart and Hand Benefit Society (Great Milton 317) and this club. The
registration was cancelled on 11 June 1912 on amalgamation with Court
Ashurst (Great Milton 315). It is unclear how the rules permitting five-year
division were accepted by the Registrar as registration took place after 1875,
and dividing societies could not register anew after this date.

317.   Heart and Hand Benefit Society

Status: Registered, OXF 102   **Type:** 7-year dividing friendly society
Established: 1844   **Registered:** 23 September 1844   **Dissolved:** 1844
Headquarters: Bull Inn (1844)
Minimum age at entry: 16 Maximum age at entry: 35
Membership: 44 members in 1844
Primary Sources: Rulebook of 1844, TNA, FS 1/578/102; TNA, FS 4/42/102
Notes: The rules state division could take place after five years if members
agreed even though it was a seven-year dividing society. A letter of 18 May
1857 stated, 'The club only lasted for a few months. There has been no club at
this house since 1844' (TNA, FS 1/578/102).

Great Tew

No. of societies and members 1802/3 – None
No. of members of a friendly society 1813/14/15 – 4, 4, 3

318.   Great Tew Friendly Society

Status: Registered, OXF 76 **Type:** Permanent friendly society

Established: 1842   **Registered:** 1842   **Dissolved**: 31 July1936
Headquarters: Falkland Arms Inn (1842-1936)
Anniversary/feast day: First Monday in June
Maximum age at entry: 30
Membership: 46 members in 1864, 54 in 1866, 67 in 1877, 75 in 1878, 67 in 1885, 98 in 1899, 95 in 1905, 74 in 1913, 37 in 1836
Primary Sources: Rulebook of 1842, TNA, FS 15/1041
Notes: The society entered the provisional scheme under the National Insurance Act 1911. Quinquennial returns were made until 1936. The society dissolved with 37 members and £455 9s 5d funds. (See also appendix 2, Crimes 81).

Hailey

No. of societies and members 1802/3 – None
No. of members of a friendly society 1813/14/15 – None
Notes: Hailey had four unregistered friendly societies and each demonstrated fierce independence through not registering and refusing to become a branch of an affiliated order. Club days continued until 1914. (See appendix 2, Crimes 115 and 183).

319.   Bird in Hand Benefit Club

Status: Unregistered   **Type:** 5-year dividing friendly society
Established: 1886 **Dissolved**: Last known 1914
Headquarters: Bird in Hand, Whiteoak Green (1886-1914)
Anniversary/feast day: Whit Thursday, Whit Monday (from 1903)
Membership: 40 members in 1899

320.   Carpenter's Arms Benefit Club

Status: Unregistered   **Type:** 5-year dividing friendly society
Established: 1852 **Dissolved**: Last known 1914
Headquarters: Carpenters Arms (1852-1914)
Anniversary/feast day: Whit Thursday
Membership: 30 members in 1899, 40 in 1907

321.   Lamb and Flag Benefit Society

Status: Unregistered   **Type:** 5-year dividing friendly society
Established: 1851 **Dissolved**: Last known 1914
Headquarters: Lamb and Flag (1851-1914)

Anniversary/feast day: Whit Thursday
Membership: Between 50-60 members in 1899
Notes: Described as the oldest club in the village in 1893 (WG, 27 May 1893). A speaker at the annual dinner in 1912 discussed the option of the club joining a large society, but concluded it would be like, 'throwing in their lot with those who lived in urban areas and whose employment caused them more illness and rendered them shorter lived' (WG, 1 June 1912). There was clearly a belief that urban or industrial life was less healthy and town members had a greater amount of sickness and if the club joined a large society they would be paying greater subscriptions. Consideration was also given to form a juvenile branch in 1914 (WG, 6 June 1914).

322.   Roebuck Friendly Society

Status: Unregistered   **Type:** 5-year dividing friendly society
Established: First known in 1893 **Dissolved**: Last known 1893
Headquarters: Roebuck Inn, Delly End (1893)
Anniversary/feast day: Whit Thursday

Hanborough

No. of societies and members 1802/3 – 1, 52
No. of members of a friendly society 1813/14/15 – 125, 125, 130
Notes: An assault occurred on club day 1878 but it is not clear which club was celebrating that year (see appendix 2, Crimes 82).

323.   Church Hanborough Friendly Society

Status: Enrolled, number OXF 107   **Type**: Permanent friendly society
Established: 6 September 1794   **Registered:** 2 October 1810   **Dissolved**: Last known 1854
Headquarters: House of James Brain Church Hanborough (1794), Hand & Shears Inn, Church Hanborough [1822-1854)
Anniversary/feast day: Whit Monday (1794), changed to 29 May (in 1836), and back to Whit Monday before 1854
Maximum age at entry: 35 (1794), 40 (from 1836)
Membership: 18 members in 1846, 39 in 1850
Primary Sources: Manuscript rules of 1794 and printed rulebook of 1836, TNA, FS 1/578/107; TNA, FS 4/42/107; Manuscript rules of 1794, OHC, OA, QSD/R/21

324.   Court King George

Status: Branch of an affiliated order   **Type**: AOF **Branch No.** 9407
Established: 1912 **Dissolved**: Post 1918
Headquarters: Bell Inn (1912-post 1918)
Notes: Oxford District of AOF.

325.   Long Hanborough Sick and Benefit Society (1890), Benefit Society (1893)

Status: Unregistered   **Type**: Permanent friendly society
Established: First known 1890 **Dissolved**: Last known 1904
Headquarters: Bell Inn (1890-1904)
Anniversary/feast day: Whit Monday
Notes: A new, purpose-built clubroom was built at the Bell Inn in 1891, holding 200 people (JOJ, 23 May 1891). It was reported that the club was about to register in 1893 (JOJ, 3 June 1893) but it did not do so. Approximately 100 people sat down for the club dinner in 1896 (JPJ, 30 May 1906).

Hanwell

No. of societies and members 1802/3 – 1, 40
No. of members of a friendly society 1813/14/15 – 53, 59, 61

326.   Hanwell Amicable Society

Status: Enrolled, OXF 158 **Type**: Diving friendly society, becoming permanent
Established: 1829   **Dissolved**: Last known 1901
Headquarters: Red Lion [1862-1901)
Anniversary/feast day: Second Friday in June
Maximum age at entry: 36
Membership: 45 members in 1861, 60 in 1865, 40 in 1879, 35 in 1889
Primary Sources: Rulebook of 1858, FS 1/579/158; BPP 1874, XXIII, (c.997), section 3, p.119
Notes: A maximum of 81 members was permitted by the early rules. The Assistant Commissioner reported that the club was a society of labourers. It was a dividing club in its early years but by 1872 no longer divided. It had £200 funds invested in Cobbe's bank (BPP 1874, XXIII, (c.997), p.119). An old flag that was painted for Mrs Longe's women's club at Banbury by

Messrs Chayney and Gublin in 1808 (Banbury 44) was used by Hanwell Amicable Society in 1879 (BG, 5 June 1879). It is probable this society was a continuation of Hanwell 327.

327.   Hanwell Friendly Society

Status: Unregistered   **Type**: Permanent friendly society
Established: 1799 **Dissolved**: Last known 1799
Notes: This society appears to be the pre-enrolment society of the Hanwell Amicable society, (Hanwell 326) established in 1829, and is likely to have been the society in existence in 1803 and 1815.

Headington

No. of societies and members 1802/3 – None
No. of members of a friendly society 1813/14/15 – None

328.   Britannia (Club) Benefit Society

Status: Enrolled, OXF 29   **Type**: Permanent friendly society
Established: 1839   **Registered:** 15 July 1839   **Dissolved**: Last known 1860
Headquarters: Britannia (1839-1859]
Anniversary/feast day: Whit Tuesday
Minimum age at entry: 15, increased to 17 **Maximum age at entry**: 40
Primary Sources: TNA, FS 4/42/29
Notes: A special meeting of the society was called on 27 August 1860 as funds had decreased 'due to misunderstanding between officers and members of the club as to who is entitled to relief' (JOJ, 1 September 1860). There is no record of the society after this date. No file for this society can be located in the Registrar's records at TNA. (See also appendix 2, Crimes 83, 85 and 86).

329.   Britannia Benefit Society, also Headington Benefit Society

Status: Unregistered   **Type**: Permanent friendly society
Established: 1884 **Dissolved**: Last known 1884
Headquarters: Britannia (1884)
Notes: A case before Oxford County Court in 1884 caused adverse comment on the club by the Judge (appendix 2, Crimes 90).

Chequers Club – see Headington Quarry Benefit Society, Headington 335

330.   Court Alice Blacklair Cutler

Status: Female branch of an affiliated order   **Type:** AOF **Branch No.** 9602
Established: 1912 **Dissolved:** Post 1918
Headquarters: Schoolroom, Headington Quarry (1912-post 1918)
Membership: 16 members in 1912
Notes: Oxford District of AOF. A female-only club.

331.   Court Napoleon

Status: Branch of an affiliated order   **Type:** AOF **Branch No.** 6829
Established: 1881 **Dissolved:** Post 1918
Headquarters: Chequers Inn (1882-1906], Schoolroom [1912-post 1918)
Membership: 22 members in 1882, 54 in 1890, 93 in 1895, 105 in 1900, 117
in 1905, 129 in 1910
Notes: Oxford District of AOF.

332.   Court Napoleon, Juvenile Branch

Status: Juvenile branch of an affiliated order   **Type:** AOF
Established: First known 1893 **Dissolved:** Last known 1895
Notes: Juvenile branch of Headington 331. The club was involved in the
Headington Hospital Sunday Parades in 1893, 1894, and 1895.

> **Headington Benefit Society** – see Britannia Benefit Society,
> Headington 329

333.   Headington Benefit Society

Status: Registered, OXF 153   **Type:** Permanent friendly society
Established: 1856   **Registered:** 25 November 1856   **Dissolved:** February
1871
Headquarters: Britannia Inn (1856-1871)
Anniversary/feast day: Whit Tuesday
Minimum age at entry: 17 Maximum age at entry: 40
Membership: 44 members in 1871
Primary Sources: Rulebook of 1856, TNA, FS 1/579/153; TNA, FS 4/42/153
Notes: The society dissolved with 44 members and £60 funds. (See also
appendix 2, Crimes 88).

334.   Headington Quarry Benefit Society

Status: Registered, OXF 205   **Type**: Permanent friendly society
Established: 1857   **Registered:** 9 September 1858   **Dissolved**: January 1884
Headquarters: Chequers Inn (1857-1884)
Anniversary/feast day: Whit Tuesday
Minimum age at entry: 15 **Maximum age at entry**: 45
Primary Sources: Rulebook of 1850, TNA, FS 1/581/205; TNA, FS 4/42/205
Notes: The Registrar's file for this society contains rules dated 1850 relating to the society dissolved in 1857, the Headington Quarry Friendly Society (Headington 335). A letter to the Registrar dated 2 June 1862 explained that when this society was established, £200 was received from the dissolved Headington Quarry Friendly Society (Headington 335). Members of the old society transferred to this new one (TNA, FS 1/581/205). Sickness benefit was reduced in 1867. A letter to the Registrar dated 23 January 1884 stated the society had died out after 40 years. It stated that within one week of writing, sickness claims would wipe out all funds and the society would cease to exist (TNA, FS 4/42/205).

335.   Headington Quarry Friendly Society, also Chequers Club or Quarry Club

Status: Enrolled, OXF 21   **Type**: Permanent friendly society
Established: 1838   **Registered:** 21 November 1838   **Dissolved:** 1857
Headquarters: Chequers (1838-1843]
Anniversary/feast day: Whit Tuesday
Minimum age at entry: 15 Maximum age at entry: 45
Membership: 127 members in 1846, 128 in 1850, 136 in 1857
Primary Sources: Rulebook of 1838, TNA, FS 1/574/21; TNA, FS 42/4/21; rulebook of 1850, TNA, FS 1/581/205
Notes: When dissolved in 1857, £200 was left with the treasurer for the formation of a new club, the Headington Quarry Benefit Society (Headington 334). A rulebook of 1850 relating to this club is contained in the Registrar's file of that society (TNA, FS 1/581/205). (See also appendix 2, Crimes 84).

336. **Headington Quarry Seven Years Benefit Club, then Quarry Union Benefit Society (from July 1875)**

Status: Registered, OXF 240   **Type:** 7-year dividing friendly society, then permanent society from 1875
Established: 11 June 1855   **Registered:** 30 October 1861   **Dissolved:** 27 October 1906
Headquarters: Six Bells Inn (1855-1906)
Anniversary/feast day: Whit Tuesday
Minimum age at entry: 14 Maximum age at entry: 45
Membership: 66 members in 1862, 81 in 1891, 63 in 1899, 52 in 1905
Primary Sources: Rulebook of 1861, TNA, FS 3/321/234; TNA, FS 4/42/240
Notes: This society was unregistered for its first six years from 1855 to 1861, then continued as a dividing society until July 1875 when it changed its name and became a permanent society. The society dissolved with 50 members and £452 5s 11½d funds. (See also appendix 2, Crimes 87).

337. **Headington Subordinate Division**

Status: Branch of an affiliated order   **Type:** OSOT **Branch No.** 721
Established: 1890 **Dissolved:** Last known 1910
Headquarters: British Workman (1890-1910)
Membership: 84 members in 1905, 122 in 1910

338. **Loyal Havelock Lodge**

Status: Branch of an affiliated order, OXF 237   **Type:** IOOFMU **Branch No.** 4820
Established: 1859   **Registered:** 1861   **Dissolved:** Post 1918
Headquarters: Black Boy (1860), Plough Inn (1861-1864], White Hart Inn (1866-1868), Britannia Inn [1870-post 1918)
Membership: 11 members in 1859, 24 in 1865, 50 in 1868, 71 in 1875, 94 in 1878, 150 in 1886, 190 in 1891, 246 in 1899, 318 in 1905, 374 in 1910, 483 in 1913
Notes: Oxford District of IOOFMU. (See also appendix 2, Crimes 89).

339. **Loyal Havelock Lodge, Juvenile Branch**

Status: Juvenile branch of an affiliated order, OXF 372   **Type:** IOOFMU
Established: 1891 **Dissolved:** Post 1914

Headquarters: Britannia Inn (1891-1914)
Membership: 55 members in 1891, 102 in 1899, 112 in 1905, 92 in 1910

> **Quarry Club** – see Headington Quarry Benefit Society, Headington 335

> **Quarry Union Benefit Society** – see Headington Quarry Seven Years Benefit Club,

> Headington 336

Henley on Thames

No. of societies and members 1802/3 – None
No. of members of a friendly society 1813/14/15 – 95, 97, 100

340.   Broad Gates Club

Status: Unregistered   **Type:** Friendly society
Established: First known 1848 **Dissolved**: Last known 1849
Headquarters: Broad Gates (1848-1849)
Anniversary/feast day: Whit Monday

341.   Court Pride of the Thames

Status: Branch of an affiliated order, OXF 198   **Type:** AOF **Branch No.** 2880
Established: 1857   **Registered:** 1857   **Dissolved**: Post 1918
Headquarters: White Horse and Star, Northfield End (1857-1861), Bull Inn, Bell Street (1861-1871), Assembly Rooms (1872-1876), Bear Inn, Bell St (1877-post 1918)
Membership: 39 members in 1860, 90 in 1862, 124 in 1865, 207 in 1866, 149 in 1870, 174 in 1880, 297 in 1885, 360 in 1890, 438 in 1895, 496 in 1905, 482 in 1910
Notes: Buckinghamshire and Middlesex District of AOF.

342.   Court Pride of the Thames Juvenile Sick and Funeral Society

Status: Juvenile branch of an affiliated order, OXF 339 **Type:** AOF
Established: 1879   **Registered:** 1879   **Dissolved**: Post 1913
Headquarters: Foresters' Rooms, Bell St (1880-1910]

Membership: 23 members in 1880, 14 in 1885, 28 in 1890, 31 in 1895, 23 in 1900, 36 in 1905, 53 in 1910

343.   Excelsior Juvenile Tent

Status: Juvenile branch of an affiliated order   **Type**: IORSU **Branch No.** 671
Established: 1888   **Dissolved**: Last known 1910
Headquarters: 23 Bell Street [1905-1910)
Membership: 230 members in 1905, 223 in 1910

344.   Henley and Nettlebed Medical Benefit Society

Status: Unregistered   **Type**: Friendly society
Established: First known 1883 **Dissolved**: Last known 1883
Notes: A special meeting of the society was held at the Bull Inn on 18 June 1883 to appoint a medical officer (HA, 23 June 1883).

345.   Henley Congregational Benefit Society

Status: Enrolled, OXF 33   **Type**: Permanent friendly society
Established: 1838   **Registered:** 24 October 1839 **Dissolved**: Last known 1878
Headquarters: Vestry of Congregational Chapel, Henley-on-Thames (1839-1865], Southfield End Schoolroom [1871-1878)
Anniversary/feast day: Whit Tuesday, from 1873 Whit Monday
Membership: 119 members in 1846, 130 in 1850, 153 in 1855, 150 in 1865, 182 in 1875, 177 in 1878
Primary Sources: File is not present in the Registrar's papers at TNA but is indexed at TNA, FS 1/575/33; TNA, FS 4/42/33; Treasurer's bonds dated 30 August 1849, OHC, QSD/R/35
Notes: The monthly meetings were held at the vestry of the chapel 'to avoid the temptations of the ale-house' (JOJ, 6 June 1857). However, the annual dinners were held at a public house (Catherine Wheel in 1857, the Bull in 1871).

346.   Henley Provident Society

Status: Enrolled, OXF 65   **Type**: Permanent friendly society
Established: First known 1835   **Registered:** 21 January 1835 **Dissolved**: Last known 1835
Minimum age at entry: 14 **Maximum age at entry**: 50

Primary Sources: Rulebook of 1835, TNA FS 1/577/65; TNA, FS 2/9
Notes: The society was open to male and female members. Married women could only become members with the written permission of their husband. A female examining committee of three was established for sick visiting. The 1835 rules state the club covered Henley, Rotherfield Grays, Rotherfield Peppard, Harpesden, Shiplake, Bix, Hurley, Nettlebed, the Buckinghamshire parishes of Hambledon and Medmenham, and the Berkshire parishes of Remenham and Wargrave.

347.   Henley United Friendly Society

Status: Enrolled, OXF 121   **Type:** Permanent friendly society
Established: 1842   **Registered:** 13 July 1847 **Dissolved:** 24 March 1897
Headquarters: Bear Inn (1842-1855], Mr W Harris, Northfield End [1876-1885]
Anniversary/feast day: First Monday in June
Maximum age at entry: 40
Primary Sources: Rulebook of 1847, TNA, FS 3/319/121; TNA, FS 4/42/121

348.   Henley Wharf Club

Status: Unregistered   **Type:** Friendly society
Established: First known 1881 **Dissolved:** Last known 1881
Notes: The society was for employees at the Henley wharf (JOJ, 17 December 1881). (See also appendix 2, Crimes 91.)

349.   Hope of Henley Tent

Status: Branch of an affiliated order **Type:** IORSU **Branch No.** 1836
Established: 1888   **Dissolved:** Last known 1910
Headquarters: Henley Coffee House, Market Place (1888), 23 Bell St [1905-1910)
Membership: 56 members in 1905, 64 in 1910

350.   Loyal Bud of Hope Juvenile Lodge

Status: Juvenile branch of an affiliated order, OXF 321 **Type:** IOOFMU
Established: 1871   **Registered:** 1873   **Dissolved:** Post 1918
Headquarters: St Mary's Hall, New Street (1873-1878], White Hart Inn [1880-1885], Grey's Hall, Grey's Road [1899-1904), White Hart Hotel (1905-1910]

Minimum age at entry: 10 **Maximum age at entry**: 18
Membership: 46 members in 1874, 54 in 1880, 79 in 1885, 104 in 1891, 122 in 1899, 82 in 1905, 62 in 1910

351.   Loyal Good Samaritan Lodge

Status: Branch of an affiliated order, OXF 146   **Type**: IOOFMU **Branch No.** 3388
Established: 1843 **Dissolved**: Post 1918
Headquarters: White Hart Inn (1846-1888), Grey's Hall, Greys Road (1891-1908]
Membership: 15 members in 1846, 24 members in 1858, 40 in 1860, 70 in 1862, 114 in 1863, 164 in 1870, 272 in 1875, 322 in 1879, 467 in 1887, 593 in 1896, 692 in 1905, 616 in 1914
Notes: Wokingham District of IOOFMU (1846-1860), Reading District (1862-post 1918).

352.   Northfield End Friendly Society, also White Horse and Star club

Status: Enrolled, OXF 188   **Type:** Permanent friendly society
Established: 7 April 1806   **Registered:** 1815   **Dissolved:** Last known 1849
Headquarters: White Horse & Star Inn (1806-1849)
Anniversary/feast day: Whit Monday
Minimum age at entry: 16 Maximum age at entry: 40 (1806), 35 (1815)
Membership: 65 members in 1815
Primary Sources: Rules 1806 and 8 January 1823, OHC QSD/R/22; Rules of 1815, TNA, FS 1/580/188; TNA, FS 4/42/188; Oxon. Cal. QS iii, p.642
Notes: The rules of 1815 were signed by 65 members. On the death of a member, a cape, hatband, and gloves were required be worn at the funeral. The society had a maximum permitted membership of 150. On club day members were required to wear a blue ribbon in their hat. An advertisement in *Jackson's Oxford Journal* of 25 August 1832 stated the Northfield End Friendly society would be dissolved on 1 October 1832. It is unclear if this dissolution took place but a club continued at the White Horse and Star until 1849 (JOJ, 2 June 1849). A letter from the Registrar was returned, postmarked 1866 indicating the society had 'broken up' (TNA, FS 1/580/188) but this had taken place several years before.

353.   Old Red Lion Slate Club

Status: Unregistered **Type**: Dividing friendly society
Established: First known 1899   **Dissolved**: Last known 1899
Headquarters: Red Lion (1899)
Notes: The society held their annual water trip on Sunday 23 July 1899 to Streatley on the 'River Queen' (JOJ, 29 July 1899).

354.   Onward and Upward Female Tent

Status: Female branch of an affiliated order, **Type:** IORSU **Branch No.** 2294
Established: 1893   **Dissolved**: Last known 1910
Headquarters: Coffee House, Market Place (1893), Temperance Hall, Market Place (1904), 23 Bell St (1905-1910)
Membership: 31 members in 1905, 37 in 1910

355.   Pride of Henley Lodge

Status: Branch of an affiliated order **Type**: IIOOFSLU, NIOOF from 1913 **Branch No.** 46, 1276 from 1913
Established: 1879 **Dissolved**: Post 1913
Headquarters: King's Arms Inn [1905-1913)
Membership: 38 members in 1881, 25 in 1906, 24 in 1910
Notes: East Berkshire District of IIOOFSLU (1879), Berkshire District (1881). The branch joined the South London District of NIOOF in 1913, branch number 1276.

356.   Reform Mechanics Society

Status: Enrolled, OXF 50   **Type:** Permanent friendly society
Established: 1832   **Registered:** 22 November 1834   **Dissolved:** Last known 1844
Headquarters: Bull Inn (1832-1844)
Anniversary/feast day: Whit Monday
Minimum age at entry: 18 Maximum age at entry: 35
Membership: 74 members in 1846, 77 in 1850
Primary Sources: Rulebooks of 1834 and 1844, TNA, FS 1/576/50; TNA, FS 4/42/50

Notes: The society admitted only 'mechanics' with a minimum weekly pay of 16s. Painters, plumbers, or anyone in a trade of a dangerous or pernicious nature could not join (TNA, FS 1/576/50).

357.   Reform Union Friendly Society

Status: Enrolled, OXF 27   **Type**: Permanent friendly society
Established: First known 1833   **Registered:** 14 October 1833   **Dissolved**: Last known 1833
Headquarters: Three Tuns, Market Place (1833)
Primary Sources: TNA, FS 4/42/27
Notes: No records are present in the Registrar's papers at TNA although indexed at TNA, FS 1/575/27

358.   Royal Jubilee Lodge

Status: Branch of an affiliated order **Type**: AOD **Branch No.** 469
Established: First known 1892   **Dissolved**: Last known 1904
Headquarters: Broad Gates (1904)
Notes: A special meeting was held at the Town Hall in May 1892 due to the large numbers expected to attend (HA, 28 May 1892).

359.   South Oxfordshire Friendly Society

Status: Enrolled, OXF 62   **Type**: Permanent friendly society
Established: First known 1841   **Registered:** 3 May 1841 **Dissolved**: 1889
Headquarters: Savings Bank, Bell St [1855-1890)
Membership: 145 members in 1864, 89 in 1878, 61 in 1885
Primary Sources: TNA, FS 4/42/62
Notes: The society was managed like a county society with control by the honorary members. A branch of the society was established in 1872 at Nettlebed (HA, 18 May 1872). A note on Registrar's index states the society was illegally dissolved in 1889 (TNA, FS 4/42/62). A letter from William Hews, clerk to the Registrar, dated 20 May 1890 stated that the society was formally dissolved on 29 May 1890.

> **White Horse and Star club** – see Northfield End Friendly Society, Henley on Thames 352

Hensington

No. of societies and members 1802/3 – None
No. of members of a friendly society 1813/14/15 – None

360.   Hensington United Brethren Benefit Society

Status: Registered, OXF 254   **Type**: Permanent friendly society
Established: 1863   **Registered:**   7   November   1863   **Dissolved**:   28
September 1865
Headquarters: Old White House (1863-1865)
Anniversary/feast day: Whit Monday
Membership: 9 members in 1865
Primary Sources: Rulebook of 1863, TNA, FS 1/582/254; TNA, FS 4/42/254
Notes: The society dissolved with nine members and £6 2s 6½d funds.

Hethe

No. of societies and members 1802/3 – None
No. of members of a friendly society 1813/14/15 – None
Notes: (See appendix 2, Crimes 92 and 93).

361.   Hethe Friendly Society

Status: Registered, OXF 28   **Type**: 7-year dividing friendly society
Established: First known 1839   **Registered:** 12 June 1839   **Dissolved**: 1871
Headquarters: Whitmore Arms (1839-1871)
Anniversary/feast day: Whit Monday
Membership: 39 members in 1862, 49 in 1866, 57 in 1871
Primary Sources: TNA, FS 4/42/28
Notes: No file in relation to this society can be located in the Registrar's papers
at TNA although the index indicates it should be present at TNA, FS 1/575/28.
The society appears to have continued as an unregistered society (Hethe 362).

362.   Hethe Friendly Society

Status: Unregistered   **Type**: 7-year dividing friendly society
Established: First known 1872 **Dissolved**: Last known 1884
Headquarters: National Schoolroom (1872-1884)
Anniversary/feast day: Whit Monday
Membership: 45 members in 1883

Notes: The society appears to be a continuation of a registered club (Hethe 361) that ceased to exist in 1871. On club day in 1884 E. Slater-Harrison urged the society to register (BicA, 6 June 1884) and this led to the formation of a new society (Hethe 363).

363.   Hethe Friendly Society

Status: Registered, OXF 357   **Type:** Permanent friendly society
Established: 1885   **Registered:** 1885   **Dissolved:** 15 July 1916
Headquarters: Whitmore Arms (1885-1916)
Anniversary/feast day: Whit Monday
Minimum age at entry: 16 Maximum age at entry: 50
Membership: 52 members in 1885, 70 in 1890, 79 in 1899, 73 in 1903, 62 in 1913
Primary Sources: Rulebook of 1885, TNA, FS 15/580
Notes: The society was formed from Hethe 362 on registration. The society's clubhouse was a building at the rear of the Whitmore Arms. New members were required to reside within five miles of Hethe. The society had members from Cottisford, Fringford, and Newton Purcell in 1886. The club room was decorated with azaleas and rhododendrons on club day. Dr. Farmer was the medical officer for the club for over 40 years. In 1903 it was reported that the Fringford club had improved and had taken some of the Hethe members with it (BicA, 5 June 1903). The society registered under the provisional scheme of National Insurance Act 1911. It dissolved with 52 members and £489 funds.

Heythrop

No. of societies and members 1802/3 – None
No. of members of a friendly society 1813/14/15 – None

364.   Holy Guild and Friendly Society of St Joseph and Our Blessed Lady, for the Catholic Congregation of Radford and Heythrop

Status: Enrolled, OXF 112   **Type:** Permanent friendly society
Established: 1846   **Registered:** 29 January 1848   **Dissolved:** Last known 1848
Minimum age at entry: 17 (sick and annuity funds), 9 (mortuary fund)
Maximum age at entry: 50 (sick and annuity funds), 64 (mortuary fund)
Primary Sources: Rulebook of 1848, TNA, FS 1/578/112; TNA, FS 1/578/112

Notes: The society was open to male and female members. Ordinary members were required to be Roman Catholic but honorary members could be of any denomination. Only male members could join the sickness fund, but both sexes could join the annuity and mortuary funds. Any member found 'tipsy' was fined 2s 6d. If this occurred twice within twelve months then the member received a fine of 5s, and three times, 7s 6d. A fourth such misdemeanour in twelve months meant the member was expelled. Tipsy was defined by the rules thus: 'whilst in drink, shouting or singing in the street, not being able to walk, or other conduct bringing disgrace upon the religion'.

Hook Norton

No. of societies and members 1802/3 – 1, 54
No. of members of a friendly society 1813/14/15 – 48, 59, 59

365.   Court Pride of Hook Norton

Status: Branch of an affiliated order   **Type**: AOF **Branch No.** 7826
Established: 1889 **Dissolved**: Post 1918
Headquarters: Bell Inn [1889-post 1918)
Anniversary/feast day: Tuesday before Whit Sunday
Membership: 10 members in 1890, 26 in 1891, 29 in 1895, 59 in 1900, 69 in 1905, 78 in 1910
Notes: Banbury District of AOF.

Hook Norton Benefit Society – see Hook Norton United
Provident Society, Hook Norton 365

366.   Hook Norton and Adderbury Sick Club, also Ironstone Works Sick Club

Status: Unregistered   **Type**: Friendly society, possibly a shop club
Established: First known 1893 **Dissolved**: Last known 1893
Notes: The society was connected with the ironstone industry. The employer, the Hook Norton Ironstone Partnership, held a dinner for the society at the Sun Inn in 1893 and 70 people attended (BG, 1 June 1893).

367.   Hook Norton Friendly Society

Status: Enrolled   **Type**: Permanent friendly society
Established: 1 May 1780 **Dissolved**: Last known 1794

Headquarters: Red Lion Inn (1780-1794]
Anniversary/feast day: First Monday in June
Primary Sources: Manuscript rules of 1 May 1790, OHC, QSD/R/23
Notes: A maximum of 111 members was permitted.

368.   Hook Norton United Provident Society, (then from 1897) Hook Norton Benefit Society

Status: Registered, OXF 215   **Type:** 5-year dividing friendly society, then annual dividing friendly society
Established: 1859   **Registered:** 1859   **Dissolved:** 31 December 1914
Headquarters: Bell Inn [1870-1883), National School (1883-1885], Bell Inn [1889), National School (1889-1897), Sun Inn (1897-1914)
Anniversary/feast day: Tuesday before Whit Sunday
Minimum age at entry: 16 Maximum age at entry: 40
Membership: 48 members in 1862, 67 in 1865, 92 in 1870, 117 in 1874, 131 in 1878, 130 in 1885, 109 in 1891, 96 in 1899, 74 in 1905, 43 in 1914
Primary Sources: Rulebooks of 1859 and 1880, TNA, FS 15/567; BPP 1874, XXIII, (c.997), p.117
Notes: The Assistant Commissioner stated the society was initially a five-year dividing club but changed to annual division. He reported 67 of the 104 members resided within distance of the doctor giving 37 distant members. No rent was paid to the landlord and no compulsory beer money was payable. In 1873 the society owned twelve acres, three roods and twelve perches of land (BPP 1874, LXXII, [c.1097], Oxford p.8 [1874]). It had a bright blue banner. Club day was almost the only holiday villagers kept during the year (BG, 20 May 1875). The society dissolved with 43 members and £111 15s 4½d funds.

Ironstone Works Sick Club – see Hook Norton and Adderbury Sick Club, Hook Norton 366

369.   Loyal General Gordon Lodge

Status: Branch of an affiliated order   **Type**: IOOFMU **Branch No.** 7510
Established: 1899 **Dissolved**: Post 1918
Headquarters: Sun Inn Assembly Rooms (1899-1912)
Anniversary/feast day: Tuesday before Whit Sunday
Membership: 35 members in 1901, 50 in 1907, 95 in 1910, 82 in 1914
Primary Sources: Lodge rulebook, 1900, Chipping Norton Museum
Notes: Banbury District of IOOFMU.

Horley

No. of societies and members 1802/3 – None
No. of members of a friendly society 1813/14/15 – None

370.   Court Old House at Home

Status: Branch of an Affiliated Order   **Type:** AOF **Branch No.** 1928
Established: 1846 **Dissolved**: 1858
Headquarters: Red Lion Inn (1846-1849), Thomas Borton's private house
(1850), Red Lion Inn (1851-1858)
Notes: Wellingborough and Higham Ferrers District of AOF (1847-1858).
This was the first AOF branch in Oxfordshire.

371.   Horley Friendly Society

Status: Registered, OXF 319   **Type:** Permanent friendly society
Established: 1873   **Registered:** 13 February 1873   **Dissolved:** June 1912
Headquarters: Schoolroom (1873-1912)
Anniversary/feast day: Third Friday in July
Minimum age at entry: 18 Maximum age at entry: 40
Membership: 23 in 1874, 24 in 1878, 24 in 1885, 31 in 1891, 33 in 1899, 40
in 1905, 37 in 1910
Primary Sources: Rulebook of 1873, FS 15/576
Notes: The registration of the society was cancelled by request as it had
dissolved in June 1912 with £119 assets.

372.   Horley Friendship and Unity Benefit Society

Status: Enrolled, OXF 53   **Type**: Permanent friendly society
Established: 1834   **Registered:** 27 October 1837   **Dissolved**: Last known
1843
Headquarters: Red Lion Inn (1834-1843)
Anniversary/feast day: Second Friday in May
Maximum age at entry: 35
Primary Sources: Rulebook of 1837, TNA, FS 1/576/53; TNA, FS 4/42/53
Notes: A letter of 7 October 1878 stated the society no longer existed (TNA,
FS 4/42/53).

373.   Horley General Insurance Society, also Royal Horley Insurance Society

Status: Registered, OXF 212   **Type:** Permanent friendly society
Established: 1858 **Registered:** 28 December 1858 **Dissolved:** Last known 1871
Headquarters: Red Lion Inn (1858), Schoolroom (1871)
Anniversary/feast day: Third Friday in July
Minimum age at entry: 15 Maximum age at entry: 40
Membership: 19 members in 1872
Primary Sources: Rulebook of 1858, TNA, FS 1/581/212; TNA, FS 4/42/212; BPP 1874, XXIII, (c.997), p.119
Notes: The Assistant Commissioner reported that the schoolmaster was club secretary and there were 19 members.

> **Royal Horley Insurance Society** – see Horley General Insurance Society, Horley 373

Hornton

No. of societies and members 1802/3 – 1, 44
No. of members of a friendly society 1813/14/15 – None
Notes: (See appendix 2, Crimes 94 and 95).

374.   Court Temple of Friendship

Status: Branch of an affiliated order, OXF 279   **Type:** AOF **Branch No.** 4783
Established: 1865   **Registered:** 1867   **Dissolved**: Post 1918
Headquarters: Bell Inn (1865-1880], Schoolroom [1893-post 1918)
Membership: 17 members in 1872, 31 in 1874, 50 in 1880, 58 in 1885, 60 in 1890, 80 in 1895, 91 in 1900, 113 in 1905, 119 in 1910
Notes: Northamptonshire, Wellingborough, and Higham Ferrers District of AOF (1865-post 1918).

375.   Court Temple of Friendship, Juvenile Branch

Status: Juvenile branch of an affiliated order   **Type**: AOF
Established: 1877 **Dissolved**: Last known 1895
Headquarters: Schoolroom (1895)
Minimum age at entry: 6 **Maximum age at entry**: 16

Membership: 5 members in 1885

376.   Hornton Friendly Society

Status: Enrolled   **Type:** Permanent friendly society
Established: 3 January 1784   **Registered:** 15 November 1794   **Dissolved:**
Last known 1794
Headquarters: Bell Inn (1794)
Anniversary/feast day: Third Friday in June
Maximum age at entry: 40
Notes: Manuscript rules of 3 January 1874, OHC, QSD/R/24

377.   Hornton Friendly Society

Status: Registered, OXF 261   **Type:** 3-year dividing friendly society
Established: 1865   **Registered:** 23 February 1865   **Dissolved:** 1866
Headquarters: Red Lion (1865-1866)
Minimum age at entry: 15 **Maximum age at entry:** 35
Primary Sources: Rulebook of 1865, TNA, FS 1/582/261; TNA, FS 4/42/261
Notes: At division, the rules stated 21s per member was to be retained in
society funds. A letter of 30 January 1866 stated the society had dissolved as
the funds were exhausted (TNA, FS 1/582/261).

378.   Hornton New Insurance Society

Status: Registered, OXF 270   **Type:** Permanent friendly society
Established: 1866   **Registered:** 27 April 1866   **Dissolved:** 17 May 1901
Headquarters: Red Lion Inn (1866-1901)
Anniversary/feast day: Monday following the first Sunday after Midsummer
Day
Minimum age at entry: 15 Maximum age at entry: 40
Membership: 19 members in 1866, 27 in 1871, 18 in 1872, 32 in 1878, 37 in
1885, 35 in 1891, 31 in 1901
Primary Sources: Rulebook of 1866, TNA, FS 3/321/270; TNA, FS 4/42/270;
BPP 1874, XXIII, (c.997), p.119).
Notes: The Assistant Commissioner reported that the club was kept by Mr C.
Webb, son of the keeper of another society in the village held at the school
(Hornton 379). The club had suffered from much sickness and some accidents
and was not well off. The society was dissolved with 31 members and £196
6s 9d funds.

379.   (Hornton Old Club)

Status: Unregistered   **Type**: Friendly society
Established: First known 1872 **Dissolved**: Last known 1872
Headquarters: National school (1872)
Primary Sources: BPP 1874, XXIII, (c.997), p.119
Notes: The Assistant Commissioner reported the society was kept by Mr J. Webb, father of C.Webb who runs the registered club (Hornton 378). It had only 25 members and was not a well off club. It clearly had a significant history but no records survive of its earlier years.

380.   **Mollington Refuge Friendly Society, Hornton Branch, also Refuge Club**

Status: Branch of a registered society, OXF 235   **Type**: Friendly society
Established: First known 1872 **Dissolved**: Last known 1872
Membership: 20 members in 1872
Primary Sources: BPP 1874, XXIII, (c.997), p.118
Notes: The Assistant Commissioner described the club as a branch of the Refuge Friendly Society held at Mollington (Mollington 441). He called it a 'teapot club', referring to the fact it had a tea party instead of a feast for its annual celebration.

> **Refuge Club** – see Mollington Refuge Friendly Society, Hornton Branch, Hornton 380

Horspath

No. of societies and members 1802/3 – None
No. of members of a friendly society 1813/14/15 – None

381.   **Court Victoria's Jubilee**

Status: Branch of an affiliated order   **Type**: AOF **Branch No.** 7626
Established: 1887 **Dissolved**: Post 1918
Headquarters: Chequers Inn (1887–post 1918)
Membership: 20 members in 1888, 34 in 1889, 42 in 1890, 72 in 1895, 80 in 1900, 76 in 1905, 94 in 1910
Notes: Oxford District of AOF.

Horton cum Studley

No. of societies and members 1802/3 – None
No. of members of a friendly society 1813/14/15 – None
Notes: (See appendix 2, Crimes 96).

> **Studley Benefit Society** – see Studley Hand in Glove Benefit
> Society, Horton cum Studley 383

382.   Studley and Horton Benefit Society

Status: Enrolled, OXF 82   **Type**: Permanent friendly society
Established: First known 1844   **Registered:** 22 January 1844   **Dissolved**:
Last known 1848
Headquarters: King's Arms Inn (1844)
Anniversary/feast day: Ascension Day
Maximum age at entry: 45
Primary Sources: Rulebook of 1844, TNA, FS 1/577/82; TNA, FS 4/42/82
Notes: The club was under the control of the trustees who had to approve
any rule change and any division of funds. A letter of 25 January 1870 to the
Registrar stated the old club was 'done away with years ago' and that another
club had started in the last twelve months but members could not agreed if it
should be registered (Horton cum Studley 383) (TNA, FS 1/577/82).

383.   Studley Hand in Glove Benefit Society, (and from 12
December 1889) Studley Benefit Society

Status: Registered, OXF 314   **Type:** Permanent friendly society
Established: 1869   **Registered:** 1872   **Dissolved:** 31 December 1925
Headquarters: King's Arms Inn (1872-1926)
Anniversary/feast day: Ascension Day
Minimum age at entry: 16 Maximum age at entry: 45
Membership: 42 members in 1878, 35 in 1891, 35 in 1899, 46 in 1905, 35 in
1913
Primary Sources: Rulebooks of 1872 and 1917, TNA, FS 15/575; rulebook of
1872, Bodl. G.A. OXF 8° 688(1); TNA, FS 1/577/82
Notes: A letter of 25 January 1870 to the Registrar stated the old club (Horton
cum Studley 382) was 'done away with years ago' and that another club had
started in the last twelve months but members could not agreed if it should
be registered (TNA, FS 1/577/82). On the valuation of 1912 the occupation
of members was described as mostly agricultural. It entered the provisional

scheme and then on 5 January 1917 was adopted as a scheme under section 72 National Insurance Act 1911. The valuation at 1922 showed a surplus above potential payout of £339 and recommended increasing benefits. The society dissolved with 23 members and £317 9s 7¼d funds.

Iffley

No. of societies and members 1802/3 – 1, 47
No. of members of a friendly society 1813/14/15 – None
Notes: (See appendix 2, Crimes 99).

384.   Court Hearts of Oak

Status: Branch of an affiliated order, OXF 298   **Type**: AOF **Branch No.** 5183
Established: 1868   **Registered:** 1869   **Dissolved**: Post 1918
Headquarters: (The) Tree Tavern (1868-post 1918)
Anniversary/feast day: First Wednesday in June
Membership: 27 members in 1869, 42 in 1870, 60 in 1872, 58 in 1875, 95 in 1877, 142 in 1885, 192 in 1890, 233 in 1895, 271 in 1900, 306 in 1905, 296 in 1910
Notes: Independent of any district of AOF.

385.   Hope of Iffley Juvenile Foresters Friendly Society

Status: Juvenile branch of an affiliated order, OXF 370   **Type**: AOF
Established: 1890   **Registered:** 1890   **Dissolved**: Post 1918
Headquarters: Schoolroom (1890-post 1914)
Minimum age at entry: 4 Maximum age at entry: 16
Membership: 14 members in 1891, 31 in 1895, 42 in 1900, 27 in 1905, 12 in 1910
Notes: Juvenile branch of Court Hearts of Oak (Iffley 384).

> **Iffley and Oxford New Benefit Society** – see Iffley New Benefit Society, Iffley 387

386.   Iffley Friendly Benefit Society

Status: Enrolled, OXF 17   **Type**: Permanent friendly society
Established: 1837   **Registered:** 12 May 1838   **Dissolved**: Last known 1838
Headquarters: The Tree (1838)
Anniversary/feast day: First Wednesday in June

Minimum age at entry: 16 **Maximum age at entry**: 35
Primary Sources: Rulebook of 1838, TNA, FS 1/574/17; TNA, FS 4/42/17
Notes: A maximum of 120 members was permitted.

387.   **Iffley New Benefit Society, (and from 1870) Iffley and Oxford New Benefit Society**

Status: Enrolled, OXF 56   **Type**: Permanent friendly society
Established: 1835   **Registered:** 16 March 1837   **Dissolved**: 3 October 1892
Headquarters: A room formerly used as a chapel, Iffley (1835-1837), St Leonard's Schoolroom, Rose Hill (1837-1855], Schoolroom [1860-1870), 6 Walton St, Oxford (1870-1878), Cheltenham House, Kingston Rd, Oxford (1879-1892)
Maximum age at entry: 45, 40 (from 1846)
Membership: 75 members in 1855, 107 in 1860, 108 in 1870, 131 in 1878, 85 in 1885, 52 in 1892
Primary Sources: Rulebook of 1835, 1858 and 1877, TNA, FS 3/319/56; TNA, FS 4/42/56; BPP 1874, XXIII, (c.997), p.95
Notes: In 1867 a member of the club was charged with stealing £6 16s 6d from the society (see appendix 2, Crimes 98). The Assistant Commissioner reported in 1872 that the society absorbed clubs from Longworth and Cumnor. Members were scattered about the villages and were mostly agricultural labourers and artisans. New members mostly came from Oxford after a new society opened in Iffley, Court Hearts of Oak, AOF (Iffley 384). The New Benefit Society moved to Oxford in 1870. The Assistant Commissioner reported that between eight and ten members were on the verge of default of payments. There were losses to funds between 1870 and 1879 of an average £19 11s 3d per annum due to cost of the doctor, who in 1859 was voted £20 per annum for attendance to members. There were 38 outlying, or distant members in 1880 representing 29 per cent of all members. The society dissolved with 52 members and £1,760 funds. (See also appendix 2, Crimes 97).

Islip

No. of societies and members 1802/3 – None
No. of members of a friendly society 1813/14/15 – None

388.   **Court Edward the Confessor**

Status: Branch of an affiliated order **Type**: AOF **Branch No.** 9035
Established: 1901 **Dissolved**: Post 1918

Headquarters: Red Lion Inn (1901-post 1918)
Anniversary/feast day: Whit Monday
Membership: 11 members in 1902, 23 in 1903, 33 in 1905, 37 in 1910
Notes: Oxford District of AOF.

Fox Benefit Society – see Union Fellowship Society, Islip 390

389.   Islip Friendly Institution, also Swan club

Status: Enrolled, OXF 93   **Type:** Permanent friendly society
Established: 8 November 1843 **Registered:** 1843 **Dissolved:** 29 November 1913
Headquarters: Swan Inn (1845-1913)
Anniversary/feast day: Whit Monday
Minimum age at entry: 14, 7 (from 1911) Maximum age at entry: 45, 35 (from 1862)
Membership: 52 members in 1862, 51 in 1870, 62 in 1875, 75 in 1880, 82 in 1890, 91 in 1895, 89 in 1902, 77 in 1905, 65 in 1913
Primary Sources: Rulebook of 1845 and 1911, TNA, FS 15/563; rulebook of 1862 and 1875, Bodl. G.A. OXF 8° 1305;
Notes: A new flag was purchased by subscription for the 50th Jubilee anniversary in 1894 for eleven guineas and contained the words, 'Islip Friendly Institution established November 6th 1843 Jubilee year - Fear God, honour the king, love the brotherhood' (BicA, 18 May 1894). Members were admitted to the society by 'crowning' which involved holding a large can of beer upon the head of the person to be admitted whilst he was lustily cheered, before and after which he was expected to take draught of the contents. The society dissolved with 65 members and £284 19s 2d funds.

Swan club – see Islip Friendly Institution, Islip 389

390.   Union Fellowship Society, also Fox Benefit Society

Status: Unregistered   **Type:** 7-year dividing friendly society
Established: 12 July 1847 **Dissolved:** Last known 1886
Headquarters: Fox and Grapes [1849-1886)
Anniversary/feast day: Whit Monday
Maximum age at entry: 35
Membership: 35 members in 1880, 60 members in 1881
Primary Sources: Undated rulebook, Bodl. G.A. OXF. 8° 1255(4)

Notes: The society permitted a maximum of 100 members with payments of 4s 6d a quarter. On division of funds two years' membership was retained in society. The rules also stated that 'One pint of beer only allowed each member before going to church'. A new flag was obtained for the society in 1849 (JOJ, 2 June 1849). The society did not take part in club day of 1886 as it was said to be recruiting members (BicA, 18 June 1886). However, it had ceased to exist by the following year when it was reported the Islip Friendly Institution (Islip 389) was the only club left in the village (BicA, 3 June 1887). (See also appendix 2, Crimes 100 and 101).

Kidlington

No. of societies and members 1802/3 – 1, 101
No. of members of a friendly society 1813/14/15 – 149, 171, 171
Notes: (See appendix 2, Crimes 103, 105 and 106).

391. Court Denford

Status: Branch of an affiliated order   **Type:** AOF **Branch No.** 7607
Established: 1887 **Dissolved:** 1888
Headquarters: Red Lion (1887-1888)
Membership: 9 members in 1888
Notes: Oxford District. Closed by the division of funds with nine members.

392. Court Duke of York

Status: Branch of an affiliated order   **Type:** AOF **Branch No.** 8545
Established: 1895 **Dissolved:** Post 1918
Headquarters: Foresters' Hall [1903-post 1918)
Anniversary/feast day: First Thursday in June
Membership: 34 members in 1897, 52 in 1998, 76 in 1900, 107 in 1905, 81 in 1910
Notes: Oxford District of AOF.

393. Independent Mutual Brethren Friendly Society, Kidlington branch

Status: Branch of a registered society, MDX 4880   **Type:** Permanent friendly society
Established: First known 1884 **Dissolved:** Last known 1884
Headquarters: Red Lion Inn (1884)

Anniversary/feast day: First Thursday in June

394.   Kidlington Benefit Society, also King's Arms Benefit Society

Status: Enrolled, OXF 220   **Type:** 7-year dividing friendly society
Established: 1858 **Registered:** 7 September 1859   **Dissolved:** 13 June 1892
Headquarters: King's Arms Inn [1865-1892)
Anniversary/feast day: First Thursday in June
Minimum age at entry: 14 Maximum age at entry: 45
Membership: 31 in 1860, 34 in 1864, 55 in 1865, 68 in 1866, 90 in 1871, 84 in 1877, 106 in 1880, 103 in 1885, 22 in 1892
Primary Sources: Rulebook of 1858, TNA, FS 3/321/220; TNA, FS 4/42/220
Notes: The club was suspended by the Registrar on 11 August 1887 for three months, and again on 11 November 1887 for the same period. It dissolved with 22 members and £30 16s 10½ funds. All but one of the final members had been a member for more than 13 years.

395.   Kidlington Friendly Society

Status: Enrolled, OXF 177   **Type:** Permanent friendly society
Established: 4 February 1760 **Registered:** 29 May 1805 **Dissolved**: Last known 1805
Headquarters: Black Horse Inn
Anniversary/feast day: First Tuesday in May
Maximum age at entry: 30
Primary Sources: Undated rules, TNA, FS 1/580/177; TNA, FS 4/42/177
Notes: It was described as being at Kidlington on the Green and was likely to have been the society with substantial membership in 1813-15 but had ceased to exist by 1839 when another society of the same name was established (Kidlington 396).

396.   Kidlington Friendly Society

Status: Enrolled, OXF 31   **Type:** Permanent friendly society
Established: 1839 **Registered:** 1839 **Dissolved:** 3 February 1914
Headquarters: National Schoolroom (1839-1914)
Anniversary/feast day: First Thursday in June
Minimum age at entry: 10 (1839), 16, (under 16s accepted after 1901)
Maximum age at entry: 60 (1839), 45

Membership: 25 members in 1839, 99 in 1846, 134 in 1849, 90 in 1854, 89 in 1860, 114 in 1864, 98 in 1870, 97 in 1877, 95 in 1879, 83 in 1880, 153 in 1891, 144 in 1900, 125 in 1910, 101 in 1914
Primary Sources: Rulebooks of 1839, 1878 and 1901, TNA, FS 15/561; rulebook of 1839, Bodl. G.A. OXF 8° 942
Notes: The society was open to male and female members but married women needed the consent of their husband to join. Minors could be members with their parents' permission but could not vote until aged ten years. It was for residents of the parish of Kidlington and its neighbourhood and had graduated payments dependent upon age of joining. The Vicar of Kidlington was the President of the society and he had a veto on all decisions. In 1860 there were 41 honorary members and they continued to hold a separate anniversary dinner on the first Thursday in May. The colours of the club were red, white, and blue (14 June 1856) and the clubroom was decorated with daisies, leaves, flowers, and old postage stamps (25 June 1859). It was thought at its formation that membership would reach 1,000 (JOJ, 17 June 1854). Funds grew considerably and division was first considered in 1866. In 1878 benefit members began to take control of the club. Various rules were changed and a confrontation ensued with the vicar. A number of court cases followed but the actions of the benefit members stood and on 14 June 1879 the division of £1,100 took place. After that date, there was to be a three-year division of all funds over £1,000 even though this technically made the club insolvent because of future projected benefits. The vicar left the parish. The society entered the provisional scheme under the National Insurance Act 1911. It dissolved with 101 members and £989 9 7¼d funds. (See also appendix 2, Crimes 104 and 107).

King's Arms Benefit Society – see Kidlington Benefit Society, Kidlington 394

Kingham

No. of societies and members 1802/3 – 1, 50
No. of members of a friendly society 1813/14/15 – 67, 63, 66

397.   Kingham Friendly Society

Status: Unregistered   **Type:** Permanent friendly society
Established: 1842 **Dissolved**: Last known 1905
Headquarters: Plough Inn [1900-1905)
Anniversary/feast day: Ascension Day

Notes: Club day at Kingham affected attendance at church services on Ascension Day in neighbouring villages, such as Daylsford and Sarsden (CNDM, July 1885 and 1886). Mowbray Jackson was surgeon in 1879 and he also served several other friendly societies in the area, namely United Christian Benefit Society (Chipping Norton 207), Churchill and Sarsden Benefit Society (Churchill 209), Chipping Norton United Provident Society (Chipping Norton 194), the Loyal Old Elm Tree Lodge (Chipping Norton 198) and the Old Guildhall Club (Chipping Norton 204) (JOJ, 12 July 1879).

Kingston Blount

No. of societies and members 1802/3 – None
No. of members of a friendly society 1813/14/15 – None

398.   (Cherry Tree Friendly Society)

Status: Unregistered   **Type:** Friendly Society
Established: First known 1871 **Dissolved**: Last known 1871
Headquarters: Cherry Tree (1871)
Anniversary/feast day: Whit Monday
Notes: The society was in existence in 1871 when the *Thame Gazette* reported on its club day (TG, 6 June 1871).

399.   Kingston Blount Friendly Society

Status: Unregistered   **Type:** 7-year dividing friendly society
Established: First known 1887 **Dissolved**: Last known 1894
Headquarters: Shoulder of Mutton (1887-1894)
Anniversary/feast day: Whit Monday
Notes: The division of funds took place in 1894 with £2 16s payable to those who had been members for the full seven year (HSOS, 18 May 1894).

400.   Kingston Friendly Society

Status: Enrolled, OXF 180   **Type:** Permanent friendly society
Established: 4 April 1825   **Registered:** 25 October 1828 **Dissolved**: Last known 1829
Headquarters: White Hart (1828)
Anniversary/feast day: Whit Monday
Minimum age at entry: 18 **Maximum age at entry**: 35

Membership: Primary Sources: rulebook of 1828, TNA, FS 1/580/180; TNA, FS 1/574/3; TNA, FS 4/42/180; Oxon. Cal. QS iii, p. 682; **Notes:** Rules enrolled at Michaelmas Quarter Session 1828. All named people recorded against the application were from Aston Rowant. A letter dated 20 August 1829 from John Holland (vicar of Lewknor) regarding this club, and requesting the bearer be provided with a copy of the rules, is misfiled in the Registrar's records (TNA, FS 1/574/3). George Jones, schoolmaster from Kingston, was requested to leave the rules at Lewknor.

401.   Kingston Friendly Society

Status: Registered, OXF 284   **Type:** 7-year Dividing friendly society
Established: 1867   **Registered:** 13 November 1867 **Dissolved**: 1875
Headquarters: Red Lion (1867-1875)
Anniversary/feast day: Whit Monday
Minimum age at entry: 16 **Maximum age at entry**: 45
Membership: Primary Sources: Rulebook of 1867, TNA, FS 1/582/284; TNA, FS 4/42/284; TNA, FS 4/42/22
Notes: A letter of 16 May 1880 from H. Savill Young, the vicar of Aston Rowant stated no such society then existed (TNA, FS 4/42/284). A letter from Richard Wakelin, late of the Red Lion Inn, Kingston Blount and dated 16 December 1878 was misfiled in the Registrar's papers under reference TNA, FS 4/42/22. It stated the Red Lion Inn had closed three years earlier and the club broke up in 1875.

402.   Mutual Benefit Society

Status: Unregistered   **Type:** 7-year dividing friendly society
Established: 1894 **Dissolved**: Last known 1894
Headquarters: (Red) Lion (1894)
Anniversary/feast day: Whit Monday
Minimum age at entry: 14 **Maximum age at entry**: 50
Notes: The *Henley Standard* reported that a new society had been formed at Kingston Blount. New members had to reside within ten miles and the society provided different classes of benefit based upon age and contribution (HSOS, 18 May 1894).

Kirtlington

No. of societies and members 1802/3 – 1, 47
No. of members of a friendly society 1813/14/15 – 97, 95, 94

Notes: (See appendix 2, Crimes 108).

Hawkes' Benefit Society – see Kirtlington Provident Friendly Society, Kirtlington 403

403.   **Kirtlington Provident Friendly Society, also Hawkes' Benefit Society**

Status: Enrolled, OXF 250   **Type:** Permanent friendly society
Established: 1 November 1809 **Dissolved:** 1902
Headquarters: Dashwood Arms Inn (c.1846), Schoolroom [1863-1902)
Anniversary/feast day: Easter Monday, (from c.1860) Trinity Monday
Minimum age at entry: 14 (1866), 16 (1884) Maximum age at entry: 30 (1863), 50 (from 1866)
Membership: 52 members in 1811, 39 in 1820, 90 in 1859, 78 in 1864, 66 in 1870, 60 in 1875, 86 in 1881, 67 in 1885, 84 in 1889, 70 in 1897, 63 in 1902
Primary Sources: Undated rules c.1846, Bodl. G.A. a.126; rulebooks of 1863, 1866 and 1884, Bodl. G.A. OXF 8° 1298(1-3); rulebook of 1884, OHC COS, KIRT 334.5
Notes: In the c.1846 rulebook the society was described as a 'friendly society meeting at the Dashwood Arms Inn', with a maximum of 61 members. No age limits were given. The 1884 rules describe the society as being for mechanics, servants, labourers, and others, with both male and female members permitted but there was no sickness insurance for women. The president of the society was always the vicar of the parish. In 1858 the Kirtlington Lamb Ale and the club feast came together and were both celebrated on Trinity Monday (BicA, 28 May 1880). The club day and Lamb Ale were described as, 'A popular holiday amongst poorer residents of this district of Oxfordshire' (BicA, 12 June 1896). In 1900 it was reported that about 20 men had left the village and moved away from the area and that many young members joined the Foresters because if they moved away they could transfer their membership (BicA, 15 June 1900). Mr Hawkes was President of the society and was associated with it for 45 years. The club became the Loyal Major Dashwood branch of the AOF (Kirtlington 404) in 1902. No file for this society exists in the Registrar's papers at TNA although it is indexed at FS 1/581/250. There is no card present in TNA, FS 4/42.

404.   **Loyal Major Dashwood Lodge**

Status: Branch of an affiliated order **Type:** IOOFMU **Branch No.** 7695
Established: 1902 **Dissolved**: Post 1918

Headquarters: Schoolroom (1902-post 1918)
Anniversary/feast day: Trinity Monday
Membership: 106 members in 1902, 110 in 1905, 108 in 1910, 118 in 1914
Notes: Oxford District of IOOFMU. The branch was formed from the Kirtlington Provident Friendly society (Kirtlington 403).

405.   Loyal Valentia Lodge

Status: Branch of an affiliated order, OXF 120   **Type:** IOOFMU Branch No. 4291
Established: 1850 **Registered:** 24 June 1853   **Dissolved:** 1861
Headquarters: Red Lion, Bletchingdon (1850), Oxford Arms Inn, Kirtlington (1853-1860)
Minimum age at entry: 18 Maximum age at entry: 36
Membership: 17 members in 1850, 9 in 1858, 6 in 1860
Primary Sources: Rulebook of 1853, TNA, FS 1/578/120; TNA, FS 4/42/120
Notes: Oxford District of AOF. The society was initially based in Bletchingdon. A letter dated 1 August 1861 was sent to the Registrar stating the society would close in a fortnight as members had gone to various parts of the country.

406.   Oxford Arms Friendly Society

Status: Registered, OXF 223   **Type:** 7-year dividing friendly society
Established: 1859 **Registered:** 14 December 1859   **Dissolved:** 20 July 1897
Headquarters: Oxford Arms (1859-1897)
Anniversary/feast day: Easter Monday, (from c.1860) Trinity Monday
Minimum age at entry: 12, 16 (from 1884) Maximum age at entry: 40, 42 (from 1884)
Membership: 16 members in 1860, 40 in 1862, 56 in 1866, 50 in 1880, 60 in 1885, 40 in 1890, 21 in 1891, 12 in 1894
Primary Sources: Rulebooks of 1859 and 1884, TNA, FS 3/321/223; rulebook of 1859, Bodl. G.A. OXF 8° 1308(6); TNA, FS 4/42/223
Notes: On division, 18 months' subscription per member was retained in the society. The society was suspended for three months by the Registrar on 24 December 1883, on 24 March 1884, on 24 June 1884 and registration was due to be cancelled on 24 August 1884 for failing to make a valuation of assets and liabilities but this was not acted upon (FS 4/42/223). The society dissolved with £28 1d 5d funds.

407.   Oxford Arms Friendly Society

Status: Unregistered **Type:** Friendly society
Established: 1914 **Dissolved**: Last known 1914
Headquarters: Oxford Arms (1914)
Anniversary/feast day: Trinity Monday
Notes: The club was formed in 1914 and for national insurance purposes it was associated with an unidentified county society (BicA, 12 June 1914).

Langford

No. of societies and members 1802/3 – None
No. of members of a friendly society 1813/14/15 – None

408.   Langford United Benefit Society

Status: Registered, OXF 340   **Type**: Permanent friendly society
Established: 1863   **Registered:** 15 December 1863   **Dissolved**: 3 March 1891
Headquarters: Schoolroom (1863-1891)
Anniversary/feast day: Whit Tuesday
Minimum age at entry: 16 **Maximum age at entry**: 45
Primary Sources: Rulebook of 1863, TNA, FS 3/321/340; TNA, FS 4/42/340
Notes: New members were required to reside within seven miles of Langford. An undated letter to the Registrar stated the society dissolved at a meeting on 3 March 1891 as funds were insufficient to meet demand of benefits (TNA, FS 4/42/340).

409.   True Britons Friendly Society

Status: Unregistered **Type**: Permanent friendly society
Established: 1858 **Dissolved**: Last known 1870
Headquarters: Crown [1861-1866], Old Bell (1870)
Anniversary/feast day: Whit Wednesday
Notes: Club day 1870 was described as the second anniversary of the True Britons Friendly Society (JOJ, 18 July 1870). It is likely the society had divided its funds in 1868 and reformed at the Old Bell. A main attraction of the feast that year was a leg of mutton suspended from a greased pole fifty feet high, with the first to climb it able to claim the meat.

Launton

No. of societies and members 1802/3 – None
No. of members of a friendly society 1813/14/15 – None

410.   Launton Provident Society, (from 1882) Launton United Brethren Provident Society, also The Parson's Club

Status: Registered, OXF 251   **Type:** 5-year dividing friendly society, then permanent by 1898
Established: 6 July 1863   **Registered:** 1863   **Dissolved:** 11 March 1916
Headquarters: National schoolroom [1880-1911]
Anniversary/feast day: Whit Tuesday
Minimum age at entry: 14 Maximum age at entry: 50
Membership: 23 members in 1864, 31 in 1865, 48 in 1871, 67 in 1874, 84 in 1877, 86 in 1882, 100 in 1884, 131 in 1899, 141 in 1905, 128 in 1913
Primary Sources: Rulebooks of 1863 and 1898, TNA, FS 15/570; OHC COS, LAUN 334.7; rulebook of 1894, 1896 and 1898, Bodl. G.A. OXF 8° 1306
Notes: The society was founded by the Rev. C. Coker and was under the control of the vicar and honorary members of the society who had a majority vote. It was for working men residing in the parish of Launton at the time of admission. Annual club day involved a tea at the rectory until 1881 when it changed to dinner at schoolroom. It entered as a provisional scheme under National Insurance Act 1911 but dissolved in 1916 with 99 members and £1549 0s 11d funds.

> **Launton United Brethren Provident Society** – see Launton Provident Society, Launton 410

> **The Parson's Club** – see Launton Provident Society, Launton 410

Leafield

No. of societies and members 1802/3 – 1, 92
No. of members of a friendly society 1813/14/15 – 92, 100, 110
Notes: Leafield feast continued over two days with club day being on Whit Friday but the village festivities lasted into Whit Saturday.

411.   Court Wychwood Forest

Status: Branch of an affiliated order   **Type**: AOF **Branch No.** 9610
Established: 1912 **Dissolved**: Post 1918
Headquarters: Fox Inn (1912-post 1918)
Membership: 83 members in 1912
Notes: Oxford District of AOF.

> **Forest Union Benefit Society** – see Leafield Friendly Society,
> Leafield 415

412.   Fox Benefit Society

Status: Unregistered   **Type**: Friendly society
Established: 1845 **Dissolved**: Last known 1862
Headquarters: Fox Inn (1845-1862)
Anniversary/feast day: Whit Friday
Membership: 100 members in 1856, 137 in 1857, 159 in 1859

413.   Fox Inn Benefit Society

Status: Unregistered   **Type**: Friendly society
Established: 1864 **Dissolved**: Last known 1867
Headquarters: Fox Inn (1864-1867)
Anniversary/feast day: Whit Friday

414.   (Fox Inn Benefit Society)

Status: Unregistered   **Type**: Friendly society
Established: First known 1907 **Dissolved**: Last known 1907
Headquarters: Fox Inn (1907)
Anniversary/feast day: Whit Friday
Minimum age at entry: 16 **Maximum age at entry**: 40
Membership: 50 members in 1907

415.   Leafield Friendly Society, from 1861 Forest Union Benefit Society, also Old George Benefit Society

Status: Enrolled, OXF 252   **Type**: Permanent friendly society
Established: 3 January 1785   **Registered:** 1794   **Dissolved**: 1864

Headquarters: George Inn (1785-1864)
Anniversary/feast day: Whit Friday
Maximum age at entry: 35
Membership: 319 members in 1857, 160 in 1864
Primary Sources: Printed rules of 1785 and rulebook of 1863, TNA, FS 1/581/252; rules of 1794, OHC, QSD/R/25; TNA, FS 4/42/252
Notes: Initially there was a maximum of 101 members but this rule was later rescinded. It had nine honorary members in 1859. Expenditure, especially on older members, was twice the income and all assets were sold and funds divided between the 160 members when the society dissolved in 1864. The dissolution of this society appeared especially contentious. There were several exchanges of correspondence with the Registrar. A full list of members, including date of joining and other correspondence appear in the papers. The sale of two cottages and outbuildings, a silk flag, pole, staves, banners, 30 dozen knives and forks, and other artefacts belonging to the society was advertised in *Jackson's Oxford Journal* on 16 July 1864 and subsequent dates. The Registrar was invited to attend a meeting at Leafield concerning the dissolution of the society and he agreed to do so on 23 July 1864, but there is no account of his attendance. A new society, the Old George Benefit Society (Leafield 417) was established on dissolution.

416.   Leafield Independent Friendly Benefit Society

Status: Registered, OXF 352   **Type:** 5-year dividing friendly society
Established: 1884   **Registered:** 5 August 1884   **Dissolved:** 4 June 1900
Headquarters: Fox Inn (1884-1900)
Anniversary/feast day: Whit Friday
Minimum age at entry: 16 Maximum age at entry: 40
Membership: 39 members in 1885, 43 in 1891, 30 in 1894, 32 in 1902
Primary Sources: Rulebook of 1884, TNA, FS 3/322/352
Notes: The society dissolved with 30 members and £67 funds. (See also appendix 2, Crimes 109).

> **Old George Benefit Society** – see Leafield Friendly Society, Leafield 415

417.   Old George Benefit Society

Status: Registered, OXF 355   **Type:** Friendly society
Established: 1864   **Registered:** 1885   **Dissolved:** 28 July 1913
Headquarters: George Inn (1864-1914)

Anniversary/feast day: Whit Friday
Minimum age at entry: 16 Maximum age at entry: 40
Membership: 29 members in 1885, 43 in 1991, 92 in 1899, 94 in 1900, 129 in 1905, 152 in 1910, 138 in 1912
Primary Sources: Rulebook of 1885, TNA, FS 15/579
Notes: The society was formed after dissolution of a previous society held at the George (Leafield 415) and registered some years later. The annual return of 1912 stated most members were engaged in agriculture. The society registered under the provisional scheme of the National Insurance Act 1911 but dissolved in 1913 with 139 members and £229 5s 0½d funds.

418. Potter's Arms Friendly Society

Status: Unregistered   **Type**: 5-year dividing friendly society
Established: First known 1892 **Dissolved**: Last known 1907
Headquarters: Potters Arms (1892-1907)
Anniversary/feast day: Whit Friday
Minimum age at entry: 16 **Maximum age at entry**: 40
Membership: 80 members in 1899, 85 in 1900, 30 in 1907

Lew

No. of societies and members 1802/3 – None
No. of members of a friendly society 1813/14/15 – 6, 6, 6
Notes: No friendly societies are recorded as being located in Lew.

Lewknor

No. of societies and members 1802/3 – None
No. of members of a friendly society 1813/14/15 – None

419. Lewknor Friendly Society

Status: Registered, OXF 356   **Type:** 7-year dividing friendly society
Established: 1885   **Registered:** 19 September 1885   **Dissolved:** 15 May 1912
Headquarters: Fox Inn (1885-1902), National School (1902-1912)
Anniversary/feast day: Whit Monday
Minimum age at entry: 16 Maximum age at entry: 45
Membership: 19 members in 1891, 16 in 1899, 10 in 1902, 10 in 1912
Primary Sources: Rulebook of 1885, TNA, FS 3/322/356; TNA, FS 4/42/356

Notes: It is unclear how the society was able to divide as this was not permitted for clubs registered after 1875. In 1891 full seven-year members received £5 15s on division (TG, 2 June 1891).The society dissolved with ten members and £49 17s 1d funds.

Little Haseley

No. of societies and members 1802/3 – None
No. of members of a friendly society 1813/14/15 – None

420.   Little Haseley Benefit Society

Status: Unregistered   **Type**: Friendly society
Established: First known 1890 **Dissolved**: Last known 1890
Anniversary/feast day: Whit Monday
Notes: Club day dinner was held at a barn lent by G. Atkinson (TG, 3 June 1890).

Little Milton

No. of societies and members 1802/3 – None
No. of members of a friendly society 1813/14/15 – None

421.   Hand in Hand Benefit Society

Status: Registered, OXF 111   **Type:** 5-year dividing friendly society
Established: 6 April 1847   **Registered:** 30 June 1847   **Dissolved:** 17 January 1896
Headquarters: Lamb Inn (1847-1896), National School (1896-1899), Lamb Inn (1889)
Anniversary/feast day: Whit Monday
Minimum age at entry: 15 Maximum age at entry: 40
Membership: 43 members in 1863, 51 in 1865, 61 in 1872, 76 in 1878, 105 in 1880, 103 in 1885, 32 in 1891, 25 in 1892
Primary Sources: Rulebooks of 1847 and 1853, TNA, FS 3/319/111; TNA FS 1/578/111
Notes: The landlord was required to provide a fire and candles between Michaelmas and Lady Day, as well as paper and ink for the club officials. The society was to continue as long as 50 members wanted it to. A letter to the Registrar dated 6 December 1853 stated the first club was broken up in April 1852. A new one was then established in January 1853. The new society

continued to use the same registration number. It dissolved with 25 members and £26 8s 6d funds.

Little Tew

No. of societies and members 1802/3 – None
No. of members of a friendly society 1813/14/15 – 4, 4, 4
No friendly societies present.

Littlemore

No. of societies and members 1802/3 – None
No. of members of a friendly society 1813/14/15 – None

422.   Littlemore Friendly Society

Status: Unregistered   **Type:** Friendly society
Established: First known 1830 **Dissolved**: Last known 1830
Membership: 64 in 1830
Notes: The friendly society was thought to be a contributory factor to there being few poor people in the parish (VCH, Parishes: Littlemore, *A History of the County of Oxford: Volume 5: Bullingdon hundred* [1957], pp. 206-214).

423.   National Deposit Friendly Society, Littlemore Branch

Status: Branch of a registered society   **Type**: Permanent friendly society
Established: First known 1905 **Dissolved**: Last known 1913

Long Hanborough – see Hanborough

Lower Heyford

No. of societies and members 1802/3 – None
No. of members of a friendly society 1813/14/15 – None

Heyford and Aston Friendly Society – see Steeple Aston 613

Lower Heyford and Steeple Aston Friendly Society – see Steeple Aston 614

424.   Lower Heyford Subordinate Division

Status: Branch of an affiliated order   **Type**: OSOT **Branch No.** 843
Established: First known 1905 **Dissolved**: Last known 1913
Headquarters: Methodist Free Church [1905-1910]
Membership: 61 members in 1905, 73 in 1910

Mapledurham

No. of societies and members 1802/3 – None
No. of members of a friendly society 1813/14/15 – None

425.   Mapledurham Friendly Society

Status: Enrolled, OXF 181   **Type**: Permanent friendly society
Established: First known 1838 **Dissolved**: Last known 1838
Headquarters: The house of Mr Brinn (landlord) (undated)
Anniversary/feast day: Whit Monday
Minimum age at entry: 16 Maximum age at entry: 35
Primary Sources: Handwritten draft of rules, interspersed with printed rules
(undated but accompanied by a letter dated 1838), TNA, FS 1/580/181
Notes: Once 60 members had been enrolled, only those residing in
Mapledurham were permitted to join. Any dispute had to be resolved by the
minister, churchwardens and overseer.

426.   Mapledurham Friendly Society

Status: Unregistered   **Type**: 5-year dividing friendly society
Established: 1846   **Dissolved**: Last known 1878
Headquarters: King's Arms Inn (1857)
Anniversary/feast day: Whit Monday
Minimum age at entry: 15 Maximum age at entry: 40
Primary Sources: Rules dated 1857, TNA, FS 1/580/181; TNA, FS 4/42/181
Notes: A letter to the Registrar, dated 5 October 1878 from John Hall, stated
that this society had never registered and that the Registrar had been notified of
this in previous years. It appears to have followed on from the enrolled society
of the same name.

Marsh Baldon

No. of societies and members 1802/3 – None
No. of members of a friendly society 1813/14/15 – None

427.   Mutual Friendly Society

Status: Unregistered   **Type**: Friendly society
Established: 1835   **Dissolved**: Last known 1895
Headquarters: Seven Stars [1885-1895)
Anniversary/feast day: Whit Thursday

Marston

No. of societies and members 1802/3 – None
No. of members of a friendly society 1813/14/15 – None

428.   Loyal Duke of Albany Lodge

Status: Branch of an affiliated order   **Type**: IOOFMU **Branch No.** 6571
Established: 30 July 1883 **Dissolved**: Post 1918
Headquarters: Red Lion Inn (1883-1893), Schoolroom (1894-1900), White Hart Inn (1901-1912)
Anniversary/feast day: Whit Monday
Membership: 31 members in 1883, 43 in 1866, 56 in 1891, 65 in 1901, 83 in 1907, 109 in 1910, 118 in 1914
Notes: Oxford District of IOOFMU. Several members from the Marston Friendly Benefit Society (Marston 429) left that society and formed this branch.

429.   Marston Friendly (Benefit) Society

Status: Registered, OXF 234   **Type**: 7-year dividing friendly society
Established: 1853   **Registered:** 1 March 1861   **Dissolved**: Last known 1883
Headquarters: Three Horseshoes [1870-1880), Red Lion Inn (1878), White Hart Inn (1880-1883)
Anniversary/feast day: Whit Monday
Maximum age at entry: 45
Membership: 44 members in 1863, 48 in 1864, 69 in 1870, 99 in 1878, 81 in 1883
Primary Sources: Rulebook of 1861, TNA, FS 3/321/234; TNA, FS 4/42/234

Notes: The society was formed on the dissolution of Marston Friendly Society (Marston 430). The meeting place for 1878 is unclear with reports of both the Three Horseshoes and the Red Lion being headquarters for that year. The society was taken to court on four occasions by members between 1875 and 1883 for non-payment of benefits (see appendix 2, Crimes 111, 112, 113 and 114).The society had severe problems in 1883 and it was reported that due to the failure of the society, many members left to form the Duke of Albany Lodge, IOOFMU (Marston 428), (JOJ, 4 August 1883). A returned pro-forma letter to the Registrar dated 8 March 1894 stated the society no longer existed (TNA, FS 4/42/234). (See also appendix 2, Crimes 110).

430.   Marston Friendly Society

Status: Enrolled, OXF 78   **Type**: 7-year dividing friendly society
Established: 1845   **Registered:** 21 March 1846   **Dissolved**: 1853
Headquarters: White Hart Inn (1845-1853)
Anniversary/feast day: Whit Monday
Maximum age at entry: 45
Primary Sources: Rulebook of 1845. TNA, FS 1/577/78; TNA, FS 4/42/78
Notes: Members were required to wear red, white, and blue ribbons on club day. Marston Friendly Society was formed on its dissolution (Marston 429).

431.   Marston Good Intent Benefit Society

Status: Registered, OXF 360   **Type:** Permanent friendly society
Established: 1886   **Registered:** 1 March 1886   **Dissolved:** 12 May 1892
Headquarters: National schoolroom (1886-1892)
Minimum age at entry: 16 Maximum age at entry: 40
Membership: 15 members in 1891, 15 in 1892
Primary Sources: Rulebook of 1886, TNA, FS 3/322/360; TNA, FS 4/42/360
Notes: The society dissolved with 15 members and £114 1s 8d funds.

Middle Barton – see Westcote Barton

Milton under Wychwood

No. of societies and members 1802/3 – None
No. of members of a friendly society 1813/14/15 – None

432.   **Cirencester Working Men's Conservative Society, Milton Branch**

Status: Branch of a registered society   **Type:** Permanent friendly society
Established: 1891 **Dissolved:** Last known 1907
Headquarters: Quart Pot (1901-07)
Anniversary/feast day: Whit Monday
Membership: 94 members in 1900, 120 in 1902, 128 in 1903
Notes: The anniversary meetings were held at the Beaconsfield Hall and the society was described as a cross between a friendly society and a savings bank (JOJ, 27 May 1899).

> **Milton, Shipton and Ascott United Provident Society** – see Shipton under Wychwood 568

433.   **Milton under Wychwood Benefit Club**

Status: Unregistered   **Type:** 5-year dividing friendly society
Established: 1855 **Dissolved:** Last known 1886
Headquarters: Butchers Arms (1855-1884]
Anniversary/feast day: Whit Monday
Membership: Over 80 members in 1858
Notes: The society was described as being a savings bank with relief for death, illness or affliction (JOJ, 28 April 1855). A new flag was obtained in 1856, and club day in 1857 was swelled by a large number of workers from the Oxford, Worcester, and Wolverhampton railway (JOJ, 24 May 1856 and 16 May 1857). In 1860, after its first division, a separate provident branch of the society was formed for savings (JOJ, 14 April 1860). A new five-year cycle was commenced in 1886.

Minster Lovell

No. of societies and members 1802/3 – 1, 60
No. of members of a friendly society 1813/14/15 – 96, 96, 101
Notes: (See appendix 2, Crimes 115 and 183).

434.   **Minster Lovell Friendly Society**

Status: Enrolled, OXF 169   **Type:** Permanent friendly society
Established: 14 June 1800   **Registered:** 1800   **Dissolved:** 1840

Headquarters: Swan Inn (1800)
Anniversary/feast day: Whit Wednesday
Maximum age at entry: 30
Primary Sources: Rules of 1800, TNA, FS 1/580/169; undated rules, TNA, FS 1/577/70; TNA, FS 4/42/169
Notes: There was confusion in the records of the Registrar, and documents relating to this society appear under both FS 1/577/70 and FS 1/580/169. The rules of 1800 required the innkeeper to keep a 'good fire' for club nights from Michaelmas to the Annunciation (29 September to 25 March). The society ceased to exist in 1840 and two new societies were formed, Minster Lovell 435 and Minster Lovell 436.

435.   Minster Lovell Friendly Society

Status: Enrolled, OXF 49   **Type:** Permanent friendly society
Established: 1840   **Registered:** 7 April 1843   **Dissolved:** 1861
Headquarters: White Hart Inn [1843-1855]
Anniversary/feast day: Whit Wednesday
Maximum age at entry: 40 at establishment, then 30
Primary Sources: Rulebook of 1840, TNA, FS 1/576/49
Notes: This society was for the industrious and provident of the labouring classes and mechanics. New members were required to reside in Minster Lovell or its neighbourhood. A male-only club, although female honorary members were permitted. If an existing member lived greater than 50 miles from Minster Lovell, they had up to six months to pay subscriptions. The society stated it was established on 14 June 1800 indicating this was a continuation of a previous society (Minster Lovell 434).

436.   Minster Lovell Friendly Society

Status: Enrolled, OXF 70   **Type:** Permanent friendly society
Established: 1 June 1840   **Registered:** 1840   **Dissolved:** Last known 1859
Headquarters: White Hart Inn (1843), Swan Inn (1843-1859)
Anniversary/feast day: Whit Wednesday
Maximum age at entry: 35
Primary Sources: Rulebook of 1840, TNA/FS 1/577/70; TNA, FS 4/42/70; OHC, QSD/R/27
Notes: The rules were amended on 26 May 1843 (TNA, FS 4/42/70). An envelope from the Registrar was returned, dated 13 January 1882 stating society had broken up.

437.   Minster Lovell Friendly Society

Status: Unregistered   **Type**: 7-year dividing friendly society
Established: 1861 **Dissolved**: May 1913
Headquarters: White Hart [1890-1913]
Anniversary/feast day: Whit Wednesday
Membership: 60 members in 1890, 60 in 1899, 55 in 1903
Notes: A new banner was purchased through subscriptions in 1899 (JOJ, 27 May 1899). It was claimed the society was established in 1800 (WG, 17 June 1905 and 5 June 1909) and indicates a continuation of Minster Lovell 434 and 435. The club broke up and divided its funds due to the National Insurance Act (WG, 17 May 1913). (See also appendix 2, Crimes 116 and 117.)

Mixbury

No. of societies and members 1802/3 – None
No. of members of a friendly society 1813/14/15 – None

438.   The Church Benefit Society of Mixbury

Status: Registered, OXF 256 **Type**: Annual dividing friendly society
Established: 15 June 1862   **Registered:** 5 April 1864   **Dissolved**: Last known 1877
Minimum age at entry: 16 **Maximum age at entry**: 60
Primary Sources: Rulebook of 1862, TNA, FS 1/581/250; TNA, FS 4/42/256
Notes: The papers are misfiled in the Registrar's records at TNA in FS 1/581/250. The society was established in 1862, with a guarantee of £20 from the Rev. G.H. Palmer. It was open to the inhabitants of Mixbury only. On the annual holiday (date not stated) the society processed from schoolroom to church.

439.   Mixbury Benefit Society

Status: Registered, OXF 381 **Type:** Permanent friendly society
Established: 1892   **Registered:** 18 July 1893   **Dissolved:** 5 October 1908
Headquarters: Parish Room, Rectory (1892-1908)
Anniversary/feast day: Last Tuesday in May
Minimum age at entry: 16 Maximum age at entry: 35
Membership: 18 members in 1899, 14 in 1905, 10 in 1908
Primary Sources: Rulebook of 1892, TNA, FS 3/322/381; TNA, FS 4/42/381

Notes: The annual feast was held at the Rectory. There were ten members and £212 14s 5d funds when the society dissolved.

Mollington

No. of societies and members 1802/3 – None
No. of members of a friendly society 1813/14/15 – None
Note: The parish was two-thirds in Oxfordshire and one-third in Warwickshire until 1895.

440.   (Mollington Old Club)

Status: Unregistered   **Type**: Permanent friendly society
Established: 1844 **Dissolved**: Last known 1872
Primary Sources: BPP 1874, XXIII, (c.997), p.118
Notes: The Assistant Commissioner reported this to be a registered club but no trace of registration can be found in either county. It was one of two clubs in the village. He reported that Mr Boote, a cooper and landlord of the inn kept the accounts. It was suspected this society had a 'free' quarter where one quarter's payments went towards the annual feast. The Assistant Commissioner appears to have confused two clubs as he describes the other society, The Refuge (Mollington 441), as being unregistered (See also appendix 2, Crimes 118).

441.   Refuge Friendly Society

Status: Registered, OXF 235 **Type:** Permanent friendly society
Established: 3 April 1860   **Registered:** 30 March 1861   **Dissolved:** 23 February 1882
Headquarters: Primitive Methodist Chapel (1861-1882)
Anniversary/feast day: Last Friday in May
Minimum age at entry: 16 Maximum age at entry: 35
Membership: 18 members in 1860, 30 in 1864, 41 in 1866, 30 in 1871, 27 in 1875, 22 in 1882
Primary Sources: Rulebook of 1861, FS 1/581/235; TNA, FS 4/42/235; BPP 1874, XXIII, (c.997), p.118
Notes: The society held a public tea on its anniversary. The Assistant Commissioner reported this society to be a chapel club run on temperance principles. He also stated this club to be unregistered but there appears to have been confusion between this and the other, unregistered Mollington club (Mollington 440). He stated the society would divide funds if they ever became

large enough. On dissolution, it had 22 members and £155 5s 9 d funds. This society had a branch at Hornton (Hornton 380).

Neithrop

No. of societies and members 1802/3 – None
No. of members of a friendly society 1813/14/15 – None

442.   The Loyal Union Friendly Society

Status: Enrolled, OXF 8 **Type**: Permanent friendly society
Established: 1829   **Registered:** 4 April 1831   **Dissolved**: Last known 1831
Headquarters: Weaver's Arms (1829-1831)
Anniversary/feast day: Last Friday in May
Minimum age at entry: 16 **Maximum age at entry**: 35
Primary Sources: Rulebook of 1831, TNA, FS 1/574/8; TNA, FS 4/42/8
Notes: The society was for out pensioners (those not in the workhouse) and others who had served in His Majesty's Service. Members were only admitted if they lived within ten miles of Banbury. Benefits were superannuated at age 70, but recipients must have been members for at least 20 years.

Nettlebed

No. of societies and members 1802/3 – None
No. of members of a friendly society 1813/14/15 – None

443.   Court Pride of Nettlebed

Status: Branch of an affiliated order   **Type**: AOF **Branch No.** 8324
Established: 1894 **Dissolved**: Post 1918
Headquarters: Red Lion Inn (1894-1900], Bull Hotel [1905-1911]
Anniversary/feast day: Whit Monday
Membership: 26 members in 1895, 30 in 1900, 71 in 1905, 67 in 1910
Notes: Buckinghamshire District of AOF. The annual fete was held in Mr Glasspool's meadow in 1906, a meadow next to the parish church in 1907, and Robert Fleming's ground in 1910.

> **Henley and Nettlebed Medical Benefit Society** – see Henley on Thames 344

444.   (Nettlebed club)

Status: Unregistered   **Type:** Friendly society
Established: First known 1848 **Dissolved:** Last known 1848
Anniversary/feast day: Whit Monday
Notes: *Jackson's Oxford Journal* reported the burglary of a house during club day 1848 (JOJ, 17 June 1848).

445.   Nettlebed Juvenile Sick and Funeral Society

Status: Juvenile branch of an affiliated order, OXF 387   **Type:** AOF
Established: 1895 **Registered:** 1895 **Dissolved:** 1912
Headquarters: Foresters' Room, Red Lion (1895-1902], Bull Hotel [1905-1912)
Minimum age at entry: 8 **Maximum age at entry:** 18
Primary Sources: Rulebook of 1895, TNA, FS 15/581
Notes: Registration was cancelled in 1912 when the society joined with Court Pride of Nettlebed (Nettlebed 443), of which it had been the juvenile branch.

446.   South Oxfordshire Friendly Society, Nettlebed Branch

Status: Branch of a registered society, OXF 62   **Type:** Permanent friendly society
Established: 1872 **Dissolved:** Last known 1874
Anniversary/feast day: Whit Monday
Notes: The society was a branch of the South Oxfordshire Friendly Society (Henley on Thames 359). The club anniversary was held at Soundess Farm, Nettlebed, and 500 people attended in 1874 (HA, 30 May 1874).

Newington

No. of societies and members 1802/3 – None
No. of members of a friendly society 1813/14/15 – None

447.   Heart and Hand Benefit Society

Status: Enrolled, OXF 67   **Type:** 5-year dividing friendly society
Established: 1840   **Registered:** 24 March 1842   **Dissolved:** Last known 1842
Headquarters: Chequers Inn, Berrick Prior (1840-1842)

Anniversary/feast day: Whit Monday
Minimum age at entry: 15 **Maximum age at entry**: 45
Primary Sources: Rulebook of 1842, TNA, FS 1/577/67; TNA, FS 1/576/67

North Leigh

No. of societies and members 1802/3 – 1, 88
No. of members of a friendly society 1813/14/15 – 94, 92, 95
Notes: Club day in North Leigh was known as the 'famous fourth'. The *Witney Gazette* lamented in 1914, that it was 'no longer the "famous fourth" as it used to be'; the band turned up late and there was no church parade (WG, 13 June 1914). (See also appendix 2, Crimes 119).

448.   East End Club, also (Old) Bottle club

Status: Unregistered   **Type**: Friendly society
Established: First known 1850   **Dissolved**: Last known 1920
Headquarters: Leather Bottle, East End [1856-1908]
Anniversary/feast day: 4 June
Membership: 85 members in 1890
Notes: The oldest club in North Leigh (JOJ, 14 June 1890) and was the sole surviving society in 1914. The club lasted into the 1920s. There was a call in the early twentieth century for the two village clubs to merge (with North Leigh 451) but it did not take place.

> **Leviathan Club** – see North Leigh Friendly Benefit Society, North Leigh 451

449.   Macclesfield Friendly Institution

Status: Unregistered   **Type**: Friendly society
Established: 4 June 1849   **Dissolved**: Last known 1857
Headquarters: Parker Arms Inn (1849-1857)
Anniversary/feast day: 4 June
Notes: The society had a new flag for club day in 1849, bearing the arms of the patron, Lord Macclesfield (JOJ, 9 June 1849).

450.   (North Leigh club)

Status: Unregistered   **Type**: Friendly society
Established: First known 1841   **Dissolved**: Last known 1842

Anniversary/feast day: 4 June
Notes: *Jackson's Oxford Journal* reported advance notice of club day for 1841 and 1842 but little further detail was recorded (JOJ, 29 May 1841). The society had clearly been in existence before 1841 and was possibly the society that existed in 1802.

451.   North Leigh Friendly Benefit Society, also West End Club, School Club and Leviathan Club (from 1903)

Status: Registered, OXF 291   **Type:** Friendly society
Established: 1868   **Registered:** 30 September 1868   **Dissolved:** 30 September 1913
Headquarters: Schoolroom (1867-1906), Harcourt Arms (1906-1913)
Anniversary/feast day: 4 June
Minimum age at entry: 15 (16 from 1906) Maximum age at entry: 45
Membership: 70 members in 1878, 117 in 1890, 81 in 1900, 64 in 1912, 58 in 1913
Primary Sources: Rulebooks of 1867 and 1906, TNA, FS 15/572;
Notes: The 1906 rules limited medical aid for members resident in North Leigh, Hanborough, and Freeland. The society dissolved with 58 members and £263 13s 11d funds. Almost three-quarters of members were aged over 51 years. There was call in the early-twentieth century for the two village clubs to merge (with North Leigh 448) but it did not take place.

> **School Club** – see North Leigh Friendly Benefit Society, North Leigh 451

> **West End Club** – see North Leigh Friendly Benefit Society, North Leigh 451

North Newington

No. of societies and members 1802/3 – None
No. of members of a friendly society 1813/14/15 – None

452.   Broughton and North Newington Benefit Society

Status: Registered, OXF 301   **Type:** Friendly society
Established: 1869   **Registered:** 13 September 1869   **Dissolved:** 1913
Headquarters: Schoolroom, North Newington (1875-1910)
Anniversary/feast day: Monday after Ascension Day

Minimum age at entry: 16 Maximum age at entry: 40
Membership: 57 members in 1871, 47 in 1872, 74 in 1878, 76 in 1886, 63 in 1891, 86 in 1899, 94 in 1905, 72 in 1913
Primary Sources: BPP 1874, XXIII, (c.997), p.117
Notes: The Assistant Commissioner reported in 1872 that the club replaced two older ones that broke-up and was formed to meet under the auspices of Lord Saye and Sele, and other gentry. The society had a feast but had difficulty in paying for it. The honorary subscriptions amounted to £10 a year but the secretary expressed concern that this may not continue due to the activities of the Agricultural Labourers' union. He warned farmer contributions might be withdrawn as wages had risen from 10s to 12s a week.

453.   Court Saye and Sele

Status: Branch of an affiliated order   **Type**: AOF **Branch No.** 7934
Established: 1891   **Dissolved**: Post 1918
Headquarters: Butchers Arms (1891), School House [1905-post 1918]
Membership: 14 members in 1892, 20 in 1894, 27 in 1900, 42 in 1905, 78 in 1910
Notes: Banbury District of AOF. Named after the Patron, Lord Saye and Sele of Broughton Castle.

454.   (Hutching's Friendly Society)

Status: Unregistered   **Type**: Friendly society
Established: First known 1865   **Dissolved**: Last known 1865
Headquarters: Mr Hutching's Beerhouse (1865)
Anniversary/feast day: Monday after Ascension Day
Membership: 30 members in 1865
Primary Sources: BPP 1874, XXIII, (c.997), p.117
Notes: One of two unregistered clubs in 1865. The report of club day stated 'Both clubs had ample supply of beef, pudding and beer' (BG, 1 June 1865). The society probably broke up in 1869 and was one of the two clubs described by the Assistant Commissioner in 1872.

455.   (Roebuck Friendly Society)

Status: Unregistered   **Type**: Friendly society
Established: First known 1865   **Dissolved**: Last known 1865
Headquarters: Roebuck (1865)
Anniversary/feast day: Monday after Ascension Day

Membership: 44 members in 1865
Primary Sources: BPP 1874, XXIII, (c.997), p.117
Notes: One of two unregistered clubs in 1865. The society probably broke up in 1869 and was one of the two clubs described by the Assistant Commissioner in 1872.

North Stoke

No. of societies and members 1802/3 – None
No. of members of a friendly society 1813/14/15 – None

456.   North Stoke Friendly Benefit Society

Status: Enrolled, OXF 81   **Type**: Annual dividing friendly society
Established: 1845   **Registered:** 1 August 1845 **Dissolved**: Last known 1845
Headquarters: White Horse Inn (1845)
Anniversary/feast day: First Monday after 19 July
Minimum age at entry: 15 Maximum age at entry: 40
Primary Sources: Rulebook of 1844, TNA, FS 1/577/82; TNA, FS 4/42/80
Notes: Records for this society are misfiled in the Registrar's records at the TNA under reference FS 1/577/82. On club day members were required to wear deep red and sky blue colours in their hat.

Nuffield

No. of societies and members 1802/3 – None
No. of members of a friendly society 1813/14/15 – None

457.   Nuffield Benefit Society

Status: Unregistered   **Type**: Friendly society
Established: First known 1891 **Dissolved**: Last known 1895
Anniversary/feast day: Whit Wednesday
Notes: The *Henley Standard* made a comparison of a dull, quiet Whit Monday at Nettlebed and a usual (lively) club gathering at Nuffield (HSOS, 14 June 1895).

Nuneham Courtenay

No. of societies and members 1802/3 – None
No. of members of a friendly society 1813/14/15 – None

458.   National Deposit Friendly Society, Nuneham Branch

Status: Branch of a registered society   **Type**: Permanent friendly society
Established: First known 1905 **Dissolved**: Last known 1913

459.   Nuneham Courtenay Friendly Society

Status: Enrolled, OXF 19   **Type**: Permanent friendly society
Established: 1837   **Registered:** 22 June 1838 **Dissolved**: 1859
Headquarters: Harcourt Arms Inn (1837-1859)
Anniversary/feast day: Whit Wednesday
Minimum age at entry: 14 **Maximum age at entry**: 40
Primary Sources: Rulebook of 1837, TNA, FS 1/574/19; TNA, FS 4/42/19
Notes: A maximum of 100 members was permitted according to the rules. The
society gave a benefit of superannuation at age 65 of 4s 6d per week. A letter
from Levi Besley to the Registrar dated 7 November 1878 stated the society had
'broken up' in 1859 when some members formed a new, unregistered seven-
year dividing society (Nuneham Courtenay 460). Members of this society had
protection of membership, a guarantee of acceptance in the new club (TNA, FS
4/42/19). (See also appendix 2, Crimes 120).

460.   (Nuneham Courtenay Friendly Society)

Status: Unregistered   **Type**: 7-year dividing friendly society
Established: 1859 **Dissolved**: Last known 1878
Headquarters: Harcourt Arms Inn [1866-1878]
Anniversary/feast day: Whit Monday
Primary Sources: TNA, FS 4/42/19
Notes: A letter from Levi Besley to the Registrar dated 7 November 1878
stated the registered society (Nuneham Courtenay 459) had 'broken up' in
1859 when some members formed this society. Members of the old society
were guaranteed membership if they wished to join. The society divided in
1866 and 1873 and was due to divide in 1880 (TNA, FS 4/42/19). *Jackson's
Oxford Journal* reported that a large number of Marsh Baldon residents were
at the Nuneham club feast on Whit Monday in 1866. A fire broke out at Marsh
Baldon and club members left their dinner at the Harcourt Arms and went to
the village to help quell the fire, as did members of the Garsington club (JOJ,
26 May 1866).

Oddington

No. of societies and members 1802/3 – None
No. of members of a friendly society 1813/14/15 – None

461.   (Oddington club)

Status: Unregistered   **Type:** Friendly society
Established: First known 1881 **Dissolved:** Last known 1881
Notes: The Oddington friendly society played a cricket match versus Charlton
on club day in 1881 (BicA, 24 June 1881).

Oxford

No. of societies and members 1802/3 – 7, 591
No. of members of a friendly society 1813/14/15 – 751, 748, 747
Notes: Unsurprisingly, Oxford had the greatest volume and variety of friendly
societies. It supported a remarkable 14 box-clubs in 1762. There is no evidence
of one traditional club day in the city with a parade of societies, although the
marching to bands did exist. The affiliated orders had processions of lodges,
such as the Oxford District of the IOOFMU in 1842, when it was commented,
'We most readily bear our testimony that such a demonstration was never
before witnessed in Oxford' (JOJ, 27 August 1842). Friendly societies were
also involved in parades to commemorate new buildings such as the laying of
the foundation stone of Oxford High School for Boys (JOJ, 10 April 1880) and
Hospital Sunday in 1890 although the latter was not a permanent feature of the
1890s as in other Oxfordshire towns.

462.   (Amalgamated) Protective and Provident Society of Women

Status: Unregistered   **Type:** Female permanent trade society
Established: 1881 **Dissolved:** Last known 1899
Headquarters: 37 New Inn Hall Street (1884), Wesleyan Lecture Room
(1887)
Minimum age at entry: 16
Membership: 58 members in 1886, 79 in 1891, 69 in 1899
Primary Sources: Rulebooks of 1884, Bodl. 24786 e.11(9)
Notes: The society was for women working in trades in Oxford. New
members were recommended by two existing members who vouched for their
'competent workwoman'. Benefit was paid for sickness and unemployment,

up to a maximum of eight weeks benefit per year. An employment register was kept for the benefit of members, keeping a record of available jobs in shops.

463.   Amalgamated Society of Railway Servants

Status: Branch of a friendly society   **Type**: Friendly society
Established: 1872 **Dissolved**: Last known 1880
Notes: In late 1871 the Amalgamated Society of Railway Servants agreed the rules of a new society. It was open to engine drivers, guards, signalmen, porters, ticket takers, firemen, policemen, etc. in the employ of any railway company. It was a combination of a benefit society and a society to look after the interests of its members. The Oxford branch opened in 1872 and subscribed £3 3s to the Radcliffe Infirmary in 1874 (JOJ, 21 March 1874). Much of the work of the society was promoting railway safety. Edward Beale of Osney, secretary of the society was charged with embezzling funds in 1876 (see appendix 2, Crimes 128). It is possible this was the same society as the Locomotive Friendly Society, known in 1881 (Oxford 501).

464.   Amicable Society

Status: Unregistered   **Type**: Friendly society
Established: First known 1762 **Dissolved**: Last known 1762
Headquarters: Wheatsheaf, High St (1762)
Notes: One of 14 societies listed as in existence at Oxford in 1762 (JOJ, 22 May 1762).

465.   Ancient Order of Druids, Albion Lodge

Status: Branch of an affiliated order **Type**: AOD **Branch No.** 59
Established: 21 May 1812 **Dissolved**: Post 1918
Headquarters: Oxford Arms Inn, George Street, re-named the Druid's Head Inn (1812-1836), Wheatsheaf Inn, High Street (1836-post 1918), temporary move to The Market Vaults (1896) whilst the Wheatsheaf was being refurbished
Notes: The Albion Lodge was not a friendly society within the meaning of this calendar but is included for completeness. It was a mixture of a fraternal organization, a philanthropic organization and a spiritual one. *The official souvenir of the centenary of the Albion lodge, Oxford, no. 59. Ancient Order of Druids, 1812-1912*, (Oxford, 1912*), records the history of the branch. There was a split in the movement in 1834 when several provincial lodges seceded and formed the United Ancient Order of Druids and initiated a sick and funeral fund. However, the Albion lodge and other Oxfordshire lodges

appear to have all remained true to the original principles that did not include any insurance aspect. In 1908, The Rt. Hon. Winston Churchill, then First Lord of the Admiralty, was admitted to the lodge, remaining a member for a short time. (See also Oxford Lodges, Ancient Order of Druids, Oxford 528).

466.   (The Blenheim Lodge)

Status: Unregistered   **Type**: An Oddfellows society
Established: First known 1833 **Dissolved**: Last known 1833
Headquarters: Blenheim, St Ebbe's (1833)
Notes: The only evidence of the existence of this society is from a court case of 1833 (see appendix 2, Crimes 121).

467.   (Blue Boar club)

Status: Unregistered   **Type**: Friendly society
Established: First known 1762 **Dissolved**: Last known 1762
Headquarters: Blue Boar, Cornmarket (1762)
Notes: One of 14 societies listed as in existence at Oxford in 1762 (JOJ, 22 May 1762).

468.   (Bowling Green club)

Status: Unregistered   **Type**: Friendly society
Established: First known 1762 **Dissolved**: Last known 1762
Headquarters: Bowling Green, Holywell (1762)
Notes: One of 14 societies listed as in existence at Oxford in 1762 (JOJ, 22 May 1762).

469.   Central Oxfordshire Friendly Society

Status: Registered, OXF 226   **Type:** 5-year dividing friendly society
Established: 1859 **Registered:** 18 January 1859 **Dissolved:** 1894
Headquarters: Oxford (1859-1894)
Anniversary/feast day: Third Wednesday in July
Minimum age at entry: 15 Maximum age at entry: 50
Membership: Total membership was 211 in 1862, 316 in 1866, 289 in 1875, 305 in 1878, 190 in 1880, 203 in 1885, 138 in 1891
Primary Sources: Rulebook of 1859, TNA, FS 3/321/226; TNA, FS 4/42/226; rulebook of 1860, Bodl. G.A. OXF 8° 208(1); rulebook of 1860, OHC COS, P/334.7

Notes: The intention to form the society was made by the Rev. J. Slatter at a meeting at Oxford Town Hall on 7 December 1859 when John Tidd Pratt, Registrar of Friendly Societies gave a lecture (JOJ, 10 December 1859), although it appears to have been registered a year earlier. Members left the society at 60 years of age but received superannuation. The society was managed by honorary members and was similar to a county society, although a dividing society. It had branches at Great Milton, Stoke Talmage and Drayton St Leonard, with members well represented in Little Milton, Dorchester, Clifton Hampden, Lewknor and Wheatfield (TG, 7 June 1859 and JOJ, 6 June 1863). A letter dated 11 March 1894 stated the society was dissolved in 1894 and had been managed on a voluntary basis by the Rev. Slatter of Whitchurch (FS 4/42/226).

> **Cherwell Lodge, Ancient Order of Druids** – see Oxford Lodges, Ancient Order of Druids, Oxford 528

470.   City of Oxford Subordinate Division

Status: Branch of a an affiliated order   **Type**: OSOT **Branch No.** 361
Established: 1873   **Registered:**1873 **Dissolved**: Last known 1910
Headquarters: Wesleyan Chapel, New Inn Hall Street (1890), Good Templar's Hall, Pembroke St (dates not known), University Gymnasium, Alfred St (1905), Rectory Room, Pembroke St (1910)
Maximum age at entry: Post 1912
Membership: 306 adult and 111 juvenile members in 1900

471.   Civil Society

Status: Unregistered   **Type**: Friendly society
Established: First known 1762 **Dissolved**: Last known 1762
Headquarters: Salutation, near All Saints (1762)
Notes: One of 14 societies listed as in existence at Oxford in 1762 (JOJ, 22 May 1762).

472.   Civis Society, Friendly Society of the Freemen of the City of Oxford (from 1817), Young Freemen's Friendly Society (from 1843)

Status: Enrolled, OXF 73   **Type:** Friendly society
Established: 9 August 1773   **Registered:**1811 **Dissolved:** 1869

Headquarters: Wheatsheaf and Anchor, St Aldate's (1773), Chequers Inn [1821-1828], Cross Keys [1836-1842), Wheatsheaf Inn, High St. (1842-1869)
Anniversary/feast day: Last Monday in September (1773), then third Monday (undated) and second Monday (by 1828)
Minimum age at entry: 18 Maximum age at entry: 35 (1773), 40 (from 1817), 30 (from 1843)
Membership: 90 members in 1849, 34 in 1865, 28 in 1869
Primary Sources: Manuscript rules of 1773, rulebooks of 1811, 1821 and 1843, TNA, FS 1/577/71; manuscript rules of 1773, Bodl. G.A.OXF a.101(4-5); rulebook of 1850, Bodl. G.A. OXF 16° 65; Oxon. Cal. QS iii, p.650
Notes: The Civis Society was a club of Freemen established in 1773. Members were required to be freemen of the City of Oxford, or if not free, with a right to vote in parliamentary elections. There was a maximum membership of 100, increased to 150 until the rule was removed in 1843. There was no fee at joining except 4d to the 'house' for wet rent and 4d for a copy of the rules. When the society had grown to 50 members, an entry fee of 5s was to be charged and, at 80 members, 10s 6d. Sickness benefit was 8s a week to a maximum of £14, then 5s a week until total claims were £21, then 3s a week until aged 65. Superannuation was payable at age 65 at the same rate as sickness benefit provided a maximum amount of £21 had not been claimed, in which case 2s a week was paid. Undated rules changed the feast day and reduced superannuation to age 60 years (G.A.OXF a.101(5)). Dinner on club day was at the expense of the society, but with no beer served at society expense after 10.00 p.m. The rules of 11 February 1818 were amended at Easter Quarter Session 1819. The rules of 1850 report the society was established in 1817 but it is clear this was in fact a continuation of the original Civis Society. It was dissolved in 1869 with 28 members who received £20 each from the division of funds. A Freemen Society, a forerunner of this society, was in existence in 1762 (Oxford 489).

473.   College Servants' Benefit Society

Status: Enrolled, OXF 39   **Type:** Permanent friendly society
Established: 7 October 1813   **Registered:** 17 October 1831   **Dissolved:** 1904
Headquarters: Ship Inn (1813-1823], Ancient Druid Tavern, George St (1831-1845), Chequers Inn, High St (1845), Ancient Druid Tavern (1849), Exchequer Inn (1855-1902]
Anniversary/feast day: Held on various days in late July or early August
Maximum age at entry: 36

Membership: 150 members in 1871, 141 in 1874, 138 in 1880, 142 in 1885, 146 in 1891, 136 in 1899, 126 in 1902
Primary Sources: TNA, FS 1/575/39; Oxon. Cal. QS iii, pp.643, 663; rulebook of 1849, Bodl. G.A. OXF 8° 124(2); BPP 1874, XXIII, (c.997), p.93-94; personal papers of James Trundle including rulebook of 1842 and accounts, OHC COS, P OXFU/58
Notes: Rules were enrolled at Epiphany Quarter Session 1817 and revised rules of 4 April 1823 enrolled at Michaelmas Session 1823. Initially, the rules limited the society to 101 members. The society was for persons employed in any capacity in the colleges or halls of Oxford University, and former servants who had served for three years and were over 21 years of age. Members of 25 years without any claim received 5s a week for a year. The Assistant Commissioner reported that Dr Godfrey, the medical attendant in 1872, stated this rule saved the society a lot of money as men did not claim for trivial sickness absence. Only a very small number of dons were honorary members. In 1870, W.F. Thurland held £13 10s of the society's money when he absconded having embezzled a large amount from the College Servants' Provident Institution (Oxford 474), (see appendix 2, Crimes 127). Thurland, the former treasurer of the society, was declared bankrupt in 1870. The sum owing was recovered in bankruptcy before the County Court, the society being a preferential creditor as it was registered. The committee was independent of its honorary members. Anniversary dinners were held in a meadow adjacent to Worcester College, a field next to Holywell church, Merton College cricket ground, Christ Church College cricket ground, Balliol College cricket ground, Headington Hill Hall and the Swan brewery grounds. In 1872 it was reported that since its formation there had been 440 members of which 186 had died, 109 had left, leaving 145 existing members. It became the Loyal College Servants Lodge, a branch of the IOOFMU (Oxford 505) in 1904. (See also appendix 2, Crimes 126).

474.　College Servants' Provident Institution (or Society)

Status: Enrolled, OXF 281　　**Type**: Permanent friendly society
Established: 9 January 1841　　**Registered:** 20 August 1841 **Dissolved**: 13 July 1889
Headquarters: Exchequer Inn (Chequers Inn), High Street (1841-1874), 12 Leckford Road, St Giles (1875-1878), Chequers Inn, High St (1878-1889)
Maximum age at entry: 55
Membership: 122 members in 1849, 145 in 1871, 172 in 1877, 171 in 1880, 150 in 1885, 137 in 1889
Primary Sources: TNA, FS 1/575/39; TNA, FS 1/582/281 TNA, FS 4/42/281; copy of the personal papers of James Trundle, a member comprising a rulebook

of 1850 and various receipts (1845-1865); OHC, P OXFU/58; BPP 1874, XXIII, (c.997), p.96

Notes: Some papers relating to this society are mistakenly filed in the Registrar's files at TNA under FS 1/575/39, being the College Servants' Benefit Society file (Oxford 473). This confusion also occurs in the printed list of societies to 1855 (OHC, QSD / R/28 and TNA, FS 2/9). Members were any persons employed in any capacity in colleges or halls of residence of Oxford University, or had been so employed. It was a burial insurance society, not for sickness, and received four or five honorary member payments a year. The governing committee comprised eleven elected members. Honorary members had no vote and could hold no office except treasurer or trustee. The society could divide funds when the amount accrued exceeded liabilities. The society loaned £2,000 to Oxford Town Council for waterworks improvement at four per cent interest in 1862 (JOJ, 4 January 1862). In 1870, the society had a defaulting treasurer, W.F. Thurland, who embezzled over £500 (see appendix 2, Crimes 127). The society was dissolved when funds amounting to £3,000 were transferred to the Legal and General Life Assurance Society which covered the liabilities of the members. (See also appendix 2, Crimes 133).

475.   Commercial Society

Status: Unregistered   **Type**: Permanent friendly society
Established: 5 January 1861 **Dissolved**: Last known 1762
Headquarters: Wheatsheaf & Anchor (1761-1762)
Anniversary/feast day: First Monday in January
Maximum age at entry: 35
Primary Sources: Printed rules, Bodl. G.A.OXF a.101(1)
Notes: This was a society for tradesmen and artificers with a maximum membership of 101. Gentlemen, servants, labourers, soldiers, sailors, bailiffs and bailiff's followers were exempted from membership. It was established at Thomas Galton's The Wheatsheaf and Anchor in St Aldate's. Subscriptions were 1s 2d a month and 4d to the 'house' as wet rent. Superannuation of 3s 6d was paid at age 65, and £10 was payable on death. The annual dinner was paid from the 'box'. It was one of 14 societies listed as in existence at Oxford in 1762 (JOJ, 22 May 1762).

476.   Compton Pilgrims Friendly Society, Oxford branch

Status: Branch of a registered society, BRK 86   **Type**: Permanent friendly society
Established: 1906 **Dissolved**: 1908

Membership: 4 members in 1907, 5 in 1908

477. County of Oxford Loyal Independent Lodge of Odd Fellows, (from 1812) Oxford Loyal and Independent Order of Odd Fellows

Status: Unregistered   **Type**: An order of oddfellows **Branch No.** 25
Established: 18 September 1804 **Dissolved**: Last known 1832
Headquarters: Ship Inn (1804], Alfred's Head Inn [1807-1810), Chequer Inn (1810], Saddlers' Arms, Lincoln Lane [1812-1816), King's Head, Holywell (1816-1830), University Arms (1830-1832)
Anniversary/feast day: Various dates until 1819, then the First Monday in July
Primary Sources: Blank membership form, Bodl., 247911 f.6/3; rulebook containing the articles of the lodge (1830), Bodl. G.A.OXF a.101(10)
Notes: The earliest Oddfellows society known in Oxfordshire. It was not a friendly society in that members received no benefit during sickness or on death but is included for completeness. This branch moved its headquarters on several occasions. The history of the order is unknown and the only other identified branch in the county was the Loyal Wellington Lodge at Banbury, branch no. 27, established 1817 (Banbury 75). The nature of the society was that it was established for fraternal and charitable purposes (Bodl., 247911 f.6/3). The rules contain no indication of a connection with any parent body or any other lodges. The method of delivery of charity was not specified in the rules, other than felons were excluded from receiving it. The rule book is inscribed in ink that it belonged to Brother William Richard Hobbs who was admitted to the lodge on 2 November 1832. A blank printed membership form for lodge number 25, is held at Bodl. G.A.OXF a.101(10).

478. Court Duke of Cornwall

Status: Branch of an affiliated order, OXF 262   **Type**: AOF **Branch No.** 4338
Established: 1864 **Registered:** 1865   **Dissolved**: Post 1918
Headquarters: Prince of Wales Inn, Cowley Road (1865-1871), Coach and Horses Inn, St Clements (1872-1883], Cape of Good Hope Inn, St Clements [1885-post 1918),
Membership: 49 members in 1865, 92 in 1870, 143 in 1880, 204 in 1885, 275 in 1890, 312 in 1895, 316 in 1900, 333 in 1905, 326 in 1910
Notes: This society was not part of any district in AOF. In 1878 Joseph Nutt was summonsed for not producing the accounts of the club and was later

charged with embezzlement of at least £41 (see appendix 2, Crimes 129). The court was suspended and reinstated by the AOF in 1879.

479.   Court Isis

Status: Branch of an affiliated order   **Type:** AOF **Branch No.** 2317
Established: 1849 **Dissolved:** 1852
Headquarters: Bell & Crown, Magdalene Street (1849-1852)
Notes: Not linked to any AOF district.

480.   Court King's Coronation

Status: Branch of an affiliated order **Type:** AOF **Branch No.** 9047
Established: 1902 **Dissolved:** 1905
Headquarters: Plough Inn, St Aldate's (1902-1905)
Membership: 19 members in 1904, 14 in 1905
Notes: Oxford District of AOF.

481.   Court Lord Nelson

Status: Branch of an affiliated order   **Type:** AOF **Branch No.** 7932
Established: 1891 **Dissolved:** 1895
Headquarters: New Inn, Jericho (1891-1895)
Membership: 13 in 1891, 15 in 1895,
Notes: Oxford District of AOF. It amalgamated with Court St Frideswide (Oxford 484) in 1895.

482.   Court Loyal Oxonian

Status: Branch of an affiliated order, OXF 208   **Type:** AOF Branch No. 2991
Established: First known 1858 **Registered:** 1858 **Dissolved:** Post 1918
Headquarters: Ancient Druid's, George Street (1858-1859), New Inn, St Aldate's (1860-1865), Anchor Inn (Hotel), New Road (1866-1870), Three Cups Hotel (1871-1876), Crown and Thistle Inn, Market Street (1877), 15 Commercial Rd (1878-1885), Crown and Thistle Inn (1886-1887], Red Lion [1889-1896], Bell Inn [1900-1905], 36a New Inn Hall Street (1909), Northgate Tavern (1910-post 1918)
Anniversary/feast day: As agreed by the society, and held on various dates in June or July
Minimum age at entry: 15, 16 (from 1896) Maximum age at entry: 40

Membership: 12 members in 1858, 142 in 1864, 247 in 1869, 263 in 1874, 302 in 1878, 337 in 1886, 402 in 1894, 460 in 1900, 505 in 1905, 522 in 1910
Primary Sources: Rulebooks of 1889 and 1896, Bodl. G.A. OXF 8° 1293(1); financial reports of 1887, 1902, 1905, 1908 and 1909, Bodl. 24785 e.28
Notes: Not linked to any AOF district. Loyal Oxonian Juvenile Friendly Society (Oxford 508) amalgamated with the branch in 1912. The higher order was Sanctuary Loyal Oxonian (Oxford 534).

483.   Court Princess Christian

Status: Female branch of an affiliated order **Type**: AOF **Branch No.** 8593
Established: 1896 **Dissolved**: Post 1918
Headquarters: St Peter-le-Bailey Schoolroom, New Inn Hall St [1905-post 1918)
Membership: 22 members in 1898, 38 in 1900, 41 in 1905, 33 in 1910
Notes: Not part of any AOF district. A society for young women.

484.   Court St Frideswide

Status: Female branch of an affiliated order   **Type**: AOF **Branch No.** 7166
Established: February 1884 **Dissolved**: Post 1918
Headquarters: Holly Bush Inn, Bridge Street, Osney (1884-1905], Greyhound (1910)
Membership: 8 members in 1883, 31 in 1884, 135 in 1886, 235 in 1890, 310 in 1895, 413 in 1905, 426 in 1910
Notes: Oxford District of AOF. Court Lord Nelson, (Oxford 481) amalgamated with this court in 1895.

485.   Court Victoria

Status: Female branch of an affiliated order **Type**: AOF **Branch No.** 8877
Established: 1899 **Dissolved**: Post 1918
Headquarters: Victoria Coffee House, High Street (1899-1902), Old British Schoolroom [1905-post 1918)
Membership: 16 members in 1900, 31 in 1905, 58 in 1910

486.   East Oxford Slate Club

Status: Unregistered **Type**: Friendly society
Established: First known 1899 **Dissolved**: Last known 1899

Notes: Played a cricket match against Court The Abbey, Eynsham (Eynsham 270) in 1899 (JOJ, 27 May 1899).

487.   East Oxford Subordinate Division

Status: Branch of an affiliated order   **Type**: OSOT **Branch No.** 725
Established: 1890 **Dissolved**: Post 1912
Headquarters: Mission Hall, Magdalene St [1905-post 1912)
Membership: 141 in 1905, 137 in 1910

488.   Elderly Society

Status: Unregistered   **Type**: Permanent friendly society
Established: 7 December 1758 **Dissolved**: Last known 1762
Headquarters: Mitre Inn, High Street (1758-1761), New Wheatsheaf & Anchor, St Aldate's (1761-1762]
Minimum age at entry: 35 **Maximum age at entry**: 45
Notes: An advertisement in *Jackson's Oxford Journal*, on 2 December 1758 stated that benefit clubs lately established in the county saw people excluded due to a maximum age of entry of 35 years. Notice was given for the formation of a society 'for those more advanced in age' at the Mitre Inn. It was to consist of no more than 101 members. The first meeting was held on 7 December 1758. In 1861 the society removed to the New Wheatsheaf & Anchor as the landlord, Mr Galton had relocated to those premises. Forty-six members agreed to hold future meetings there, supported by many other members who could not be present due to the harvest. This caused a split in the membership and some continued to meet at the Mitre (JOJ, 22 August 1861). The club at the New Wheatsheaf & Anchor met on 2 October 1761, and a further advertisement on their behalf stated, 'And whereas divers falsehoods and ridiculous reflections have from time to time been industriously handed about, in print and otherwise, and many illegal measures pursued; it is necessary to observe, that whether they were the effects of folly or ill design, can at present only be determined in their own breasts; Yet as rancour malice and falsehood may be found almost in every sentence, appearances are at last very unfavourable on the part of those who thus strenuously uphold and inflame the differences subsisting within the society' (JOJ, 5 September 1761). Two Elderly Societies, one held at the Mitre and other at the New Wheatsheaf & Anchor, continued to meet in 1762 and was counted as one of 14 societies listed as in existence at Oxford in 1762 (JOJ, 22 May 1762).

489.   Freemen Society

Status: Unregistered   **Type**: Friendly society
Established: First known 1762 **Dissolved**: Last known 1762
Headquarters: Turk's Head, Cornmarket (1762)
Notes: One of 14 societies listed as in existence at Oxford in 1762 (JOJ, 22 May 1762). It was probably the forerunner of the Civis Society, established 1773 (Oxford 472).

490.   Friendly Society of Carpenters and Joiners

Status: Enrolled, OXF 157   **Type**: Permanent friendly society
Established: 1810 **Dissolved**: Last known 1810
Minimum age at entry: 20
Primary Sources: Undated rulebook, TNA, FS 1/579/157
Notes: Members of the society had to have worked at the trade of carpenter or joiner for a minimum of seven years before they were eligible to join. Benefits insured were for the fire of shops, buildings or dwellings, tools of the trade to a maximum of three guineas, accident, sickness and robbery. A carpenter or joiner who came to the City of Oxford could join but was required do so within one month of first residence. The society later became a trade union.

> **Friendly Society of the Freemen of the City of Oxford** – see Civis Society, Oxford 472

491.   Friendly Society of Operative Stonemasons

Status: Unregistered   **Type**: Friendly society
Established: 1873 **Dissolved**: Last known 1873
Notes: The Oxford branch of the society wrote an open letter to *Jackson's Oxford Journal* concerning stonemason's wages in 1873 (JOJ, 10 May 1873).

492.   Friendly Union Tradesmen's Society

Status: Registered, OXF 26   **Type**: Friendly society
Established: First known 1833   **Registered:** 16 July 1833 **Dissolved**: Last known 1833
Headquarters: University Arms (1833)
Primary Sources: TNA, FS 4/42/26

Notes: No file exists in the Registrar's papers at TNA although it is indicated in the index at TNA, FS 1/574/26.

493.   Good Intent Lodge, Oxford Independent Order of United Brothers

Status: Enrolled, OXF 109   **Type**: Permanent friendly society
Established: 1846   **Registered:** 26 November 1846   **Dissolved**: 1859
Headquarters: Bell & Crown Inn, Magdalene St (1846-1850), University Arms, Red Lion Square (1850), Bell & Crown Inn, Magdalene St (1850-1855]
Minimum age at entry: 15 **Maximum age at entry**: 35
Primary Sources: Rulebook of 1846, TNA, FS 1/578/109; TNA, FS 4/42/109; rulebook of 1846, Bodl. G.A. OXF 16° 65(2); (BPP 1874, XXIII, (c.997), p.92).
Notes: The society was previously the Loyal Good Intent Lodge of the IOOFMU (Oxford 506) until it seceded from the Oddfellows in 1846 after there had been disagreement with the Oxford District Grand Master. When he died, the society rejoined the IOOFMU and reverted to their original name of Good Intent Lodge. It was governed by honorary members who held the positions of President, Vice-President, and Secretary. A letter from the Registrar was returned, dated 23 May 1879, and stated the society had broken up (FS 4/42/109).

494.   (Greyhound club)

Status: Unregistered   **Type**: Friendly society
Established: First known 1762 **Dissolved**: Last known 1762
Headquarters: Greyhound (1762)
Notes: One of 14 societies listed as in existence at Oxford in 1762 (JOJ, 22 May 1762).

> **Iffley and Oxford New Benefit Society** – see Iffley New Benefit Society, Iffley 387

495.   Industrious Society

Status: Unregistered   **Type**: Friendly society
Established: First known 1762 **Dissolved**: Last known 1762
Headquarters: Wheatsheaf, High St (1762)
Notes: One of 14 societies listed as in existence at Oxford in 1762 (JOJ, 22 May 1762).

496.   The Industrious Society

Status: Enrolled, OXF 9   **Type**: Permanent friendly society
Established: 1831   **Registered:** 4 April 1831 **Dissolved**: Last known 1831
Headquarters: Cross Keys (1831)
Minimum age at entry: 16 **Maximum age at entry**: 36
Primary Sources: Rulebook of 1831, TNA, FS 1/574/9; TNA, FS 4/42/9
Notes: The society permitted a maximum of 121 members.

497.   Integrity Life Assurance and Sick Benefit Society, Bath District

Status: Registered   **Type**: Collecting friendly society
Established: First known 1882 **Dissolved**: Last known 1882
Notes: This was a collecting society with an agent in Oxford, Thomas Gardener, who was charged with embezzlement of funds in 1882. Integrity Life is now part of Western and Southern Financial Group. (See also appendix 2, Crimes 130).

> **Isis Lodge, Ancient Order of Druids** – see Oxford Lodges, Ancient Order of Druids, Oxford 528

498.   Juvenile Society of Oxford District

Status: Juvenile branch of an affiliated order   **Type**: AOF
Established: January 1884 **Dissolved**: Post 1914
Headquarters: St Peter le Bailey schoolroom, New Inn Hall St [1905-post 1914)
Membership: 80 members in 1884, 180 in 1885, 350 in 1890, 630 in 1895, 809 in 1900
Notes: Open to male and female members and was the juvenile society for Foresters' courts in the Oxford District.

499.   Labourers' Accident and Burial Society

Status: Registered, OXF 320   **Type**: Permanent friendly society
Established: First known 1871 **Registered:** 2 June 1871   **Dissolved**: 1876
Headquarters: White Hart Inn, Cornmarket Street (1873-1876)
Minimum age at entry: 18
Primary Sources: Rulebook of 1873, TNA, FS 3/321/340; TNA, FS 4/42/320

Notes: There was no age limits for the society but a member joining over 50 years of age received no burial cover. Registration was cancelled on 24 March 1897 as the society had ceased to exist some years earlier. A letter dated 27 November 1894 from the landlord of the White Hart stated that the society was held at the premises until 18 years before and was then broken up (TNA, FS 4/42/320).

500.   Liverpool Victoria Friendly Society, Oxford Branch

Status: Branch of a registered society   **Type:** Liverpool Victoria Friendly Society **Established:** First known 1863 **Dissolved:** Last known 1863
Anniversary/feast day: Whit Monday
Notes: A tea party was held at Cold Harbour on Whit Monday 1863 (JOJ, 30 May 1863).

501.   Locomotive Friendly Society

Status: Unregistered   **Type:** Friendly society
Established: First known 1881 **Dissolved:** Last known 1881
Headquarters: Running Horse Inn, Bridge Street (1881)
Notes: The society was in existence in 1881, and presented a marble timepiece to Mr Uriah Waters as departing secretary (JOJ, 26 November 1881). It is possible this was the same society as the Amalgamated Society of Railway Servants, known from 1872 to 1880 (Oxford 463).

502.   London Friendly Institution, Oxford Branch

Status: Branch of an enrolled society, LND 57   **Type:** Permanent friendly society
Established: December 1825 **Dissolved:** Last known 1900
Primary Sources: Rulebooks of 1841, 1869, 1882 and 1900, TNA, FS 15/1662; BPP 1874, XXIII, (c.997), P.93
Notes: An advert was placed in *Jackson's Oxford Journal* for members to join the society. The contact was W.M. Cleobury, a medical attendant of St Aldate's (JOJ, 22 October 1825, repeated in later weeks). Annual dinners were held at the Wheatsheaf, High Street or The Tree, Iffley, during the 1840s when approximately 70 people attended. In 1872 the Assistant Commissioner discovered that the society had lost money after the seceding of the Oxford Friendly Institution in 1840 (Oxford 522). Nearly all Post Office employees in Oxford were members of this society in 1872 (BPP 1874, XXIII, (c.997),

p.93). The society lists a medical attendant at Oxford in its rulebooks until 1900 indicating its continued presence until that time.

503.   Loyal Borough Lodge

Status: Branch of an affiliated order **Type:** IOOFMU **Branch No.** 6556
Established: March 1883   **Dissolved:** Post 1918
Headquarters: The Cape of Good Hope Inn (1883-post 1918)
Membership: 33 members in 1883, 53 in 1886, 101 in 1891, 122 in 1901, 148 in 1910, 194 in 1913
Notes: Oxford District of IOOFMU.

504.   Loyal Charlotte Toynbee Female Lodge

Status: Female branch of an affiliated order **Type:** IOOFMU **Branch No.** 7604
Established: 1900 **Dissolved:** Post 1912
Headquarters: St Giles Parish Hall (1900-1901], St Peter-le-Bailey Parish Room [1905-post 1912)
Membership: 2 members in 1902, 51 in 1905, 71 in 1910, 230 in 1913
Primary Sources: Declaration book, 1912 onwards, OHC, O23/2/16

505.   Loyal College Servants Lodge

Status: Branch of an affiliated order **Type:** IOOFMU **Branch No.** 7889
Established: 1904 **Dissolved:** Post 1912
Headquarters: Druid's Head Inn, George Street (1904-post 1912)
Membership: 96 members in 1905, 100 in 1907, 109 in 1910, 140 in 1914
Notes: Oxford District of IOOFMU. It was formed from the College Servants' Benefit Society (Oxford 473).

506.   Loyal Good Intent Lodge

Status: Branch of an affiliated order, OXF 203   **Type:** IOOFMU **Branch No.** 1703
Established: 1838   **Registered:** 1839 **Dissolved:** Post 1918
Headquarters: Bell and Crown Inn, Magdalene Street [1841-1846, 1859-1862), Wheatsheaf Inn, High St (1862-1884], Chequers Inn, High Street [1886-1892], Bell Inn, Cornmarket Street (1894-1897), Wheatsheaf Inn [1901-post 1918)

Membership: 92 members in 1841, 85 in 1846, 60 in 1860, 103 in 1862, 229 in 1866, 308 in 1870, 443 in 1875, 505 in 1879, 453 in 1886, 455 in 1892, 483 in 1897, 469 in 1905, 473 in 1910, 537 in 1914
Primary Sources: Minute books of 1886-1890 and 1895-1901, OHC, O23/2/3/A1; BPP 1874, XXIII, (c.997), p.92
Notes: Cheltenham District (1841-1846), Oxford District (1859-post 1918) of IOOFMU. The branch society seceded from IOOFMU in 1846 and was renamed 'The Good Intent Lodge, Oxford Independent Order of United Brothers' as an independent society (Oxford 493). There had been disagreement with the Oxford District Grand Master, but when he died the society rejoined the IOOFMU and reverted to their original name. The *Oddfellows Quarterly Report* of 1859, p.51 states society had been re-instated after suspension. Initially it was given branch number 3656, but subsequently reverted to its original branch number of 1703 (BPP 1874, XXIII, (c.997), p.92)

507.   Loyal Oxonian Juvenile Foresters

Status: Juvenile branch of an affiliated order, OXF 313   **Type**: AOF
Established: 1871 **Registered:** 23 December 1871   **Dissolved**: 1875
Headquarters: Three Cups Hotel, Queen St (1871-1875)
Minimum age at entry: 7 **Maximum age at entry**: 18
Primary Sources: rulebook of 1871, TNA, FS 1/582/313; TNA, FS 4/42/313
Notes: The benefit for those aged 7-12 years was medical attendance only. For those aged 12-15 it was 3s 6d a week. A returned letter to the Registrar of 1878 stated the society had been closed since 1875 (TNA, FS 4/42/313). The parent branch was Court Loyal Oxonian (Oxford 482).

508.   Loyal Oxonian Juvenile Friendly Society

Status: Juvenile branch of an affiliated order, OXF 383   **Type:** AOF
Established: 1894 **Registered:** 20 March 1894 **Dissolved:** 28 February 1912
Headquarters: St Michael's Schoolroom, (1894-1899), St Peter-le-Bailey Schoolroom, New Inn Hall St (1899-1912)
Minimum age at entry: 8, 5 (from 1906) Maximum age at entry: 16, 18 (from 1906)
Membership: 53 members in 1899, 45 in 1905, 41 in 1910
Primary Sources: Rulebooks of 1894, 1899 and 1906, TNA, FS 3/322/383; TNA, FS 4/42/383
Notes: Registration was cancelled on amalgamation with Court Loyal Oxonian (Oxford 482) in 1912.

509. Loyal Prince of Wales Lodge

Status: Branch of an affiliated order, OXF 243 **Type**: IOOFMU **Branch No.** 4902
Established: 1860 **Registered:** 1862 **Dissolved**: Post 1918
Headquarters: Druid's Head Inn (1862-1912)
Anniversary/feast day: Held on a date agreed in September, October or November
Membership: 22 members in 1860, 29 in 1862, 56 in 1863, 94 in 1866, 145 in 1869, 309 in 1879, 393 in 1886, 437 in 1891, 511 in 1897, 543 in 1905, 631 in 1913
Notes: Oxford District of IOOFMU. In 1872 the branch loaned £400 to the Oxford Local Board for street improvements (JOJ, 8 June 1872).

510. Loyal St Giles Lodge

Status: Branch of an affiliated order **Type**: IOOFMU **Branch No.** 6889
Established: 1889 **Dissolved**: Post 1918
Headquarters: King's Arms Inn, Summertown (1889-1912)
Membership: 42 members in 1890, 65 in 1892, 90 in 1895, 96 in 1901, 124 in 1905, 114 in 1910, 135 in 1913
Primary Sources: Minute books of 1889-1896 and 1896-1905, OHC, O23/2/12/F1/1
Notes: Oxford District of IOOFMU.

511. Loyal St Lawrence Lodge

Status: Branch of an affiliated order **Type**: IOOFMU **Branch No.** 7323
Established: 31 January 1895 **Dissolved**: Post 1914
Headquarters: The George Elliot, South Hinksey (1895), New Hinksey schoolroom (1897), (Old) White House Inn, Abingdon Rd, Oxford [1899-1910]
Membership: 25 members in 1897, 74 in 1905, 64 in 1907, 75 in 1910, 131 in 1914
Notes: Oxford District of IOOFMU. The society was established in South Hinksey (then Berkshire) but removed to the White House Inn, Abingdon Road, Oxford by 1899.

512. Loyal Society

Status: Unregistered   **Type:** Friendly society
Established: First known 1762 **Dissolved**: Last known 1762
Headquarters: Crown and Fleece, Old Butcher Row (1762)
Notes: One of 14 societies listed as in existence at Oxford in 1762 (JOJ, 22 May 1762).

513. Loyal Walton Lodge

Status: Branch of an affiliated order, OXF 274   **Type:** IOOFMU **Branch No.** 5385
Established: January 1866 **Registered:** 1866   **Dissolved**: Post 1918
Headquarters: Jericho House, Walton Street (1866-post 1918)
Membership: 65 members in 1866, 92 in 1868, 143 in 1871, 169 in 1875, 226 in 1880, 263 in 1886, 308 in 1891, 372 in 1897, 461 in 1901, 550 in 1905, 602 in 1910, 688 in 1913
Notes: Oxford District of IOOFMU. In the early 1880s the lodge jointly organized an annual outing by Great Western Railway to Portsmouth and the Isle of Wight with the Loyal Bower Lodge, Abingdon. In 1882, 750 people attended in 18 carriages. The train arrived at 9.30 a.m. and the travellers enjoyed visiting the naval dockyard, including HMS Victory, bathing at Southsea and travelling to the Isle of Wight by steamer. The train arrived back in Oxford at 11.00 p.m. (JOJ, 15 July 1882). In 1885 a similar outing was undertaken to Liverpool, Blackpool, and Southport with the London and North Western Railway (JOJ, 11 July 1885).

514. Loyal Wellington Lodge

Status: Branch of an affiliated order, OXF 117   **Type:** IOOFMU **Branch No.** 2662
Established: 1841   **Registered:** 1841 **Dissolved**: Post 1918
Headquarters: Ancient Druid Inn [1842-1860), Crown and Thistle, Market Street (1860-1864), Druid's Head Inn, George Street (1865-post 1918)
Membership: 38 members in 1842, 50 in 1846, 19 in 1855, 39 in 1858, 71 in 1859, 122 in 1860, 172 in 1865, 234 in 1870, 266 in 1875, 334 in 1880, 401 in 1886, 415 in 1891, 412 in 1901, 401 in 1907, 380 in 1910, 372 in 1914
Notes: Oxford District of IOOFMU.

515.   Mechanical Benefit Society

Status: Enrolled, OXF 2   **Type:** Permanent friendly society
Established: 1818   **Registered:** 1827   **Dissolved:** 1887
Headquarters: Ship Inn, St Michaels parish [1826-1834], Chequers (1834-1855], Ship Inn [1860-1870], Chequers Inn, High St [1875-1885]
Minimum age at entry: 18 Maximum age at entry: 30, 36 (from 1830)
Membership: 112 members in 1846, 100 in 1850, 92 in 1855, 80 in 1860, 67 in 1864, 51 in 1870, 45 in 1875, 29 in 1880, 22 in 1885, 19 in 1887
Primary Sources: Rulebook of 1826, TNA, FS 1/574/2; TNA, FS 4/42/2; rulebook of 1830 and accounts for 1855, Bodl. G.A. 8° 566; OHC, QSD/R/38; Oxon. Cal. QS iii, p. 679; BPP 1874, XXIII, (c.997),p.95
Notes: The society enrolled at the Michaelmas Quarter Session 1827. The rules permitted a maximum of 121 members. Members were required to be of a handicraft calling with no timber sawyers, painters, colour grinders, plumbers or glaziers to being admitted (Bodl. G.A. 8° 566). In 1852, Joseph Nutt, a steward of the society was charged with defrauding the society of £3 16s (see appendix 2, Crimes 123). In 1855 a further member was charged with embezzlement from the society of £6 10s (see appendix 2, Crimes 124). Accounts of the society for year ending August 1855 showed £1,557 in stock and £109 in the box. The Assistant Commissioner described the Mechanical Benefit Society as a small club with 40-50 members and closed to new entrants in 1872. It had no honorary members and never held a feast day. On dissolution there was £502 in funds.

516.   (New Wheatsheaf club)

Status: Unregistered   **Type**: Friendly society
Established: First known 1762 **Dissolved**: Last known 1762
Headquarters: New Wheatsheaf (1762)
Notes: One of 14 societies listed as in existence at Oxford in 1762 (JOJ, 22 May 1762).

517.   Onward Section, Cadets of Temperance

Status: Juvenile branch of an affiliated order   **Type**: OSOT **Branch No.** 181
Established: 1886 **Dissolved**: Last known 1886
Headquarters: Temperance Hall, Pembroke St (1886)

518.   Osney Working Men's Benefit Slate Club

Status: Unregistered **Type**: Friendly society
Established: 31 January 1895 **Dissolved**: Last known 1899
Headquarters: Hollybush Inn, Bridge St (1895-99)
Anniversary/feast day: January
Notes: Seventy people attended the annual dinner held at the clubroom adjoining the Hollybush Inn, held on Saturday 29 January 1899 (JOJ, 4 February 1899).

519.   Oxford Cab-Drivers' Benefit Club

Status: Unregistered   **Type**: Annual dividing friendly society
Established: 1887 **Dissolved**: Last know 1910
Headquarters: St Giles' (south) shelter (1910)
Membership: 32 members in 1887, 50 in 1891, 71 in 1897, 83 in 1902, 110 in 1909, 95 in 1910
Primary Sources: Rulebook of 1905 and financial accounts, OHC COS, OXF 388.3
Notes: All members were required to be cab-drivers, tram-drivers, stable-men or men connected with the cab trade. Membership was 6d a week. A statement of accounts for 1910 shows a financial account since the commencement of the society in 1887.

520.   Oxford District Agricultural Labourers' Union Sick and Benefit Society

Status: Registered, OXF 330   **Type**: Permanent friendly society
Established: 1875   **Registered:** 3 June 1875 **Dissolved**: Last known 1876
Headquarters: Hythe Bridge St (1875-1876)
Primary Sources: Rulebook of 1875, TNA, FS 1/582/330; TNA, FS 4/42/330
Notes: A committee meeting of Oxford District of the Agricultural Labourers' Union in 1875 decided to have a sick benefit society to be commenced immediately (Pamela Horn, *Agricultural trade unionism in Oxfordshire, 1872-81* [Oxfordshire Record Society, v.48, 1974], p.82). There was no age stipulation in the rules. All members had to be a member of the National Agricultural Labourers Union. A letter dated 4 February 1880 was returned to Registrar stating the society had ceased to exist.

521.   Oxford District Juvenile Branch

Status: Juvenile branch of an affiliated order, OXF 373   **Type**: IOOFMU
Established: 10 January 1891 **Registered:** 1891   **Dissolved**: Post 1914
Headquarters: St Peter-le-Bailey Schoolroom, New Inn Hall St (1891-post 1914)
Membership: 189 in 1891, 348 in 1899, 296 in 1905, 272 in 1910
Notes: Juvenile branch for lodges in the Oxford District of the IOOFMU.

522.   Oxford District of IOOFMU

Status: District of an Affiliated Order, OXF 221   **Type**: IOOFMU
Established: 1841   **Registered:** 1859 **Dissolved**: Post 1918
Headquarters: Ancient Druid Tavern (1859-1877]
Notes: This was registered as a friendly society with the Registrar but was a district structure and had no direct members. Affiliated branches in the district pooled their financial resources to spread risk.

523.   Oxford District Widow and Orphan Society

Status: Branch of an affiliated order, OXF 294   **Type:** IOOFMU
Established: 1869 **Registered:** 27 January 1869   **Dissolved:** 30 April 1913
Headquarters: Druid's Head Inn, George St [1875-1878), White Hart Inn, Cornmarket St (1878-1889), Druid's Head Inn, George St (1889-1913)
Anniversary/feast day: January
Minimum age at entry: 18 (from 1910) Maximum age at entry: 45, 40 (from 1890)
Membership: 162 members in 1875, 184 in 1877, 144 in 1880, 133 in 1885, 127 in 1891, 76 in 1899, 63 in 1905, 52 in 1910, 44 in 1913
Primary Sources: Rulebooks of 1869, 1890 and 1910, TNA, FS 3/321/294; TNA, FS 4/42/294
Notes: A district society, open to existing members of IOOFMU only. The object of society was to 'Grant relief to widows and orphans of deceased members'. It dissolved with 44 members and £791 funds.

524.   Oxford Friendly Institution

Status: Enrolled, OXF 43   **Type:** Permanent friendly society
Established: 1840   **Registered:** 8 December 1840 **Dissolved:** 6 April 1882

Headquarters: No. 4 Church St, St Giles (1846), Wheatsheaf Inn, High St [1854-1860], 32 Pembroke St (1862), Wheatsheaf Inn (1865-1870], St Aldate's [1875-1877), 29 Pembroke St (1876-1882)
Minimum age at entry: 20 (from 1854) Maximum age at entry: 45, reduced to 40 (1840), reduced to 35 (1854)
Membership: 271 members in 1855, 309 in 1860, 317 in 1867, 299 in 1871, 283 in 1874, 233 in 1882
Primary Sources: Rulebooks of 1840 and 1854, TNA, FS 1/576/43; TNA, FS 4/42/43; rulebooks of January 1843 and 1865, treasurers bonds of 8 April 1841, 17 November 1849, 12 September 1854 and 1 March 1877, OHC, QSD/R/37; BPP 1874, XXIII, (c.997), pp.12, 92
Notes: New members were required to reside in the Borough of Oxford and have a minimum income of 6s a week. The society seceded from the London Friendly Institution (Oxford 502) after a difference in the ideas of local and central management. It was initially supported by local 'gentlemen' but a secretary of the society stole monies from the club over a number of years amounting to between £285 and £500. At an adjourned AGM on 1 March 1882, a government appointed official decided the society should be dissolved. He cited two reasons, namely that payments had been fixed too low by the original founders and that the amount paid out was too much, with too lax views on the rules (JOJ, 4 March 1882). The society dissolved with 233 members and £1,900 funds.

525.   Oxford Friendly Society

Status: Unregistered   **Type**: Friendly society
Established: First known 1872 **Dissolved**: Last known 1872
Membership: 31 members in 1872
Primary Sources: (BPP 1874, XXIII, (c.997), p.92)
Notes: The Assistant Commissioner reported the presence of this small society in 1872 with 31 member and £16 funds.

526.   Oxford Hearts of Oak Benefit Society (medical agency)

Status: An independent society, associated with a registered society without branches **Type**: HOO
Established: 1873 **Dissolved**: Last known 1889
Headquarters: Druid's Head Inn (1889)
Membership: 23 members in 23 members, 60 in 1879, 130 in 1889
Notes: This was a medical agency in association with the Hearts of Oak Benefit Society. The HOO did not have branches and was a collecting society.

527.   Oxford Juvenile Society

Status: Registered, OXF 379   **Type:** Female juvenile friendly society
Established: 10 January 1893 **Registered:** 12 May 1893 **Dissolved:** 5 December 1899
Headquarters: 37 New Inn Hall Street (1893-1896), 21 George Street [1898] 81 Southmoor Road (1898-99)
Minimum age at entry: 12, 8 (from 1898) **Maximum age at entry:** 16
Primary Sources: Rulebook of 1893, TNA, FS 3/322/379; TNA, FS 4/42/379
Notes: A female juvenile society, in association with the Working Women's Club (Oxford 547), with which it amalgamated on 5 December 1899.

528.   Oxford Lodges, Ancient Order of Druid's

Status: Branches of an affiliated order   **Type:** AOD
Notes: The Albion Lodge (Oxford 465) was the dominant Oxford Lodge of AOD, and similarly other Oxford lodges were not friendly societies within the meaning of this calendar. They were a mixture of a fraternal organizations, philanthropic organizations and spiritual ones. A lodge at Jericho House (Lodge 421) was suspended in 1878, Isis Lodge (Lodge 580) was established at the Northgate Tavern in 1907 and the Cherwell Lodge (Lodge 588) opened in 1908 at the Cape of Good Hope.

> **Oxford Loyal and Independent Order of Odd Fellows** – see
> County of Oxford Loyal
>
> Independent Order of Odd Fellows, Oxford 477

529.   Oxford Phoenix Benefit Society

Status: Enrolled, OXF 46   **Type:** Permanent friendly society
Established: 16 February 1805   **Registered:** 1819   **Dissolved:** 1877
Headquarters: Three Goats Inn, Cornmarket Street (1827-1841], New Inn, St Aldate's [1844-1850], Woodstock Arms, Magdalene St [1855], Crown Inn, Cornmarket St (1855-1877)
Minimum age at entry: 20 Maximum age at entry: 35
Membership: 60 members in 1846, 56 in 1850, 44 in 1855, 34 in 1860, 26 in 1865, 24 in 1870, 16 in 1877
Primary Sources: Rulebooks of 1827 and 1837, TNA, FS 1/576/46; TNA, FS 4/42/46; rulebook of 1827 and 1850, Bodl. G.A. 8° 565; rulebook of 1827,

OHC, QSD/R/39; Oxon. Cal. QS iii, pp.650, 678; (BPP 1874, XXIII, (c.997), pp.14, 94)
Notes: The rules of 9 February 1818 were enrolled at the Easter Quarter Session 1819 and amended at Easter Session 1827. The society was established for printers. Subscriptions of 6d were collected weekly with quarterly meetings. The collector had responsibility to question prospective new members and make recommendations regarding entrance to the society (Bodl. G.A. 8° 565). The society flourished until 1840 when unlimited allowances were paid to sick members and superannuated members drew heavily on the funds. In 1849 a committee was set up to revise the rules and these were registered and implemented the following year. In the rule changes, superannuation was reduced and a maximum of £100 total benefit per member was set. The club still consisted entirely of compositors and those in the printing trade. The society had ceased to take in new members and the average age of the society was between 54 and 55 years when the Assistant Commissioner investigated in 1872 for the Royal Commission. No person was permitted to become a member of another society and four were non-residents of Oxford (BPP 1874, XXIII, (c.997), p.94). It was dissolved in 1877 with assets of £399 16s 10d.

> **Oxford Tradesmen's Benefit Society** - see Tradesmen's Society, Oxford 543

530.   Oxford United Brethren Friendly Society

Status: Registered, OXF 361   **Type:** Friendly society
Established: 1887 **Registered:** 22 June 1887 **Dissolved**: 2 June 1896
Headquarters: Crown Inn, Cornmarket Street (1887-1893), Leopold Arms, Cornmarket St (1893-1896)
Minimum age at entry: 17 **Maximum age at entry**: 40
Membership: 75 members in 1891, 42 in 1894, 42 in 1896
Primary Sources: Rulebook of 1887, Bodl. G.A. OXF 16° 136(3); TNA, FS 3/322/361; TNA, FS 4/42/361
Notes: Benefits included to 'grant relief to members in distressed circumstances'. Honorary members controlled the society. It dissolved on with 42 members and £88 13s 4d funds.

> **Protective and Provident Society of Women** – see Amalgamated Protective and Provident Society of Women, Oxford 462

531.   The Queen's College Servants Benevolent Society

Status: Unregistered   **Type**: Permanent friendly society
Established: 1860 **Dissolved**: Last known 1872
Headquarters: The Queen's College (1860-1872)
Primary Sources: BPP 1874, XXIII, (c.997), p.95
Notes: The Assistant Commissioner reported in 1872 that 24 employees of the college had joined together twelve years previously to form a benevolent society. It was founded by William Owen, principal buttery clerk at The Queen's College. Members paid 6d a month and if they were sick during term time the society paid out 10s a week for a substitute. The money was paid direct to the substitute worker so members could belong to another society, something excluded by many rules, and it was so designed as it was believed it made it not able to be registered under the Friendly Societies Act. There were a few honorary payments.

532.   St Clements Union Friendly Society

Status: Enrolled, OXF 132   **Type**: Permanent friendly society
Established: 3 October 1816   **Registered:** 4 August 1846   **Dissolved**: Last known 1847
Headquarters: Black Horse Inn, St Clements (1816-1846)
Anniversary/feast day: First Thursday in September
Maximum age at entry: 36
Primary Sources: Rules of 1816, TNA, FS 3/319/132; rulebook of 1846, TNA, FS 1/579/132; TNA, FS 4/42/132
Notes: The society initially had a maximum of 101 members. No labourers, soldiers, sailors or sheriff's bailiffs could belong as a benefit member. The landlord was paid 2s rent with a fire for exclusive use of the room on club nights. A letter dated September 1866 indicated the society had 'broken up' but with no indication when. A court case on 23 March 1847 ended with Mr London, a club steward, stating the society was to be broken up (see also appendix 2, Crimes 122), (JOJ, 27 March 1847).

533.   Sanctuary Duke of Cornwall

Status: Branch of an affiliated order, OXF 280   **Type**: AOS **Branch No.** 4338
Established: 1870   **Registered:** 16 December 1870   **Dissolved**: November 1890

Headquarters: Prince of Wales Inn, Cowley Road, Cowley St John (1870-1872), Coach and Horses Inn, High St, Oxford (1872-1880), Cape of Good Hope, Iffley Road (1880-1889)
Anniversary/feast day: As agreed by the society
Minimum age at entry: 18 **Maximum age at entry**: 40
Primary Sources: Rulebook of 1870, TNA, FS 3/321/280; TNA, FS 4/42/280
Notes: A letter from Charles Holley, dated 14 November 1894 explains the demise of the club was due to sickness and lack of funds (TNA, FS 4/42/280). The society ceased to exist in November 1890 although registration was not cancelled until 14 March 1897.

534.   Sanctuary Loyal Oxonian

Status: Branch of an affiliated order, OXF 253   **Type**: AOS **Branch No.** 2991
Established: 1863 **Registered:** 1863   **Dissolved**: Last known 1863
Headquarters: New Inn, St Aldate's (1863), Anchor Hotel (undated), 23 Union St, Jericho [1876-1885), Crown and Thistle Inn (1886)
Notes: This society was registered separately with the Registrar but was the higher order membership of the Court Loyal Oxonian, AOF (Oxford 481), using the same branch number. The Ancient Order of Shepherds were Foresters, in this case they had to be a member of the Court Loyal Oxonian, and paid a greater contribution than normal members for increased benefits.

535.   Shoemakers Benefit Society

Status: Unregistered **Type**: Friendly society
Established: 1872 **Dissolved**: Last known 1872
Headquarters: Anchor Inn, New Road (1872)
Primary Sources: (BPP 1874, XXIII, (c.997), p.96).
Notes: Funds of the society were devoted to pay a small amount of relief and travelling pay to wandering 'brothers'. The object was to persuade competition to leave the town. It was not part of the Amalgamated Union of Shoemakers and had disagreements with it. The Masters in Oxford only recognized members of this society to undertake work for them and hence had the appearance of being a trade association as well as a friendly society.

536.   Sociable Society

Status: Enrolled, OXF 165   **Type**: Friendly society
Established: 16 March 1801   **Registered:** 11 August 1826 **Dissolved**: Last known 1826

Headquarters: Cross Keys, St Peter-le-Bailey (1801), Anchor Inn, St Peter-le-Bailey (1826)
Anniversary/feast day: Second Monday in July
Maximum age at entry: 38
Primary Sources: Printed rules of 1801, TNA, FS 3/320/165; TNA, FS 4/42/165
Notes: The society had a maximum of 101 members. The rules of the Unanimous Society (Oxford 544), established in 1770, were included in the file of this society under TNA, FS 3/320/165. It appears the Sociable society either merged or was taken over by this society after 1809. Enquiries by the Registrar in 1895 proved negative and it was deduced the society had ceased to exist before 1876 (TNA, FS 4/42/165). No returns were ever received by the Registrar indicating it probably dissolved before 1855. No newspaper reports of the society exist.

> **Society of Tradesmen and Artificers** - see Tradesmen's Society, Oxford 543

537.   (Sot's Hole club)

Status: Unregistered   **Type**: Friendly society
Established: First known 1762 **Dissolved**: Last known 1762
Headquarters: Sot's Hole, St Aldate's (1762)
Notes: One of 14 societies listed as in existence at Oxford in 1762 (JOJ, 22 May 1762).

538.   South Oxford Working Men's' Club and Institute

Status: Registered, OXF 295   **Type**: Working Men's' Club
Established: January 1869 **Registered:** 23 March 1869   **Dissolved**: Last Known 1876
Headquarters: 37 Pembroke Street, Oxford (1869)
Minimum age at entry: 18
Primary Sources: Rulebook of 1869, TNA, FS 3/321/295; TNA, FS 4/42/295
Notes: Although a Working Men's club, it was registered under the Friendly Societies Act in 1869. It was a society for 'social intercourse, reading, refreshments and relaxation of working men'.

539.   Star of Hope Tent

Status: Female branch of an affiliated order **Type**: IORSU **Branch No.** 2835

Established: 1898 **Dissolved**: Post 1912
Headquarters: 7 Adelaide St [1905-1910]
Membership: 9 members in 1905, 10 in 1910

540. Summertown Benefit Society (1858), Summertown St John's Unity Benefit Society

Status: Registered, OXF 211   **Type:** Permanent friendly society
Established: 9 August 1858 **Registered:** 1858 **Dissolved:** 30 June 1899
Headquarters: Red Lion Inn, Summertown (1858-1859), Parochial (National) Schoolroom, Summertown (1859-1898)
Anniversary/feast day: Third Wednesday in July
Minimum age at entry: 15 Maximum age at entry: 40
Membership: 70 members in 1862, 72 in 1866, 86 in 1871, 98 in 1875, 109 in 1877, 109 in 1885, 89 in 1891, 58 in 1899
Primary Sources: Rulebooks of 1858 and 1890, TNA, FS 3/320/211; rulebook of 1858, Bodl. G.A. OXF 8° 1132(4)
Notes: The society was formed after a meeting on 9 August 1858, coinciding with the extension of St John's church. The landlord of the Red Lion, Richard Hicks, refused to hand over the box of the society. He had enlarged the public house at considerable expense to accommodate the club when it removed to the schoolroom but he was taken to court and ordered to return the box (see appendix 2, Crimes 125), (JOJ, 14 January 1860). The banner of the society contained the words, 'Unity is Strength' (JOJ, 26 June 1869). Charles Hawkins was a Trustee of the society and in 1895 was declared bankrupt. He owed £332 10s to the society for money he was holding on their behalf but had used for his own benefit (see appendix 2, Crimes 134), (JOJ, 2 November 1895). It was dissolved with 58 members and £574 18s 8d funds. (See also appendix 2, Crimes 131). The Registrar's file at TNA in relation to this society also includes papers relating to the earlier Summertown Friendly Society (Oxford 541) (TNA, FS 3/320/211).

541. Summertown Friendly Society

Status: Enrolled, OXF 14   **Type**: Permanent friendly society
Established: 1831   **Registered:** 28 October 1831 **Dissolved**: Last known 1831
Headquarters: King's Arms Inn, Summertown (1831)
Anniversary/feast day: Whit Monday
Minimum age at entry: 16 **Maximum age at entry**: 40
Primary Sources: Rulebook of 1831, TNA, FS 3/320/211

Notes: No separate file exists for this society in the records of the Registrar at TNA. However, a rulebook is retained in the file of the Summertown Benefit Society (Oxford 540). This was a society for men who were parishioners or inhabitants of Summertown, Godstow, Wolvercote, Wytham, Yarnton, Water Eaton, and Marston. The rules stated the annual feast should be held on Whit Monday or the day of consecration of the church then being built. The society probably ceased to exist in 1858 with the formation of the new club (Oxford 540).

Summertown St John's Unity Benefit Society – see Summertown Benefit Society, Oxford 540

542.   Temple of Friendship Lodge

Status: Branch of an affiliated order   **Type:** IOOFMU
Established: 1841 **Dissolved**: 1850
Headquarters: Wheatsheaf Inn, High Street (1841-1842), Prince Albert Hotel, Queen Street (1843-1847], White Hart Inn, Cornmarket [1850]
Membership: 19 members in 1841, 45 in 1843, 60 in 1846, 44 in 1850
Notes: Cheltenham District of IOOFMU. The society closed in 1850 by the division of lodge funds.

543.   Tradesmen's Society, also Oxford Tradesmen's Benefit Society and Society of Tradesmen and Artificers

Status: Enrolled, OXF 38   **Type:** Friendly society
Established: 11 May 1801   **Registered:** 2 April 1816   **Dissolved**: Last known 1843
Headquarters: Cross Keys, Queen St (1801-1843)
Anniversary/feast day: First Monday in July
Minimum age at entry: 15 **Maximum age at entry**: 35, reduced to 30 (1839)
Primary Sources: Rulebooks of 1834 and 1839, TNA, FS 3/319/38; TNA, FS 4/42/38; Oxon. Cal. QS iii, p.641
Notes: This was a society of tradesmen and artificers. Rules of 2 April 1816 were enrolled at the Easter Quarter Session 1816. Those excluded from membership included gentlemen, servants, labourers, soldiers, sailors, bailiffs, publicans, and those belonging to another benefit society. At the time of joining, members were required to reside in Oxford, the suburbs of Oxford or the parish of St Clements. The rules were last amended in 1843 and a returned letter from the Registrar dated 17 February 1867 stated it was believed the society had broken up (TNA, FS 4/42/38).

544.   Unanimous Society

Status: Unregistered   **Type**: Friendly society
Established: 14 June 1770 **Dissolved**: Last known 1809
Headquarters: Anchor Inn, St Peter-le-Bailey (1770-1806)
Anniversary/feast day: First Thursday in July
Maximum age at entry: 38
Primary Sources: Manuscript rules of 1770 and 1775, Bodl. G.A.OXF a.101(2-3); Printed rules of 1809, TNA, FS 3/320/165;
Notes: The society had a maximum of 101 members but the rule had been rescinded by 1809. Monthly fees of 1s 2d and 4d were for the 'house' as wet rent. Superannuation benefit of 4s was payable at age 65, and £10 on death. The rules were reprinted in 1775 with the right to superannuation removed. The rules of 1809 are found in the records of the Sociable Society (Oxford 536) at TNA under reference FS 3/320/165. It is probable this society merged or was taken over by the Sociable society after 1809 as the Unanimous Society was not enrolled and there was no other reason for its rules to be in TNA.

545.   Union Society of Oxford

Status: Enrolled, OXF 163   **Type**: Permanent friendly society
Established: 20 April 1758 **Registered:** 18 May 1825 **Dissolved**: Last known 1826
Headquarters: Wheatsheaf (1762), Cross Keys Inn, Old Butchers Row (1826)
Anniversary/feast day: Third Tuesday in June
Maximum age at entry: 35
Primary Sources: set of printed rules, undated, TNA, FS 1/579/163; TNA, FS 4/42/163; Oxon. Cal. QS iii, p.663
Notes: Rules of the society were revised on 13 November 1825 and approved at the Epiphany Quarter Session 1826 (Oxon. Cal. QS iii, p.663). A note in the calendar states no-one could be a member who had not had the small pox. One of 14 societies listed as in existence at Oxford in 1762 (JOJ, 22 May 1762).

Useful Benefit Society – see Useful Society, Oxford 546

546.   Useful Society, also Useful Benefit Society, also the Young Civis Society

Status: Unregistered   **Type**: Friendly society
Established: First known 1762 **Dissolved**: Last known 1834

Headquarters: Ben Serjeant's, near Brocado (1762), Lamb and Flag, St Thomas's [1830-1834]
Anniversary/feast day: Second Monday in July
Maximum age at entry: 36 (1834)
Primary Sources: Printed rules of 1834, Bodl. OXF 8° 900
Notes: A society for tradesmen and freemen with a maximum of 100 members. One of 14 societies listed as in existence at Oxford in 1762 (JOJ, 22 May 1762). Approximately 120 people attended the annual dinner in 1832 (JOJ, 4 August 1832).

547.   Working Women's Benefit Society

Status: Registered, OXF 351   **Type**: Female Permanent friendly society
Established: First known 1883   **Registered:** 1883   **Dissolved**: Post 1912
Headquarters: Wesleyan Lecture Room, 37 New Inn Hall St (1883-1899), 81 Southmoor Rd (1899-1902], 6 Lonsdale Rd (1905), 92 Walton St (1910)
Membership: 97 members in 1885, 110 in 1889, 125 in 1891, 157 in 1895, 149 in 1900
Notes: The Oxford Juvenile Society (Oxford 527) amalgamated with this society when it dissolved in 1899 (TNA, FS 4/42/379).

Young Civis Society – see Useful Society, Oxford 546

Young Freemen's Friendly Society – see Civis Society, Oxford 472

Piddington

No. of societies and members 1802/3 – None
No. of members of a friendly society 1813/14/15 – None
Notes: (See appendix 2, Crimes135 and 136).

548.   Piddington Division

Status: Branch of an affiliated order   **Type**: OSOT **Branch No.** 820
Established: First known 1905 **Dissolved**: Last known 1913
Headquarters: National School (1905-1913)

Piddington Friendly Institution - see Piddington Friendly Society, Piddington 549

549.   Piddington Friendly Society, also Piddington Friendly Institution

Status: Registered, OXF 248   **Type:** Permanent friendly society
Established: 1862   **Registered:** 10 December 1862 **Dissolved:** 14 August 1894
Headquarters: Seven Stars Inn (1862-1894)
Anniversary/feast day: First Tuesday in June
Minimum age at entry: 18 Maximum age at entry: 35
Membership: 39 members in 1865, 42 in 1874, 50 in 1876, 70 in 1878, 82 in 1881, 81 in 1885, 60 in 1891
Primary Sources: Rulebook of 1862, TNA, FS 3/321/248: TNA, FS 4/42/248
Notes: It was reported in 1874 that proceedings were less harmonious than normal and the Rev. C.E. Bagshaw, the chairman of the society, was not treated courteously. Some of the members wanted to divide a portion of the funds but this was not permitted by the registered rules (BH, 5 June 1874). Registration was cancelled by the Registrar in 1894 due to that society not complying with the requirement to provide a valuation of its assets (TNA, FS 3/321/248).

550.   Piddington Friendly Society

Status: Unregistered   **Type:** Friendly society
Established: First known 1897 **Dissolved:** Last known 1901
Headquarters: Seven Stars Inn (1897-1901)
Anniversary/feast day: First Tuesday in June
Notes: A dispute arose in 1897 concerning the carrying of the flag on club day. Frank Reynolds, a club member, engaged in a quarrel over who should carry the flag as his father had done so for many years (see appendix 2, Crimes 136).

Postcombe

No. of societies and members 1802/3 – None
No. of members of a friendly society 1813/14/15 – None

551.   Postcombe Friendly Benefit Society

Status: Unregistered   **Type:** Friendly society
Established: First known 1890 **Dissolved:** Last known 1901
Headquarters: New Inn (1890-1901)
Anniversary/feast day: Whit Monday, Whit Tuesday (1898)

Notes: On club day the society paraded the settlements of South Weston, Wheatfield, and Adwell as well as Postcombe. (JOJ, 7 June 1890 and HSOS, 10 June 1898).

Pyrton

No. of societies and members 1802/3 – 1, 45
No. of members of a friendly society 1813/14/15 – None
No friendly societies known.

Ramsden

No. of societies and members 1802/3 – 1, 43
No. of members of a friendly society 1813/14/15 – 50, 52, 54
Notes: On 23 June 1864 the vicar, R. Lowbridge Baker wrote to the Registrar, John Tidd Pratt. He had heard that the Registrar would be visiting nearby Leafield and wrote, 'I hope you will allow me the pleasure of meeting you, that I may have the benefit of your opinion with reference to the formation of a club in my parish' (TNA/FS 1/581/252).

552.   Cirencester Conservative Benefit Society, Ramsden Branch

Status: Branch of a registered society   **Type**: Permanent friendly society
Established: 1900 **Dissolved**: Last known 1900

553.   (Ramsden club)

Status: Unregistered   **Type**: Friendly society
Established: 1902 **Dissolved**: Last known 1902
Headquarters: Stag and Hounds Inn (1902)
Anniversary/feast day: Whit Wednesday
Notes: The 'revival of the old village club' was reported in *Jackson's Oxford Journal* on 24 May 1902.

554.   Ramsden Friendly Society

Status: Registered, OXF 41   **Type**: Friendly society
Established: 1837   **Registered:** 19 January 1841   **Dissolved**: Last known 1841
Headquarters: Mr B Sheppard's, Royal Oak (1841)
Anniversary/feast day: Whit Tuesday

Maximum age at entry: 45 years at formation, then 35
Primary Sources: Rulebook of 1841, TNA, FS 1/576/41;
Notes: A society for the industrious and productive among the labouring classes, namely labourers, mechanics and artisans not belonging to any other friendly society. A letter from Joseph Hicks, secretary, dated 20 October 1878 stated there was no society at Mr Shepherd's as he has been dead for several years (FS 4/42/41). It was dissolved by the Registrar that year. It is unclear when this society ceased to exist but was likely to have been before the vicar wrote to the Registrar in 1864 (TNA/FS 1/581/252).

555.   Ramsden Friendly Society

Status: Registered, OXF 273   **Type:** 5-year dividing friendly society
Established: 1866   **Registered:** 19 June 1866   **Dissolved:** 21 December 1895
Headquarters: Royal Oak Inn (1866-1895)
Anniversary/feast day: Whit Wednesday
Minimum age at entry: 15 Maximum age at entry: 40
Membership: 35 in 1872, 36 in 1875, 32 in 1880, 39 in 1885, 26 in 1891, 18 in 1895
Primary Sources: Rulebook of 1866, TNA, FS 3/321/273; TNA, FS 4/42/273
Notes: The society dissolved in 1895 with 18 members. Assets included, 'A tattered flag, twelve poles and a box worth 4/-' (TNA, FS 3/321/273).

556.   Ramsden Working Men's' Benefit Society

Status: Registered, OXF 354   **Type:** 5-year dividing friendly society
Established: 1885   **Registered:** 20 June 1885   **Dissolved:** 1 May 1897
Headquarters: Stag and Hounds Inn (1885-1897)
Anniversary/feast day: Whit Wednesday
Minimum age at entry: 16 Maximum age at entry: 45
Membership: 58 members in 1885, 75 in 1891, 13 in 1897
Primary Sources: Rulebook of 1885, TNA, FS 3/322/354; TNA, FS 4/42/354
Notes: The society dissolved with 13 members and £11 7s 7d funds. The flags, box, and other items were valued at £1 (TNA, FS 3/322/354).

Rotherfield Grays

No. of societies and members 1802/3 – None
No. of members of a friendly society 1813/14/15 – None

Notes: Club day was celebrated in Rotherfield Grays in 1866 but it is not known what friendly society it related to (see appendix 2, Crimes 138 and also Crimes 137).

Rotherfield Peppard

No. of societies and members 1802/3 – None
No. of members of a friendly society 1813/14/15 – None

557.   Peppard Union Society

Status: Registered, OXF 162   **Type**: Permanent friendly society
Established: 1823   **Registered:** 1824   **Dissolved**: Last known 1824
Headquarters: Dog Inn (1823)
Anniversary/feast day: Whit Tuesday
Maximum age at entry: under 45
Primary Sources: Rulebook of 1824, TNA, FS 1/579/162; further rulebook of 1824, TNA, FS 3/320/162; TNA, FS 4/42/162
Notes: The society paid for a member's funeral out its funds, and any excess up to the amount of benefit due was then paid to the widow or other beneficiary.

Salford

No. of societies and members 1802/3 – None
No. of members of a friendly society 1813/14/15 – None

558.   Salford Friendly Society

Status: Registered, number OXF 257   **Type:** Permanent friendly society
Established: 1864   **Registered:** 1864   **Dissolved:** 23 July 1928
Headquarters: Black Horse Inn (1864-1904), The Old Schoolroom in the vicarage (1904-1916), Council schoolroom (1916-1928)
Anniversary/feast day: Third Friday in July
Minimum age at entry: 16 Maximum age at entry: under 50
Membership: 55 members in 1876, 29 in 1878, 37 in 1885, 52 in 1899, 37 in 1905, 35 in 1910
Primary Sources: Rulebooks of 1864 and 1905, TNA, FS 15/571
Notes: The registration was cancelled in 1928 after a request to dissolve the society was received by the Registrar as funds were exhausted due to the sickness of older members. (See also appendix 2, Crimes 139).

Sandford on Thames

No. of societies and members 1802/3 – None
No. of members of a friendly society 1813/14/15 – 4, 0, 0
Notes: (See appendix 2, Crimes 140 and 141).

559.   Sandford Independent Heart and Hand Friendly Society, (and from 1886) Sandford Independent Life Society

Status: Registered, OXF 222   **Type:** 7-year dividing friendly society
Established: 14   September   1858   **Registered:**   13   September
1859   **Dissolved:** 11 March 1918
Headquarters: King's Arms Inn, Sandford Ferry (1858-1910]
Anniversary/feast day: First Monday in July, then third Friday in July
Minimum age at entry: 16, changed to 1 year in 1905 (17 to receive full
benefits) Maximum age at entry: 40
Membership: 37 members in 1860, 68 in 1865, 76 in 1870, 91 in 1875, 128
in 1880, 150 in 1885, 160 in 1899, 131 in 1905, 124 in 1910 and 80 in 1918
Primary Sources: Rulebook of 1858 and 1905, valuation, dissolution papers,
TNA, FS 15/568
Notes: The society continued to insure against sickness and death after its
change of name. Members wore oak apples in their button holes on club day.
It was accepted within the provisional national insurance scheme in 1913. The
society dissolved in 1918 with 80 members and £588 17s 1d assets that were
divided amongst the remaining members. (See also appendix 2, Crimes 142).

Shenington

No. of societies and members 1802/3 – None
No. of members of a friendly society 1813/14/15 – 4, 0, 0
Notes: (See appendix 2, Crimes 143, 144 and 146).

560.   Shenington Amicable Lodge

Status: Branch of an affiliated order   **Type**: IOOFMU **Branch No.** 8586
Established: 1912 **Dissolved**: Post 1918
Headquarters: Schoolroom [1914]
Anniversary/feast day: Trinity Monday
Notes: Banbury District of IOOFMU. It was formed from the Shenington
Amicable Society (Shenington 561).

561.   Shenington Amicable Society

Status: Registered, OXF 348   **Type**: Permanent friendly society
Established: 7 June 1841 **Dissolved**: 1912
Headquarters: Schoolroom [1876-1910]
Anniversary/feast day: Trinity Monday and Tuesday, Trinity Monday (after 1872), both days reinstated by 1878 and then just Trinity Monday by 1880
Maximum age at entry: 35
Membership: 52 members in 1857, 56 in 1858, 80 in 1866, 54 in 1872, 45 in 1874, 43 in 1876, 38 in 1884, 45 in 1890, 52 in 1899, 55 in 1905, 64 in 1910
Primary Sources: Manuscript rules of 1841, OHC, O129/A1; rulebooks of 1841, 1872 and 1885, OHC, Misc. Clifton 1/1-2; Banbury Savings Bank book for the society, 1872-1885, OHC, O129/F1; BPP 1874, XXIII, (c.997), p.119
Notes: A maximum of 121 members was permitted in the early years of the society. The Assistant Commissioner reported that in 1872 the society had never divided its funds. The club owned two cottages, described as very poor and with 'not an inch of garden'. They brought in about 1s a week although one was frequently empty. Members only paid 2s 6d towards the feasts, which did not cover the costs. A new parson arrived in 1868 and threatened to make members pay back money from the funds that had been put towards the feast as it was against the rules of registration. About nine members left the club because of it. Two or three gentlemen helped finance a feast in 1871 but they withdrew from the society because the labourers joined the Agricultural Labourers' Union. It was reported this action raised wages 2s or 3s a week. The new rules in 1872 noted that the annual feast had become a tea. The new secretary, a young shoemaker, stated that there were only eight members left plus four new ones that had just been admitted. He stated that of 61 members in 1872, and all except twelve were agricultural labourers (although this figure appears to include honorary members). Membership never again reached pre-dispute levels. The feast had previously been held on two days but has reduced to just one and was frequently held at the Rectory after this date. A new, unregistered society was formed in 1873 (Shenington 562). In 1877 there were eleven honorary members, compared to 43 benefit members (BG, 31 May 1877) and it remained at that high level until 1890 when five honorary members left (BG, 5 June 1890). The society became a branch of the IOOFMU in 1912 (Shenington 560). (See also appendix 2, Crimes 145).

562.   Shenington New Friendly Society

Status: Unregistered   **Type**: Friendly society

Established: 1873 **Dissolved**: Last known 1875
Headquarters: Bell Inn [1875)
Anniversary/feast day: Trinity Monday
Membership: 32 members in 1874
Notes: The society was formed at a time of change in the Shenington Amicable Society (Shenington 561). In 1874 the dinner was held on the village green (BG, 11 June 1874) and the following year it was said to provide more generous benefit to members than any other society in the neighbourhood (BG, 3 June 1875).

Shillingford – see Warborough

Shilton

No. of societies and members 1802/3 – None
No. of members of a friendly society 1813/14/15 – None
Notes: The village maintained a traditional club day feast until at least 1912. (See also appendix 2, Crimes 147).

563.   Shilton Mutual Benefit Society

Status: Unregistered   **Type**: 5-year year dividing friendly society
Established: 1878 **Dissolved**: Last known 1912
Headquarters: Rose and Crown [1894-1912)
Anniversary/feast day: Whit Tuesday
Membership: nearly 50 members in 1892, 39 in 1899, 50 in 1903, 55 in 1909

Shiplake

No. of societies and members 1802/3 – None
No. of members of a friendly society 1813/14/15 – None

564.   Court Pride of the Hill

Status: Branch of an affiliated order, OXF 286 **Type**: AOF **Branch No.** 5044
Established: 1867 **Dissolved**: Post 1918
Headquarters: Plough Inn (1868-post 1918)
Membership: 23 members in 1870, 33 in 1872, 46 in 1874, 60 in 1876, 87 in 1880, 102 in 1885, 107 in 1890, 114 in 1895, 127 in 1900, 109 in 1905, 101 in 1910

Notes: London United District of AOF (1867-post 1918).

565.   Shiplake Friendly [Provident] Society

Status: Unregistered   **Type:** Friendly society
Established: First known 1877 **Dissolved:** Last known 1878
Headquarters: White Hart Inn (1877-1878)
Anniversary/feast day: Whit Monday
Notes: The society held its anniversary dinner in a tent near Miss Allum's house and at the White Hart (HA, 26 May 1877).

Shipton under Wychwood

No. of societies and members 1802/3 – 1, 80
No. of members of a friendly society 1813/14/15 – 100, 100, 100

566.   Loyal Wychwood Forest Lodge

Status: Branch of an affiliated order   **Type:** IOOFMU **Branch No.** 6221
Established: 6 March 1877 **Dissolved:** 1968
Headquarters: Red Horse Inn (1877-1912)
Anniversary/feast day: Whit Wednesday
Membership: 28 members in 1877, 44 in 1879, 54 in 1881, 66 in 1886, 82 in 1892, 84 in 1901, 89 in 1905, 103 in 1910, 104 in 1913
Notes: Banbury District of IOOFMU. The first anniversary fete was held in 1878 at Shipton Court and 1,200 people attended who paid for admission (JOJ, 10 August 1878). In 1881 additional Great Western Railway trains stopped at Shipton station to facilitate those attending, by which time attendance had risen to 1,700 people paying 6d entry (JOJ, 13 August 1881 and CNDM, September 1881). It amalgamated with the Old Elm Tree Lodge, Chipping Norton (Chipping Norton 198) in 1968.

567.   Loyal Wychwood Forest Lodge, Juvenile Branch

Status: Juvenile branch of an affiliated order, OXF 365   **Type:** IOOFMU
Established: 1889 **Dissolved:** Post 1910
Headquarters: National Schoolroom (1889-1910)
Membership: 7 in 1899, 2 in 1910
Notes: The juvenile branch of Shipton under Wychwood 566.

568. Milton, Shipton and Ascott United Provident Society

Status: Unregistered   **Type:** Friendly society
Established: 1863 **Dissolved:** Last known 1899
Headquarters: Baptist Chapel, Shipton under Wychwood (1899)
Anniversary/feast day: February
Membership: Over 100 in 1899
Notes: A non-denominational society established so members did not have to pay 'wet rent' or be tempted to buy alcohol (JOJ, 4 February 1899). It was reported to have Baptist, Methodist (Wesleyan and Primitive), Anglican, and Roman Catholic members.

569. Red Horse Friendly Society, then Shipton-under-Wychwood Friendly Society also Shipton Old Club

Status: Registered, OXF 18   **Type:** Permanent friendly society
Established: 1811   **Registered:** 22 May 1838   **Dissolved:** 1874
Headquarters: Red Horse (1811), Crown Inn (1838-1860)
Anniversary/feast day: Whit Wednesday
Maximum age at entry: 35
Membership: 46 members in 1811, 43 in 1815, 39 in 1820, 48 in 1826, 25 in 1830, 49 in 1837, 58 in 1843, 54 in 1846, 29 in 1872
Primary Sources: Rulebooks of 1812 and 1838, list of members at division 1860, TNA, FS 1/574/18; TNA, FS 4/42/18; membership book, account of division of funds 1874, list of members fees for club day 1871, invoice of provisions for club day 1870 and 1871, disbursement of club funds on dissolution 1874 and statement of account, OHC PAR/236/13/A7/1-5
Notes: There was a division of assets of £568 15s 8d on 5 September 1860 between 65 members, including David Porter, a butcher and founder member (TNA, FS 1/574/18). The society continued under the same registration number and formally dissolved in 1874 with 29 members and £633 13s 9½d assets. (See also appendix 2, Crimes 148).

570. Shipton Female Benefit Society

Status: Unregistered   **Type:** 5-year year dividing friendly society, annual dividing friendly society by 1881
Established: 1860 **Dissolved:** Last known 1902
Headquarters: Lamb Inn (1859-1863], National Schoolroom (1870-1878], Beaconsfield Hall (1889-1901]

Anniversary/feast day: Whit Wednesday, then last Thursday in July (from 1890)
Membership: 23 members in 1890, 25 in 1891
Notes: The society was one of only five independent all-female societies in Oxfordshire. It followed the usual pattern of celebration on club day with a parade, church service and dinner followed by entertainment, including archery, dancing and music (JOJ, 8 August 1863). It was described as being a club for 'young married women' (CNDM, June 1881). Payments were 2s 6d per quarter, providing benefit of 4s a week during sickness. In 1881, two stewards and members of the club identified in the *Chipping Norton Deanery Magazine* were Sarah Hart, aged 61, the wife of a farm labourer, and Harriet Davis, a gloveress, and also the wife of a farm labourer (CNDM July 1881). The date of the club day was changed in 1890 as previously it had clashed with the Oddfellows fete (JOJ, 10 August 1889). A plea for more members was made in 1902 (CNDM, September 1902).

571.   **Shipton Friendly Society also Shipton Old Friendly Society**

Status: Registered, OXF 390   **Type:** Friendly society
Established: First known 1902   **Registered:** 31 July 1902   **Dissolved:** 14 March 1913
Headquarters: Crown Inn (1902-1913)
Anniversary/feast day: Whit Wednesday
Minimum age at entry: 12 Maximum age at entry: 40
Membership: 59 members in 1905, 38 in 1910 and 33 in 1913
Primary Sources: Rulebook of 1902, TNA, FS 3/322/390; TNA, FS 4/42/390
Notes: The society was initially an unregistered club and claimed to be 40 years old in 1902 (CNDM, June 1902). That year, rumours surfaced of the club's insolvency and that it was 'on its last legs' (JOJ, 24 May 1902). A meeting was called and it was agreed to amend the rules and register the club immediately. An application to register was made on 22 July. There is no record of this society prior to 1902 and it dissolved in 1913 with 33 members and £104 5s 2d funds. It is possible the society was founded after the dissolution of the Shipton under Wychwood Friendly Society (Shipton 569).

Shipton Old Club - see Red Horse Friendly Society, Shipton 569

Shipton Old Friendly Society - see Shipton Friendly Society, Shipton 571

Shipton-under-Wychwood Friendly Society - see Red Horse
Friendly Society, Shipton 569

Shutford

No. of societies and members 1802/3 – None
No. of members of a friendly society 1813/14/15 – None
Notes: The village feast declined in 1898 when the Shutford Friendly Society
replaced the club dinner and band with a tea.

572.   Court King George

Status: Branch of an affiliated order   **Type**: AOF **Branch No.** 9583
Established: 1912   **Dissolved**: Post 1918
Headquarters: Band Room, West Street (1912)
Membership: 45 members in 1912
Notes: Banbury district of AOF.

573.   Shutford Friendly Society

Status: Enrolled, OXF 116   **Type:** Permanent friendly society
Established: 1852   **Registered:** 20 August 1852   **Dissolved:** 1862
Headquarters: House of William Coles (1852)
Anniversary/feast day: First Friday in June
Minimum age at entry: 14 Maximum age at entry: 35
Membership: 13 members in 1862
Primary Sources: Rulebook of 1852, TNA, FS 1/578/116; TNA, FS 4/42/116
Notes: A letter of 20 October 1865 from William Coles stated the society
became very weak in 1862 and was unable to support sickness benefit
payments. It was broken up in 1862, and at dissolution had 13 members and £7
16s (TNA, FS 1/578/116).

574.   Shutford Friendly Society

Status: Registered, OXF 268   **Type**: Friendly society
Established: 1864   **Registered:** 1866   **Dissolved**: Last known 1914
Headquarters: The dwelling house of Mr William Coles [1866-1910],
Foresters Hall (1914)
Anniversary/feast day: First Friday in June
Membership: 23 members in 1866, 30 in 1872, 41 in 1874, 43 in 1878, 44 in
1885, 39 in 1891, 23 in 1896, 20 in 1899, 23 in 1910, 49 in 1914

Primary Sources: BPP 1874, XXIII, (c.997), p.118
Notes: The Assistant Commissioner reported that in 1872 the society met at the house of the secretary, Mr Coles, a grocer and gardener. Local farmers made honorary subscriptions but no longer made a contribution of meat to the feast as they had done. It was independent of any public house but was not a temperance club. In 1884 the Rev. James Geraghty refused to preach at the club day service (BG, 2 June 1884). A meeting of the society was held and the committee decided to attend the Wesleyan chapel for divine service as they did for following years. A significant change took place in 1896 when the club day dinner was replaced by a tea and the vicar, the Rev. F.C. Chambers, became president and chair of the society (DDM, July 1896). The usual shows and entertainment were also abandoned and village club day was much quieter. Membership of the society also decreased. No file in relation to this society can be located in the Registrar's papers at TNA.

575.   Shutford Provident Institution and Friendly Society

Status: Enrolled, OXF 37   **Type**: Permanent friendly society
Established: First known 1834   **Registered:** 7 October 1834   **Dissolved**: Last known 1834
Headquarters: George and Dragon (1834-1834)
Primary Sources: TNA, FS 4/42/37; BPP 1874, XXIII, (c.997), p.118
Notes: No file exists in TNA under reference FS 1/575/37 although it is indicated in the index. A letter of 5 October 1878 stated the club broke up ''ears ago' (TNA, FS 4/42/37). The Assistant Commissioner reported in 1872 that the society 'broke-up long ago'.

Sibford Gower

No. of societies and members 1802/3 – None
No. of members of a friendly society 1813/14/15 – 5, 5, 5
Notes: Club day was still attracting 'a substantial crowd from neighbouring villages' in 1914 (BG, 4 June 1914).

576.   Sibford Benefit Friendly Society then from 1890 Sibford Gower Friendly Society

Status: Registered, OXF 201   **Type:** Permanent friendly society
Established: 1857   **Registered:** 1858   **Dissolved:** 30 June 1944
Headquarters: Endowed School (1858-1912), Council school (1912-1944)
Anniversary/feast day: First Monday in June

Minimum age at entry: 16 Maximum age at entry: 40 until membership exceeded thirty, then the maximum was 35, from 1890 it was 40
Membership: 88 members in 1860, 91 in 1862, 99 in 1865, 112 in 1870, 109 in 1874, 124 in 1875, 125 in 1879, 133 in 1885, 90 in 1891, 82 in 1895, 80 in 1900, 69 in 1905, 75 in 1910, 105 in 1911
Primary Sources: Rulebook of 1858 and 1915, TNA, FS 15/1830; BPP 1874, XXIII, (c.997), p.117
Notes: This society was a continuation of Sibford Friendly Society (Sibford Gower 578), claiming the same date of establishment of 1839 but with substantial new rules in 1857. Membership was open to men and women. The Assistant Commissioner reported that the society had always met at the schoolroom except for a short period when it was unavailable, when they met at a beer-house. Most of the 109 members were agricultural labourers in 1872. In March 1877 a dispute arose at the club when many members wanted to use club plates, knives, etc. for an Agricultural Labourers' Union dinner when Joseph Arch was due to attend. The Trustees and most of the honorary members who were farmers objected (unpublished diary of the Rev. Edward T. Stevens, vicar of Sibford from 1874 to 1898, held by Sibfords History Society). No farmers attended the club day in 1877 and they withdrew from the society in protest at the action of some of the Union members of the club. There was some drunkenness and fighting and Stevens told the officers of the club that unless they made rules to prevent drunkenness and disorder at the dinner the following year he would refuse them the use of the school room. On 2 December 1878, the tee-total members of the society proposed the abolition of wet rent payments. The motion was narrowly defeated and the abstainers took their beer and poured it onto the road. After this time, the Rev. Stevens entertained members at the Vicarage and parades through the village gradually died out.

In 1879, all members 'belonged' to Sibford or Swalcliffe (BG, 12 June 1879). The name of society changed in 1890 at the time of introduction of a new set of rules (BG, 29 May 1890). There were 26 honorary members in 1891 and they continued at that number into the twentieth century. In 1911, Mr Frank Lascelles, master of the Empire Pageant at Crystal Palace, presented a new banner to the society (BG, 8 June 1911). Lascelles, whose real name was Frank William Thomas Charles Stevens, was the third son of the Reverend Edward Stevens. The banner is on display at Holy Trinity Church, Sibford Gower. It has a painted picture of a knight in armour with a red heart on his chest, sword in hand and a woman in front of him. The words, 'The Greatest of these is Charity' and 'Sibford Friendly Society' appear at the top and bottom respectively. It has a dark blue, velvet background with ornate gold edging to the picture. Cotton material roses in pink, or possibly faded red, mounted on card, frame the picture. It is backed with cotton. A further banner with a cotton back and white-colour-washed linen front displays the heading 'Sibford Friendly Society' and '1839-1920'. Lettering is in black, red, and gold and the body of the banner reads, 'I shall pass this way but once, if there is any good deed I can do before I go, any kind word I can speak, any joy I can give, or any weaker brother I can help, let me do it now, For I shall not pass this way again'. (The saying is largely attributed to Stephen Grellet [1773-1855], a prominent Quaker, but it is has a disputed provenance). The society was provisionally registered under the National Insurance Act 1911. The society dissolved in 1944 with 16 members and £260 6s 8d funds.

577.　Sibford Benefit Friendly Society, Juvenile Branch

Status: Juvenile branch of a registered society　**Type**: Juvenile friendly society
Established: 5 June 1893　**Dissolved**: Last known 1901
Membership: 16 members in 1894, 18 in 1896, 12 in 1901

578.　Sibford Friendly Society

Status: Enrolled, OXF 86　**Type**: Permanent friendly society
Established: 3 June 1839　**Registered:** 21 June 1843　**Dissolved:** 1857
Headquarters: Alternately at Bishop's Blaize Inn, Burdrop and Wickham Arms Inn, Sibford Gower (1839)
Anniversary/feast day: First Monday in June
Minimum age at entry: 15 Maximum age at entry: 40 until membership exceeded 30, then the maximum was 35
Membership: 27 members in 1846, 28 in 1848, 25 in 1850, 37 in 1855
Primary Sources: Rulebook of 1839, TNA, FS 3/319/86; TNA, FS 4/42/86
Notes: It appears this society submitted new rules in 1857, approved in 1858 and the Registrar allocated a new number of OXF 201 during the early days of the Registry (see Sibford Gower 576).

> **Sibford Gower Friendly Society** – see Sibford Benefit Friendly Society, Sibford Gower 576

579.　Sibford New Friendly Society

Status: Registered, OXF 271　**Type**: Permanent friendly society
Established: 1866　**Registered:** 27 April 1866　**Dissolved**: 1869
Headquarters: Bishop Blaize Inn (1866-1869)

Anniversary/feast day: First Monday in June
Minimum age at entry: 12 **Maximum age at entry**: 35
Primary Sources: Rulebook of 1866, TNA, FS 1/582/271; TNA, FS 4/42/271
Notes: A letter dated 21 June 1869 to the Registrar stated, 'The paucity of members and the continual sickness of some rendered it impossible to make headway' and the society had ceased to exist (TNA, FS 1/582/271).

Somerton

No. of societies and members 1802/3 – None
No. of members of a friendly society 1813/14/15 – None

580.   Jersey Lodge

Status: Branch of an affiliated order   **Type**: IOOFMU **Branch No.** 8666
Established: 1912   **Dissolved**: Post 1918
Headquarters: Schoolroom (1912)
Notes: The society was named after 7th Earl of Jersey.

581.   Somerton Friendly and Benefit Society

Status: Registered, OXF 245   **Type:** Permanent friendly society
Established: 1863   **Registered:** January 1863   **Dissolved:** Last known 1914
Headquarters: Schoolroom (1863-1889], Railway Tavern (1892), Schoolroom [1899-1914)
Anniversary/feast day: Various days including first Tuesday in June, last Tuesday in July, and Whit Monday
Minimum age at entry: 14 Maximum age at entry: 50 (1873), then 35 (from 1884)
Membership: 37 members in 1866, 116 in 1871, 196 in 1874, 250 in 1877, 310 in 1878, 280 in 1880, 193 in 1885, 192 in 1894, 186 in 1902, 174 in 1905, 152 in 1910
Primary Sources: Rulebooks of 1873, 1884 and 1892, OHC COS, SOME 334.7; rulebook of 1873, Bodl. G.A. OXF 8° 1300; rulebook of 1892, Bodl. 24786 e.11(23)
Notes: The society was established in 1862 by Rev. William Price (BicA, 20 May 1892). It was a society for men and women of Somerton and adjacent parishes, or residing in a 'reasonable distance' of Somerton. Female members were admitted for medical attendance and death benefit only. Mechanics and servants as well as labourers were admitted. The rules permitted the appointment of local agents. The anniversary could be held in any of the parishes from

which members were drawn. The rulebook of 1884 listed the places and hours for receipt of the monthly contributions, namely Upper Heyford (1st Monday), Somerton (1st Monday), North Aston (1st Monday), Fritwell (1st Tuesday), Caulcott (1st Wednesday), Lower Heyford (1st Wednesday), Deddington (1st Thursday), Middleton Stoney (1st Friday), and Steeple Aston (1st Saturday). A proposal was made in 1894 not to hold the annual feast in the future but this was defeated by 22 votes to 19 (BicA, 1 June 1894). No file exists in TNA for this society. A medal commemorating the institution of the society in 1863 depicts a bee-skep and bees, symbolizing community and collaborative industry, with a pair of clasped right hands below, representing mutual help, responsibility and reciprocity (Victoria Solt Dennis, *Discovering Friendly and Fraternal Societies: Their badges and regalia* [Oxford 2005], p.53). Around the edge is inscribed 'Let everyone of you lay by him in store' and 'Bear ye one another's burdens' (I Corinthians 16:2 and Galatians 6:2), (OXCMS : 1989.83.2). (See also appendix 2, Crimes 149.)

582.   Somerton Friendly Society

Status: Registered, OXF 131   **Type:** 5-year dividing friendly society
Established: 1855   **Registered:** 29 December 1855   **Dissolved:** 13 May 1873
Headquarters: Railway Tavern Inn (1855-1873)
Anniversary/feast day: First Tuesday in June
Minimum age at entry: 15 Maximum age at entry: 35
Membership: 72 members in 1862, 82 in 1866, 85 in 1872, 79 in 1873,
Primary Sources: Rulebook of 1855, TNA, FS 1/579/131; TNA, FS 4/42/131; rulebooks of 1855, belonging to James Andrews (dated 2 May 1859), and 1872, Bodl. G.A. OXF 8° 1297
Notes: There was division of surplus funds every five years (JOJ, 27 March 1867). The society dissolved in 1873 with 79 members. There were 136 votes for and 18 against dissolution (TNA, FS 1/579/131).

Souldern

No. of societies and members 1802/3 – None
No. of members of a friendly society 1813/14/15 – None

583.   Souldern Friendly Society

Status: Enrolled, OXF 77   **Type:** Permanent friendly society
Established: 6 June 1816 **Registered:** 1816   **Dissolved:** 1875

Headquarters: Bull's Head Inn (1816-1875)
Anniversary/feast day: 29 May
Minimum age at entry: 10 Maximum age at entry: 35, 31 (from 1864)
Membership: 41 members in 1846, 36 in 1850
Primary Sources: Rules of 1816, OHC, QSD/R/29; member's rulebook of 1843 and 1864 in the name of William Finch, Bodl. G.A. 8° 1302; TNA, FS 4/42/77;
Notes: Initially there was a maximum of 121 members. Excluded occupations included merchants of the East India Company. In 1844, Mr Gee of Aynho, the medical attendant was presented with a silver snuff box for his service to the society (JOJ, 1 June 1844). In 1875, the Registrar refused to sanction a division of funds by the society. A new vote was taken and dissolution was agreed by five-sixths of the society. Each member received £3 13s and £1 per member was left in the fund for the new society (BG, 8 June 1876). A letter to the Registrar dated 3 March 1894 stated the society ceased to exist in 1875 (TNA, FS 4/42/77). It explained a fresh society, also called Souldern Friendly Society (Souldern 584) was formed in 1876 but had never been registered. On 29 December 1896 the Registrar gave a warning notice of dissolution which activated on 24 March 1897 (FS 3/319/77), although the society had ceased to exist many years earlier. (See also appendix 2, Crimes 150 and 151).

584.　Souldern Friendly Society

Status: Unregistered　**Type:** 5-year dividing friendly society
Established: 1875 **Dissolved:** Last known 1911
Headquarters: Bull's Head (1875-1880), National School (1880-1911]
Anniversary/feast day: 29 May
Minimum age at entry: 14 Maximum age at entry: 50, 35 (from 1881)
Membership: 62 members in 1876, 66 in 1879, 84 in 1881,
Primary Sources: Rulebooks of 1876 and 1881, Bodl. G.A. 8° 1302; TNA/ FS 4/42/77;
Notes: A letter to the Registrar dated 3 March 1894 stated that this unregistered society commenced in 1875 (TNA/FS 4/42/77). The Registrar refused to sanction the rule on division of funds of the old society (Souldern 583) (BG, 8 June 1876) and the club made a fresh start in 1875, becoming a five-year dividing society (JOJ, 3 June 1881). This is confirmed in the rules of 1876 which stated it was established that year from the surviving members of the one founded in 1816. On division, £1 per member was retained in the funds. However, any member of the old society who had drawn more than two years sick pay was excluded from the new society (Bodl. G.A. 8° 1302). The club was described as being managed by the 'working men of the village' (BG, 2

June 1881). In 1884 the old banner of 1816 was worn out and anew one was needed (BicA, 6 June 1884). (See also appendix 2, Crimes 152 and 153).

585.   Souldern United Division

Status: Branch of an affiliated order   **Type**: OSOT **Branch No.** 865
Established: First known 1911 **Dissolved**: Last known 1913
Headquarters: Wesleyan school room (1911-1913)

South Stoke

No. of societies and members 1802/3 – None
No. of members of a friendly society 1813/14/15 – None

586.   South Stoke Mutual Benefit Society

Status: Enrolled, OXF 75   **Type**: Annual dividing friendly society
Established: 1841   **Registered:** 10 February 1842 **Dissolved**: Last known 1842
Headquarters: Cross Keys Inn (1841-1842)
Anniversary/feast day: Whit Thursday
Minimum age at entry: 15 **Maximum age at entry**: 40
Primary Sources: Rulebook of 1841, TNA, FS 1/577/75; TNA, FS 4/42/75
Notes: The landlord was required to provide fire, ink and pens on club nights. Members were not permitted by the club rules to leave home by more than one mile (church or society meeting excluded) when claiming sick benefit. No honorary members were permitted to attend meetings except on the annual club day.

Spelsbury

No. of societies and members 1802/3 – 1, 47
No. of members of a friendly society 1813/14/15 – 66, 61, 60

587.   Spelsbury Friendly Society

Status: Enrolled **Type**: Permanent friendly society
Established: 31 May 1779 **Registered:** 1794 **Dissolved**: Last known 1794
Headquarters: Chequers Inn (1779-1794)
Anniversary/feast day: Ascension Day
Primary Sources: Manuscript rules of 1794, OA, QSD/R/30

Notes: A maximum 101 members was permitted.

Stadhampton

No. of societies and members 1802/3 – None
No. of members of a friendly society 1813/14/15 – None

588.   Brookhampton Benefit Society

Status: Enrolled, OXF 5 **Type**: Friendly society
Established: First known 1830 **Registered:** 12 July 1830 **Dissolved**: Last known 1830
Headquarters: The Bear and Ragged Staff Inn, Brookhampton (1830)
Primary Sources: TNA, FS 4/42/5
Notes: No file exists for this society in TNA.

589.   Brookhampton Hand and Heart Friendly Society

Status: Enrolled, OXF 89 **Type:** Dividing friendly society
Established: 1 January 1846 **Registered:** 1846 **Dissolved:** 31 December 1920
Headquarters: Bear and Ragged Staff Inn, Brookhampton (1846-55], Mr J Payne's [1876-1880], Bear (and Ragged Staff) Inn [1885-1911]
Anniversary/feast day: Whit Tuesday
Minimum age at entry: 15, 16 (from 1890) Maximum age at entry: 45, 40 (from 1890)
Membership: 84 members in 1872, 97 in 1877, 105 in 1880, 87 in 1885, 53 in 1891, 64 in 1899, 63 in 1902, 33 in 1905, 28 in 1910, 23 in 1913, 15 in 1920
Primary Sources: Rulebooks of 1846 and 1890, TNA, FS 15/562
Notes: On club day the society attended Newington church and paraded Brookhampton, Chiselhampton, and Stadhampton (SON, 30 May 1891 and TG, 2 June 1891). The club feast was abandoned in 1903, having once been one of the largest in the area, it was then much smaller (JOJ, 6 June 1903). In 1906 the juvenile branch (Stadhampton 590) amalgamated with the main club. The society entered provisional scheme under National Insurance Act 1911. It dissolved in 1920 with 15 members and £139 13s 4½d funds. (See also appendix 2, Crimes 154).

590.   Brookhampton Hand and Heart Juvenile Friendly Society

Status: Juvenile branch of a registered society, OXF 376 **Type:** Juvenile friendly society

Established: 1891 **Registered:** 8 April 1892   **Dissolved:** 17 December 1906
Headquarters: Bear and Ragged Staff Inn, Brookhampton (1892-1906)
Anniversary/feast day: First Monday in June
Minimum age at entry: 6 Maximum age at entry: 16
Membership: 5 members in 1899
Primary Sources: Rulebook of 1891, TNA, FS 3/322/376; TNA, FS 4/42/376
Notes: The juvenile branch of Stadhampton 589. Registration was cancelled in 1906 on amalgamation with its parent society.

591.   **Court Hampton**

Status: Branch of an affiliated order **Type**: AOF **Branch No.** 6697
Established: 1880 **Dissolved**: Post 1918
Headquarters: Crown Inn (1880-post 1918)
Anniversary/feast day: First Monday in June, Whit Monday (from 1893)
Membership: 19 members in 1880, 38 in 1885, 56 in 1890, 78 in 1893, 100 in 1900, 128 in 1905, 148 in 1910
Notes: London United District of AOF. Twenty-two new members joined in 1893 (HSOS, 26 May 1893). The Court had a juvenile branch (Stadhampton 592).

592.   **Court Hampton, Juvenile Branch**

Status: Juvenile branch of an affiliated order **Type**: AOF
Established: 1886 **Dissolved**: Last known 1900
Headquarters: The Crown (1886-1900]
Membership: 16 members in 1886, 20 in 1895, 25 in 1900
Notes: Juvenile branch of Court Hampton (Stadhampton 591).

593.   **Stadhampton Associated Providential Benefit Society**

Status: Enrolled, OXF 4 **Type**: Permanent friendly society
Established: First known 1830 **Registered:** 12 July 1830 **Dissolved**: Last known 1831
Headquarters: Crown Inn (1830-1831)
Anniversary/feast day: Whit Thursday
Maximum age at entry: 35
Primary Sources: rulebook of 1830, TNA, FS 1/574/4; TNA, FS 4/42/4
Notes: A notice was placed in the *Jackson's Oxford Journal* on 21 May 1831 stating that it had been 'wilfully reported by evil-disposed persons that the

Stadhampton club was broken up'. It corrects that rumour and gives notice of the club feast on the following Whit Thursday at the Crown Inn.

Standlake

No. of societies and members 1802/3 – 2, 163
No. of members of a friendly society 1813/14/15 – None
Notes: (See appendix 2, Crimes 155).

594.   Court Star of Standlake

Status: Branch of an affiliated order **Type**: AOF **Branch No.** 8039
Established: 1892 **Dissolved**: Post 1918
Headquarters: Black Horse Inn (1892-post 1918)
Membership: 25 members in 1894, 30 in 1900, 32 in 1905, 39 in 1910
Notes: Oxford District of AOF. Club day was 'revived' on Whit Wednesday by the branch and Loyal Harcourt Lodge of IOOFMU (Standlake 595) in 1908 (JOJ, 23 May 1908). A banner for this court is housed by the Oxfordshire Museum service (OXCMS, 1974.78.1). It is double-sided with a yellow border, one side of two Foresters flanking a central roundel with a Good Samaritan scene. The reverse comprises a central cartouche with angels.

595.   Loyal Harcourt Lodge

Status: Branch of an affiliated order **Type**: IOOFMU **Branch No.** 7158
Established: 1892 **Dissolved**: Post 1918
Headquarters: Bell Inn (1892-post 1918)
Membership: 29 members in 1894, 32 in 1897, 43 in 1901, 53 in 1905, 46 in 1910, 42 in 1914
Notes: Oxford District of IOOFMU.

596.   Loyal Harcourt Lodge, Juvenile Branch

Status: Juvenile branch of an affiliated order **Type**: IOOFMU
Established: 1893 **Dissolved**: Post 1914
Notes: Juvenile branch of Standlake 595.

597.   Standlake Benefit Society

Status: Enrolled, OXF 176 **Type**: Permanent friendly society
Established: 24 January 1761 **Dissolved**: Last known 1866

Headquarters: Bell Inn (1761-1866]
Anniversary/feast day: Year end
Minimum age at entry: 18 **Maximum age at entry**: 41
Primary Sources: Manuscript rules of 1761, TNA, FS 1/582/275; FS 4/42/176; undated rules, OHC, O 117/X/1
Notes: No file for this society exists in the Registrar's records at TNA. The rules of 1761 were misfiled in the Registrar's papers under OXF 275, Standlake Friendly Society (Standlake 600). This indicates continuity of the two societies and this society had probably ceased to exist in 1866 when the new one at the Bell Inn commenced. Rules permitted a maximum of 101 members.

598.   Standlake Friendly Society

Status: Enrolled, OXF 13 **Type**: Friendly society
Established: 1795 **Registered:** 1824   **Dissolved**: Last known 1831
Headquarters: Black Horse Inn [1831)
Maximum age at entry: 41
Primary Sources: Rulebook of 1831, TNA, FS 1/574/13; FS 4/42/13
Notes: The society was open to all labourers, servants, mechanics, manufacturers, tradesmen, and other industrious classes. Members had to reside in Standlake or within two miles on admission.

599.   Standlake Friendly Society

Status: Enrolled, OXF 48 **Type**: Permanent friendly society
Established: 1837 **Registered:** 21 May 1840   **Dissolved**: Last known 1840
Headquarters: The Golden Balls (1837-1840)
Anniversary/feast day: Whit Wednesday
Minimum age at entry: 14 **Maximum age at entry**: 35
Primary Sources: Rulebook of 1840, TNA, FS 1/576/48; TNA, FS 4/42/48

600.   Standlake Friendly Society

Status: Registered, OXF 275 **Type**: 7-year dividing friendly society
Established: 1866 **Registered:** 3 October 1866   **Dissolved**: 1882
Headquarters: Bell Inn (1866-1880]
Anniversary/feast day: Whit Wednesday
Primary Sources: Rulebook of 1866, TNA, FS 1/582/275; TNA, FS 4/42/275
Notes: New members were admitted up to Whit Wednesday 1868. A misfiled letter under reference TNA, FS 4/42/176 (Standlake 596) to the Registrar, dated 13 January 1882 stated this society had ceased to exist. A further letter

was returned to the Registrar dated 9 January 1883 stating no such society existed.

Stanton Harcourt

No. of societies and members 1802/3 – None
No. of members of a friendly society 1813/14/15 – None
Notes: A meeting was held at the Harcourt Arms on Monday 11 June 1860 with a view to forming a permanent friendly society due to the preponderance of seven-year dividing societies in the towns and villages (JOJ, 16 June 1860). There is no indication a society was established.

601.   Court Welcome

Status: Branch of an affiliated order **Type**: AOF **Branch No.** 6686
Established: 1880 **Dissolved**: Post 19187
Headquarters: Fox Inn (1880-post 1918)
Anniversary/feast day: Whit Thursday
Membership: 33 members in 1880, 37 in 1881, 57 in 1885, 67 in 1886, 86 in 1890, 117 in 1895, 117 in 1900, 133 in 1905, 141 in 1910
Notes: Banbury District of AOF.

602.   Fox Inn Savings Club

Status: Unregistered   **Type**: 5-year dividing friendly society
Established: First known 1899 **Dissolved**: Last known 1899
Headquarters: Fox Inn (1899)
Membership: 32 members in 1899

603.   Fox Friendly Society

Status: Registered, OXF 229 **Type**: 5-year dividing friendly society
Established: 1860 **Registered:** 11 August 1860 **Dissolved**: 1870
Headquarters: Fox Inn (1860-1870)
Anniversary/feast day: Whit Monday
Membership: 47 in 1862, 81 in 1865
Primary Sources: Rulebook of 1865, TNA, FS 1/581/229; TNA, FS 4/42/229
Notes: New members were admitted until Whit Monday of the second year of the society. It was dissolved on Whit Monday 1870 after two divisions, with £342 2s 8d funds. The 1865 rules required the society to dissolve after that

five-year cycle. A new society was formed on dissolution (Stanton Harcourt 604).

604. Fox Friendly Society

Status: Registered, OXF 305 **Type**: 5-year dividing friendly society
Established: 1870 **Registered:** 20 July 1870 **Dissolved**: 17 May 1880
Headquarters: Fox Inn (1870-1880)
Anniversary/feast day: Whit Monday
Membership: 100 in 1871, 110 in 1872, 104 in 1878
Primary Sources: Rulebook of 1870, TNA, FS 1/582/305; TNA, FS 4/42/305
Notes: The society was formed on the dissolution of the Fox Friendly Society (Stanton Harcourt 603). New members were admitted until Whit Monday of the second year of the society. There were no age limits at time of entry. A letter dated 11 March 1881 to the Registrar from Mark Burden, secretary of a new Fox Friendly Society (Stanton Harcourt 605), stated the society dissolved Whit Monday 1880 and a new unregistered club commenced at the same time (Stanton Harcourt 605), (TNA, FS 4/42/305).

605. Fox Friendly Society

Status: Unregistered   **Type**: 5-year dividing friendly society
Established: 17 May 1880 **Dissolved**: Last known 1880
Headquarters: Fox Inn (1880)
Notes: A letter dated 11 March 1881 to the Registrar from Mark Burden, secretary of this society, stated the registered club (Stanton Harcourt 604) was dissolved on Whit Monday 1880 and this new, unregistered club commenced at the same time (TNA, FS 4/42/305). This club may be the same society as the Fox Inn Savings Club (Stanton Harcourt 602) that was in existence in 1899 but there is no evidence of continuity.

606. Harcourt Arms Benefit Society

Status: Unregistered   **Type**: Friendly society
Established: First known 1895 **Dissolved**: Last known 1899
Headquarters: Harcourt Arms (1895-1899)
Membership: 26 members in 1899

Stanton St John

No. of societies and members 1802/3 – None

No. of members of a friendly society 1813/14/15 – None

607.   Heart in Hand Benefit Society

Status: Registered, OXF 293   **Type:** Permanent friendly society
Established: 29 October 1868 **Registered:** 29 October 1868 **Dissolved:** 26
May 1913
Headquarters: Star Inn (1868-1870), Schoolroom (1870-1913)
Anniversary/feast day: Second Monday in July
Minimum age at entry: 15 Maximum age at entry: 45
Membership: 28 members in 1871, 37 in 1872, 48 in 1877, 63 in 1880, 81 in
1885, 65 in 1891, 86 in 1899, 71 in 1905, 65 in 1908, 59 in 1913
Primary Sources: Rulebook of 1868, TNA, FS 3/321/293; TNA, FS 4/42/293
Notes: The Society was under the management of the honorary members. It
dissolved in 1913 with 59 members and £618 18s 8½d funds. The society had
a juvenile branch (Stanton St John 608).

608.   Heart in Hand Benefit Society, Juvenile Branch

Status: Juvenile branch of a registered society   **Type:** Juvenile friendly
society
Established: First known 1899 **Dissolved:** Last known 1899
Anniversary/feast day: Second Monday in July
Membership: 14 members in 1899
Notes: Juvenile branch of Hand in Hand Benefit Society (Stanton St John 607).
The report of club day 1899 referred to the juvenile branch of 14 members
(JOJ, 15 July 1899).

609.   Stanton St John Providential Benefit Society

Status: Enrolled, OXF 20   **Type:** Friendly society
Established: 1837 **Registered:** 23 November 1838 **Dissolved:** Last known
1865
Headquarters: Chequers Inn (1838-1865)
Minimum age at entry: 16 Maximum age at entry: 45
Membership: 25 members in 1846, 44 in 1850, 47 in 1855, 48 in 1860, 54 in
1865
Primary Sources: TNA, FS 4/42/20
Notes: No file exists for this society in the Registrar's records at TNA.

610.   Star of Stanton

Status: Branch of an affiliated order **Type**: AOF **Branch No.** 7748
Established: 1889 **Dissolved**: Post 1918
Headquarters: The Star (1890-post 1918)
Anniversary/feast day: Whit Thursday
Membership: 17 members in 1890, 35 in 1891, 59 in 1895, 91 in 1899, 100 in 1905, 118 in 1910
Notes: Oxford District of AOF.

Steeple Aston

No. of societies and members 1802/3 – None
No. of members of a friendly society 1813/14/15 – None
Notes: (See appendix 2, Crimes 156, 158, 160, 161 and 162).

611.   Court Robin Hood's Pride

Status: Branch of an affiliated order   **Type**: AOF **Branch No.** 8883
Established: 1899 **Dissolved**: Post 1918
Headquarters: Red Lion Inn, Steeple Aston (1899-post 1918)
Membership: 19 members in 1903, 140 in 1905, 157 in 1910
Notes: Banbury District of AOF.

612.   Court Royal Queen Mary

Status: Female branch of an affiliated order   **Type**: AOF **Branch No.** 9597
Established: 1912 **Dissolved**: Post 1918
Headquarters: Infant school (1912-post 1918)
Membership: 19 members in 1914
Notes: Banbury District of AOF.

613.   Heyford and Aston Friendly Society

Status: Registered, OXF 57   **Type:** Permanent friendly society
Established: 1875 **Registered:** 1875 **Dissolved:** 1 October 1901
Headquarters: Red Lion Inn, Steeple Aston [1879-1901)
Anniversary/feast day: Ascension Day, then (from 1856) third Wednesday in May
Minimum age at entry: 16 Maximum age at entry: 30

Membership: 63 members in 1885, 31 in 1891, 7 in 1899, 7 in 1901
Primary Sources: TNA, FS 3/319/57; TNA, FS 4/42/57; rulebook of 1879, Bodl. G.A. OXF 8° 1304
Notes: The society was formed after the previous society dissolved (Steeple Aston 614) but continued to use the same registration number of OXF 57. It dissolved in 1901 with 7 members and no funds.

Labourers' Friendly Society – see Steeple Aston 614

614.   **Lower Heyford and Steeple Aston Friendly Society, also Labourers' Friendly Society and Poor Man's Club**

Status: Enrolled, OXF 57   **Type:** Permanent friendly society
Established: 26 July 1836 **Registered:** 5 April 1837 **Dissolved:** 1 May 1875
Headquarters: Alternately at the Wesleyan Chapel, Lower Heyford and Radcliffe School, Steeple Aston (1843), Red Lion Inn, Steeple Aston (1845), Wesleyan Chapel, Lower Heyford (1855), Red Lion Inn, SA [1865-1875)
Anniversary/feast day: Ascension Day, then (from 1856) third Wednesday in May
Minimum age at entry: 16 Maximum age at entry: 50
Membership: 25 members in 1846, 37 in 1848, 56 in 1850, 108 in 1853, 118 in 1856, 143 in 1858, 177 in 1861, 218 in 1863, 235 in 1864, 207 in 1871
Primary Sources: Rulebook of 1837, TNA, FS 3/319/57; TNA, FS 4/42/56; rulebooks of 1851, Bodl. G.A. OXF 8° 1304; treasurers Bond dated 20 February 1838, OHC, QSD/R/36
Notes: The original rules were printed in *The Guardian, or Monthly Poor Law Register* in December 1838. A handwritten note of a rule change in the 1851 rulebook excluded benefit to anyone leaving the United Kingdom. In the 1879 rulebook, one of the stated aims of the society was, 'To promote peace, love and unity'. No sick payments were made to anyone suffering from smallpox unless they had previously been inoculated and an annuity was payable at age 65 of 3s a week. No subscriptions were required after that age. Three guineas was paid to the Radcliffe Infirmary, Oxford, from the annual subscription to secure benefit for its members (JOJ, 29 December 1855). The club was comprised mainly of agricultural labourers (BG, 30 April 1857). The location of club day was migratory and held in one of the villages where members lived, mainly in Steeple Aston, Steeple Barton, Lower Heyford, and Upper Heyford. The annual feast was described as a 'kettledrum' party in 1864 (BG, 26 May 1864) and did not include attendance at divine service until 1856 when club members attended Upper Heyford church (JOJ, 24 May 1856). In 1875 a significant dispute arose within the club. The founder and honorary member, William

Wing, was excluded by the society for selling land under value and refusing the division of funds of the society (BG, 22 April 1875). A four-bedroom freehold property at Combe, valued at £165 had been sold by Wing, a land agent, for £160 and he had also objected to the division of £1,000 of funds between its members. At the quarterly meeting, Wing tendered his quarterly subscription but it was refused. There followed an agreement to dissolve on 1 May 1875. It was agreed that £1,300 was to be divided between the members and the surplus was to remain towards the re-establishment of a new society (TNA, FS 3/319/57). The dispute led to exchanges of letters published in the *Banbury Guardian* (6 and 13 May) and *Bicester Herald* (4 June and 11 June). William Wing wrote in the *Annals of Steeple Aston and Middle Aston* (1875) stating the society had experienced 'unprecedented popularity and success' with 143 members in 1857 and £1,221 funds. However, he also stated that a rector in a neighbouring parish assailed the society, denouncing it as unsound. This led to the withdrawal of several honorary members, and the benefit members agreed on the division of £1,000 at a cost of £50 in solicitor's fees. The society re-formed as Heyford and Aston Friendly Society (Steeple Aston 613).

Poor Man's Club – see Steeple Aston 614

615.   Steeple Aston Friendly Society, also Tradesmen's Friendly Society

Status: Enrolled, OXF 24   **Type:** Permanent friendly society
Established: 1831 **Registered:** 15 December 1832 **Dissolved:** 1887
Headquarters: Red Lion Inn (1831-1887)
Anniversary/feast day: First Wednesday in May
Minimum age at entry: 15 Maximum age at entry: 35, 30 from 1861
Membership: 54 members in 1846, 60 in 1847, 74 in 1850, 84 in 1860, 74 in 1862, 59 in 1873, 30 in 1887
Primary Sources: Rulebook of 1861, TNA, Bodl. G.A. OXF 8° 1308(6); TNA, FS 1/574/24; TNA, FS 4/42/24; treasurer's bond for Richard Southam dated 31 January 1849 with further bonds dated 30 April 1859 and 16 May 1877, OHC, QSD/R/42
Notes: In 1842 the society advertised in *Jackson's Oxford Journal* offering to place a loan of funds for investment purposes to an amount between £300 and £400 (JOJ, 5 February 1842). In 1845 the Rev. Burrows, vicar excluded the use of the parish church at Steeple Aston for a club day service (BG, 15 May 1845). The vicars of Steeple Barton and Upper Heyford both offered the use of their church. *Jackson's Oxford Journal* reported in 1874 under a heading 'Disestablishment spreads' that the society, though prosperous, had decided

to disestablish their yearly parade to church and band at the club day (JOJ, 2 May 1874). In 1882 the society was described as being in a 'tottering position' (BicA, 9 June 1882) and it dissolved in 1887 with £374 5s 4d funds distributed between 30 members. (See also appendix 2, Crimes 157).

616.   Subscription Fire Engine Society

Status: Enrolled, OXF 106   **Type**: Benevolent society
Established: 1831 **Registered:** 29 March 1839 **Dissolved**: 29 November 1919
Headquarters: Hopcroft's Holt Inn (1839-1919)
Anniversary/feast day: Annual meeting held in December
Membership: 64 members in 1905, 46 in 1910
Primary Sources: Undated rulebook, TNA, FS 15/564
Notes: As a consequence of the riots in the agricultural districts in 1830-1, the 'Swing Riots', and in particular the visit by Swing rioters to Steeple Barton on 24 November 1830, a society was formed for the purchase of a fire engine for Steeple Aston and seven neighbouring parishes (William Wing, *Annals of Steeple Aston and Middle Aston* [1875]). The rules stated the society was for the purpose of the purchase and maintenance of a fire engine for the benefit of its benefit members and occupiers of their property. An effective engine was purchased for £120 with funds raised by subscription of amounts varying between 2s 6d and 10s. Members could be either individuals or corporate bodies. The area covered was Middle, North and Steeple Aston, Steeple Seswell (Steeple Barton parish), Middle and Westcote Barton, Upper and Lower Heyford, Duns Tew, and Rousham. Subscription was set each year depending on the previous year's expense. Deployment of the fire engine to members was free but non-members were charged a fee of between £5 and £7 (JOJ, 9 December 1976). An engineer and six firemen were retained at £2 per annum plus a fee for each call out. In 1850 it was considered extending the area to Tackley and Somerton but the proposal was rejected (JOJ, 7 December 1850). In 1852, landlord members included the Oxford colleges of Brasenose, New and Corpus Christi as well as the Farmer's Fire Insurance Company (JOJ, 11 December 1852). In 1859 it was reported that many societies had been set up based upon the experience and rules of the Steeple Aston society. These included Burford, Buckingham, Brackley (Northamptonshire) and Rendcombe (Gloucestershire) (JOJ, 10 December 1959). Response time at a test was found to be six minutes (JOJ, 7 December 1861). In November 1878 it was proposed that the society was dissolved and fire engine sold as the 'voluntarism of the aggregate of parishes no longer works' (JOJ, 30 November 1878). It appears several parishes owed their annual subscriptions but all had paid up by the December annual meeting and the society continued. Registration of the

society was eventually cancelled in 1919 as no annual returns had been filed (TNA, FS 15/564).

Tradesmen's Friendly Society – see Steeple Aston 615

Stoke Lyne

No. of societies and members 1802/3 – None
No. of members of a friendly society 1813/14/15 – None

617.   Stoke Lyne Friendly Society

Status: Unregistered   **Type**: Friendly society
Established: First known 1879 **Dissolved**: Last known 1911
Headquarters: Peyton Arms (unspecified)
Anniversary/feast day: Various days including Rogation Tuesday (1879), Trinity Wednesday (1880) and third Monday in July (from 1899)
Membership: Between 70 and 80 members in 1899
Notes: Sir Algernon Peyton was President and Trustee of the society that in 1899 had funds of £433 1s 11d (JOJ, 22 July 1899). The society flag had the Union flag in the top left quarter and the words, 'Stoke Lyne Friendly Society. We assist our Distressed Brethren' (OCCPA, D259844a).

Stoke Row

No. of societies and members 1802/3 – None
No. of members of a friendly society 1813/14/15 – None

618.   (Stoke Row club)

Status: Unregistered   **Type**: Friendly society
Established: First known 1895 **Dissolved**: Last known 1895
Notes: The *Henley Standard* of 14 June 1895 made a comparison between a quiet Whit Monday at Nettlebed and a usual club gathering at Stoke Row.

Stoke Talmage

No. of societies and members 1802/3 – None
No. of members of a friendly society 1813/14/15 – None

619.   **Central Oxfordshire Friendly Society, Stoke Talmage and Wheatfield branch**

Status: Branch of a registered society, OXF 500   **Type**: Permanent friendly society
Established: First known 1863 **Dissolved**: 1894
Anniversary/feast day: Whit Wednesday
Membership: 22 members in 1884
Notes: This was a branch of the Central Oxfordshire Friendly Society (Oxford 469). The fifth anniversary of the Central Oxfordshire Friendly society was held at Wheatfield Park and over 200 people attended (TG, 9 June 1863). On dissolution of the society in 1894, the members of the Stoke Talmage and Wheatfield branch presented the Rev. C. Vere Spencer, Rector of Stoke Talmage with an inscribed ink stand. He had been branch secretary for 30 years (17 February 1894).

Stokenchurch

No. of societies and members 1802/3 – None
No. of members of a friendly society 1813/14/15 – 4, 5, 6
Note: It is likely there was continuity between the independent societies in Stokenchurch from Stokenchurch 622, to 623, 624 and then 621. However, there are gaps in the evidence to prove this.

620.   **Court Hayman**

Status: Branch of an affiliated order, OXF 334   **Type**: AOF **Branch No.** 6047
Established: 1874   **Registered:** 1875 **Dissolved**: Post 1918
Headquarters: Barley Mow Inn [1876-1885], Old King's Arms Inn [1901-1905]
Anniversary/feast day: Whit Monday
Membership: 85 members in 1878, 185 in 1891
Notes: Buckinghamshire and Middlesex Division of AOF. The foresters' fete was held in a meadow at Chalk Farm (TG, 4 June 1901).

Red Lion Benefit Society – see Stokenchurch 621

621.   Stokenchurch Benefit Society, also Red Lion Benefit Society

Status: Unregistered   **Type**: Friendly society
Established: First known 1879 **Dissolved**: Last known 1901
Headquarters: Red Lion (1879-1901]
Anniversary/feast day: Whit Tuesday
Membership: 80 members in 1892

622.   Stokenchurch Friendly Society

Status: Enrolled, OXF 1   **Type**: Permanent friendly society
Established: 1828   **Registered:** 17 October 1831 **Dissolved**: Last known 1831
Headquarters: Barley Mow (1828-1831)
Anniversary/feast day: Whit Tuesday
Minimum age at entry: 18 **Maximum age at entry**: 35
Primary Sources: Rulebook of 1828, TNA, FS 1/574/1; TNA, FS 4/42/1
Notes: The duties of the landlord of the Barley Mow were set out in the rules: 'The room wherein the society meet, shall be kept in decent order, and shall have in it a clock, watch, or hour-glass, by which the society is to regulate its time of sitting. And from Michaelmas to Lady Day a fire and candles shall be ready at the appointed time of meeting, in default of which the innkeeper shall forfeit one shilling.'

623.   Stokenchurch Friendly Society

Status: Enrolled, OXF 103   **Type**: Permanent friendly society
Established: 1843   **Registered:** 16 April 1844 **Dissolved**: Last known 1844
Headquarters: King's Head Inn (1844)
Minimum age at entry: 16 **Maximum age at entry**: 35
Notes: No file exists for this society in TNA.

624.   Stokenchurch Friendly Society

Status: Registered, OXF 194   **Type**: Permanent friendly society
Established: 1857   **Registered:** 1 July 1857 **Dissolved**: Last known 1872
Headquarters: King's Arms Inn (1857-1872)
Anniversary/feast day: Whit Monday
Minimum age at entry: 16 Maximum age at entry: 35

Membership: 66 members in 1872
Primary Sources: Rulebook of 1857, TNA, FS 1/580/194; TNA, FS 4/42/194
Notes: Soldiers, sailors and bargemen were excluded from membership. The rules also required the landlord to provide a room, furnished with a clock or watch, a fire and candles. A note dated 13 May 1882 on a letter returned to the Registrar stated no society was held at the King's Arms (FS 4/42/194).

Stonesfield

No. of societies and members 1802/3 – 1, 86
No. of members of a friendly society 1813/14/15 – 91, 93, 95

625.   Court Black Head

Status: Branch of an affiliated order   **Type:** AOF **Branch No.** 9513
Established: 1912 **Dissolved:** Post 1918
Headquarters: Black Head (1912-post 1918)
Anniversary/feast day: 29 May
Maximum age at entry: 30
Membership: 90 members in 1913
Primary Sources: Rulebook 1917, OHC, STON., III/ii/2 & 3; sickness benefit records, OHC, STON/i/12 & 14; accounts 1913-1924, OHC, STON I/vi/1; National health insurance books, post 1912, OHC, STON II/iv/1; sickness payment sheets 1913-1917, OHC, STON II/i/1-17; AOF authority to pay book 1913-1916, OHC, STON I/iii/1; National insurance receipt book, OHC, STON I/iii/2
Notes: Oxford District of AOF. Formed when Stonesfield Friendly Society (Stonesfield 626) became a branch of the AOF.

626.   Stonesfield Friendly Society

Status: Enrolled, OXF 72   **Type:** Permanent friendly society
Established: 5 November 1765   **Registered:** 1794 **Dissolved:** 1912
Headquarters: Rose and Crown (1765-1823], Black Boy/Black Head [1836-1912)
Anniversary/feast day: 29 May
Maximum age at entry: 30
Membership: 63 in 1777, 79 in 1782, 84 in 1790, 78 in 1851, 87 in 1855, 115 in 1860, 118 in 1865, 117 in 1870, 131 in 1875, 146 in 1879, 126 in 1885, 120 in 1891, 105 in 1892, 89 in 1893, 74 in 1895, 69 in 1899, 66 in 1901, 77 in 1902, 69 in 1905, 64 in 1910

Primary Sources: Manuscript rules of 1765, OHC, QSD/R/31; manuscript rules of 1823, OHC, STON III/i/1; rulebook 1898, OHC, STON III/ii/1; membership and account book 1766-1798, OHC, STON I/ii/b/1; membership book 1850-1896, OHC, STON I//a/1; membership book 1900-1912, OHC, STON I/i/a/2; sickness payment book 1771-1846, OHC, STON I/v/9a/1; sickness payment book 1860, OHC, STON I/ii/a/1; sickness payment books 1888-1896 and 1903-1911, OHC, STON I/ii/b/3 & 5; accounts and minute books 1851-1875 & 1875-1893, OHC, STON I/ii/b/2 & 4; Club rent book, OHC, STON I/iv/1; Oxon. Cal. QS iii, p.662

Notes: The Stonesfield Friendly Society was the longest-lasting society in the county and the records held at OHC are the most comprehensive of any Oxfordshire society. It was enrolled at the Michaelmas Quarter Sessions, 1794 (Oxon. Cal. QS iii, p.662). The rules were amended on 5 May 1823 and approved at Trinity Quarter Sessions. In 1790 the society had over £295 on loan to twelve people (OHC, STON I/iv/1). In April 1817, the society invested £150 in Lord Churchill's bank at 5 per cent interest. Mr Hawkins was elected club doctor in 1856, and he was to attend members who lived within four miles of the clubhouse or his residence in Woodstock for the fee of £12 per annum. The fee increased to £15 in 1869. The rent of the club room at the Black Head was £3 per annum in 1864 and 'wet rent' increased from 2d a quarter to 2d monthly. Club funds of £159 were kept in the Woodstock Savings Bank in 1864.

A flag for the society was purchased for £15 in 1780 and repaired in 1789 at a cost of 2s 6d. A new flag was needed in 1873 and the committee agreed that Robert Milling should be tasked to find one, 'the new flag to be the same size as the old one with the same paining on it as it is now except the rose and crown and for the hammer and pick to show both sides' (OHC, STON I/ii/b/2). The image represented tools of the local craft of Stonesfield slate production. G.H. Powell (*Stonesfield* [Stonesfield, 1975] p. 33) states the flag was purple and gold. The cost of the flag and pole was £10 and needed repair in 1886, but was still in existence in 1975 in a frail state. It no longer survives. On club day, 'during the feast the flag hung from an upper window [of the Black Head], the lads congregated below making it a point to toss up their hats and try to lodge them on the spike at the top' (Powell [1975], p.33). In 1879 Dr F Stockwell was surgeon to the club as well as to societies at Combe (219), Woodstock (727) and Tackley (632). There was a division of funds above £300 in 1880. The society became a branch of the AOF, Court Black Head (Stonesfield 625) in 1912.

A part history of the society has been written by David Eastwood, 'The Benefits of Brotherhood: The First Century of the Stonesfield Friendly Society, 1765-1865', *Oxfordshire Local History*, vol. 2, no. 5, (1986). One of the main sources cited by Eastwood is a book entitled 'Stonesfield Club Book 1860' that he identifies as a membership book and records 88 names (OHC, STON/I/ ii/a/1). However, this is not a membership book but a claim or benefit book and lists those members making claims and receiving benefits on the club for 1860 and several years afterwards. This error calls into question the reliability of the conclusions. Eastwood also takes a glance at early Oxfordshire societies and whilst recognising the series of enrolled rules in the Quarter Session papers at OHC, QSD/R/1-44, he was not able to determine these were only part of the enrolled societies, and many were not included in the formal statistics of the Registrar of Friendly Societies.

627. Stonesfield Permanent Mutual Benefit Society

Status: Registered, OXF 349   **Type:** Permanent friendly society
Established: November 1882   **Registered:** 11 May 1883 **Dissolved:** 3 November 1894
Headquarters: Wesleyan Schoolroom (1883-1894)
Anniversary/feast day: 29 May
Minimum age at entry: 16 Maximum age at entry: 35
Membership: 33 members in 1885, 37 in 1891, 24 in 1893
Primary Sources: Undated rulebook, TNA, FS 3/322/349; TNA, FS4/42/349
Notes: The society dissolved in 1894 with 24 members and £83 funds with members receiving between £6 and 19s.

Stowood

No. of societies and members 1802/3 – None
No. of members of a friendly society 1813/14/15 – None

628. Beckley Friendly Society (until 1852), then Stowood Friendly Society

Status: Enrolled, OXF 80   **Type:** Permanent friendly society
Established: First known 1839 **Registered:** 16 May 1845 **Dissolved:** 24 November 1873
Headquarters: Royal Oak Inn, Stowood (1845-1855]
Minimum age at entry: 14 **Maximum age at entry:** 35
Primary Sources: Rulebooks of 1845 and 1852, TNA, FS 1/577/80; TNA, FS 4/42/80

Notes: On dissolution of the society all assets were to be sold including the box, flag, and other items (TNA, FS 1/577/80). (See also appendix 2, Crimes 163).

Stowood Friendly Society – see Stowood 628

Stratton Audley

No. of societies and members 1802/3 – None
No. of members of a friendly society 1813/14/15 – None

629.   Stratton Audley Benefit Friendly Society

Status: Registered, OXF 246   **Type:** 7-year dividing friendly society
Established: 5 August 1862   **Registered:** 1862 **Dissolved:** 21 December 1948
Headquarters: Schoolroom (1862-1948)
Anniversary/feast day: Whit Tuesday
Minimum age at entry: 16 Maximum age at entry: 30
Membership: 60 members in 1864, 74 in 1871, 86 in 1872, 94 in 1874, 91 in 1878, 98 in 1880, 93 in 1885, 77 in 1899, 75 in 1905, 69 in 1910, 21 in 1948
Primary Sources: Rulebooks of 1862 and 1902, valuations, correspondence and dissolution documents, TNA, FS 15/1877; Minute Book 1862-1948, OHC, P 8/2/A1/1
Notes: The society was open to new members who lived within five miles of Stratton Audley. It entered the provisional scheme under the National Insurance Act 1911 and was confirmed on the scheme on 4 July 1916. The society was dissolved in 1948 with 21 members and £597 0s 5d funds and was the last independent society in Oxfordshire.

Swerford

No. of societies and members 1802/3 – None
No. of members of a friendly society 1813/14/15 – None

630.   Loyal Masons' Arms Lodge

Status: Branch of an affiliated order   **Type:** IOOFMU **Branch No.** 7346
Established: 1895 **Dissolved:** Post 1918
Headquarters: Masons Arms (1895-1901], The Schoolroom [1905-post 1918)
Anniversary/feast day: On a Tuesday in late May or June

Membership: 26 members in 1901, 44 in 1905, 38 in 1907, 79 in 1910, 62 in 1914
Notes: Banbury District of IOOFMU.

Swinbrook

No. of societies and members 1802/3 – None
No. of members of a friendly society 1813/14/15 – None

631.   Swinbrook Mutual Benefit Society

Status: Unregistered   **Type:** Friendly society
Established: First known 1857 **Dissolved:** Last known 1857
Headquarters: Swan Inn (1857)
Notes: An inauguration dinner was held on 16 January 1857 (JOJ, 24 January 1857).

Tackley

No. of societies and members 1802/3 – None
No. of members of a friendly society 1813/14/15 – None

632.   King's Arms Friendly

Status: Registered, OXF 302   **Type:** Friendly society
Established: 1869   **Registered:** 17 January 1871   **Dissolved:** 22 October 1913
Headquarters: King's Arms Inn (1871-1913)
Anniversary/feast day: Second Thursday in July
Minimum age at entry: 12 Maximum age at entry: 40
Membership: 28 members in 1871, 31 in 1876, 37 in 1891, 60 in 1899, 74 in 1907, 76 in 1910, 68 in 1913
Primary Sources: Rulebook of 1871 and 1897, TNA, FS 15/574
Notes: The medical attendant visited all members resident within 4 miles of Woodstock. On 12 July 1879 a new surgeon was appointed to the club, Dr F. Stockwell, who was also surgeon to societies at Combe (219), Woodstock (727), and Stonesfield (626). A letter to the Registrar dated 4 August 1881 from James Cleaver questioned the appointment of three trustees (TNA, FS 15/574). It transpired that Robert Hoare, a carpenter of Tackley, had completed a new Trustees' form and submitted it to the Registrar without formal process through the society. It appointed Jesse Minn, James Hoare, and himself as Trustees in

place of James Cleaver, Anthony Adams and William Floyd. An investigation was conducted by the society and Robert Hoare admitted to submitting the form. A valuation of the society's assets and liabilities on 31 December 1911 showed an accounting deficit of £431. It dissolved in 1913 with 68 members and £689 4s 10½d funds.

633.   Sturdy's Castle Friendly Society

Status: Registered, OXF 265   **Type:** 5-year dividing friendly society
Established: First known 1865   **Registered:** 19 September 1865   **Dissolved:** 18 January 1886
Headquarters: Sturdy's Castle (1865), National Schoolroom [1870-1885], Sturdy's Castle Inn (1878)
Membership: 78 members in 1865, 63 in 1870, 54 in 1874, 44 in 1877, 50 in 1880, 26 in 1885
Primary Sources: TNA, FS 4/42/265
Notes: A letter from J.A. Sharpe, rector of Tackley to the Registrar dated 11 May 1886 explained the club had ceased as it had run out of funds and that division every five years was to blame.

Tadmarton

No. of societies and members 1802/3 – None
No. of members of a friendly society 1813/14/15 – None

634.   Empress of India Lodge

Status: Branch of an affiliated order   **Type:** IOOFMU **Branch No.** 6883
Established: 1889 **Dissolved:** Post 1918
Headquarters: Lampet Arms Inn (1889-post 1918)
Membership: 30 members in 1890, 31 in 1892, 54 in 1894, 60 in 1897, 66 in 1901, 68 in 1905, 83 in 1910, 106 in 1914
Notes: Banbury District of IOOFMU. It was unanimously agreed to form a juvenile branch in 1893 (BG, 18 May 1893) but no evidence of its existence can be found.

635.   (Tadmarton club)

Status: Unregistered   **Type:** 3-year dividing friendly society
Established: First known 1856 **Dissolved:** Last known 1872
Headquarters: Schoolroom (1857), then an unknown public house

Minimum age at entry: 10
Membership: 40 members in 1871
Primary Sources: BPP 1874, XXIII, (c.997), p.117
Notes: The Assistant Commissioner reported that when the club first commenced it was based in the schoolroom and there was no feast. The young members disliked this and left to form a new one (Tadmarton 636). The society then moved to a public house in the village. It held a feast and contributions were made from members. It was described as 'the old club'. It was further described as a 'jolly club' and the secretary, James Cartwright 'a jolly old labourer'. The feast was said to last 'a day and the next night'. The club had juvenile members at reduced contribution between ages 10-18.

636.   Tadmarton Junior Benefit Society

Status: Registered, OXF 308   **Type:** Friendly society
Established: 1856   **Registered:** 19 June 1871   **Dissolved:** 1894
Headquarters: Lampet Arms Inn (1856-1889), Schoolroom (1889-1894]
Anniversary/feast day: First Monday in May
Minimum age at entry: 15 Maximum age at entry: 35
Membership: 29 members in 1871, 25 in 1874, 24 in 1878, 36 in 1880, 39 in 1885, 33 in 1891
Primary Sources: Rulebook of 1871, TNA, FS 3/321/308; TNA, FS 4/42/308; BPP 1874, XXIII, (c.997), p.117
Notes: The Assistant Commissioner reported that the society was established by young members from an unregistered club in the village (Tadmarton 635) and it registered in 1871. At the time of registration, the funds of over £40 were divided amongst the members. The club did not engage a band for the feast after 1871 and consequently costs for the day reduced from £13 to £5. The society was suspended for three months by the Registrar on 4 October 1881 for violating the requirement of submission of a valuation. A letter dated 10 April 1896 was received by the Registrar and it stated the society was dissolved in 1894 with the consent of all the members (TNA, FS 4/42/308). Registration was cancelled on 24 March 1897 as the society had ceased to exist.

Taynton

No. of societies and members 1802/3 – None
No. of members of a friendly society 1813/14/15 – 10, 10, 10
Notes: No friendly societies are recorded as being located in Taynton.

Tetsworth

No. of societies and members 1802/3 – None
No. of members of a friendly society 1813/14/15 – None

637.   Tetsworth Friendly Society

Status: Enrolled, OXF 104   **Type:** Permanent friendly society
Established: 1844 **Registered:** 16 January 1845 **Dissolved:** 11 March 1913
Headquarters: Red Lion Inn (1844-1895), Old Schoolroom (1895-1910)
Anniversary/feast day: Whit Monday
Minimum age at entry: 12, 14 (from 1895) Maximum age at entry: 45, 40 (from 1895)
Membership: 84 members in 1862, 71 in 1866, 63 in 1871, 57 in 1877, 56 in 1880, 76 in 1885, 46 in 1899, 30 in 1905, 12 in 1910
Primary Sources: Rulebook of 1845, amended rules of 1895, TNA, FS 3/319/104; TNA, FS 4/42/104
Notes: A meeting was held at the old schoolroom on 23 May 1894 with a view to forming a juvenile branch (HSOS, 18 May 1894). The amended rules of 1895 stated adult members were aged over 20 years, whilst those aged between 14 and 20 were juvenile members. The society dissolved in 1913 with £40 funds and 13 members; three were aged between 50 and 65, ten were aged over 65.

638.   Tetsworth Hand in Hand Benefit Society

Status: Unregistered   **Type**: Friendly society
Established: First known 1889 **Dissolved**: Last known 1893
Headquarters: King's Arms Inn (1889-1893)
Anniversary/feast day: Whit Tuesday
Notes: The club day dinner and parade was reported in the local newspapers (TG, 18 June 1889, HSOS, 26 May 1893).

639.   Tetsworth Seven Years Friendly Society

Status: Enrolled, OXF 22   **Type:** 7-year dividing friendly society
Established: 5 September 1837   **Registered:** 15 December 1838   **Dissolved:** Last known 1862
Headquarters: Red Lion Inn (1838)
Anniversary/feast day: Whit Wednesday

Minimum age at entry: 12 Maximum age at entry: 40
Membership: 47 members in 1862
Primary Sources: Rulebook of 1837, TNA, FS 1/574/22; TNA, FS 4/42/22
Notes: All members residing within two miles of Tetsworth were required to attend the funeral of a member, and were entitled to one pint of beer from the club funds. A letter relating to the Red Lion, filed in the Registrar's papers under reference TNA, FS 4/42/22 relates to a different society (Kingston Blount 400).

Thame

No. of societies and members 1802/3 – None
No. of members of a friendly society 1813/14/15 – None
Notes: The parade of friendly societies and attendance at church had largely died out by the early 1870s. Some societies also abandoned hiring a band but others continued to support club day festivities. In Whitsun week, because of the lack of a town parade, the Thame Royal Band would strike up in the early morning before departing to their engagement at a nearby club day. (See also appendix 2, Crimes 165).

640.   Court British Queen

Status: Branch of an affiliated order, OXF 197   **Type:** AOF **Branch No.** 2683
Established: 1855   **Registered:** 1855   **Dissolved:** 1907
Headquarters: Anchor Inn, Middle Row, High Street (1855-1857), Six Bells, Priest End (1858-1859], Spread Eagle Hotel [1862-1879), Black Horse Inn (1879-1890], 29 East Street (1905)
Anniversary/feast day: Whit Wednesday
Membership: 93 members in 1862, 103 in 1866, 111 in 1880, 117 in 1885, 101 in 1889, 78 in 1890, 59 in 1895, 43 in 1900, 23 in 1905
Notes: The branch did not belong to a district of the AOF. It was suspended by the AOF in 1875 and reinstated in 1877. In 1879, William Scadding, court secretary, was discovered to have embezzled £500 over a number of years, having deceived auditors appointed by the Foresters (see appendix 2, Crimes 166). The 1908 AOF Directory states the society became defunct in 1907 with centralized membership when it was 'taken on the High Court Sick and Funeral Fund'.

> **Hand in Hand Benefit Society** – see Old Briton Benefit Society, Thame 644

641.   Hearts of Oak Friendly Society, Thame Branch

Status: Branch of a registered society **Type**: Permanent friendly society
Established: 1886 **Dissolved**: Last known 1886
Headquarters: Anchor Inn (1886)

642.   Independent Mutual Brethren Friendly Society, Thame Branch

Status: Branch of a registered society, MDX 4880 **Type**: IMBFS **Branch No.** 380
Established: 1879 **Dissolved**: Last known 1885
Headquarters: Black Horse (1879 - 1885)
Anniversary/feast day: Whit Wednesday

643.   Loyal Wenman Lodge

Status: Branch of an affiliated order, OXF 316   **Type**: IOOFMU **Branch No.** 5734
Established: 1869   **Registered:** 1869   **Dissolved**: Post 1918
Headquarters: Fighting Cocks Inn (1869-post 1918)
Anniversary/feast day: Whit Wednesday
Membership: 18 members in 1870, 35 in 1872, 50 in 1874, 47 in 1880, 87 in 1886, 113 in 1891, 135 in 1894, 148 in 1901, 154 in 1905, 186 in 1910, 213 in 1913
Primary Sources: Minute book (1897-1908), OHC, O23/2/10/A1/1
Notes: Oxford District of IOOFMU.

644.   Old Britons Benefit Society, also Hand in Hand Benefit Society in its early years

Status: Unregistered   **Type**: Seven-year dividing friendly society
Established: 1874 **Dissolved**: Last known 1896
Headquarters: White Horse (1874-1893), White Hart Hotel (1894-1896)
Anniversary/feast day: Whit Wednesday
Membership: 72 members in 1881, 64 in 1892
Notes: This society was formed on the dissolution of the Thame Permanent Hand in Hand Friendly Society (Thame 648) and continued to be known by the name of Hand in Hand Benefit Society for its first few years. It was described as having a tricolour banner.

645.   Thame Friendly Society

Status: Enrolled, OXF 178   **Type:** Friendly society
Established: 1 May 1797   **Registered:** 1797   **Dissolved:** Last known 1797
Headquarters: Crown Inn (1797)
Anniversary/feast day: Easter Wednesday
Maximum age at entry: 40
Primary Sources: Undated rules, TNA, FS 1/580/178; TNA, FS 4/42/178

646.   Thame Friendly Benefit Society

Status: Enrolled, OXF 42   **Type:** 7-year dividing friendly society
Established: 1841   **Registered:** 1 January 1841   **Dissolved:** Last known 1841
Headquarters: Saracen's Head Inn (1841)
Anniversary/feast day: Whit Wednesday
Minimum age at entry: 6 **Maximum age at entry:** 40
Primary Sources: Rulebook of 1841, TNA, FS 1/576/42; TNA, FS 4/42

647.   Thame Friendly Society

Status: Enrolled, OXF 40   **Type:** Permanent friendly society
Established: 1841   **Registered:** 25 February 1841   **Dissolved:** Last known 1841
Headquarters: Market Hall (1841)
Anniversary/feast day: As agreed by the society
Minimum age at entry: 6 **Maximum age at entry:** 50
Primary Sources: TNA, FS 1/576/40; TNA, FS 4/42/40
Notes: A meeting was called at the Town Hall for the purpose of forming a general benefit society in 1840 (JOJ, 29 August 1840). The society was open to male and female members of all parishes in Thame Union and all other places within five miles of Thame.

648.   Thame Permanent Hand in Hand Friendly (or Benevolent) Society

Status: Enrolled, OXF 71   **Type:** Permanent friendly society, annual dividing friendly society after 1843
Established: 1807   **Registered:** 1818   **Dissolved:** 1874

Headquarters: Spread Eagle Hotel (1840- 1863), Town Hall (1863-1864), Fighting Cocks Inn (1864-1868), Town Hall (1868), White Horse Inn (1870-1873]
Anniversary/feast day: Whit Wednesday
Minimum age at entry: 15 (1840), 18 (1855) Maximum age at entry: 40 (1840), 35 (1855)
Membership: 111 members in 1857, 128 in 1862, 135 in 1865, 158 in 1867, 20 members in 1874
Primary Sources: Oxon. Cal. QS iii, p.650; rulebooks of 1840 and 1855, TNA, FS 1/577/71; Rulebook of 1843, TNA, FS 1/578/105; TNA, 4/42/71; TNA, FS 1/578/105
Notes: Rules of this friendly society, dated 2 February 1818, were enrolled at the Easter Quarter Sessions 1819 (Oxon. Cal. QS iii, p.650). A new banner was paraded on club day in 1841 (JOJ, 5 June 1841). In 1862, new members were required to earn a minimum of 12s a week (TG, 17 June 1862), reducing to 10s a week the following year (TG, 2 June 1863). A letter of 1874 from W. Howland stated the club had 'been run badly of late' (TNA, FS 1/577/71). A Steward, Thomas Green, had defrauded the Society. He had been prosecuted and expelled in 1869 but Magistrates reinstated him (See also appendix 2, Crimes 164). As a consequence the majority of the members left. In May 1873 the treasurer became involved in misappropriating club funds to the sum of £40 and could not repay so members refused to pay subscriptions until he refunded the money. The treasurer surrendered two life policies to the value of £26 16s but a general meeting of 1874 agreed to dissolve the society. There were 20 members at dissolution, the oldest member, aged 86, stated he had been a member for 67 years, and eleven members for over 35 years. A society of the same name was registered by the Registrar as OXF 105 (Thame 649) but it appears to be a duplicate of this society. The Registrar's records contains a set of rules for 1843 and appears to have been allocated a new registration number at this time, although OXF 71 continued to be used as the registered number until dissolution (TNA, FS 1/578/105). A token, with 'Thame Hand in Hand Benevolent Society 1868' on the front, surrounding a large '3D', and clasped left hands on the rear is a rare example of a beer token to pay wet rent (Thame Museum, THMLM:2006.11.1). The clasped hands represented mutual help, responsibility and reciprocity (Victoria Solt Dennis, *Discovering Friendly and Fraternal Societies: Their badges and regalia* [Oxford 2005], p.53). The unregistered Old Britons Benefit Society (Thame 644) was a continuation of this society.

649.   Thame Permanent Hand in Hand Friendly Society

Status: Enrolled, OXF 105   **Type**: Annual dividing friendly society
Primary Sources: TNA, FS 4/42/105
Notes: The Registrar's records state the society was enrolled on 7 November 1843 (TNA, FS 4/42/105). However, this is a duplicate registration of society no. OXF 71 (Thame 648), representing a misinterpretation of the enrolment of amended rules in 1843. The only mention in parliamentary papers of this society is for 1876 with no further details provided. The registration number OXF 71 was used in all correspondence with the Registrar.

650.   Thame Temperance Provident Society

Status: Enrolled, OXF 113   **Type**: Permanent friendly society
Established: First known 1850   **Registered:** 6 June 1850   **Dissolved**: Last known 1850
Headquarters: Royal British School, Park Street (1850)
Anniversary/feast day: Easter Monday
Minimum age at entry: 6 Maximum age at entry: 35
Primary Sources: Rulebook of 1850, TNA, FS 1/578/113; TNA, FS 4/42/113
Notes: Members were required to sign the pledge of abstinence. A letter of 23 March (but no year) indicated the society was dissolved.

651.   United Brotherhood

Status: Unregistered   **Type**: Permanent friendly society
Established: 1869 **Dissolved**: 1881
Headquarters: Swan Inn (1869-1881)
Anniversary/feast day: Whit Wednesday
Notes: The society did not engage a band or parade after 1872. It dissolved with £3 3s 3d funds (JOJ, 12 November 1881).

652.   United Patriots National Benefit Society, Thame Branch

Status: Branch of a registered society **Type**: Permanent friendly Society
Branch No. 166
Established: 1879 **Dissolved**: Last known 1910
Headquarters: Mr J Dowsett's, Pristend [1905-1910]

653.   The United Relieving Officers and Masters of Workhouses Superannuation Society

Status: Enrolled, OXF 23   **Type**: Permanent friendly society
Established: 1837   **Registered:** 1 January 1838   **Dissolved**: Last known 1838
Headquarters: Fighting Cocks Inn (1837-1838)
Maximum age at entry: 60
Primary Sources: Undated rulebook, TNA, FS 1/574/23; TNA, FS 4/42/23
Notes: Benefits included a pension of £30 per annum at age 65 provided they had been a member for 20 years. If a benefit member recommended seven honorary members they received a silver medal worth 10s. There was no restriction on where the member resided at joining.

654.   Wenman Independent Friendly Society

Status: Enrolled, OXF 114   **Type**: Permanent friendly society
Established: First known 1850   **Registered:** 14 August 1850   **Dissolved**: Last known 1851
Headquarters: Fighting Cocks' Inn (1850-1851)
Anniversary/feast day: Last Thursday in July
Minimum age at entry: 18 **Maximum age at entry**: 35
Primary Sources: Rulebook of 1850, TNA, FS 3/319/114; TNA, FS 4/42/114
Notes: New members were required to earn at least 15s a week on admission.

655.   Wenman Lodge

Status: Branch of an affiliated order   **Type**: IOOFMU **Branch No.** 3229
Established: 1843 **Dissolved**: 1852
Headquarters: Fighting Cocks' Inn (1844-1852)
Membership: 44 members in 1844, 59 in 1846, 42 in 1850
Notes: Oxford District of IOOFMU (1844-1849), Witney District (1849-1852).

Upton and Signet

No. of societies and members 1802/3 – None
No. of members of a friendly society 1813/14/15 – 8, 8, 8
Notes: No friendly societies are recorded as being located in Upton and Signet.

Warborough

No. of societies and members 1802/3 – None
No. of members of a friendly society 1813/14/15 – 2, 2, 3

656.   National Deposit Friendly Society, Warborough Branch

Status: Branch of a registered society **Type:** Permanent friendly Society
Established: First known 1887 **Dissolved:** Last known 1910
Headquarters: Schoolroom (1887-1905]
Anniversary/feast day: Whit Monday
Membership: 70 members in 1889, 71 in 1904, 64 in 1905
Notes: The branch was founded by the Rev. F. Chalkery (BOA, 31 May 1901).
Shillingford members of the branch dined separately from the Warborough
residents and joined up after dinner (JOJ, 9 June 1900). A subscription fund
for a new banner was commenced in 1900 and it was displayed at the club day
parade (BOA, 8 June 1900). Club day was postponed in 1910 due to the death
of King Edward VII (BOA, 19 May 1910).

657.   Prince of Wales Friendly Society

Status: Registered, OXF 267 **Type:** 5-year dividing friendly society
Established: First known 1866   **Registered:** 18 January 1866   **Dissolved:**
1875
Headquarters: Cricketers Arms (1868)
Minimum age at entry: 14 Maximum age at entry: 47
Membership: 24 members in 1872
Primary Sources: TNA, FS 4/42/267
Notes: No file relating to this society exists in the records of the Registrar at
TNA. (See also appendix 2, Crimes 167).

658.   Shillingford Friendly Society

Status: Registered, OXF 266 **Type:** Permanent friendly society
Established: 1865   **Registered:** 7 October 1865   **Dissolved:** 1866
Headquarters: George Inn (1865-1866)
Minimum age at entry: 14 **Maximum age at entry:** 47
Primary Sources: Rulebook of 1865, TNA, FS 1/582/266; TNA, FS 4/42/266
Notes: The annual return to the Registrar for 1866 stated there were no
members of the society at 31 December 1865 or 31 December 1866. It was
marked, 'All the members have left' (TNA, FS 1/582/266).

Wardington

No. of societies and members 1802/3 – None
No. of members of a friendly society 1813/14/15 – 48, 51, 59

659.   Temple of Friendship Lodge

Status: Branch of an affiliated order, OXF 128 **Type**: IOOFMU **Branch No:**
3655
Established: 1843 **Registered:** 1852   **Dissolved**: Post 1918
Headquarters: Wheatsheaf Inn (1843-1913)
Anniversary/feast day: Whit Monday
Membership: 10 members in 1844, 19 in 1845, 24 in 1846, 22 in 1850, 26 in
1855, 41 in 1860, 40 in 1865, 35 in 1870, 34 in 1875, 43 in 1881, 53 in 1885,
65 in 1888, 66 in 1895, 69 in 1901, 60 in 1905, 74 in 1910, 84 in 1913, 72 in
1914
Primary Sources: Various documents covering period 1848-1914 including
rules and regulations of IOOFMU, correspondence and financial records.
Includes a fines book (O172/F/1) and a declaration book (O127/A9) and
Lecture Book, detailing secret rituals of the society (O127/A11), OHC, O172;
BPP 1874, XXIII, (c.997), p.114
Notes: Banbury District of IOOFMU. The Assistant Commissioner reported
that in 1872 there were 35 members scattered in the neighbourhood within about
two and a half miles of Wardington. There were only one or two agricultural
labourers who were members. He further commented, 'Practically the society
cannot be said to reach the labourers' class'. He also noted there were some
distant members living in Birmingham. The Wardington Oddfellows' fete was
held in the grounds of Mr Loveday at Williamscot in 1881 (BG, 9 June 1881).

660.   (Wardington club)

Status: Unregistered **Type**: Permanent friendly society
Established: First known 1841 **Dissolved**: Last known 1871
Headquarters: Hare and Hounds (1871)
Membership: 44 members in 1872
Primary Sources: BPP 1874, XXIII, (c.997), p.114
Notes: The Assistant Commissioner reported this was an unregistered local
club and was a permanent society. The society had been in existence for at
least 30 years.

661.   United Christian Benefit Society

Status: Registered, OXF 232 **Type:** Permanent friendly society
Established: 2 October 1860 **Registered:** 21 November 1860   **Dissolved:** 1912
Headquarters: Mr John Mainwood's dwelling house (1860-1904), Mr Thomas Watts' (1905-1910]
Anniversary/feast day: Whit Tuesday
Minimum age at entry: 15 Maximum age at entry: 30
Membership: 9 members in 1862, 19 in 1865, 23 in 1872, 32 in 1878, 42 in 1885, 51 in 1891, 51 in 1902, 62 in 1910
Primary Sources: Rulebooks of 1860 and 1894, TNA, FS 3/321/232; TNA, FS 4/42/232; BPP 1874, XXIII, (c.997), p.114
Notes: The society was managed by the president, treasurer, and secretary, all honorary members. New members were required to reside within ten miles of Wardington. The Assistant Commissioner reported that in 1872 the society kept away from public houses and there was 'no folly, no beer'. There were several chapel members but the society was non-denominational. Members were chiefly agricultural labourers but were described as a 'picked lot' indicating only selected labourers were permitted to join. Mr Mainwood, whose house was the registered office, was a carrier at Wardington. In the valuation of 1912 it was stated the society was seeking to join the Royal Oak Benefit Society.

662.   Wardington Friendly Society

Status: Enrolled **Type**: Friendly society
Established: 27 August 1819 **Registered:** 1826   **Dissolved**: Last known 1826
Headquarters: Wheatsheaf Inn (1819-1826)
Anniversary/feast day: Whit Monday
Primary Sources: Oxon. Cal. QS iii, p. 674
Notes: Rules of the society were enrolled at the Easter Quarter Sessions 1826.

Watlington

No. of societies and members 1802/3 – 1, 45
No. of members of a friendly society 1813/14/15 – 81, 90, 107
Notes: Watlington feast was celebrated on three days during Whitsun week from Monday to Wednesday. In 1887, four or five clubs met on Whit Monday and Tuesday and over 1,000 people attended the town to witness the parade

and to take part in the festivities (SON, 4 June 1887). The town supported a number of clubs and most were unregistered.

663.   Bold Fellows

Status: Unregistered **Type**: Permanent friendly society,
Established: First known 1847   **Dissolved**: Last known 1893
Headquarters: Hare and Hounds [1848-1893)
Anniversary/feast day: Whit Monday
Notes: The origin of the society appears to be that its founding members seceded from the Watlington Old Club (Watlington 674) before 1847 and then incorporated 'a younger brood' of members from the dissolved Castle Lodge of Oddfellows in 1850 (Watlington 664) (JOJ, 5 June 1852 and 2 June 1855). The club name was an amusing variation on the Oddfellows.

664.   Castle Lodge

Status: Branch of an affiliated order **Type**: IOOFMU **Branch No.** 4213
Established: 1847 **Dissolved**: 1850
Headquarters: Hare and Hounds (1847- 1850)
Anniversary/feast day: Whit Monday
Membership: 6 members in 1850
Notes: Oxford District of IOOFMU. The branch was closed in 1850 by division of funds between the branch members. Several members joined the Bold Fellows (Watlington 663).

665.   Court Hampden

Status: Branch of an affiliated order, OXF 306   **Type**: AOF **Branch No.** 5372
Established: 1869   **Registered:** 1870   **Dissolved**: Post 1918
Headquarters: Hare and Hounds (1870), Fox and Hounds (1872-1876), Hare and Hounds Hotel (1877-1912]
Anniversary/feast day: Whit Wednesday in 1881 and Whit Monday in 1882.
Membership: 34 members in 1872, 72 in 1875, 80 in 1880, 91 in 1885, 84 in 1890, 115 in 1895, 109 in 1900, 116 in 1905, 89 in 1910
Notes: London United District of AOF. In 1901 the branch celebrated club day with a dinner and fete and collected for the local cottage hospital (TG, 4 June 1901).

666.   Crown Tradesmen's Benefit Society

Status: Unregistered **Type**: 7-year dividing friendly society
Established: 25 July 1825 **Dissolved**: Last known 1856
Headquarters: (One) Crown Inn (1825-1856)
Anniversary/feast day: Whit Monday
Membership: 61 members in 1839

> **Hare and Hounds Club** – see Watlington Old Club, Watlington
> 674

> **Mechanics United** – see Watlington United Friendly Society,
> Watlington 675

667.   National Deposit Friendly Society, Watlington branch

Status: Branch of a registered society **Type**: Permanent friendly society
Established: First known 1911 **Dissolved**: post 1913
Anniversary/feast day: Whit Monday
Notes: Club day was celebrated with sports on Whit Monday (HSOS, 9 June 1911 and TG, 20 May 1913).

668.   Nephalites

Status: Unregistered **Type**: Annual dividing friendly society,
Established: 1861   **Dissolved**: 1894
Headquarters: Lecture Hall (1861-1894)
Anniversary/feast day: Whit Tuesday
Membership: 24 members in 1864, almost 240 by 1889
Notes: A non-sectarian, tee-totallers' club promoting alcohol abstinence. Club day was celebrated with a band, church, and a tea party. By 1880 it was the largest club in Watlington (JOJ, 22 May 1880). In 1884 there were 220 attendees to dinner and 500 to tea (TG, 10 June 1884). The club had its own brass band, formed in 1885 (WT, 18 June 1886). The society was valued by IORSU with a view to becoming a branch (BOA, 26 May 1893) but members decided to reform as a registered society, the United Society of Nephalites (Watlington 672).

669.   Nephalite Subordinate Division

Status: Branch of an affiliated order **Type**: OSOT **Branch No.** 1308
Established: 1908 **Dissolved**: post 1914
Headquarters: Lecture Hall (1908-1914)
Anniversary/feast day: Whit Monday
Membership: 11 members in 1894, 22 in 1890, 31 members in 1905, 45 in 1908, 54 in 1911, 61 in 1913
Notes: Formed as a branch of the OSOT from the United Society of Nephalites (Watlington 672).

670.   (New) Exhibition Club

Status: Unregistered **Type**: Friendly society,
Established: 1852   **Dissolved**: Last known 1856
Headquarters: Fox and Hounds (1852-1856)
Anniversary/feast day: Whit Monday

671.   New Wesleyan Provident Society

Status: Unregistered **Type**: Permanent friendly society,
Established: 1851   **Dissolved**: Last known 1893
Headquarters: Schoolroom (1852-1859), Lecture Hall (1860-1893)
Anniversary/feast day: Whit Monday
Membership: 86 members in 1864
Notes: The society was established in 1851 as members did not want to pay 'wet rent' to a landlord in addition to normal benefit contributions (TG, 28 May 1861). It had no music, no banner or procession and held a dinner and tea on club day. In 1860, the club headquarters was moved from the schoolroom to the Lecture room as the former was too small. Its nature was described as, 'A quieter chapel club' (TG, 9 June 1868).

Poor Mans' Club – see Watlington Old Club, Watlington 674

Tradesmen's club – see Watlington United Friendly Society, Watlington 675

672.   United Society of Nephalites

Status: Registered, OXF 384 **Type:** Permanent friendly society

Established: 1894   **Registered:** 10 May 1894 **Dissolved:** 28 May 1908
Headquarters: Lecture Hall (1894-1908)
Anniversary/feast day: Whit Monday, then varying between Whit Monday and Tuesday after c.1900
Minimum age at entry: 16 Maximum age at entry: 40
Membership: 175 members in 1898, 156 in 1899, 156 in 1900, 129 in 1905
Primary Sources: Rulebook of 1894, TNA, FS 3/322/384; TNA, FS 4/42/384
Notes: The society re-formed from the Nephalite club (Watlington 668) and registered, having decided not to join the IOORSU. Members were expelled if they broke 'the pledge'. Additional benefit for members was that they could be insured for the funeral costs of their wife. Divine service was held at the Wesleyan chapel. Registration was cancelled to amalgamate and become a branch of the Order of the Sons of Temperance (Watlington 669).

673.   Watlington Branch of Compton Pilgrims Friendly Society

Status: Branch of a registered society, BRK 86 **Type:** Permanent friendly society
Established: First known 1894 **Dissolved:** post 1914
Anniversary/feast day: Whit Monday
Membership: 11 members in 1894, 22 in 1890, 31 members in 1905, 45 in 1908, 54 in 1911, 61 in 1913
Notes: Club day was held at Compton, Berkshire.

674.   Watlington Old Club, also Poor Mans' Club, also Hare and Hounds Club

Status: Unregistered **Type:** Friendly society
Established: 1759 **Dissolved:** Last known 1852
Headquarters: Hare and Hounds [1841-1852)
Anniversary/feast day: Whit Monday
Notes: The society had their headquarters at the same public house as the Bold Fellows (Watlington 663), formed by members that seceded from the Watlington Old Club in 1847, but in a different room. (JOJ, 2 June 1849 and 5 June 1852).

675.   Watlington United Friendly Society, also Mechanics United and Tradesmen's club

Status: Enrolled, OXF 47 **Type:** Dividing friendly society, then from 1866 a permanent friendly society

Established: 1839   **Registered:** 24 December 1839 **Dissolved:** 28 July 1913
Headquarters: Greyhound (1839-1840), Hare and Hounds Inn (1840 -1913)
Anniversary/feast day: Whit Tuesday
Minimum age at entry: 16 Maximum age at entry: 35
Membership: 25 members in 1839, 53 in 1863, 55 in 1864, 37 in 1865, 19 in 1866, 61 in 1876, 50 in 1878, 56 in 1885, 73 in 1891, 81 in 1893, 63 in 1899, 49 in 1905, 50 in 1910, 67 in 1913
Primary Sources: Rulebook of 1840, TNA, FS 3/319/47; TNA, FS 4/42/46
Notes: The society was to be composed exclusively of tradesmen or persons whose weekly income bore an equal proportion. At a meeting at the Greyhound Inn on Tuesday 21 May 1839, 25 members signed up to join the club (JOJ, 1 June 1839). The rules were changed on 7 December 1866 so that in future the club was to be considered a permanent society. The society remained the only independent registered club in Watlington until 1894. It was dissolved with 67 members, 28 of whom were aged over 50 years, and £162 funds. The *Thame Gazette* reported on 20 May 1913 that 'Not for 90 years past has the Hare and Hounds Hotel been without one or two club feasts until this Whitsuntide when the United Friendly society decided not to hold its annual festival. The decline of this event was predicted some time ago but it was not realized what an effect National Insurance would have upon small and even prosperous clubs in city, towns and villages'.

Wendlebury

No. of societies and members 1802/3 – None
No. of members of a friendly society 1813/14/15 – None

> **Merton and Wendlebury Benefit Society** – see Wendlebury Benefit Society, Wendlebury 677

676.   Wendlebury Benefit Society

Status: Unregistered **Type**: 7-year dividing friendly society
Established: 1858 **Dissolved**: 9 March 1898
Headquarters: Plough Inn (1858-1898)
Anniversary/feast day: Whit Thursday
Maximum age at entry: 45
Membership: 85 members in 1880, 107 members in 1882, 64 members in 1894
Primary Sources: Undated rulebook, Bodl. G.A. 8° 1255(5)

Notes: The layout and wording of the rulebook is almost identical to the 1880 rulebook of Charlton Benefit Society (Charlton on Otmoor 183). Many of the members in the period 1880-1887 lived in Merton and other nearby villages (BicA, 3 June 1887). The club was described as being in a poor state in 1892 (BicA, 10 June 1892). The funds of the society were exhausted on 7 March 1898 and the club ceased to exist when it was declared insolvent (BicA, 10 June 1898). Wendlebury Benefit Society was formed on its dissolution (Wendlebury 677). (See also appendix 2, Crimes 168).

677.   **Wendlebury Benefit Society, also Merton and Wendlebury Benefit Society**

Status: Unregistered **Type**: 7-year dividing friendly society
Established: 1898 **Dissolved**: Last known 1911
Headquarters: Plough Inn (1858-1911)
Anniversary/feast day: Whit Thursday
Membership: 25 members in 1901
Notes: The society was formed after the dissolution of Wendlebury Benefit Society (Wendlebury 676). The clubroom was decorated with lilac on club day (BicA, 31 May 1901).

Westcote Barton

No. of societies and members 1802/3 – None
No. of members of a friendly society 1813/14/15 – None
Notes: (See appendix 2, Crimes 169 and 170).

678.   **Barton Friendly Society**

Status: Registered, OXF 227 **Type:** 7-year dividing friendly society
Established: 15 October 1858   **Registered:** 16 June 1860 **Dissolved:** 6 October 1914
Headquarters: Schoolroom, Middle Barton (1860-1914)
Anniversary/feast day: First Tuesday in July, then second Tuesday in February (from 1895)
Minimum age at entry: 16 Maximum age at entry: 40
Membership: 130 members in 1860, 148 in 1865, 154 in 1873, 150 in 1878, 183 in 1885, 192 in 1891, 169 in 1899, 150 in 1902, 118 in 1908, 99 in 1914
Primary Sources: Rulebooks of 1860 and 1894, TNA, FS 15/569; Rulebooks of 1868 and 1895, Bodl. G.A. OXF 8° 596; letter of 5 July 1878 from Edward Marshall to Barton Friendly Society, Bodl. G.A.Oxon. C22

Notes: Club colours were red, white, and blue. The society had a large number of honorary members, 35 in 1860 and 24 in 1873. After chairing the club day meeting in 1878, Edward Marshall wrote to the club suggesting that they should not apply for alcohol extensions in future years. In 1895 the club secretary, Mark Gibson, committed suicide as he could not account for £89 of club funds (see appendix 2, Crimes 171). The society had a plain banner with the words 'Barton Friendly Society 1858'. The society dissolved with 99 members and £1,859 11s 5d funds.

Weston on the Green

No. of societies and members 1802/3 – None
No. of members of a friendly society 1813/14/15 – None
Notes: A club day was held in 1914, after the last friendly society had been dissolved. The *Bicester Advertiser* commented that 'This was one day in the year when labourer, farmer and parson all came together. They realized they were all human beings, and they forgot the distinction that bothered them on other occasions' (BicA, 5 June 1914).

679.   Weston-on-the-Green Friendly Society

Status: Registered, OXF 213 **Type**: Permanent friendly society
Established: 1859   **Registered:** 2 February 1859 **Dissolved**: 29 May 1862
Headquarters: Chequers Inn (1859-1862)
Anniversary/feast day: 29 May
Minimum age at entry: 16 **Maximum age at entry**: 45
Primary Sources: Rulebook of 1859, TNA, FS 1/581/213; TNA, FS 4/42/213
Notes: A letter to the Registrar stated the society dissolved on 29 May 1862.

680.   Weston-on-the-Green Friendly Society

Status: Unregistered, then registered, OXF 388 **Type:** Permanent friendly society
Established: 5 July 1875   **Registered:** 7 January 1899 **Dissolved:** 8 April 1913
Headquarters: Schoolroom [1881-1910]
Anniversary/feast day: Whit Tuesday
Minimum age at entry: 16 Maximum age at entry: 40
Membership: Rulebook of 1898, TNA, FS 3/322/388; TNA, FS 4/42/388; rulebooks of 1877 and 1889, Bodl. G.A. 8° 1303; rulebooks of 1889 and 1899,

membership book, Roll of members 1911, photographs, solicitors' account 1894-1899 of Mallam & Co., Weston on the Green History Society archives
Primary Sources: 45 members in 1881, 60 members in 1885, 65 in 1890, 69 in 1901, 60 in 1908, 59 in 1913
Notes: This is one of the three most well documented societies in Oxfordshire with a substantial amount of surviving records. New members were required to reside in Weston-on-the-Green, and to have done so for the previous 12 months (1889 rules, not included in 1899). The society gave superannuation benefit at 70. The rector urged the society to register in 1885 but it was recognized that if it did, subscriptions for older members would need to increase (BicA, 29 May 1885). In 1894, the secretary, Edward Hicks appropriated approximately £200 (see appendix 2, Crimes 172). The society was dissolved with £988 funds.

Wheatley

No. of societies and members 1802/3 – None
No. of members of a friendly society 1813/14/15 – 50, 70, 90
Notes: In 1870, it was reported that the numbers at the Wheatley club dinners were below normal due to the bitterness of feeling between tradesmen and the labouring poor as to common rights of the parish (TG, 14 June 1870). (See also appendix 2, Crimes 179 and 181).

681.   Court Constitution

Status: Branch of an affiliated order, OXF 303 **Type:** AOF **Branch No.** 5308
Established: 1869   **Registered:** 1870 **Dissolved:** Post 1918
Headquarters: Railway Hotel (1869-1875), Court Road (1876-1877), King's Arms Inn (1878-post 1918)
Membership: 33 members in 1871, 45 in 1874, 58 in 1876, 69 in 1880, 68 in 1885, 93 in 1900, 137 in 1895, 153 in 1900, 162 in 1905, 172 in 1910
Notes: In 1891 the branch made a subscription of £3 3s to the Radcliffe Infirmary (JOJ, 6 June 1891). (See also appendix 2, Crimes175).

682.   Crown Inn Friendly Society

Status: Enrolled, OXF 101 **Type:** Permanent friendly society
Established: 5 December 1823   **Registered:** 29 July 1844 **Dissolved:** 4 January 1861
Headquarters: Crown Inn (1823-1861)
Anniversary/feast day: Whit Tuesday
Minimum age at entry: 15 (after 1845) Maximum age at entry: 45

Membership: 47 members in 1855
Primary Sources: Rulebook of 1844, TNA, FS 1/578/101; TNA, FS 4/42/101
Notes: There was a division of £284 1s 6¾d in 1854. It was dissolved in 1861 with 16 members sharing £50 10 7½ funds. The society re-formed as Wheatley 683.

683.   Crown Inn Friendly Society

Status: Registered, OXF 241 **Type:** Permanent friendly society
Established: 1861   **Registered:** 18 December 1861 **Dissolved:** 20 June 1871
Headquarters: Crown Inn (1861-1871)
Anniversary/feast day: Whit Tuesday
Minimum age at entry: 15 Maximum age at entry: 45
Membership: 43 members in 1862, 50 in 1863, 55 in 1866, 65 in 1871
Primary Sources: Rulebook of 1861, TNA, FS 1/581/241; TNA, FS 4/42/241
Notes: The society formed after the dissolution of Wheatley 682. It was dissolved in 1871 with 65 members and £320 funds.

684.   King and Queen Friendly Benefit Society (1861-1862) White Hart Benefit Society (1862-1871)

Status: Registered, OXF 238 **Type:** Permanent friendly society
Established: 1861   **Registered:** 21 August 1861 **Dissolved:** 1871
Headquarters: King and Queen Inn (1861-1862), White Hart Inn (1862-1870), Railway Hotel (1870-1871)
Anniversary/feast day: Whit Tuesday
Minimum age at entry: 18 Maximum age at entry: 45
Membership: 43 members in 1862, 50 in 1863, 55 in 1866, 65 in 1871
Primary Sources: Rulebook of 1861, TNA, FS 1/581/238; TNA, FS 4/42/238
Notes: The society dissolved in 1871 with 58 members and £258 16s funds.

685.   King and Queen Slate Club

Status: Unregistered **Type**: Annual dividing friendly society
Established: 18 February 1899 **Dissolved**: Last known 1899
Headquarters: King and Queen Inn (1899)
Membership: 15 in 1899
Notes: A meeting was held at the King and Queen public house to discuss the establishment of a slate club in 1899 with 25 people present. The rules of a High Wycombe club were discussed and amended and it was agreed to form the club. Fifteen members joined and the society agreed to meet every

Saturday. The amount of 1s 3d was to be paid on entry and members would receive a copy of the rules and a contribution card. Payments were 6d per week and after three months, sickness benefit of 8s a week could be drawn. There was an annual division of funds at Christmas (JOJ 29/7/1899).

686.   Loyal Jubilee Lodge

Status: Branch of an affiliated order **Type:** IOOFMU **Branch No.** 7068
Established: 1891 **Dissolved:** Post 1918
Headquarters: White Hart Inn (1891-post 1918)
Anniversary/feast day: July or August
Membership: 25 members in 1892, 46 in 1894, 53 in 1895, 97 in 1897, 88 in 1901, 98 in 1905, 102 in 1910, 101 in 1914
Notes: Oxford District of IOOFMU. The branch took part in Headington Hospital Sunday in 1892 (JOJ, 23 July 1892).

687.   Loyal Jubilee Lodge, Juvenile Branch

Status: Juvenile branch of an affiliated order **Type:** IOOFMU
Established: 25 April 1892 **Dissolved:** Post 1914
Headquarters: Ye Merrie Bells (1892-1893]

688.   The Orange and Blue Benefit Society

Status: Unregistered **Type:** Annual dividing friendly society
Established: First known 1899 **Dissolved:** Last known 1899
Anniversary/feast day: Whit Tuesday
Notes: The club met on Whit Tuesday but there were no stalls or band engaged (TG, 30 May 1899).

689.   Wheatley Associated Providential Benefit Society

Status: Enrolled, OXF 11 **Type:** Friendly society
Established: First known 1831   **Registered:** 27 June 1831 **Dissolved:** Last known 1850
Headquarters: White Hart Inn (1831-1850]
Minimum age at entry: 16 Maximum age at entry: 45, reduced to 40 in 1838
Membership: 65 in 1846, 70 in 1849, 56 in 1850
Primary Sources: Rulebooks of 1831 and 1838, TNA, FS 1/574/11; TNA, FS 4/42/11

Notes: The rules were enrolled at the Trinity Quarter Sessions in 1831 and Trinity 1838. In 1882 a letter from the Registrar was returned, marked, 'No Society at White Hart Inn Wheatley' (TNA, FS 4/42/11).

690.   Wheatley Friendly Society

Status: Enrolled **Type**: Friendly society
Established: 25 March 1825   **Registered:** 1826 **Dissolved**: Last known 1826
Primary Sources: Oxon. Cal. QS iii, p.672
Notes: The rules were enrolled at the Epiphany Quarter Sessions in 1826.

691.   Wheatley Friendly Society

Status: Registered, OXF 310 **Type**: Permanent friendly society
Established: First known 1871   **Registered:** 29 August 1871 **Dissolved**: Last known 1885
Headquarters: Crown Inn (1871-1881), King's Arms Inn (1881-1882), Red Lion Inn (1882-1885)
Anniversary/feast day: Whit Tuesday
Membership: 54 in 1874, 48 in 1878, 42 in 1880, 29 in 1885
Primary Sources: TNA, FS 4/42/310
Notes: No file exists in the Registrar's papers at TNA. A letter was returned to the Registrar stamped 18 January 1889 stating the society was 'dead' (TNA, FS 4/42/310).

692.   Wheatley New Benefit Society

Status: Enrolled **Type**: Friendly society
Established: 1 January 1824   **Registered:** 1826 **Dissolved**: Last known 1826
Headquarters: White Hart Inn (1824-1826)
Primary Sources: Oxon. Cal. QS iii, p.676
Notes: The rules enrolled at the Michaelmas Quarter Session in 1826.

693.   Wheatley Tradesmen's Hand-in-Hand Benefit Society

Status: Enrolled, OXF 79 **Type:** Friendly society
Established: First known 1845   **Registered:** 19 December 1845 **Dissolved:** 7 March 1892
Headquarters: King's Arms Inn (1845-1892)
Anniversary/feast day: Whit Tuesday
Minimum age at entry: 18, 17 from 1873 **Maximum age at entry:** 35

Membership: 69 in 1862, 72 in 1866, 55 in 1874, 43 in 1878, 48 in 1880, 39 in 1885, 26 in 1891
Primary Sources: Rulebooks of 1845 and 1854, TNA, FS 3/319/79; TNA, FS 4/42/79
Notes: The society required new members to be in receipt of a minimum weekly income of 12s. A steward of the club, Henry Quarterman was prosecuted for embezzlement of £19 17s 8d funds from the club in 1849 (see appendix 2, Crimes 173). The officials of the society were taken to court on four separate occasions by sick members between 1867 and 1890 for refusal to pay and illegal expulsion from the society (see appendix 2, Crimes 174, 176, 177 and 180). All cases were found in favour of the member. A letter from the Secretary, R. Ward, dated 12 March 1892 stated all funds were used up due to sickness and so the society was dissolved at a general meeting (TNA, FS 4/42/79).

White Hart Benefit Society - see King and Queen Friendly Benefit Society, Wheatley 684

694.   Ye Merrie Bells Subordinate Division

Status: Branch of an affiliated order **Type**: OSOT **Branch No.** 704
Established: 1889 **Dissolved**: Post 1914
Headquarters: Ye Merrie Bells Coffee Palace (1890-1914)
Membership: 40 members in 1905, 51 in 1910

Whitchurch

No. of societies and members 1802/3 – None
No. of members of a friendly society 1813/14/15 – 71, 73, 73

695.   Collins End Friendly Society

Status: Enrolled, OXF 88 **Type**: 5-year dividing friendly society
Established: 2 April 1840   **Registered:** 13 December 1845 **Dissolved**: Last known 1845
Headquarters: Collins End Public House (1840-1843)
Minimum age at entry: 18 **Maximum age at entry**: 40
Primary Sources: Rulebook of 1845, TNA, FS 1/578/88; TNA, FS 4/42/85; BRO, D/EX 1044/7/6
Notes: The society had a militia substitute rule with £10 being available for a member to find a substitute. It also had the role of pitchermen as officials, two

members who were responsible for pouring out and distributing the beer on club quarter-nights and on club day.

696.   Pride of Whitchurch

Status: Branch of an affiliated order   **Type**: AOF **Branch No.** 7732
Established: 1890 **Dissolved**: 1892
Headquarters: Royal Oak (1889-1892)
Membership: 18 members in 1890, 12 in 1892
Notes: Reading District of AOF. It amalgamated with Court Allnut, Goring in 1892 (Goring 306).

697.   Pride of Whitchurch, Juvenile Branch

Status: Juvenile branch of an affiliated order   **Type**: AOF
Established: 1890 **Dissolved**: 1892
Headquarters: Royal Oak (1889-1892)
Membership: 2 members in 1890

698.   Whitchurch Friendly Society

Status: Enrolled, OXF 10 **Type**: Permanent friendly society
Established: October 1830   **Registered:** 4 April 1831 **Dissolved**: Last known 1885
Headquarters: Royal Oak Inn, Ferry Boat Inn and Collin's End Public House alternately (1830), Royal Oak (1831-1855], Royal Oak Inn, Ferry Boat Inn and Collin's End Public House alternately (1876), Royal Oak Inn [1880-1885)
Minimum age at entry: 16 **Maximum age at entry**: 30
Primary Sources: Rulebooks of 1830, TNA, FS 3/319/10; TNA, FS 4/42/10
Notes: The revised rulebook of 1830 indicates the society had existed before that date. The society was open to male and female members with the latter admitted for half subscription and half benefit of male members, plus lying-in benefit of 10s. The society had ceased to exist by 1894.

699.   Whitchurch Women's Friendly Society

Status: Unregistered **Type**: Annual dividing friendly society
Established: 25 March 1860 **Dissolved**: 1882
Minimum age at entry: 18 **Maximum age at entry**: 40
Membership: 24 members in 1860, 45 in 1861, 50 in 1865, 55 in 1870, 59 in 1875, 87 in 1881

Primary Sources: Printed rules of 1860, membership and payment records 1860-1882, OHC, PAR 287/13/F3/1
Notes: This is one of only five independent all-female friendly societies in Oxfordshire and the only one where original membership records survive. The society was open to married women residing in the parish of Whitchurch. They could join at any age, though unmarried women were required to be aged 21 years. Members leaving the parish had to withdraw from the society. Lying-in benefit was paid in addition to sickness and burial benefit. Although an annual dividing society, the division at year end was given in clothing tokens rather than cash. The Rev. E. Moore was responsible for the formation of the club and the membership book indicates that after 1882 a lying-in charity was to replace it.

Wiggington

No. of societies and members 1802/3 – None
No. of members of a friendly society 1813/14/15 – None

700. Loyal Wiggington Lodge

Status: Branch of an affiliated order **Type:** IOOFMU **Branch No.** 7524
Established: 10 April 1899 **Dissolved:** Post 1918
Headquarters: National schoolroom (1899-post 1914)
Anniversary/feast day: Whit Wednesday
Membership: 39 members in 1901, 61 in 1905, 69 in 1910, 59 in 1914
Primary Sources: Record book 1889-1938, OHC, O23/1/12/A2
Notes: Banbury District of IOOFMU. The society was formed from Wiggington Labourers' Friendly society (Wiggington 702). Club day was celebrated with a tea but in 1900 it was reported 'few members were willing or able to attend' (DDM, July 1900).

701. Wiggington Friendly Society

Status: Unregistered **Type:** Friendly society
Established: First known 1876 **Dissolved:** Last known 1878
Headquarters: Schoolroom (1878)
Anniversary/feast day: Wednesday in Ascension week
Membership: 24 members in 1878
Notes: Club day was celebrated with a public tea (BG, 15 June 1876).

702.   Wiggington Labourers' Friendly Society

Status: Registered, OXF 343 **Type:** Friendly society
Established: 1881 **Registered:** 16 February 1881   **Dissolved:** 21 November 1898
Headquarters: Mr Joshua Powell's (1881-1896), National School (1896 -1898)
Anniversary/feast day: Wednesday in Ascension week
Minimum age at entry: 16 Maximum age at entry: 40
Membership: 32 members in 1885, 53 in 1891, 39 in 1898
Primary Sources: Rulebook of 1897, TNA, FS 3/321/343
Notes: At a meeting on 4 July 1898, the society resolved to apply to the Oddfellows to be admitted to the society as a registered branch (DDM, August 1898). On 29 January 1902 the society retrospectively requested the Registrar to cancel their registration from 21 November 1898, having become the Loyal Wiggington Lodge of the IOOFMU (Wiggington 700).

Witney

No. of societies and members 1802/3 – 4, 335
No. of members of a friendly society 1813/14/15 – 248, 246, 247
Notes: The oldest identified friendly society in Oxfordshire was the King's Arms Friendly Society (Witney 712), established in 1750. Witney also had the first branch of an affiliated order in the county, the Bud of Friendship Lodge of the IOOFMU (Witney 704), established in 1836. The town had the second highest number of societies in Oxfordshire in 1803 alongside Charlbury and Woodstock with four, and Oxford having most. (See also appendix 2, Crimes 182 and 183).

703.   (Blanket Hall) Friendly Society

Status: Enrolled, OXF 74   **Type**: Permanent friendly society
Established: 1834   **Registered:** 29 August 1834   **Dissolved**: Last known 1846
Headquarters: Blanket Hall (1835)
Anniversary/feast day: First Friday in July
Maximum age at entry: 30
Primary Sources: Rulebook of 1834, TNA, FS 1/577/74; TNA, FS 1/577/74
Notes: The society had twelve directors. The Treasurer and eight directors were honorary members giving overall control of club. Payments were 3d

per week. On club day the society paraded to Cogges church and in 1841, E. Earley presented the financial statement of the club (JOJ, 10 July 1841). In both 1844 and 1846 the society dined at the Marlborough Arms (JOJ, 13 July 1844 and 11 July 1846).

704. Bud of Friendship Lodge

Status: Branch of an affiliated order **Type**: IOOFMU **Branch No.** 3604
Established: 1836 **Dissolved**: 1850
Headquarters: King's Arms Inn [1844-1850)
Membership: 48 members in 1844, 77 in 1845, 91 in 1846, 72 in 1850
Notes: Oxford District of IOOFMU (1844-1846). Witney District (1850). The Bud of Friendship Lodge was the first branch of one of the affiliated orders to be established in the county. The lodge dissolved in 1850 and a new branch, The Fountain of Friendship (Witney 709) was established the same year.

705. Christian Mutual Aid (Benefit) Society

Status: Unregistered, then registered, OXF 347   **Type**: Permanent friendly society
Established: 1849   **Registered:** 24 October 1882   **Dissolved**: 21 July 1897
Headquarters: Wesleyan Chapel Schoolroom (1880-1893]
Anniversary/feast day: Whit Monday
Membership: 227 members in 1885, 224 in 1891, 98 in 1897
Primary Sources: Rulebook of 1882, TNA, FS 3/321/347; TNA, FS 4/42/347
Notes: The society was unregistered for it first 33 years of existence (WG, 15 June 1889). It was suspended for three months in April 1888 and June 1888 by Registrar for failing to make returns. The society took part in Witney Hospital Sunday parade in 1893 (WG, 27 May 1893). It was dissolved in 1897 with 98 members and £55 funds.

706. Court Windrush

Status: Branch of an affiliated order **Type**: AOF **Branch No.** 7846
Established: 1890 **Dissolved**: Post 1918
Headquarters: Bull Inn (1890-post 1918]
Membership: 35 members in 1891, 105 in 1895, 128 in 1900, 156 in 1905, 159 in 1910
Notes: Oxford District of AOF. The branch took part in Witney Hospital Sunday parades in 1890s. In 1900, the annual dinner on 6 December was 'sparsely attended' (JOJ, 29 December 1900). Francis Solomon Barnes, a

plumber of Corn Street was secretary of the society from its formation but in 1903 faced charges of embezzling £200 of the society's funds (see appendix 2, Crimes 184).

707. Cross Keys Benefit Club

Status: Unregistered   **Type**: Friendly society
Established: First known 1821 **Dissolved**: Last known 1825
Headquarters: Cross Keys Inn (1821-1825)
Primary Sources: Loan documents to William Moulder from the society, OHC, B5/44/F/1-3

> **Cross Keys Friendly Society** – see Crown Inn Friendly Society, Witney 708

708. Crown Inn Friendly Society, then (from 1874) Cross Keys Friendly Society

Status: Registered, OXF 249   **Type:** Permanent friendly society
Established: 1861   **Registered:** 17 December 1862   **Dissolved:** 26 March 1878
Headquarters: Crown Inn (1862-1874), Cross Keys Inn (1874-1878)
Anniversary/feast day: First Friday in August
Minimum age at entry: 18 Maximum age at entry: 35
Membership: 20 members in 1863, 14 members in 1865, 16 in 1870, 17 in 1874, 14 in 1878
Primary Sources: Rulebook of 1862, TNA, FS 1/581/249; TNA, FS 4/42/249
Notes: The society dissolved in 1878 with 14 members and £56 9s 4¼d funds.

709. Fountain of Friendship Lodge

Status: Branch of an affiliated order **Type**: IOOFMU **Branch No.** 4440
Established: 1850 **Dissolved**: 1850
Headquarters: Cross Keys Inn (1850)
Membership: 11 members in 1850
Notes: Witney District of IOOFMU (1850). The lodge formed after the dissolution of the Bud of Friendship Lodge (Witney 704), but did not survive one year. After the lodge closed there was no Oddfellows presence in Witney until the Loyal Garibaldi in 1864 (Witney 715).

710.   Hand-in-Hand Friendly Society

Status: Enrolled, OXF 44   **Type:** Permanent friendly society
Established: 1837   **Registered:** 4 July 1837   **Dissolved:** Last known 1837
Headquarters: Cross Keys Inn (1837)
Maximum age at entry: 35
Primary Sources: Rulebook of 1837, TNA, FS 1/576/44; TNA, FS 4/42/44
Notes: The rules stated that members at joining must earn a minimum of 6s a week.

711.   Hearts of Oak Friendly Society

Status: Branch of a registered society   **Type:** Permanent friendly society
Established: First known 1882 **Dissolved:** Last known 1894
Notes: The branch held supper at the Coffee Tavern in 1882 (JOJ, 7 January 1882) and were part of the Witney Hospital Sunday parade in the 1890s.

712.   King's Arms Friendly Society, also Witney Friendly Society

Status: Enrolled, OXF 170 **Type:** Permanent friendly society
Established: 29 September 1750   **Registered:** 1793   **Dissolved:** Last known 1794
Headquarters: King's Head (1789), King's Arms (1793), Crown Inn and King's Head Inn (1794)
Anniversary/feast day: Friday, on or before 29 September
Maximum age at entry: 30
Primary Sources: Three manuscript documents of rules, one dated 1794 and two undated, TNA, FS 1/580/170; manuscript rules dated 10 August 1793, TNA, FS 3/320/170; TNA, FS 4/42/170
Notes: The oldest recorded friendly society in Oxfordshire. All the rules stated a maximum of 100 members and the same club day. Two describe the meeting place as the Crown Inn, one as King's Head (1794).

713.   King's Head Friendly Society

Status: Unregistered   **Type:** Friendly society
Established: First known 1881 **Dissolved:** Last known 1893
Headquarters: King's Head (1881-1893)
Anniversary/feast day: Whit Monday

Notes: The society held a dinner only on club day in 1893, with no parade (WG, 27 May 1893).

714.   London Friendly Institution, Witney Branch

Status: Branch of a registered society, LND 57   **Type:** Permanent friendly society
Established: First known 1841 **Dissolved:** Last known 1882
Membership: 96 members in 1872
Primary Sources: Rulebooks of 1841, 1869 and 1882, TNA, FS 15/1662; BPP 1874, XXIII, (c.997), p.92
Notes: The rulebooks show the presence of a medical attendant for the society at Witney indicating the existence of the branch in the town. This is confirmed by *Jackson's Oxford Journal* (25 November 1848) and the Assistant Commissioner in 1872.

715.   Loyal Garibaldi Lodge

Status: Branch of an affiliated order, OXF 318 **Type:** IOOFMU **Branch No.** 5261
Established: 1864 **Dissolved:** Post 1918
Headquarters: Angel Inn (1864-1892], Town Hall [1894-post 1918)
Anniversary/feast day: Whit Monday
Membership: 50 members in 1865, 35 in 1866, 32 in 1871, 61 in 1874, 90 in 1875, 81 in 1878, 106 in 1886, 173 in 1891, 205 in 1894, 229 in 1895, 355 in 1897, 323 in 1901, 388 in 1905, 424 in 1910, 453 in 1913
Notes: Oxford District of IOOFMU (1866). At the club day dinner in 1889, W. Clinch was the speaker and revealed he had been a member of the Bud of Friendship Lodge when it was formed 53 years earlier (Witney 704) (WG, 15 June 1889). The society was engaged in Hospital Sunday at Witney from 1890 to at least 1895. The branch was named after Giuseppe Garibaldi, one of the heroes of Italian unification, who visited London in 1864.

716.   Nag's Head Friendly Society

Status: Unregistered   **Type:** Friendly society
Established: First known 1893 **Dissolved:** Last known 1893
Headquarters: Nag's Head (1893)
Anniversary/feast day: Whit Monday

Notes: The society took part in Witney Hospital Sunday parade on Whit Sunday 1893 and celebrated their club day on Whit Monday (WG, 27 May 1893).

717. The Sociable Friendly Society

Status: Enrolled, OXF 190 **Type**: Permanent friendly society
Established: 1789 **Dissolved**: Last known 1789
Headquarters: Royal Oak Inn (1789)
Anniversary/feast day: Friday, on or last one before the feast of St Michael
Primary Sources: Undated rules, TNA, FS 1/580/190; TNA, FS 4/42/190

718. Union Benefit Society

Status: Unregistered   **Type**: Friendly society
Established: 1851 **Dissolved**: Last known 1857
Headquarters: Holly Bush Inn (1857)
Anniversary/feast day: Whit Tuesday

> **Witney Friendly Society** – see King's Arms Friendly Society, Witney 712

719. Witney Friendly Society

Status: Enrolled, OXF 187   **Type**: Permanent friendly society
Established: Not known **Dissolved**: Not known
Headquarters: Golden Ball Inn (date unknown)
Anniversary/feast day: Year end
Maximum age at entry: 30
Primary Sources: Undated manuscript rules, TNA, FS 1/580/187; TNA, FS 4/42/187
Notes: Members admitted were required to earn a minimum of 6s a week. Rules are identical in appearance and style to Witney Friendly society (Witney 720) although in manuscript form. They are probably late-eighteenth century.

720. Witney Friendly Society

Status: Enrolled   **Type**: Permanent friendly society
Established: 1809 **Dissolved**: Last known 1809
Headquarters: George Inn (1809)
Anniversary/feast day: Year end

Maximum age at entry: 30
Primary Sources: Rules of 1809, OHC, QSD/R/32
Notes: The society could have a maximum 100 male members.

721. Witney Subordinate Division

Status: Branch of an affiliated order **Type:** OSOT **Branch No.** 759
Established: 1892 **Dissolved:** Post 1913
Headquarters: Coffee Tavern, High Street (1892-1905), Witney Temperance Hotel (1905-1913)
Membership: 97 members in 1905, 108 in 1910
Notes: The branch took part in Witney Hospital Sunday parades from 1892.

Wolvercote

No. of societies and members 1802/3 – None
No. of members of a friendly society 1813/14/15 – None

722. Court Fair Rosamund's Bower

Status: Branch of an affiliated order **Type:** AOF **Branch No.** 7514
Established: 1886 **Dissolved:** Post 1918
Headquarters: Red Lion Inn [1903-post 1918)
Anniversary/feast day: Whit Monday
Membership: 15 members in 1887, 27 in 1888, 71 in 1895, 83 in 1900, 110 in 1905, 135 in 1910
Notes: Oxford District of AOF. On club day, sports were also held on Wolvercote Common in Port Meadow (JOJ, 6 June 1903).

723. Independent Mutual Brethren Friendly Society, Wolvercote Lodge

Status: Branch of a registered society, MDX 4880   **Type:** Permanent friendly society **Branch No.** 202
Established: First known 1883 **Dissolved:** Last known 1883
Notes: The officers of the branch were summoned to Bullingdon Petty Session in 1883 by a member's widow for non payment of benefit (see appendix 2, Crimes 185).

Woodcote

No. of societies and members 1802/3 – None
No. of members of a friendly society 1813/14/15 – None

724.   Compton Pilgrims Friendly Society, Woodcote branch

Status: Branch of a registered society, BRK 86 **Type**: Permanent friendly
society
Established: 1892 **Dissolved**: Post 1913
Anniversary/feast day: Whit Monday
Membership: 27 members in 1893, 30 in 1895, 55 in 1900, 40 in 1904, 42 in
1908, 39 in 1913
Notes: The branch was formed in 1892 with the appointment of an agent,
steward and trustee (BOA, 17 June 1892). Club day was held at Compton,
Berkshire.

725.   Woodcote Friendly Society

Status: Registered, OXF 84   **Type**: 5-year dividing friendly society
Established: 12 June 1838   **Registered:** 19 April 1844   **Dissolved**: Last
known 1844
Headquarters: Red Lion Inn [1844)
Anniversary/feast day: Whit Monday
Minimum age at entry: 16 **Maximum age at entry**: 45
Primary Sources: Rulebook of 1844, TNA, FS 1/577/84; TNA, FS 4/42/84;
rulebook of 1844, BRO, D/EX 1044/7/7
Notes: The society had a militia substitute rule whereby if a member was
selected for militia duty, all members paid 1s towards a substitute. At division,
£1 per member was carried forward to the following club. The society also had
two pitchermen, selected each year to pour and equally distribute the beer at
club day.

Woodstock

No. of societies and members 1802/3 – 4, 294
No. of members of a friendly society 1813/14/15 – 283, 263, 247
Notes: Woodstock had the second highest number of societies in Oxfordshire
in 1803 alongside Charlbury and Witney, with Oxford having most.

726.   [Blue Boar] Friendly Society

Status: Enrolled, OXF 185   **Type**: Permanent friendly society
Established: First known 1806 **Registered:** 28 April 1806   **Dissolved**: Last known 1806
Headquarters: Blue Boar Inn (1806)
Primary Sources: TNA, FS 4/42/185
Notes: No file for this society exists in the Registrar's papers at TNA.

727.   Court Loyal Blenheim

Status: Branch of an affiliated order, OXF 304   **Type:** AOF Branch No. 5428
Established: 7 March 1870 **Registered:** 12 April 1870   **Dissolved:** Post 1918
Headquarters: Crown Inn (1870-1874), King's Arms Inn (1874-post 1918)
Minimum age at entry: 18 Maximum age at entry: 40
Membership: 20 members in 1870, 53 in 1872, 91 in 1874, 180 in 1879, 262 in 1885, 372 in 1890, 389 in 1900, 345 in 1905, 306 in 1910
Primary Sources: Rulebook of 1870, TNA, FS 1/582/304; TNA, FS2/9
Notes: The Court was not initially associated with a district of AOF, but then joined the London United District (1873-post 1918). Register no. OXF 329 is a duplicate registration of this branch by the Registrar (TNA, FS2/9). On registration, the registered office was The Crown. There was either a change of rules or change of registered office notified in 1875 and this appears to have led to OXF 329 being applied to Court Loyal Blenheim. No separate papers or records exist at TNA under that reference. An anniversary dinner was held on a Monday in March and a fete at Blenheim Park on the last Monday in July. In 1875 the landlord of the King's Arms was prosecuted for serving alcohol to members after hours (see appendix 2, Crimes 187).The 1876 fete was 'disastrous' organisationally and financially. Captain Treloar's Imperial Clown Cricketers and Clown Band had been engaged for the day but they arrived two hours late. They consisted of two or three men for the band, four shabbily dressed cricketers with three or four other men. After an argument with their 'Captain', the troop disbanded and they failed to perform in the evening (JOJ, 29 July 1876). The following year, free entry was given to inmates of the Woodstock Union workhouse and the School of Industry (JOJ, 11 August 1877). In 1879, fete day moved to August Bank Holiday on the first Monday of that month. Attendance increased to almost 4,000 people in 1886 and 5,400 in 1888 but had declined to under 2,200 by 1895. In 1879 Dr F Stockwell was surgeon to the club as well as societies at Combe (219), Tackley

(632) and Stonesfield (626). The day of the fete had changed to Whit Tuesday by 1902. The Lodge had a juvenile branch (Woodstock 728).

728.   Court Loyal Blenheim, Juvenile Branch

Status: Juvenile branch of an affiliated order   **Type**: AOF
Established: 1904 **Dissolved**: Post 1912
Headquarters: Kings Arms (1904)
Minimum age at entry: 1 Maximum age at entry: 17
Membership: 6 members in 1904
Notes: Juvenile branch of Woodstock 727.

729.   Hand and Heart Benefit Society

Status: Registered, OXF 297   **Type:** 10-year dividing friendly society
Established: 1869 **Registered:** 16 April 1869   **Dissolved:** 1869
Headquarters: White Hart Inn (1869)
Anniversary/feast day: Third Friday in July
Minimum age at entry: 16 Maximum age at entry: 40
Membership: None
Primary Sources: Rulebook of 1869, TNA, FS 1/582/297; TNA, FS 4/42/297
Notes: Notice was given of the society's club day for 2 July 1869 at the White Hart Inn (JOJ, 26 June 1869). A letter to the Registrar dated of 19 January 1871 from James Mitchell, landlord of the White Hart revealed that the society 'never came of anything as a club' (TNA, FS 1/582/297). There were two monthly meetings with no attendance and the landlord found himself out of pocket for registration, copies of the rules and other account books.

730.   London Friendly Institution, Woodstock Branch

Status: Branch of a enrolled society, LND 57   **Type:** Permanent friendly society
Established: First known 1850 **Dissolved**: Last known 1882
Primary Sources: File of LFI including rulebooks of 1869 and 1882, TNA, FS 15/1662; BPP 1874, XXIII, (c.997), p.93
Notes: In 1850 the Woodstock branch dined at the Red Lion, Bladon, in mid July (JOJ, 20 July 1850). The Assistant Commissioner noted the presence of the branch in 1872 and a medical attendant for the society was indicated as present at Woodstock in the rulebooks of 1869 and 1882.

731.   Loyal Chaucer Lodge

Status: Branch of an affiliated order   **Type:** IOOFMU **Branch No.** 6471
Established: 9 February 1882 **Dissolved**: Last known 1882
Headquarters: Star Inn (1882)
Notes: Oxford District of IOOFMU. The *Oddfellows Magazine* reported the establishment of this lodge at Woodstock in its April-June quarter, 1882 but there is no trace after that year in the Oddfellows' records. The opening of the branch was reported as due to 'demands of the Tradesmen of the town' (JOJ, 18 February 1882).

732.   Loyal Marlborough Lodge

Status: Branch of an affiliated order, OXF 118 **Type:** IOOFMU Branch No. 3927
Established: 1846 **Registered:** 21 August 1852   **Dissolved:** 1869
Headquarters: Adam and Eve (1846), Old Angel Inn [1850-1869)
Minimum age at entry: 18 Maximum age at entry: 36
Membership: 32 members in 1846, 33 in 1850, 22 in 1857, 21 in 1863, 18 in 1869
Primary Sources: Rulebook of 1852, TNA, FS 1/578/118; TNA, FS 4/42/118
Notes: Oxford District of IOOFMU (1846-1849), Witney District (1850), and Woodstock District (1858-1868). A letter to the Registrar dated 28 April 1869 stated the society dissolved with 18 members and £469 16s 8d funds.

733.   Loyal Marlborough Lodge

Status: Branch of an affiliated order   **Type:** IOOFMU **Branch No.** 8299
Established: 1912 **Dissolved**: Post 1918
Headquarters: Olivet schoolroom (1912-post 1918)
Notes: Oxford District of IOOFMU. A banner for this lodge is housed by the Oxfordshire Museum service (OXCMS, 1979.161.1). It is square, red silk with a blue border; one side has a central painted cartouche of three angels holding a round, crowned plaque with figures and the legend 'Go thou and do likewise', with the legend 'Loyal Marlborough Lodge No 8299 I.O.O.F.M.U. Woodstock'. The other side has a central painted cartouche of three female figures and a legend in scroll 'We Unite to Assist Each Other'.

734.   New Angel Friendly Society, then from 1851 Woodstock Friendly Society

Status: Enrolled, OXF 129 **Type**: Permanent friendly society
Established: June 1838 **Registered:** 10 October 1851   **Dissolved**: 4 July 1879
Headquarters: New Angel Inn (1838-1856), Marlborough Arms Inn (1856-1879)
Anniversary/feast day: First Friday in July
Maximum age at entry: 30
Membership: 69 members in 1859, 71 in 1862, 93 in 1865, 49 in 1872, 27 in 1875, 23 in 1878, 14 in 1879
Primary Sources: Rulebook of 1851, TNA, FS 3/319/129; TNA, FS 4/42/129
Notes: A letter of 6 October 1856 to the Registrar from the landlord of the New Angel stated the club was moving to another public house in Woodstock. At Oxfordshire County Court on 23 January 1857 a member claimed he was illegally excluded from the club (see appendix 2, Crimes 186). It transpired the club had moved to the Marlborough Arms after Henry Haynes, a victualler and member of the club committee also moved there after 30 years at the New Angel. However, the rules had not been amended to reflect the new registered office (JOJ, 31 January 1857). A further letter to the Registrar dated 25 February 1857 informed the Registrar of the change of name of the society to Woodstock Friendly society, held at Marlborough Arms Inn. The society ceased to exist on club day in 1879 after a division of funds and decline in membership (JOJ, 12 July 1879). Funds were divided between the remaining 14 members, whose combined age was 763 years. A letter of 3 February 1892 was returned to the Registrar and stated the society had broken up (TNA, FS 4/42/129).

735.   Sovereign Benefit Society

Status: Registered, OXF 209   **Type:** 5-year dividing friendly society
Established: 2 August 1858 **Registered:** 13 November 1858   **Dissolved:** 17 January 1893
Headquarters: Star Inn (1858-1868), Woodstock Arms Inn (1869-1876], Royal Oak (1879), Woodstock Arms (1881)
Anniversary/feast day: First Friday in July
Minimum age at entry: 17 Maximum age at entry: 47
Membership: 80 members in 1872, 73 in 1877, 65 in 1880, 62 in 1885, 42 in 1891

Primary Sources: Rulebook 1858, TNA, FS 3/320/209; final balance sheet of society, FS 4/42/209
Notes: The club collapsed and ceased to exist with £39 14s 3d being divided amongst the 27 members.

736.   United Brethren Benefit Society

Status: Registered, OXF 206   **Type:** 5-year dividing friendly society
Established: 1858 **Registered:** 9 September 1858   **Dissolved:** September 1865
Headquarters: Crown Inn (1858-1865)
Anniversary/feast day: Second Friday in July
Minimum age at entry: 12 Maximum age at entry: 40
Membership: 54 members in 1859, 56 in 1863, 53 in 1864
Primary Sources: Rulebook of 1858, TNA, FS 1/581/206; TNA, FS 4/42/206
Notes: A letter to the Registrar dated 1 January 1866 stated the society was dissolved in September 1865 as funds were exhausted. It was re-formed as Woodstock 737.

737.   United Brethren Benefit Society

Status: Registered, OXF 272   **Type:** Dividing friendly society
Established: 1866 **Registered:** 29 May 1866   **Dissolved:** Last known 1876
Headquarters: Crown Inn (1866-1867), Blandford Arms (1867), New Angel (1868-1873), Adam and Eve (1873-1876)
Anniversary/feast day: First Friday in July
Minimum age at entry: 12 Maximum age at entry: 40
Membership: 26 members in 1866, 17 members in 1871, 16 in 1872, 15 in 1874
Primary Sources: Rulebook of 1866, TNA, FS 1/582/272; TNA, FS 4/42/272
Notes: This was a re-formed society from Woodstock 736. An undated letter to the Registrar from W. Ryman, late secretary, stated the society had 'broken up for want of funds' (TNA, FS 4/42/272). It was re-formed as Woodstock 738.

738.   United Brethren Benefit Society

Status: Registered, OXF 341   **Type:** Friendly society
Established: July 1879 **Registered:** 14 February 1880   **Dissolved:** 1886
Headquarters: Crown Inn (1879-1886)
Membership: 45 members in 1881, 27 in 1885, 26 in 1887
Primary Sources: TNA, FS 4/42/341

Notes: This was a society re-formed after Woodstock 737. It dissolved with 26 members and £21 funds.

739.   United Glovers Benefit Society

Status: Registered, OXF 225   **Type**: 3-year dividing friendly society
Established: 1859 **Registered:** 16 December 1859   **Dissolved**: Last known 1860
Headquarters: Mr Godden's Factory, Woodstock (1859)
Anniversary/feast day: First Tuesday in May
Minimum age at entry: 18 **Maximum age at entry**: 45
Primary Sources: Rulebook of 1859, TNA, FS 1/581/225; TNA, FS 1/580/188; TNA, FS 4/42/225
Notes: Members were required to have been in the glove trade for twelve months before being admitted as a member, or six months if aged under 18 years. An undated return to the Registrar indicated the society had 'broken up' is misfiled under TNA, FS 1/580/188. A presentation of a gold watch and chain and other items to Rev. E. Geare in January 1860 for his various charitable work, credited him with the foundation of the society and that 'he intended to encourage thrift and sobriety among gloving men, a class difficult to influence' (JOJ, 21 January 1860).

740.   Victoria Lodge

Status: Branch of an affiliated order **Type**: IOOFMU **Branch No.** 3336
Established: 1843 **Dissolved**: 1850
Headquarters: King's Arms Inn (1844-1850)
Membership: 36 in 1845, 44 in 1846, 31 in 1850
Notes: Oxford District of IOOFMU (1844-1849), Witney District (1850). The society was suspended in 1850 due to non compliance with AOF rules and it was dissolved.

741.   Woodstock District, IOOFMU

Status: District of an affiliated order, OXF 115 **Type**: IOOFMU
Established: 1852 **Registered:** 24 July 1852   **Dissolved**: Last known 1868
Headquarters: Old Angel Inn (1852)
Primary Sources: TNA, FS 4/42/115
Notes: This was registered as a friendly society with the Registrar but was a district structure and had no direct members. Affiliated branches in the district pooled their financial resources to spread risk.

Woodstock Friendly Society – see New Angel Friendly Society, Woodstock 734

742.   Woodstock Friendly Society

Status: Enrolled, OXF 130 **Type**: Permanent friendly society
Established: First known 1851 **Registered:** 12 March 1851   **Dissolved**: Last known 1851
Headquarters: King's Arms Inn (1851)
Primary Sources: TNA, FS 4/42/130
Notes: No file exists in the Registrar's records at TNA.

743.   Woodstock New Friendly Society

Status: Enrolled **Type**: Permanent friendly society
Established: 23 May 1757 **Registered:** 1794   **Dissolved**: Last known 1794
Headquarters: Old Angel Inn (1794)
Anniversary/feast day: Friday after mid-summer's day
Maximum age at entry: 30
Primary Sources: Rules of 1794, OHC, QSD/R/33
Notes: The rules permitted a maximum 101 members who had residency qualifications in that, 'No person can be admitted unless they belong to Woodstock or Old Woodstock'. It was three years before a member could receive benefit, an unusually long time. The society claimed to be earliest box club in the county (JOJ, 19 November 1788) although the Witney Friendly society has an earlier provenance (Witney 712), making it the second oldest known friendly society in Oxfordshire.

744.   Woodstock United Permanent Benefit Friendly Society

Status: Registered, OXF 309   **Type**: Permanent friendly society
Established: 1871 **Registered:** 1871   **Dissolved**: Post 1918
Headquarters: Olivet Chapel, Schoolroom (1871-1910]
Anniversary/feast day: Whit Monday, although it was held on the first or third Fridays in July between 1874 and 1881
Membership: 74 members in 1872, 86 in 1873, 130 in 1874, 170 in 1879, 175 in 1881, 226 in 1883, 308 in 1891, 403 in 1899, 430 in 1905, 459 in 1910
Primary Sources: Mortgage dated 2 August 1888, OHC, BOR4/2/D1/30D/2
Notes: The society accrued over £1,000 capital after just 14 years. A loan by way of mortgage of £250 plus interest, dated 2 August 1888, was made to the Borough of New Woodstock and was signed by the trustees of The Woodstock

United Permanent Benefit Society, William Crute (baker), Josiah Nutt Godden (glove manufacturer), and John Banbury (draper). It concerned three pieces of meadow land forming part of Corporation Meadows, New Woodstock (OHC, BOR4/2/D1/30D/2). The society survived into 1920s but no file relating to the society exists in the records of the Registrar at TNA.

Wootton

No. of societies and members 1802/3 – 1, 83
No. of members of a friendly society 1813/14/15 – 70, 72, 84

745.   Alliance Benefit Society

Status: Registered, OXF 192   **Type:** 5-year dividing friendly society, permanent after 1879
Established: 1857 **Registered:** 11 April 1857   **Dissolved:** Last known 1885
Headquarters: Three Horseshoes Inn (1857-1885)
Anniversary/feast day: Second Wednesday in July
Minimum age at entry: 15 Maximum age at entry: 40 (reduced to 36 in 1858)
Membership: 126 in 1862, 129 in 1864, 144 in 1866, 121 in 1871, 111 in 1874, 85 in 1878, 103 in 1880, 73 in 1885
Primary Sources: Rulebook of 1857, TNA, FS 3/320/192; TNA, FS 3/320/192; TNA, FS 4/42/189
Notes: The rule regarding the division of funds was amended in 1879 and division was no longer permitted. In a letter to the Registrar, from Charles Haynes, dated 23 May 1882, concerning the Reformed Benefit Society (Wootton 747), he added a footnote that the Alliance Benefit Society was held at the Three Horse Shoes in Wootton and no valuation had been made to its effects (TNA, FS 4/42/189). An unsigned note to the Registrar dated 19 March 1894 stated the club 'has been broken up for some time' (FS 3/320/192) and registration was finally cancelled on 24 March 1897.

746.   Independent Mutual Brethren Friendly Society, Wootton Lodge

Status: Branch of a registered society, MDX 4880   **Type:** Permanent friendly society
Established: First known 1882 **Dissolved:** Last known 1882
Headquarters: Killingworth Castle Inn (1882)
Primary Sources: TNA, FS 4/42/189

Notes: A letter to the Registrar concerning the Reformed Benefit Society, dated 23 May 1882 from Charles Haynes stated he was the secretary of the lodge, held at the Killingworth Castle (TNA, FS 4/42/189).

747. Killingworth Castle Friendly Society, later Reformed Benefit Society

Status: Enrolled, OXF 189   **Type**: Permanent friendly society
Established: 5 December 1791 **Registered:** 1807   **Dissolved**: 1880
Headquarters: Killingworth Castle (1791-1880)
Maximum age at entry: 35
Membership: 117 in 1862, 117 in 1864, 94 in 1872,
Primary Sources: Rules of 1791, 1807, 1859 and various other amendments, TNA, FS 1/580/189; TNA, FS 4/42/189
Notes: The society changed its name at some stage to Reformed Friendly society, at the latest by 1859. A letter to the Registrar dated 23 May 1882 from Charles Haynes stated the society had ceased 'for more than two years' and that a lodge of the IMBFS was now meeting at the Killingworth Castle (TNA, FS 4/42/189). Haynes was secretary of that society. He also informed the Registrar that the Wootton Alliance Friendly society (Wootton 745) meeting at the Three Horseshoes had undertaken no valuation of its assets.

> **Reformed Benefit Society** – see Killingworth Castle Friendly Society, Wootton 747

748. Woodleys Mutual Benefit Society

Status: Registered, OXF 233   **Type:** 5-year dividing friendly society
Established: 16 August 1860 **Registered:** 6 February 1861   **Dissolved:** Last known 1872
Headquarters: New Inn, Woodleys (1860-1872), Horseshoe Inn (1872)
Anniversary/feast day: First Monday after 19 September
Minimum age at entry: 15 Maximum age at entry: 40
Membership: 38 members in 1862, 41 in 1864
Primary Sources: Rulebook of 1860, TNA, FS 1/581/233; TNA, FS 4/42/233

749. Wootton Jubilee Benefit Society

Status: Registered, OXF 363   **Type:** Permanent friendly society
Established: 1887 **Registered:** 15 October 1888   **Dissolved:** 22 July 1890
Headquarters: Infant Schoolroom (1887-1890)

Minimum age at entry: 16 Maximum age at entry: 40
Membership: 11 members in 1890
Primary Sources: Rulebook of 1887, TNA, FS 3/322/363; TNA, FS 4/42/363
Notes: The society dissolved with 11 members and £20 9s funds.

Wroxton

No. of societies and members 1802/3 – None
No. of members of a friendly society 1813/14/15 – None
Notes: (See appendix 2, Crimes 188).

750.   Good Intent Lodge

Status: Branch of an affiliated order, OXF 119   **Type:** IOOFMU Branch No. 3656
Established: 1844   **Registered:** 20 October 1852   **Dissolved:** 1867
Headquarters: North Arms Inn (1844-1854), White Horse Inn (1854-1867)
Minimum age at entry: 18 Maximum age at entry: 36
Membership: 11 members in 1844, 25 in 1845, 40 in 1846, 32 in 1850, 34 in 1855, 27 in 1860, 33 in 1864, 92 members in 1867
Primary Sources: Rulebook of 1852, TNA, FS 1/578/119; TNA, FS 4/42/119; BPP 1874, XXIII, (c.997), p.119
Notes: Banbury District of IOOFMU. The lodge was suspended by IOOFMU in 1864. It dissolved in 1867 with 92 members and £537 funds and reformed as Good Intent Lodge Friendly Society (Wroxton 751). The Assistant Commissioner stated the branch left the IOOFMU in 1867 over a dispute about the amount of district levies.

751.   Good Intent Lodge Friendly Society

Status: Registered, OXF 278   **Type:** Permanent friendly society
Established: 23 February 1867 **Registered:** 27 March 1867   **Dissolved**: 1882
Headquarters: North Arms Inn (1867-1882)
Minimum age at entry: 16 **Maximum age at entry**: 32
Primary Sources: Rulebook of 1867, TNA, FS 1/582/278; TNA, FS 4/42/278; BPP 1874, XXIII, (c.997), p.119
Notes: This society was formed from the Good Intent Lodge of the IOOFMU (Wroxton 750). On admission members had to have minimum earnings of 10s per week. The Assistant Commissioner stated the society was old but left the IOOFMU in 1867 over a dispute about the amount of district levies. Five hundred pounds was divided when the lodge closed, but £170 was kept back to

form this society. There were only two or three members who were agricultural labourers. A letter from the Registrar was returned, dated 15 May 1882 marked 'This society is broken up.'

752.   North Arms Friendly Society

Status: Registered, OXF 336   **Type:** Permanent friendly society
Established: 1877 **Registered:** 14 March 1877   **Dissolved:** Last known 1911
Headquarters: North Arms Inn (1877-1879), National Schoolroom (1879-1911)
Minimum age at entry: 16 Maximum age at entry: 35
Membership: 34 members in 1877, 29 in 1885, 46 in 1891, 60 in 1899, 57 in 1905, 67 in 1910, 74 in 1914
Primary Sources: Rulebook of 1879, TNA, FS 3/321/336; TNA, FS 4/42/336
Notes: In 1911 it was reported that the society was celebrating its 52nd anniversary, indicating its evolution from Wroxton Friendly Society (Wroxton 755), (JOJ, 15 June 1911). There is no indication in the file at TNA when this society ceased to exist. There was a juvenile branch (Wroxton 753).

753.   North Arms Friendly Society, Juvenile Branch

Status: Juvenile branch of a registered society   **Type**: Juvenile friendly society
Established: First known 1896 **Dissolved**: Last known 1896
Membership: 74 members in 1914
Notes: A juvenile branch of the North Arms Friendly society, Wroxton 752 (JOJ, 11 June 1896).

754.   Wroxton Friendly Society

Status: Enrolled, OXF 45   **Type**: Permanent friendly society
Established: 11 June 1816 **Registered:** 1819   **Dissolved**: Last known 1847
Headquarters: White Horse Inn (1816-1837]
Anniversary/feast day: Whit Friday
Maximum age at entry: 35
Primary Sources: Oxon. Cal. QS iii, p.650; rulebook of 1837, TNA, FS 1/576/45; TNA, FS 1/576/44; letter of 1847, OHC, QSD/R/43
Notes: The rules were enrolled on 21 April 1819 at the Easter Quarter Session. The 1837 rules permitted a maximum of 100 members. All disputes were required to go to arbitration and not before the courts. A letter to the Clerk

of the Peace, dated 21 October 1847 from John M. Davenport asked whether registration of rules was complete (OHC, QSD/R/43).

755. **Wroxton Friendly Society**

Status: Registered, OXF 231   **Type**: Permanent friendly society
Established: 1860 **Registered:** 13 November 1860   **Dissolved**: 1877
Headquarters: North Arms Inn (1860-1877)
Primary Sources: TNA, FS 4/42/231; BPP 1874, XXIII, (c.997), p.119
Notes: The Assistant Commissioner stated the society was poor and had only 20 members. The feast was partly paid from the fund with 2s 6d from each attending member. The society re-formed as the North Arms Friendly Society (Wroxton 752).

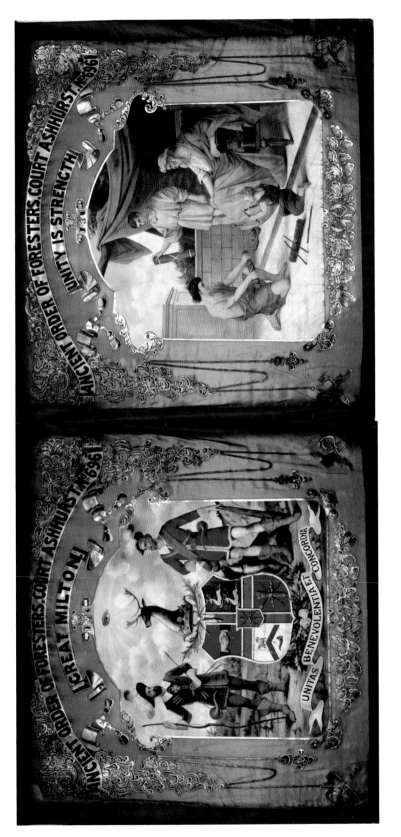

Banner of Court Ashurst, Ancient Order of Foresters, Great Milton (Calendar, Great Milton 315). (Photographs courtesy of Phil Ashworth.)

Banner of Loyal Mansfield Lodge, Independent Order of Oddfellows, Manchester Unity, Fringford (Calendar, Fringford 295). (Photographs courtesy of Peter Silver.)

BLETCHINGTON
FRIENDLY SOCIETY
ESTᴰ 1855
JUBILEE 1897.

Banner of Bletchingdon Friendly Society (Calendar, Bletchingdon 112), with detail of fringe and photograph of Bletchingdon Club Day with banner displayed. (Photographs by Shaun Morley and courtesy of Ian Gedling.)

CHALGROVE FRIENDLY SOCIETY

Established JULY 6th 1810.

Banner of Chalgrove Friendly Society (Calendar Chalgrove 168). (Photograph by Shaun Morley, courtesy of Rev. Ian Cohen.)

Club Day c.1905, Sibford Gower Friendly Society
(Calendar, Sibford Gower 576).

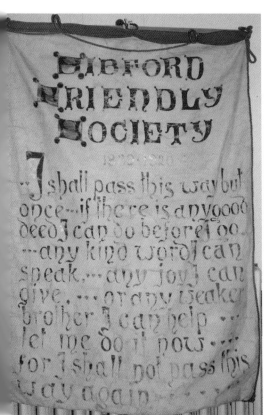

Banner of 1920
and Pole Head of
Sibford Gower
Friendly Society

(All photographs
by
Shaun Morley,
courtesy of the
Sibfords Society).

Prince of Wales Friendly Society Club Day, Clanfield 1911 (Calendar, Clanfield 213). (Photograph courtesy of Oxfordshire History Centre.)

Clanfield Club Day, 1910.
(Photograph courtesy of Oxfordshire History Centre.)

Club Day, North Arms Friendly Society, Wroxton (Calendar, Wroxton 752). (Photograph courtesy of Oxfordshire History Centre.)

Stole Lyne Friendly Society, c.1900-1910,(Calendar, Stoke Lyne 617) outside the Peyton Arms public house. (Photograph courtesy of Oxfordshire History Centre.)

Finstock Independent Friendly Society club day, outside Home Farm, School Road c.1908. (Photograph courtesy of Finstock Local History Society.)

(**Above**) Commemorative medal of Somerton Friendly and Benefit Society, 1863 (Calendar Somerton 581) (courtesy of Oxfordshire Museums Service).

(**Top left**) Beer token for the Thame Hand in Hand Benevolent Society (Calendar Thame 647) (courtesy of Thame Museum).

(**Left**) Membership token of the Compton Pilgrims Benefit Society (Berks) that had branches at Goring, Oxford, Watlington and Woodcote (courtesy of Shaun Morley).

MEMBER'S BOOK.

Months paid for.	Amount.			Initials of Manager.
	£	s.	d.	
3 Months To June 23 61		5	3 3/4	Thomas Goodey
3 Months to Sep 23 61		5	3 3/4	J. G.
3 Months to Dec 23 61		5	3 3/4	J. G.
3 Months to March 23 62		5	3 3/4	J. G.
3 Months to June 23 62		5	3 3/4	J. G.
3 Months to Sep 23 62		5	3 3/4	J. Goodey
3 Months to Dec 23 62		5	3 3/4	J. G.
3 Months to March 23 63		5	3 3/4	J. Goodey

Extract of membership card of Oxfordshire Friendly and Medical Benefit
Society, Charlbury (Calendar Charlbury 178). Member number 86,
James Claridge of Finstock, 1861-1875.
(courtesy of Jim Claridge, great-grandson of the member.)

Appendix 1   Glossary of terms

Term	Description
Accumulating society	A permanent society that did not divide its funds.
Affiliated order	A national organization comprised of independent or semi-autonomous branches, sometimes divided into districts. The individual affiliates or branches retained a degree of independence although as the nineteenth century progressed standardised rules and actuarial tables were adopted.
Agent	A local collector of subscriptions. This could be for a collecting society or in isolated areas covered by an independent friendly society.
Arbitration committee	A specified group of people to arbitrate on the interpretation of rules and validity of benefit claims, sometimes specified in the rules to prevent cases being taken to court.
Articles	The printed or manuscript rules or constitution of a society.
Beadle	The doorkeeper.
Bed-lying pay	Full sickness benefit.
Beer token	A metal disk given to a member at club meetings in exchange for a compulsory fee, often 3d, and exchanged for beer at the club-house. Part of the act of enforcing 'wet rent' (q.v.).
Benefit club, benefit society	A friendly society.
Benefit member	A member of a friendly society who paid an agreed regular subscription in return for defined benefits, normally receivable after a period of time defined in the rules of the society.
Bondsman	A person providing financial surety for the secretary.

Box	A locked box of wood or metal, usually kept at the clubhouse and secured by a number of locks, often three or five. The key for each lock was held by different club officials.
Box club	A friendly society where the books of the club and cash balance were retained in the box.
Box member	A benefit member of a box club.
Cash and check steward	Assisted the secretary in receiving contributions and fines from members.
Ceased to exist	A phrase used when a society came to a natural end, usually at the point when all funds of the society were exhausted and benefit payments could not be met by subscriptions.
Chairman	The chair of the managing committee.
Class	A division of membership subscription, often a graded system of increasing payments in return for increased benefit payments.
Clerk	Kept account of monies received and paid.
Club	A friendly society.
Club Day	The annual anniversary of a friendly society that could encompassed a parade to church for divine service, the hiring of a brass band, a club dinner for members and entertainment for the whole village.
Club room	The meeting place of a friendly society. It was frequently a room at a public house and in some cases, a purpose built or adapted clubroom. It could also be a schoolroom, a public building or occasionally a dwelling house.
Collector	Received subscriptions and paid out expenditure.
Compulsory beer	The requirement for a club member to expend a set amount on beer on a club night. Also known as 'wet rent' (q.v.).
Court	A branch of the Ancient Order of Foresters.
Court room	The meeting place of a Court.
Director	A member of the managing committee, usually an honorary member.

Dissolved by instrument	The formal dissolution of a registered friendly society in accordance with the rules of the club and Registrar of Friendly Societies.
Dividing society	A friendly society that intended to divide all or part of the remaining funds of the society at the end of a specified period, usually three, five, or seven years. Either the club would start afresh, or a set amount per member would be retained in the club to provide a balance of funds to pay benefits in the early years of a new society.
Doorkeeper	Controlled entry at the door, only allowing members in and preventing drunkenness.
Enrollment	The voluntary act of a friendly society to deposit the rules of a friendly society with Justices of the Peace after 1793 in return for which they were granted additional legal protection, until registration began in 1846.
Father	1. The senior member of the club, either by age or length of membership, 2. The chairman, or, 3. The honorary head of a friendly society, sometimes a Trustee; also known as the President.
Feast	A village festival held annually, usually on a particular day of the year, and the one or two days following. A great annual occasion for family gatherings and the entertainment of residents and visitors from a distance.
Flagman (Flagmen)	The man or men chosen to carry the club flag or banner.
Free member	A benefit member who was entitled to receive benefit having subscribed for the period required by the rules.
Friendly society	A mutual association, the members of which paid fixed contributions to insure pecuniary help in sickness or old age, and provision for their families in the event of death.
Governor	A member of managing committee, but not an honorary member.
Guardian	A doorkeeper.
Honorary member	A member of a friendly society who paid an agreed minimum annual sum but who was not entitled to draw benefit.
Kettledrum party	An afternoon tea-party on a large scale held instead of club day.

Lodge	A branch of the Independent Order of Oddfellows Manchester Unity or other oddfellow society.
Lodge room	The meeting place of a lodge.
Non-free member	A benefit member who had not served the required amount of time to be able to draw benefit.
Pay steward	The steward responsible for making sick and other benefit payments to members.
Pitcherman	A member designated to pour and equally distribute beer at monthly meetings and the annual meeting on club day. Stewards could assist after the collection of subscriptions.
President	The honorary head of a friendly society, sometimes a Trustee.
Provident club, Provident society	Either a friendly society or a savings club.
Purse club	A dividing friendly society.
Registered club	A club that had rules certified by The Registrar of Friendly Societies, and registered with the Registrar, available after 1846.
Registrar	The Registrar of Friendly Societies, the head of the government department. After 1875, the Chief Registrar.
Registration	The voluntary act of a friendly society to register with the Registry of Friendly Societies, in return for which they were granted additional legal protection.
Registration cancelled by request	The formal cancellation of the registration of a registered society, usually granted on the merger with another club or on becoming a branch of an affiliated order.
Relieving officer	A designated member who visited the sick and gave sick pay. A pay steward (q.v.).
Removal	1. The act of moving the club house or registered place, 2. The act of a member of an affiliated order moving from one branch to another.
Rose's Act	An Act for the Encouragement and Relief of Friendly Societies, 1793, promoted by George Rose.
Sanctuary	The branch of the Ancient Order of Shepherds, a higher order of the Ancient Order of Foresters where members paid higher subscription for increased benefit.

Secretary	An honorary or salaried role that frequently incorporated the treasurer's role. The secretary was not a benefit member of the society. The role of the secretary varied greatly but was responsible for the management of the club in accordance with the rules, including the accurate record of all business transactions.
Shop club	An unregistered sick club, with compulsory membership for a defined set of employees of a company or business.
Sick list	A list of members receiving sickness benefit.
Sickness papers	The papers prepared and presented to a friendly society by a distant member to prove sickness in order to obtain benefit. Normally, club rules would specify that they needed to be signed by a medical practitioner and a churchwarden, or other local official.
Slate club	An informal, annually-dividing friendly society generally held at a public house. Subscriptions paid were kept on a chalk board in the public house or on a basic paper record. The division of remaining funds was normally made at Christmas.
Steward	Collected fines and ensured order in the clubroom at club meetings and on club day. The post was usually selected on a rotation basis from the list of members, with those refusing to hold office paying a fine.
Subordinate division	A branch of the Order of Sons of Temperance.
Subscriber	A benefit or an honorary member (q.v.).
Surgeon	Medical attendant to the society, paid either by a fixed retainer or by individual attendance.
Teapot club	A society having an annual tea without alcohol instead of a feast.
Tent	A branch of the Independent Order of Rechabites, Salford Unity.
Treasurer	Responsible for the management of the finances of the society, but rarely the collection of monies.
Trustee	Provided financial guarantees for the society.
Tyler	A doorkeeper.
Walking pay	Half or part sickness benefit.

Warden	A steward.
Wet rent	The arrangement whereby a meeting room was provided by the landlord in exchange for the guaranteed expenditure on beer by club members.
Woodward	A steward.

Appendix 2   Crimes, courts, disputes and dishonesty

This appendix comprises 188 events concerning friendly societies in Oxfordshire where there was interface with the civil or criminal courts, dishonesty that did not reach that stage or a range of other disputes. The information is largely derived from newspapers as few records of court cases survive from formal court records. They are presented in alphabetical order of place and provide a brief resume of the reported episode. This section is not a comprehensive record of all such events but provides an extensive record of the variety of incidents, exposing the interaction between friendly societies and the law. Some cases were brought by members of a society, some by the society themselves, whilst cases of assault or disorder may have been instigated by the Police or an individual complainant. In some instances there was no dispute between the parties, such as in cases where a registered society sought clarification on rules or the law regarding payments, or claimed their position as priority creditor where an official of the club held monies but had been declared bankrupt. Registration gave far greater benefit and protection from the law than that given to unregistered societies.

Through these cases several themes can be followed. Disorder at club feasts, the misappropriation of money by officials and disputes over the non-payment of benefit all feature heavily. The decision making of the court officials, and perhaps potential bias, can be detected through these events. The growing role of the courts, increasing legislation and the role of the police can all be observed as the nineteenth century progressed.

Adderbury

1.   **7 December 1839 (Geoffrey Smedley-Stevenson,** *Early Victorian Squarson: The Diaries of William Cotton Risley, Vicar of Deddington, 1835-1848* **[Banbury Historical Society, v. 29, 2007])**

A summons was granted to Richard Hawkins, senior, by Rev. William Cotton Risley against the stewards of the Adderbury Amicable Society (Adderbury 1) for excluding him from the club without sufficient reason. The summons was to appear at Banbury court. No details of the outcome can be located.

2.   **Banbury Petty Session Division, 10 November 1864 (JOJ, 12 November 1864)**

John Dorsett of Adderbury, a member of the Tradesmen's Benefit Society (Adderbury 10), preferred a charge against the officers of the society for illegally expelling him. He was in receipt of sick pay in September when some of the officers of the society saw him drinking at a public house until nearly midnight. The committee expelled him for breach of the rules which stated that any member, whilst sick, being intoxicated was liable to be expelled. No evidence could be produced that he was drunk and the club was ordered to reinstate Dorsett.

3.   **Banbury Petty Session Division, 21 June 1877 (JOJ, 23 June 1877)**

William Merry, landlord of the Red Lion, Adderbury, was summoned for assault on Henry Flint of Adderbury. On the evening of Adderbury club feast day, the defendant allegedly seized Flint by the throat and scratched him without provocation. Witnesses were called for the defence who contradicted the evidence and claimed Flint was the aggressor. The case was dismissed.

Aston

4.   **Witney Petty Session Division, (JOJ, 27 March 1847)**

Richard Waite of Aston appeared at court having been arrested at Southampton for misappropriating monies from the Universalist Friendly Society (Aston 24), held at the Red Lion Inn. He was committed for trial.

> 4.1. Oxfordshire Summer Assizes, 13 July 1847 (JOJ, 17 July 1847)
> Richard Waite was charged with embezzlement of diverse sums of money totalling £3, belonging to the members of the Universalist Friendly Society. It was commented that with the recently amended law the charge would be difficult to prove, 'however guilty he might be, and of which there was no doubt'. The case was heard on Tuesday 13 July 1847. Waite pleaded not guilty to several indictments for embezzlement. The Judge was of the opinion that the prosecution could not be sustained and the only remedy he could see was by civil action. Verdicts of not guilty on each indictment were returned.

Banbury

5.   **Banbury Magistrates (JOJ, 29 September 1849)**

The case of Lovell versus the Loyal British Queen Lodge of the IOOFMU (Banbury 72), had been before the magistrates many times previously. Lovell, a benefit member, had claimed weekly sick pay but other members resented it and determined to break up the club rather than pay him. The matter was reported as having been settled, but with no explanation how.

6.   **Banbury Borough Police Court, 5 June 1854 (BG, 8 June 1854)**

Thomas Parteger and Thomas Merchant, stewards of the Conservative Friendly Society (Banbury 59) were summoned by Elizabeth Burchell to show cause why the society refused to pay her husband 12s a week benefit in accordance with the rules. Burchell had been seen by the club doctor concerning insanity but then he appears to have attempted suicide (a criminal offence). The defence of the club officials relied on the exemption of payment whereby the illness was caused by the member's own act. The Magistrates found the complainant was entitled to relief and the society was ordered to pay 10s costs.

7.   **Banbury Petty Session Division, 21 July 1859 (JOJ, 23 July 1859)**

William Butler of Crouch Farm, near Banbury, charged his man-servant, William Taylor with absenting himself from his service. Butler had given Taylor leave to go home to his club feast, but instead of staying the agreed two days he stayed away for four. When he returned, Taylor refused to work. He was ordered to pay 15s 6d and forfeit £2 wages. The complainant refused to take Taylor back in his employment again.

8.   **Banbury Petty Session Division, 12 July 1873 (JOJ, 15 July 1873)**

Moses Walker and Henry French were charged with having damaged a rick cloth that was being used as a canopy for a booth erected in the White Hart yard for the Conservative Benefit Society (Banbury 61). On Wednesday 7 July 1873, at 12 o'clock midnight a large party had assembled at the booth for dancing. A hole was cut in the covering and stones dropped in, to the alarm of the company. The two prisoners were seen and were caught in the act. The men were fined 5s, plus damages and 11s costs.

Beckley

9.   **Bullingdon Petty Session Division, 26 November 1870 (JOJ, 23 December 1870)**

Abraham Hillsden summoned the club officials of the (United) Beckley Friendly Society (Beckley 88) for failing to pay 10s sick pay. Hillsden had been observed going to Thame and entering a public house contrary to the rules. The Justices found in favour of the complainant and the club was ordered to pay the amount due plus costs.

10.   **Bullingdon Petty Session Division, Oxford, 11 May 1889 (JOJ, 18 May 1889)**

A. Sumner, a labourer of Beckley, was summoned by John Blake, a farmer of Murcott, for assault on him on 30 January 1889. Blake was a member of the Farmers' Home Lodge of the IOOFMU (Beckley 87) and attended a meeting at the Abingdon Arms, Beckley. After the business of the lodge concluded Blake called for a half pint of beer but the landlord refused to draw it as licensed closing time had passed. About 30 club members were outside when Blake got into his cart to drive away but someone held the horse's head while others held onto the wheels of the cart. He stopped, and someone let down the tailboard and removed fish from the rear. Blake alighted and walked away up a hill but was followed by four men. It was alleged the defendant, Sumner, caught hold of him and threw him to the ground. A jar of oil in the cart was knocked over and smashed. Blake suffered a broken leg and injured ankle and he was 'laid up' for several weeks. Blake said he was sober at the time. However, witnesses alleged that when he arrived at 9.30 p.m. he was drunk. He used abusive language and was warned by the club secretary that he was liable to be fined for using bad language. Blake had been claiming sickness benefit from the club following his injuries until two weeks before the court case, but the stewards had now refused to pay. The case was dismissed by the Justices and costs were awarded in favour of all witnesses.

Benson

11. Watlington Magistrates Court, 7 June 1890 (BOA, 13 June 1890 and JOJ, 14 June 1890)

Henry Richard Dandridge and Thomas Rush appeared for being Drunk and Disorderly on club feast day on 27 July 1890 (Benson 89). They had been drinking all day and were involved in disturbances and quarrels. When the Police were called to the Crown Inn at 8.55 p.m., the two men were still causing trouble, being drunk. The Police asked them to leave the Crown Inn where a crowd of over 200 had gathered. The landlord of the Crown, Fred Pease said the men had been drinking at the pub since early morning. Dandridge had attempted to take the flowers out of the coats of two club members. Both men were found guilty. Dandridge was fined 10s and 13s costs; Rush was fined 10s and 12s costs, or either to serve 14 days hard labour in default with seven days to pay.

Bicester

12. Bicester Old Friendly Society (JOJ, 13 June 1835)

During the night of Thursday 11 June 1835 the Dog Inn, the club house of the Old Friendly Society (Bicester 105), was broken into and £10 stolen from the club box.

13. Ploughley Petty Session Division, Bicester, 25 July 1856 (JOJ, 2 August 1856)

The stewards of the Friendly Society of Tradesmen at Bicester (Bicester 100) attended court for a decision from the Magistrates relating to sick pay to John Fathers of Hethe, a member of the club. There was some irregularity in Fathers sending his sick papers during his absence from home. The bench decided the club should pay 13 weeks sickness benefit to Fathers.

14. Ploughley Petty Session Division, Bicester, 30 January 1857 (JOJ, 7 February 1857)

William Bonham was charged with withholding and misappropriating funds entrusted to his care as a steward of the Friendly Society of Tradesmen

(Bicester 100) to pay sick members, to the amount of £3 0s 7d. He was ordered to repay the amount and was fined 10s with costs, or five weeks imprisonment in default.

15. Ploughley Petty Session Division, Bicester, 10 May 1861 (JOJ, 18 May 1861)

William Parker, a labourer of Bicester, was charged with the violent assault of James Timms of Steeple Aston in Sheep Street, Bicester on 2 March. Parker had six previous convictions for violence. Both men had been drinking at the Angel Inn. Parker was quarrelsome but Timms refused to fight. Parker knocked him down so violently he broke his arm and was disabled for some time afterwards. As Timms was a member of an un-named friendly society from which he received relief, it was necessary he preferred a charge against Parker, who had absconded, to maintain his benefit payments from the club. Parker was found guilty in his absence and fined £5 or two months hard labour.

16. Ploughley Petty Session Division, 24 January 1862, Bicester (JOJ, 1 February 1862)

The stewards of the Friendly Society of Tradesmen (Bicester 100) were charged by William Bradbury with refusing to pay 16s for 8 days sickness benefit on the grounds he worked in the meantime, contrary to the rules of the club. The case was adjourned.

> 16.1. Ploughley Petty Session Division, 7 February 1862 (JOJ, 15 February 1862)
> The case of William Bradbury against the stewards of the Friendly Society of Tradesmen was brought forward. The Magistrates found in favour of the stewards.

17. Bicester Provident Society (BicA, 1 June 1883)

The Bicester Provident Society (Bicester 95) ceased to exist after nine years when £30 was stolen from the club cash-box. The Bicester Medical Aid Club, a voluntary subscriber association for medical attendance only, incorporated the members of the Bicester Provident Society.

Bletchingdon

18.   **Ploughley Petty Session Division, Bicester, 21 September 1877 (JOJ, 29 September 1877)**

C. Bullock, senior, C. Bullock, junior, and George Bullock, all of Bletchingdon, summoned the stewards of the Valentia Club (Bletchingdon 113) concerning why they should not be reinstated to the club having been expelled. C. Bullock, junior, also claimed £6 15s sick pay. The decision of the Justices was that they were illegally expelled and an order was made to reinstate them and pay the sickness benefit due within 14 days.

19.   **Valentia Club (JOJ, 16 February 1884)**

A notice of suspension of the Valentia Club (Bletchingdon 113) by the Registrar of Friendly Societies for three months from 13 February 1884 appeared in the newspaper. The club was held at the school room and had failed to submit a valuation of assets and liabilities as required by the Registrar.

Bloxham

20.   **Banbury Petty Session Division, 3 June 1858 (JOJ, 5 June 1858)**

Henry Raven of South Newington appeared at court charged with assault on Police Constable William Morgan at a Bloxham club. Several witnesses were called but their evidence was conflicting, some stating the policeman himself was not sober at the time. However, Raven was found guilty and was fined 10s with 16s costs. The case against Louisa Smith, 'a loose woman', who was charged with rescuing Raven after the policeman had taken him into custody, was discharged.

21.   **Wootton North Petty Session Division, Bicester, 3 May 1867 (JOJ, 11 May 1867 and BH, 17 May 1867)**

Caleb Charles (Chief Ranger), Alfred West (Secretary) and John Bates (Treasurer) of Court British Lion of the AOF (Bloxham 119), lately of the Hawk and Partridge Inn were summoned. Some time ago the landlady of the Hawk and Partridge got into difficulty and they decided to remove the society's box, of which each had a key and were responsible for its contents. Instead of removing the box to another house, Bates, a butcher kept possession of it and applied the £67 money it contained to his own use. Caleb Charles and Alfred West pleaded guilty; John Bates did not appear. After consulting, the bench decided that unless the money was handed over within one month, each would be sentenced to three months imprisonment.

22.   Banbury Petty Session Division, 4 June 1868 (JOJ, 6 June 1868)

Henry Hancock and Thomas Dunn of Banbury were charged with assaulting Police Constable Pinnell at Bloxham club day. Both men were found guilty and each was fined 6s without costs, or seven days imprisonment in default.

23.   Banbury Petty Session Division, 4 June 1868 (JOJ, 6 June 1868)

Thomas Knibb and William Cooper were charged with assault on Police Constable John Webb at Bloxham club day. The case had been heard before and adjourned. The case was withdrawn against Knibb and he was discharged. There was a disturbance at the club on club day and while arresting Knibb the officer was struck from behind. Witnesses stated it was Cooper, who was found guilty and was fined 5s, or seven days imprisonment in default.

24.   Banbury Petty Session Division, 18 June 1868 (JOJ, 20 June 1868)

Frederick Sabin, a butcher of Bloxham was charged with assault on Charles Carter, an old man of North Newington at an unspecified Bloxham friendly society. Carter attended the meeting to sell nuts and on entering the public house, Sabin called him a rogue and threw him out, injuring him severely. Sabin was found guilty, fined 5s and ordered to pay 10s costs, or 14 days imprisonment in default.

25.   Banbury Petty Session Division, 22 June 1876 (JOJ, 24 June 1876)

James Robinson, a baker of Bloxham was summoned for assault on Samuel Heath of Bloxham, shoemaker. Robinson's son kept a public house and Heath went there on the evening of the Bloxham club feast. Being drunk, Heath was refused to be served. Later, Heath abused Robinson and it is alleged Robinson then struck him with a stick, inflicting severe wounds to the face. The assault was denied by Robinson. The Justices found the evidence unsatisfactory and the case was dismissed.

Bodicote

26.   Article entitled 'Club Riot' (BG, 13 June 1844)

An article appeared in the *Banbury Guardian* in 1844 that twenty years before a serious riot took place on club day and many inhabitants of Bodicote were attacked and beaten by a body of strangers. It continued the same happened on Friday 31 May 1844 at the club feast of the Bodicote Friendly Society (Bodicote 126). In the late evening between 30 and 50 men from Northamptonshire, Banbury and other parts appeared at Bodicote and were 'most boisterous'. At 11.00 p.m. the landlord of the White Hart Inn refused to serve them and as a result furniture and windows of the public house were broken. The Police were called and on arrival the lights of the pub were extinguished and the staves were taken off the police. The rioters agreed to leave if they were given beer outside the White Hart, which it was. However, the men forced their way back in to the public house and caused more damage. The riot went on for two to three hours and was 'one scene of riotous drunkenness'. Warrants were issued against many parties.

> 26.1. County Magistrates Court, 7 June 1844 (JOJ, 15 June 1844)
> Richard Horne, William Long, James Young, James Nutt, George Southam and William Fairfax were all committed to Oxford Quarter Sessions court for being concerned in the riot at Bodicote on 31 May 1844. The outcome of the case is unknown.

27.   Banbury Petty Session Division, 20 June (JOJ, 22 June 1867)

David Barnwell, an innkeeper of Banbury, John Warr, John Wells and Leonard Hyam, labourers of Neithrop were all charged with assault on Police Constables Webb and Fox in the execution of their duty at Bodicote. After leaving the public house on the Bodicote club day, a number of Banbury men were described to have 'amused themselves' and had a 'set to' with the police. All four men named were fined with costs totalling 19s each or 14 days imprisonment in default. All paid the fine and costs.

28.   Banbury PSD, 5 May 1870 (JOJ, 7 May 1870)

Frederick Green summoned the officials of Bodicote Friendly Society (Bodicote 126) for arrears of sick pay to the amount of £5 4s. The officials of the club stated they had no funds, but after questioning by the Justices it transpired the society owned some land. Once this was established, the only issue then for the Justices was whether full or half pay was payable to Green according to the rules. Ultimately, an order was made to pay £2 12s (half pay) and 10s costs.

29.   Banbury Petty Session Division, 16 June (JOJ, 18 June 1870)

William Clarke, a tall powerful man from America, was charged with assaulting the police and others at Bodicote club day in 1870. He made a disturbance and wanted a fight with everyone. He kicked a police officer in a violent manner and knocked down the parish Constable. Clarke was found guilty of three assaults and sentenced to five months imprisonment.

30.   Banbury Petty Session Division, 28 July 1870 (JOJ, 13 August 1870)

John Morris summoned officials of the Bodicote Friendly Society (Bodicote 126) for arrears of sick pay amounting to £7 12s. The defence of the club was that it simply did not have any money to pay but promised to do so when the club did have sufficient funds, land owned by the club having been sold. The case was dismissed.

31.   County Police Court, 26 October 1899 (BG, 2 November 1899)

The case concerned the misappropriation of funds of Court Hand in Hand, AOF (Bodicote 127). George Bailey, 37, a labourer of Banbury was summoned for misapplying £61 14s 2½d of funds on 9 July 1899 and before. Bailey was former secretary of the court and landlord of the Plough Inn, Bodicote. An order was agreed for him to repay £50 and he agreed to pay 2s 6d a week, or serve three months imprisonment in default. No costs were awarded.

31.1. County Police Court, Neithrop, 25 April 1901 (BG, 2 May 1901)
An application appeared before the court concerning George Bailey, former secretary of the Court Hand in Hand, AOF (Bodicote 127). On 26 October 1899 Bailey pleaded guilty to applying to his own use the sum of £50 of club funds. He was sentenced to three months imprisonment, suspended as long as he paid 2s 6d a week. Bailey had paid £6 10s to the court but owed £9 15s that should have been paid. The AOF Executive Council had struck out the money in the accounts of the Bodicote branch but this was for accounting purposes. Bailey stated he thought he did not have to pay as the money had been written off. The case was adjourned.

31.2. Letter to the Editor from the secretary of the Ancient Order of Foresters (BG, 16 May 1901)
The Executive Council of the AOF had considered the Court Hand in Hand case before the County Police Magistrates Court that was due on 9 May. The ex-secretary of the Bodicote branch, George Bailey, was summoned to appear in default of payments under an order of a previous appearance. The letter explained the Executive Council never sanctioned any activity with a view to interfering with any actions the Magistrates might deem to take. There was no further explanation but it appears there was confusion in that the Banbury District of the AOF had underwritten the loss suffered by Court Hand in Hand but had not written off the debt itself.

31.3. County Police Court, Neithrop, 9 May 1901 (BG, 16 May 1901)
George Bailey, ex-secretary of the Court Hand in Hand, AOF (Bodicote 127) appeared. At the last hearing, an application had been made by Mr A. Stockton, representing the AOF, for the committal of Bailey to prison in default of a payment order made by the Justices. It had been adjourned for two weeks to enable the District Secretary of the Foresters to attend. H.R. Webb of Banbury District of AOF gave evidence that the Banbury District of the AOF had struck out the money owed to the branch but it was an accounting procedure and they had written off the debt. Bailey had owed £50 but had only paid £6 10s. The bench committed Bailey to prison in default of his payment, but reduced the period from three months to two months in lieu of the money he had repaid.

Bourton

32.   **Banbury Petty Session Division, 11 June, 1857 (JOJ, 20
       June 1857)**

William Allitt, William Humphris and Edward Upton, all of Great Bourton,
and Isaac Eden of Mollington were charged with assaulting Israel Bunton,
George Bull and Thomas Webb, foundry-men of Banbury, at Bourton club
feast on 31 May. They were found guilty and each was fined £2, including
costs, or six weeks imprisonment in default.

Brize Norton

33.   **Bampton West Petty Session Division, Burford, 2 July 1881
       (JOJ, 16 July 1881)**

James Whiting of Shilton and Charles Hunt of Curbridge were summoned for
being drunk and disorderly at Brize Norton Club day on Whit Monday, 6 June
1881. Hunt also assaulted a Police Officer. He was fined £1 2s 6d with 15s
6d costs. Whiting was fined 17s 6d and 15s 6d costs. If the fines were not
paid within six weeks, the sentence was three months imprisonment with hard
labour in default.

Burford

34.   **Burford Petty Session Division, 17 January 1849 (JOJ, 20
       January 1849)**

Mr W. Pearn, secretary of Burford Friendly Society (Burford 143) was
summoned by Thomas Rogers, a member of the society as the club had refused
to pay him sickness benefit. Rogers had suffered from an accident but he was
apparently in a state of intoxication at the time. A witness to the accident
refused to testify, and the society was ordered to pay the benefit due.

Chadlington

35.   Chadlington Petty Session Division (JOJ, 25 March 1899)

The Magistrates gave approval for a license extension for the Sandy's Arms Public House at the club feast to be held on Easter Monday 1899.

Chalgrove

36.   Watlington Petty Session Division, 12 September 1871 (JOJ, 30 September 1871)

George Smith of Chalgrove, shoemaker, charged the trustees of the Chalgrove Friendly society held at the Red Lion (Chalgrove 167) with unjustly and illegally expelling him. The Justices dismissed the case after hearing the evidence.

37.   Watlington Petty Session Division, 1 December 1900 (JOJ, 8 December 1900)

William Phelps was held in custody, having been arrested in Nottingham, charged with misappropriation of funds of the Chalgrove Friendly Society (Chalgrove 168) to the amount of £4 4s. He held the money to pay the medical officer. Phelps pleaded guilty and in mitigation he stated he had suffered a severe attack of influenza. He was ordered to pay £3 to the society, 4s 6d fine and 15s 6d costs.

Charlbury

38.   Oxfordshire County Court, Oxford, 27 September 1862 (JOJ, 4 October 1862)

Thomas Brooks brought an action against the Old Club (Charlbury 171). The plaintiff was a member of the club and was expelled when claiming sickness benefit due to an alleged complaint of working on an allotment when sick. He cut down thistles with a hoe. The Judge decided expulsion was not justified for a trivial offence and the club was ordered to reinstate Brooks within 28 days or pay £8 15s. It was also ordered to pay £1 15s arrears of sick pay and the costs of the case.

39.   Chadlington Petty Session Division, Chipping Norton, 16 July 1884 (JOJ, 19 July 1884)

William Dolloway, the proprietor of a merry-go-round, was fined 15s including costs for assaulting Jesse Pratley, a swing boat proprietor, at Charlbury club day on 3 July.

40.   Chadlington Petty Session Division, Chipping Norton, 19 August 1891 (JOJ, 22 August 1891)

Henry Forrest of Burford, swing-boat proprietor, was charged with obstruction of the footpath at Charlbury club day on 10 July. The Police and the Highway Board Surveyor attended Church Street and saw the swing-boat completely obstructed the footpath, measuring 34' x 8'. Forrest said his father had placed the swing-boat in the same place for 28 years and he had done so for eight years. The Justices found him guilty and fined him 5s with 10s costs.

41.   Sudden death (JOJ, 29 July 1893)

William Ayres, aged 76 of Old Baywell Toll Gate visited Charlbury club day feast on 7 July 1893. He indulged freely in intoxicants and was later found lying dead in his bed.

Charlton on Otmoor

42.   Incident involving landlord (BG, 13 June 1844)

Charlton club feast day was held on Thursday 30 May 1844. In the evening, Mr Kirby of the George and Dragon public house attempted to eject a troublesome customer but in doing so was thrown down some stairs and broke his leg.

43.   Bicester Petty Session Division, 14 May 1869 (BH, 21 May 1869)

George Powell, the son of a farmer at Charlton on Otmoor was charged with being drunk and riotous at Charlton club day (Charlton 183) on 6 May 1869. He pleaded not guilty. Powell approached PC Yeats between 7.00 p.m. – 8.00

p.m. and accused him of telling lies about his brother. He challenged PC Yeats to a fight but was led away by his brother. However, Powell came back and it was said in evidence that he was drunk and swearing. Witnesses for the defence stated he was not drunk or abusive. Powell was found not guilty by the Justices but provocation was recognized so he was ordered to pay costs of 2s 6d.

44.   Bicester Petty Session Division, 26 May (BH, 2 June 1876)

Richard Crawford, a machinist of Charlton on Otmoor was charged with drunk and riotous behaviour at Charlton club day feast (Charlton 183) on 4 May 1876. The disorderly conduct charge was withdrawn and proceedings for being drunk only continued. He pleaded not guilty. It was alleged he was drunk in the street, opposite the Crown Inn and was arrested by police at approximately 9.45 p.m. One witness to the events was working on a cake stall all day at the feast. The case was proven, but it was dismissed in the hope Crawford would not appear before the court again.

Chesterton

45.   Inquest at Little Chesterton (JOJ, 25 June 1892)

An inquest was held at Little Chesterton on Saturday 18 May 1892. Chesterton feast was held on Monday 13 June 1892 and John Westbury, aged 52, had been to the club day dinner. He was returning to see the band in the evening when he had an accident, falling from a five-barred gate, and he died from his injuries.

Chinnor

46.   Theft of Gold (TG, 1 June 1858)

The True Britons Friendly Society (Chinnor 189), a three-year dividing society, held their club day on Wednesday 26 May 1858 at the Royal Oak Inn. All went well until the following day when the division of the funds was about to take place. Instructions were given to open a packet of gold worth £41, retained in the box since the start of the three year cycle, as part of the division. The package was taken from the box and opened. It was found to contain a piece of lead of the exact size and shape as the gold and had been carefully substituted. The gold was kept in a three-key box and so must have been substituted for the lead on a general meeting club night when all three club officials were present with their key. Suspicion immediately fell on an un-named steward who had requested a loan from the club, but it had been refused for want of proper sureties. He suddenly left the club and emigrated to America although he had been destitute immediately prior to this. The secretary and others had urged the cash value of the gold to be invested but this had been ignored by the committee of the society.

Chipping Norton

47.   **Chadlington Petty Session Division, Chipping Norton, 30 June 1886 (JOJ, 3 July 1886)**

An occasional license was granted to Fox Hotel for the Oddfellows fete to be held on Tuesday 6 July 1886, club day for the Old Elm Tree Lodge (Chipping Norton 198).

48.   **Unspecified court, Chipping Norton, 7 July 1886 (JOJ, 10 July 1886)**

On Wednesday 7 July 1886, the day after club day, cases were heard before the Mayor and Deputy Mayor of Chipping Norton. George Harris of Chipping Norton was held in custody on a charge of being drunk and riotous on club day. He was fined £1 with 5s 6d costs, or 21 days imprisonment with hard labour in default.

Churchill

49.   **Chadlington Petty Session Division, Chipping Norton, 16 June 1886 (JOJ, 19 June 1886)**

An application for an extension of the license at Chequers Inn (Churchill 209) for club day was granted.

Combe

50.   **Woodstock Petty Session Division, 10 November 1885 (JOJ, 14 November 1885)**

The secretary of the Combe Friendly Society (Combe 220) was summoned for refusing to pay benefit to William Floyd of Bladon the sum of £4 7s incurred by him in consequence of medical attendance. The Justices ordered the society to pay the amount with 11s costs.

Cowley

51.   **Bullingdon Petty Session Division, Oxford (JOJ, 8 April 1899)**

William Churchill, an engine driver of Cowley and official of the club, was charged with withholding over £30 from the Court Knight of the Temple, AOF (Cowley 224). He pleaded guilty. Churchill was fined £2, required to refund £15 2s 2d, or serve six weeks imprisonment with hard labour in default.

Deddington

52.   **Deddington Union Beneficial Society (Geoffrey Smedley-Stevenson,** *Early Victorian Squarson: The Diaries of William Cotton Risley, Vicar of Deddington, 1835-1848* **[Banbury Historical Society, v. 29, 2007])**

On 15 May 1837, T. Austin called upon the Rev. William Cotton Risley of Deddington, magistrate, about his son, William Austin. He had refused to give the Deddington Union Beneficial Society (Deddington 242) possession of the book of account. The society had removed from William Austin's Plough Inn to the Tuns Public House. Risley advised Austin that his son should give up what was required.

53.   Committee meeting of Union Beneficial Society (JOJ, 14 January 1860)

The committee of the Union Beneficial Society (Deddington 242) met at the Unicorn Inn to investigate a charge against Mr Henry West, Carpenter of Upper Heyford, for breach of the rules by officiating at a wedding while receiving sickness benefit from the society. Rule 21 stated that any sick member must not transact any business. The committee found West had breached the rules and expelled him from the society.

53.1. Wootton North Petty Session Division, Woodstock, 3 February 1860 (JOJ, 11 February 1860)
An appeal was held in a case of alleged illegal expulsion of a member from the Union Beneficial Society (Deddington 242). The request was for the reinstatement of Mr West. In addition there was a new case and Charles Moon and Joseph Woolgrove, stewards of the society, were summoned to answer a charge that they refused to receive membership payment from West. The decision of the bench was that West was illegally expelled and the stewards were wrong in refusing to take his money. Each party was ordered to pay their own costs.

53.2. Committee meeting of Union Beneficial Society, 6 June 1860 (JOJ, 14 June 1860)
The committee of the Union Beneficial Society (Deddington 242) met at the Unicorn Inn to investigate a charge against Henry West, carpenter and Parish Clerk of Upper Heyford. It was alleged he breached the rules of the club by officiating at a wedding whilst on the funds of the society, in breach of rule 21 that forbid the transaction of business during periods of sickness. West said he fulfilled his duties as a Parish Clerk and was not working. An agricultural labourer could not attend to officiate at the wedding as it was a week day and he did not see this as transacting business. The committee decided West had breached the rules and excluded him from the club.

53.3. Wootton North Petty Session Division, Deddington, 7 September 1860 (JOJ, 15 September 1860)
Henry West charged the stewards of Deddington Union Beneficial Society (Deddington 242) with neglecting to enforce the rules of

the club against a member, J. Hopcroft for using scurrilous language towards West on 20 June. He also charged the stewards with refusing to pay him 6s 6d sick benefit. West said that he was coming from church on club day and J. Hopcroft called him a 'shabby rascal'. The Justices made an order for the payment of the 6s 6d that had been improperly stopped, with 4s for West's expenses and 6s costs. No outcome was recorded for the allegation of neglecting to enforce the rules.

53.4. Wootton North Petty Session Division, Deddington, 7 June 1861 (JOJ, 15 June 1861)
Henry West of Upper Heyford summoned John Calcutt, trustee of Deddington Union Beneficial Society (Deddington 242) for unlawfully misappropriating £4 16s 4d from the funds of the society. West stated a great proportion of the amount was incurred by employing a solicitor, Mr Kilby, regarding a dispute between West and the club. Calcutt said that he had been in the club 44 years and no member had given so much trouble as West. The society was on the verge of breaking up rather than keep West as a member. West also summoned Calcutt for £4 10s 4d for his legal costs incurred in previous matters. The Justices dismissed both cases against the club.

54.   **Wootton North Petty Session Division, Deddington, 4 June 1869 (BH, 11 June 1869)**

Deverill Hoare, a labourer, was charged with assaulting Henry Wilkins at Deddington on 19 May 1869, club day. There was a counter summons for assault and it was alleged Hoare went into the Exhibition beer house and Wilkins gave him a 'blow on the nose'. Justices dismissed both cases.

55.   **Disappearance of Henry Churchill (JOJ, 25 June 1870)**

It was reported in *Jackson's Oxford Journal* that Henry Churchill, a solicitor of Deddington and partner in Messrs. Field and Churchill, had not been seen since the morning of Wednesday 8 June 1870. He held various positions of office including Coroner, Clerk to the Justices for Wootton North Petty Session Division, agent to W. C. Cartwright, MP, solicitor, treasurer to the Deddington Prosecution Association and secretary of a Deddington friendly society. It soon transpired that Churchill was insolvent and various meetings were held of interested parties. His liabilities were approximately £6,000. It is not known which Deddington friendly society he was treasurer for but was one of the three registered societies in the town which afforded preferential creditor status in cases of bankruptcy.

> 55.1. Oxford County Court, Thursday 13 April 1871 (JOJ, 15 April 1871)
> Henry Churchill, solicitor, late of Deddington and formerly treasurer of a friendly society, had absconded with £106 of friendly society money a month before being made bankrupt. The club was granted an order by the Judge, His Honour, J.B. Parry, that £106 be repaid from his estate as preferential creditor under friendly society legislation.

56. **Wootton North Petty Session Division, Deddington 27 June 1879 (JOJ, 5 July 1879)**

John Wheeler of the Crown and Tuns Public House, Deddington was charged with having an iron box in his possession, the property of the Deddington General Friendly Institution (Deddington 240) and withholding the same. The club formerly met at the Crown and Tuns but on Whit Wednesday members had decided by a majority to move to the Exhibition Inn. Wheeler alleged £3 10s was owing to him for rent but the Society stated it owed no rent. The defendant was ordered to hand over the box immediately upon payment of an amount admitted to be owed for refreshments.

57. **Wootton North Petty Session Division, Deddington 8 August 1879 (JOJ, 16 August 1879)**

William Grace and Thomas Seeney, late stewards of the Deddington Friendly Society (Deddington 246) were charged with misappropriating £30, advanced for payment to sick members in November 1878. The defendants objected as they claimed due to the limitation of proceedings, they should have been summoned within six months of the event. The case was adjourned for two weeks but there is no further record of proceedings.

58. **Deddington Petty Session Division, 17 June 1892 (BG, 23 June 1892)**

Robert Callow, a labourer, was charged with being drunk and disorderly at Deddington club feast on 8 June 1892. He was fined 2s 6d with 8s costs.

59. Wootton North Petty Session Division, Deddington, 25 May 1894 (BG, 31 May 1894)

William Hawtin of Hempton, labourer, was fined 1s with 7s costs for being drunk and disorderly at Deddington club day on 16 May 1894.

Dorchester on Thames

60. Bullingdon Petty Session Division, Oxford, 21 January 1888 (JOJ, 28 January 1888)

Vincent Cobb, a tailor, was charged with embezzlement of £1 18s 4d on 16 May 1887 and other days, the monies of the Royal Oxonian Branch of the Bath and Bristol Friendly Society (Dorchester 250). Cobb was arrested on 20 January and placed on bail for one month.

> 60.1. Bullingdon Petty Session Division, Oxford, 28 January 1888 (JOJ, 4 February 1888)
> Vincent Cobb, treasurer of the Dorchester branch of the Bath and Bristol Friendly Society (Dorchester 250), appeared charged with stealing 10s on 24 January 1887. He signed individual's books as receipt of the monies but he did not account for money paid to him. This was a sample charge. Cobb had been club secretary until May 1887. He was sentenced to one month's hard labour.

61. Bullingdon Petty Session Division, Oxford, 7th December 1895 (JOJ, 14 December 1895)

John Cobb, secretary of the Dorchester Friendly Society (Dorchester 253) was summoned by the Registrar of Friendly Societies for failing to submit an annual return. Cobb did not appear and the case had been adjourned once so he could comply. In his absence, he was fined 50s with 4 guineas costs, and 21 days imprisonment in default.

Drayton

62.   Banbury Petty Session Division, 21 May 1868 (JOJ, 23 May 1868)

Walter Sansbury, George Hone and Charles Fowler, all of Banbury, were charged with assaulting Police Constable Noah Pratt at the club feast (Drayton 259). There was a fight at the public house and Pratt went to stop it. The three defendants knocked him down and struck him. Sansbury had left home and the summons had not been served. The case was adjourned until the next meeting in order that he may be present.

> 62.1. Banbury Petty Session Division, 18 June 1868 (JOJ, 20 June 1868)
> This case had been twice adjourned. Sansbury, Hone and Fowler were all charged with assault on police. There was conflicting evidence whether the officer was acting in the execution of his duty and so the case was dismissed.

63.   Banbury Petty Session Division, 16 September 1875 (JOJ, 25 September 1875)

The officers of the Drayton Friendly Society (Drayton 259) were summoned by William Webb for allegedly misapplying funds. The positions or names of the defendants were not mentioned. Members had agreed to divide the funds of the society without completing the forms of statute or satisfying Webb, who at the time was receiving sick pay. A receipt for £4 10s was produced by the complainant's attorney for discharge of all claims on the society. This led to an angry altercation between the attorneys, and the case was adjourned for one month to enable the parties to meet and adjust their differences.

> 63.1. Banbury Petty Session Division, 14 October 1875 (JOJ, 16 October 1875)
> This case appeared again after an adjournment. William Webb, a member, was ill and entitled to sick pay. Members of the Drayton Friendly Society (Drayton 259) held a meeting, unknown to Webb, and divided the funds without satisfying him and without completing the forms required by law. Since the last hearing, the defendant's solicitor had prepared an agreement in accordance with statutes but

the Magistrates held it did not cure the defect. The case was against the treasurer, secretary and other officers of the club (all un-named). The defendants were committed to prison for seven days, much to their surprise. Later in the day, the Magistrates reconsidered their decision and thought a fine and an order to refund the money would meet the justice of the case. It was further adjourned for two weeks.

63.2. Banbury Petty Session Division, 28 October 1875 (JOJ, 30 October 1875)
The Drayton Friendly Society (Drayton 259) case appeared before the magistrates again. The attorney for William Webb attended and stated the matter had been arranged between the parties and the charge was withdrawn.

Duns Tew

64.   Deddington Petty Session Division, 5 May 1854 (BG, 11 May 1854, JOJ, 13 May 1854))

Richard Lewis of North Aston was charged with assaulting Thomas Hatton, Constable of Duns Tew at the club feast on 2 May 1854 (Duns Tew 262). There was a disturbance at the village Inn and Hatton was called to a fight at 11 p.m. to intervene. Hatton attempted to stop the fight but Lewis took hold of Hatton's arm and attempted to take his staff. Lewis was found guilty, fined 2s with 8s costs or 21 days imprisonment in default.

65.   Deddington Petty Session Division, 18 May 1888 (JOJ, 24 May 1888)

Alfred Barret and Henry Newman, both of Steeple Barton, were charged with being drunk and disorderly at the club feast on 1 May 1888 (Duns Tew 262). The defendants were fighting in the evening and refused to go home as required by the police. They were very unruly in the dock and the chairman felt they were drunk in court. Barret and Newman were sentenced to 21 days imprisonment with hard labour at Oxford prison without the option of a fine. The defendants were surprised as they were expecting a small fine.

Enstone

66.   Chadlington Petty Session Division, 24 August 1864 (JOJ, 27 August 1864)

The treasurer of the Enstone Friendly Society (Enstone 265) was summoned by Daniel Baughan of Enstone for refusal to pay £9 4s benefit for 23 weeks sick between 20 February and 30 July 1864. The club was ordered to pay for the period of 20 April to 30 July at 8s a week, and 10s costs.

67.   Chadlington Petty Session Division, Chipping Norton, 25 May 1892 (JOJ, 28 May 1892)

Tow licensing applications were made for the Swan and Crown Inns, Enstone. Each was granted a one-hour extension for the club feast.

Eynsham

68.   Wootton South Petty Session Division, Woodstock, 13 November 1856 (JOJ, 22 November 1856)

Betherel Riddle, a steward of the Eynsham Friendly Society (Eynsham 271) held at the Maltster & Shovel, was summoned for non-payment of 42s to Kezia Batts on the death of her husband. Magistrates gave a verbal order for the society to pay.

Fencott and Murcott

69.   Ploughley Petty Session Division, Bicester, 18 July 1873 (JOJ, 26 July 1873)

John Honor, late landlord of Marlake House, Murcott was charged with stealing £10 from the Murcott & Fencott Friendly Society (Fencott and Murcott 281). The case was dismissed as the Justices decided it was not taken with felonious intent.

Fifield

70.   **Chadlington Petty Session Division, Chipping Norton, 9 May 1894 (JOJ, 12 May 1894)**

Mr Toy applied on behalf of Mr R. Smith of Westcote for an occasional license to sell refreshments in a shed at Fifield at Fifield Friendly Society (Fifield 283) club day on 21 May. The application was granted.

Finmere

71.   **Confrontation at club day averted (BicA, 3 June 1887)**

A serious disturbance was avoided by the sagacity of the Police at Finmere Friendly Society club day. The club was parading the village when the Salvation Army and the Skeleton Army both appeared. The Skeleton Army was a loose group that operated mainly in southern England in the late nineteenth century and opposed views of the Salvation Army. It challenged and marched against the Salvation Army's views on alcohol and disrupted their activities, especially marches. The Police persuaded the Salvation Army not to hold their service and both 'armies' dispersed and left Finmere club day in peace.

Finstock

72.   **Chadlington Petty Session Division, 30 May 1864, Chipping Norton (JOJ, 2 June 1864)**

George and Alfred Thornett, both of Finstock, were charged by PC Frewin with being drunk and riotous on club day (Finstock 288) on 10 May. They were convicted, with fine and costs of £2 or seven days imprisonment in default.

73.   **Chadlington Petty Session Division, 18 March 1891 (JOJ, 21 March 1891)**

James Bowell, aged 72 of Finstock summoned the secretary of the Finstock Independent Friendly Benefit Society (Finstock 288) for non-payment of sickness benefit. He had been a member for 26 years and claiming sickness benefit for four years. A report had been received by the society that he was working in his garden on 30 September 1890, contrary to the rules. A meeting of the society was held and 35 of the 46 members were present. They decided he should be excluded from the club. The court made no decision on the case.

74.   Chadlington Petty Session Division, Chipping Norton, 25 April 1894 (JOJ, 28 April 1894)

An occasional license was granted to S. Langford of the Crown Inn to serve beer in a barn for Finstock club day on 3 May 1894.

Forest Hill

75.   Bullingdon Petty Session Division, Oxford, 7 June 1884 (JOJ, 14 June 1884)

Michael, Thomas, Walter and Frederick Soanes (father and three sons) were charged with assaulting Police Constable Williams at Forest Hill on 2 June 1884, the evening of club day (Forest Hill 292). Several police were present. The case was an alleged unprovoked attack by Thomas Soanes when PC Williams went to the club room at the King's Arms Inn. He alleged he was assaulted and there were further incidents. There was conflicting evidence and the case was dismissed by the Justices.

Fritwell

76.   Bicester Petty Session Division, 9 June 1871 (BH, 16 June 1871)

John Bolton, a labourer of Fritwell, was charged with being drunk and disorderly at Fritwell club feast (Fritwell 297) on 30 May. Police Sergeant Wharton found Bolton in the street in Fritwell. He was very drunk, using bad language and was abusive. He struck out at Sergeant Wharton twice. Bolton did not attend court and was fined 2s 6d with 11s costs plus Police fees of 4s, or 14 days imprisonment.

Garsington

77.   Oxford County Court (JOJ, 27 July 1872)

John Cooper, plaintiff, who was a member of the Garsington Benefit Society (Garsington 302), brought a case against Thomas Smith, a steward of the club. The claim was for 18s due in sickness benefit. The judge decided Cooper had not complied with the rules of the club and was therefore not entitled to receive the money. However, the case was adjourned.

78.   Oxford County Court, 20 August 1872 (JOJ, 24 August 1872)

Cooper, the plaintiff, was 70 years old and a member of the society and brought a case against Smith the younger, secretary of the Garsington Benefit society (Garsington 302). The club refused to pay sick pay on the grounds that the medical certificate was not signed by the club doctor, but by another doctor from Oxford. Objection was also raised as it had not been signed by the Vicar, Churchwarden, and Overseer as required by the rules. The case had been adjourned from the last Court. The court decided the rules had been complied with and the society should pay what was owed.

79.   Oxford County Court, 20 August 1872 (JOJ, 24 August 1872)

James Quarterman, a member of the Garsington Benefit Society (Garsington 302), claimed he was owed £1 10s by the society for six weeks sick pay. He was an old man, and his certificate was not signed by the churchwardens and overseers. Smith was representing the club, and two or more of the parties involved were relatives of Smith. The case was adjourned so the defendant could negotiate with the club.

80.   Bullingdon Petty Session Division, Oxford, 23 September 1876 (JOJ, 30 September 1876)

Henry Hilsden summoned the stewards of the Garsington Benefit Society (Garsington 302) for non-payment of £1 9s sick pay. The defence of the society was that a rule had been added after the rulebook had been published that a member of the society, being ill and receiving relief from any charitable institution would forfeit their claim on the society. The complainant had been a patient at the Radcliffe Infirmary. The rule was found to have been illegally added and the stewards were ordered to pay the amount of sick pay due and costs of the court.

Great Tew

81.   Wootton North Petty Session Division, Deddington, 13 February 1880 (JOJ, 21 February 1880)

Richard Spencer, a labourer of Great Tew, summoned the officers of the Great Tew Friendly Society (Great Tew 318) for non-payment of sickness benefit. The issue was whether he was capable of work. The club doctor said he was not incapacitated and so the case was dismissed by the Justices.

Hanborough

82.   Wootton South Petty Session Division, Woodstock, 13 August 1878 (JOJ, 17 August 1878)

Walter Laitt of Hanborough, a carpenter summoned George Woodward with having assaulted him at Hanborough on 20 July 1878. Woodward, with two others, was going along the road on club day and met Laitt, who had complained of friendly society matters. It was claimed Laitt spat in his hand and wanted to fight, putting his hands in Woodward's face. It is alleged Woodward then 'put him in the ditch'. Witnesses were called and stated they did not see any blows. The case was dismissed on the payment of 8s costs.

Headington

83.   County Court, Oxford, 2 June 1849 (JOJ, 9 June 1849)

At the Headington club feast on 29 May 1849, a late hours drinking license had been granted until 2.00 a.m. for the Britannia Inn (Headington 328). Charles Petty forced himself over the bar having been refused beer and he was followed by his brother Stephen. They beat Mrs Buggins, landlady, and she received black eyes and serious injuries. Her daughter was also assaulted. The Petty brothers were committed for trial at the County Assizes.

83.1. Oxford County Quarter Sessions (JOJ, 7 July 1849)
Charles Petty was found guilty of common assault and sentenced to 6 months imprisonment. Stephen Petty was found not guilty.

84.   Bullingdon Petty Session Division, Oxford 27 December 1851 (JOJ, 3 January 1852)

Jabez Clare, complainant summoned the officers of Headington Quarry Friendly Society (Headington 335) for refusing to pay him 5s due as a sick member on 20th December 1851. Clare, a tailor, worked for Messrs Hyde & Co, clothiers, until his sight became so impaired he could no longer fulfil his occupation. Clare placed himself under an oculist, Mr Cleobury, and followed his instructions. He was declared sick and was allowed 5s a week as a sick member. It was thought likely he would be permanently sick and some members attempted to get him struck off the register altogether. The only way of the society avoiding payment was to show he was not sick and could follow his calling as a tailor. Witnesses were called by the club. On 6 December 1851 Clare was seen with a pig bucket and a stick to stir it. He was also seen picking up straw after the pig had been killed and he had shut the shutters of his home. The bench was of the opinion this was a 'very trumpery case' and no evidence was brought forward by the club to justify withholding the weekly payment of 5s. The officers of the club were ordered to reinstate Clare and pay him his allowance, plus the costs of the case.

85.   Bullingdon PSD, Oxford, 29 December 1855 (JOJ, 5 January 1856)

The stewards of the Britannia Benefit Society (Headington 328) were summoned for refusing to pay Robert Bateman, an old member of 76 years, 5s a week sickness benefit. After hearing the evidence, the Justices ordered Bateman to be paid the three weeks due.

86.   Bullingdon Petty Session Division, Oxford, 2 June 1860 (JOJ, 9 June 1860)

This was a case of assault on a police officer at the Headington club feast on the evening of 29 May 1860 (Headington 328). A great many people were drinking at the Britannia public house at midnight. James Witt, a private with the 23rd Regiment of Foot had been at the feast for the purpose of enlisting recruits. He became drunk and quarrelsome and the landlord called the police.

The police requested Witt leave the premises but he took off his belt and beat two policemen around the face and eyes. Three other drunk men, William Bough, Richard Luckett and John Perry, assisted the soldier and got him away from the policemen. All four were charged with assaulting the police officers. The policemen were hurt and one lost his hat and his handcuffs were broken. Bough was fined £6 10s or two months imprisonment in default, Luckett was fined £5 10s or two months imprisonment in default, and Witt and Perry were each fined £3 10s or one month imprisonment in default.

87. Bullingdon Petty Session Division, Oxford, 8 March 1862 (JOJ, 15 March 1862)

Charles Hedges summoned the Stewards of the Headington Quarry Seven Years Benefit Club (Headington 336) for non-payment of money due on the death of his second wife. The case was dismissed as the rules of the society stated that disputes must be settled by an arbitrator.

88. County Court, Oxford, 9 October 1866 (JOJ, 13 October 1866)

The plaintiff, Stevens, was a former member of the Headington Benefit Society (Headington 333) held at the Britannia Public House. He had been expelled as he refused to pay his share of expenses for the club dinner in Whitsun week. The action was brought to compel the society to reinstate him. The judgement was that the society had acted illegally. A registered society could not force a member to pay if he did not attend. The judge commented that J. Tidd Pratt would never have given his sanction to such a rule and that this was a case that should have gone to arbitration. Stevens was reinstated.

89. Bullingdon Petty Session Division, Oxford, 6 June 1874 (JOJ, 20 June 1874)

Edward Matthews, landlord of the Britannia Inn, Headington was charged with keeping his house open for the sale of liquor during prohibited hours on 26 May 1874, anniversary of the Loyal Havelock Lodge, IOOFMU (Headington 338). Police Constable Harrison stated that at 11.30 p.m. there were a number of people drinking in the tap room. There was also a room full of guests upstairs served by the defendant's son and in a field nearby, where a large group had gathered. There was no licensing extension as it had been refused by the court. The defendant stated he drew no fluid after 11.00 p.m. However, the Justices found Matthews guilty, and he was fined £1 with 13s 6d costs.

90.   County Court, Oxford, 17 July 1884 (JOJ, 19 July 1884)

J. Sims, the plaintiff, of Floyds Row, Oxford, brought the case against J. Adams, secretary of the Britannia Benefit Society (Headington 329). He sued the society for £6 8s for unpaid sickness benefit. The defence of the society was that the man was old and his condition old age, not sickness. The judge described this as a disgraceful defence but he was bound by the rules of the society. The non submission of a doctor's certificate meant he had to order a non-suit but no costs were awarded to mark his sense of disapprobation. He suggested a new suit was needed if a certificate could be obtained. The judge further commented that unregistered societies should be 'swept away as poor people were being swindled of money'.

Henley on Thames

91.   Town and County Magistrates, Henley on Thames, 12 December 1881 (JOJ, 17 December 1881)

The case was alleged assault by George and John Mellett, brothers and blacksmiths, against George Smith, a boat builder. All parties worked at Timber Wharf, Henley. John Mellett had been 'on the box' of the Wharf Club (Henley on Thames 348) for 16 weeks and when Smith saw him he accused him of 'skulking' on the funds. John Mellett then assaulted Smith in Duke Street. The Police came and advised all parties to go home. However, Smith followed the Mellett brothers instead and the younger brother turned and knocked Smith down. His injuries were severe, sustaining a broken jaw and nose and a 'pummelled' face. Both men were convicted and sentenced to 21 days imprisonment with hard labour.

Hethe

92.   Ploughley Petty Session Division, Bicester, 14 June 1865 (JOJ, 24 June 1865)

Phillip Hatwell of Hethe was charged by Mary Jones, wife of William, with assault on 5 June 1865. Her husband and Hatwell were arguing at Hethe club day supper. She grabbed hold of Hatwell, pulling him away from her husband but Hatwell hit her in the mouth. He was fined 1s, ordered to pay 10s 6d costs and 4s police fees or serve 14 days imprisonment in default. The money was paid by Hatwell.

93.   Ploughley Petty Session Division, Bicester 19 June 1868 (BH, 26 June 1868)

Edward Haydon, labourer of Hethe, was charged with being drunk and riotous on 1 June 1868 at Hethe feast day. Haydon was not present in court. During the evening, Police Constable Brooks was on duty when Haydon approached him, challenged him to a fight and was very abusive. He was found guilty in his absence, with a fine and costs totalling £2 1s, or six weeks imprisonment with hard labour in default.

Hornton

94.   Banbury Petty Session Division, 16 July 1857 (JOJ, 18 July 1857)

Thomas Gilks, John Dove, Isaac Horsley and William Gardner were all charged with assault on police and resisting arrest at Hornton on 13 July 1857. Constable James Cooke was on duty at Hornton club day. Gilks was very drunk and abusive in the street and Constable Cooke attempted to remove him. Gilks resisted, assaulted Cooke and the other defendants attempted to help Gilks. All four were fined £5 each or two months imprisonment with hard labour in default.

95.   Banbury Petty Session Division, 31 July 1873 (JOJ, 16 August 1873)

Henry Hone of Adderbury and George Bennett of Banbury were charged with assault on Police Constable George Judge at Hornton club feast in the evening. It was a long case. The two defendants were musicians in rival bands and after the music there was a quarrel and fight. In trying to separate the men, Police Constable Judge received some severe blows. Each defendant was fined 1s with 12s costs. The magistrates expressed the view the police officer had shown great forbearance in not using his staff and had acted very properly.

Horton cum Studley

96.   **Bullingdon Petty Session Division, Oxford, 11 June 1870
(BH, 17 June 1870)**

'Drunk and pugilistic at Horton feast'. William Oakley of Brill was charged by
Police Constable Fry with being drunk and disorderly at Horton cum Studley
on 26 May. It was Horton club day and he struck a man named Black and
challenged another to a fight. He was fined 5s with costs 19s 6d or 14 days
imprisonment with hard labour in default.

Iffley

97.   **Bullingdon Petty Session Division, Oxford, 4 November
1854 (JOJ, 11 November 1854)**

Thomas Castell of Thame, made a complaint against the stewards of Iffley
New Benefit Society (Iffley 387) for unlawfully excluding him. The matter
was not fully explored by the Magistrates but they were of the opinion the
complainant had not been legally expelled and the case was dismissed.

98.   **Bullingdon Petty Session Division, Oxford, 27 July 1867
(JOJ, 3 August 1867)**

John Widows, a labourer, pleaded guilty to misappropriating monies to the
amount of £6 16s 6d from the Iffley New Benefit Society (Iffley 387). He
stated he would pay the money back but did not have it. He was fined £3, with
costs of 13s 6d or two months imprisonment in default. 'The bench commented
on the impropriety of allowing men of straw to occupy responsible positions
in societies'. The magistrates on the day comprised the Rev. Dr. Wynter, J.H.
Ashurst, G. Gammie-Maitland, and Guy Thomson, Esqrs., Major Ruck-Keane
and Captain Fane.

99.   **Bullingdon Petty Session Division, Oxford, 8 July 1899
(JOJ, 15 July 1899)**

Henry Clarke, a labourer, appeared for assault on Edward Bampton at Iffley on
29 June 1899 at Iffley club feast. Clarke, who was not a member of a friendly
society, stopped Bampton and asked him for a drink. Bampton refused and

Clarke knocked him down. He then hit him again, giving him a black eye. The defendant was fined 2s 6d with 7s 6d costs.

Islip

100.   County Court, Oxford, 1 December 1873 (JOJ, 13 December 1873)

Watson, a labourer, took action against the secretary of the Union Fellowship Society (Islip 390), an unregistered friendly society, for non-payment of £3 12s for 16 weeks sick pay. Watson had been a member for 20 years and he had been on benefit for ten years. The case was adjourned to the next court.

> 100.1. County Court, Oxford, 19 January 1874 (JOJ, 24 January 1874) The secretary of the Union Fellowship Society (Islip 390), Mr. Webb, represented the club. The case concerned a rule that a member should only be attended by a club doctor. The club doctor, Dr. Blick had certified Watson to be fit for work. Watson attended the Radcliffe Infirmary and was given a certificate of sickness. The decision of the court was that Watson should be given half the claim and the Judge commented that he thought the rule was unreasonable.

101.   Accident at club day (BicA, 20 June 1884)

Islip club day was held on Monday 9 June 1884. David Bateman, a member of the Union Fellowship Society (Islip 390), was disabled with strengthening irons on his legs. He had 'partaken rather freely of the good things provided on club day and lost control of his lower organs' when he fell and broke his leg.

102.   Bicester Petty Session Division (BicA, 1 June 1906)

The case was reported in the 'District Tattler' column of the newspaper. Dr Hill of Islip summoned Cox of Beckley for using threats towards him. Cox was anxious to claim from the friendly society as sick, 'apparently for a rest'. Dr Hill would not certify Cox as sick and he reacted accordingly. Cox appeared at court and was ordered to pay 4s 6d costs and to give an apology to Dr Hill. It is unclear to what friendly society Cox belonged.

Kidlington

103.   **Woodstock Petty Session Division, 9 October 1848 (JOJ, 14 October 1848)**

Robert Watts, Richard Watts and William Wren were summoned in connection with their riotous conduct on the evening of the Kidlington village club feast towards members of the cricket club who were closing their holiday with a quiet dance in a private room. The defendants were fined £3 in total, including costs.

104.   **Wootton South Petty Session Division, 15 March 1864 (JOJ, 19 March 1864)**

The stewards of Kidlington Friendly Society (Kidlington 396) were summoned by George Cox for not paying him £3 12s, representing 12 weeks sick pay at 6s a week. It was stated that following an accident, sick pay from the society was made to 12 December 1863. The club officials claimed that on 12 December, Cox had recovered and he was no longer entitled to benefit. The summons was dismissed.

105.   **Wootton South Petty Session Division, Woodstock, 22 June 1875 (JOJ, 3 July 1875)**

Henry Robey of the Black Bull Inn, Kidlington was convicted of opening his public house after the hour of closing on Thursday 3 June 1875, club feast day. He was fined 6d with 11s costs. There was to be no endorsement to be made on his license.

106.   **Wootton South Petty Session Division, 4 June 1878 (JOJ, 8 June 1878)**

Henry King of the Black Bull, Kidlington made application for an extension on the following Thursday, being club day. The Magistrates decided he had failed to prove to their satisfaction that an extension was necessary, and the application was refused.

107.   **Oxford City Police Court, 6 December 1878 (JOJ, 7 December 1878)**

Richard Scott, landlord of the Anchor Inn, New Road, Oxford and George Hinton, James Street, Cowley were charged with conspiracy, a false declaration to amend the rules and giving no legal notice of a meeting of Kidlington Friendly Society (Kidlington 396). The case was brought by the former officers of the club. It was alleged that only 26 of the 52 rules published were passed by the meeting and the name put on the form to Registrar of Friendly Societies as secretary did not hold that position. The case concerned the members of the club who wished to amend the rules to take control from the Vicar of Kidlington, who was President of the society and had a veto on all aspects. The members wanted to divide funds above £1,000 held by the society among the benefit members.

> 107.1. Oxford City Police Court (JOJ, 14 December 1878)
> The court case continued against Scott and Hinton concerning the Kidlington Friendly Society (Kidlington 396). The bench decided there was no conspiracy and the summons was dismissed. An appeal was lodged.

> 107.2 Oxfordshire Assizes, Oxford 16 January 1879 (JOJ, 18 January 1879)
> The appeal in the case against Scott and Hinton of the Kidlington Friendly Society (Kidlington 396) was heard by the Grand Jury, who after deliberation threw out the indictment and both men were cleared of all charges.

Kirtlington

108.   **Ploughley Petty Session Division, Bicester, 14 June 1865 (JOJ, 24 June 1865)**

William Whitehead of London and George Clarke of Nottingham (both vagrants) were charged with attempting to pick pockets at Kirtlington club day on the evening of Monday 9 June 1865, being Kirtlington club feast. Police Sergeant Wharton saw two men acting suspiciously and he observed them as they conducted a pickpocket manoeuvre on a young girl and attempted to get in her pockets. Ann Hayward gave evidence that she was at Kirtlington feast and she discovered her purse missing with about 10s that had been in her pocket. Both men were found guilty and sentenced to 14 days imprisonment with hard labour.

Leafield

109.   **Chadlington Petty Session Division, Chipping Norton, 10 July 1889 (JOJ, 13 July 1889)**

James Faulkner, a labourer of Wychwood, was indicted for being drunk and disorderly on the highway at Leafield on 14 June, Leafield club day. The defendant made a disturbance at the Fox Inn, where the Leafield Independent Friendly Benefit Society (Leafield 416) dined, and then on the highway. He was fined 5s.

Marston

110.   **Bullingdon Petty Session Division, Oxford, 23 October 1869 (JOJ, 6 November 1869)**

William White, Edward Stringer and Isaac Couling, all of Marston, labourers, were charged with obtaining £1 15s by false pretences at Marston on 18 October 1869, the property of John Collingridge. Their defence was that money had been given to Mrs Collingridge, wife of the prosecutor and landlady of the Three Horseshoes, to keep a club of 24 members called Marston Friendly Benefit Society (Marston 429). The case was dismissed.

111.   **Bullingdon PSD, Oxford, 20 February 1875 (JOJ, 27 February 1875)**

Charles Randle summoned the stewards of the Marston Friendly Benefit Society (Marston 429) for failing to pay 10s 6d for sickness. The stewards were ordered to pay or face seven days imprisonment.

112. Bullingdon Petty Session Division, Oxford, 17 August 1878 (JOJ, 24 August 1878)

Richard Viles summoned the secretary of the Marston Friendly Benefit Society (Marston 429) for unlawfully being expelled from the society. He missed four months payment but had offered to pay the arrears. An order to reinstate Viles was made by the Justices.

113. Bullingdon Petty Session Division (WT, 1 June 1883)

George Cummings, a steward of Marston Friendly Society (Marston 429) was summoned to show good cause why he should not pay Francis Simms, a gardener of Headington £1 11s 6d sick benefit. Cummings stated the club had no money to pay him. It had £50 but he was under instruction to leave it in the bank until after a meeting of the club had been held. Cummings was ordered to pay amount due to Simms and £1 12s costs.

114. Bullingdon Petty Session Division, Oxford, 14 July (JOJ, 21 July 1883)

Joseph Miles summoned the stewards of Marston Friendly Benefit Society (Marston 429) for non-payment of sick pay amounting to £4 19s 9d. The case was adjourned.

114.1. Bullingdon Petty Session Division, Oxford, 21 July 1883 (JOJ, 28 July 1883)
Joseph Miles summoned officials of the club for non-payment of £4 19s. 9d benefit. The headquarters of the club was at the White Hart. The case was adjourned.

114.2. Bullingdon Petty Session Division, Oxford, 28 July1883 (JOJ, 4 August 1883)
The case was adjourned again.

114.3. Bullingdon Petty Session Division, Oxford, 11 August 1883 (JOJ, 18 August 1883)
The case was adjourned again.

114.4. Bullingdon Petty Session Division, 1 September, Oxford (JOJ, 8 September 1883)

The defendant, a steward of the society did not appear and payment of the money due to Miles was ordered with payment by distress if default.

114.4. Bullingdon Petty Session Division, Oxford, 6 October 1883 (JOJ, 13 October 1883)

The defendant, John Edle, a steward of Marston Friendly Benefit Society, did not appear. An order was given for payment with costs.

Minster Lovell

115.   Witney Petty Session Division (JOJ, 18 January 1851)

An order was made on Minster Lovell Benefit Society to pay William Hern, a benefit member, 5s weekly on his application (it is unclear exactly which club this relates to but is either Minster Lovell 435 or 436). He had applied to the club several times but they refused as he was ineligible. Hern produced a certificate of his inability to work. The bench found in favour of Hern and costs of the hearing were to be paid by the club.

116.   County Court, Oxford, 11 June 1880 (JOJ, 19 June 1880)

Brooks, the plaintiff, was a member of Minster Lovell Friendly Society (Minster Lovell 437). He was excluded from the society and so from a division of funds of 4s 2d. He had been a member of the club for 20 years in June 1879. The case was non-suited, and the judge recommended that the vicar act as arbiter and 'see what the result of the arbitration might be'. The society was unregistered.

117.   County Court, Witney (OCBBG, 11 July 1896)

Thomas Pratley, plaintiff sued James Cross, secretary of the Minster Lovell Friendly Society (Minster Lovell 437), an unregistered club. Pratley claimed he had been due money from the previous distribution of funds. He said he joined the society in 1885 and the club was a 7-year dividing society. The last distribution was on 9 May 1896 and he was due £1 15s. Pratley gave notice that he would leave the club at the division but he was told he must pay his subscription for the May quarter of 3s 6d before he could receive the division money due to him. This he declined to do. The Judge stated he could not adjudicate as the club was unregistered and the rules were not authorised by the Registrar. However, both parties agreed to leave the case to the Judge to decide. He awarded Pratley £1 11s 6d.

Mollington

118. Banbury Petty Session Division, 7 May 1855 (JOJ, 12 May 1855)

Thomas Talbot and John Howe of Claydon were charged with assaulting the constables at Mollington in the execution of their duty. Talbot and Howe went into the club room occupied by Mollington club (Mollington 440) about midnight, and annoyed the company. They challenged to fight anyone and broke a table. The landlord called for the constables and the Talbot and Howe each seized a leg of the table and produced pocket bludgeons. They used these on the head and body of the constables and those assisting. More than five people were injured and needed treatment from the surgeon. Talbot and Howe were taken to the Bird in Hand beer-house, Cherwell Street, Neithrop where they were held until transported to court at Banbury. They were committed to Warwick for trial on bail. A third offender, Hughes, was not captured. No outcome of the further hearing has been located.

North Leigh

119. Wootton South PSD, Woodstock, 12 June 1894 (JOJ, 16 June 1894)

Edwin Holifield of Finstock was summoned for using obscene language at North Leigh feast on 4 June 1894. Inspector Sorrell said the defendant had some swing boats, and other amusements at East End, North Leigh. A dispute arose and he used the language described. He was fined 15s including costs or 14 days imprisonment with hard labour in default. The fine was paid.

Nuneham Courtenay

120.   City Court, Oxford, 24 February 1849 (JOJ, 3 March 1849)

Frances Ahfield, widow of John, summoned the stewards of the Nuneham Courtenay Friendly Society (Nuneham Courtenay 459) for the recovery of £8 due to her as death benefit. There was no disinclination for the stewards to pay but they wanted to obtain an order from the Magistrates as the action was not clear in the rules of the society. The order was granted.

Oxford

121.   Oxford City Quarter Sessions (JOJ, 19 October 1833)

Jethro Ludlow and James Davis were charged with seven counts of stealing a mahogany box, and gold and silver coins from The Blenheim Public House, St Ebbe's, kept by Charles Dyer. They belonged to a lodge of Oddfellows (Oxford 466). On the evening of 12 August the box containing the books and assets of the society went missing. However, after consideration the Judge found the indictment flawed and dismissed the case. Indictments against several other members of the lodge who it was alleged had received part of the money out of the box also had their cases dismissed.

122.   City Court, 23 March 1847 (JOJ, 27 March 1847)

John Green, a carpenter living in St Clement's, appealed against expulsion from the St Clement's Union Friendly Society (Oxford 532) for carrying on a business and drinking in a public house during a period when he was receiving sickness benefit. He had been a member since 1816. Expulsion was not in the rules of the society and the minutes were not signed. The charges were not proved and Green was ordered to be reinstated. Mr London, the club Steward, stated the result would be that the club would be broken up. It had £300 in hand.

123.   **City Court, Oxford, 26 October 1852 (JOJ, 30 October 1852)**

Joseph Nutt of Iffley was charged with having received £3 16s as steward of the Mechanical Benefit Society (Oxford 515), and defrauding it by claiming it to have been paid to a sick member. This proved to be false. Nutt was found guilty and was ordered to pay double the deficiency, plus 10s costs by 6 November 1852.

124.   **City Court, Oxford, 28 December 1855 (JOJ, 29 December 1855)**

Charles Puddle, who did not appear, was charged with embezzlement of £6 10s he received to pay sick members as a steward of the Mechanical Benefit Society (Oxford 515). He was found guilty in his absence and fined £13 (double the amount embezzled) or three months imprisonment in default.

125.   **Bullingdon PSD, Oxford, 7 January 1860 (JOJ, 14 January 1860)**

Richard Hicks, landlord of the Red Lion, Summertown was charged by the Trustees of the Summertown Benefit Society (Oxford 540) with refusing to give up the club box and contents. The Magistrates ordered Hicks to hand over the club box but adjourned the case for a week. At considerable expense, Hicks had enlarged the public house to accommodate the club but the society had moved to the parochial school-room. The Magistrates considered that the Society should consider making some compensation to him.

126.   **City Court, Oxford, 14 April 1863 (JOJ, 18 April 1863)**

John Lewis made a complaint against the stewards of the College Servants' Benefit Society (Oxford 473) and claimed unpaid sickness benefit. He had suffered from asthma for the previous six months, and attended the Radcliffe Infirmary as an out-patient. The club stated it was an 'old mans cough' and the society took no account of age. The case was dismissed by the Justices.

127.   'Rumoured Embezzlement by College Cook' (JOJ, 14 May 1870)

W.F. Thurland, cook and manciple of New College had been missing since 4 May 1870. 'With faith in his honour and integrity', the College Servants' Provident Institution (Oxford 474) accounts had not been audited in the normal way for some time and on Thurland's disappearance it was discovered there was a £1,000 deficiency. He was at work on Tuesday 3 May but the following morning had disappeared. A warrant was issued for his apprehension. Thurland was Town Councillor for East Ward, Oxford.

127.1. 'Absconding Cook' (JOJ, 21 May 1870)
Jackson's Oxford Journal reported that nothing had been heard of Thurland and the Police were searching for him. A creditors meeting was held and £1,800 was found to be owed in addition to the £1,000 to the College Servants' Provident Institution (Oxford 474).

127.2. Bankrupt (LG, 27 May 1870)
A notice was presented of W.F. Thurland being declared bankrupt.

127.3. County Court (JOJ, 4 June 1870)
It was noted that W.F. Thurland, 97 Holywell Street and New College, a victualler, was adjudged bankrupt on 21 May 1870. A creditors meeting was due to be held on 8 June 1870. (Notice repeated 11 June).

127.4. County Court (JOJ, 11 June 1870)
A notice of the sale of several houses and furniture belonging to W.F. Thurland in Oxford was advertised as part of his bankruptcy proceedings.

127.5. Oxford County Court 11 October 1870 (JOJ, 15 October 1870).
The amount of £15 10s was ordered by the Judge to be paid to the College Servants' Benefit Society (Oxford 473) from Thurland's assets as preferential creditors.

127.6. County Court, Oxford, 8 November (JOJ, 12 November 1870) The court was asked to decide upon a point of law concerning the College Servants' Provident Institution (Oxford 474). Thurland had held £512 6s 3d of the Institution's money plus £13 10s from the College Servants' Benefit Society (Oxford 473). Losses had been incurred by Thurland over previous two or three years. It was decided that Thurland had not invested the cash as he should have done and that he owed the Provident Institution the sum stated. The sum of £512 5s 3d was ordered to be paid to the College Servants' Provident Institution. The decision on the Benefit Society funds would follow in the same manner.

128.   Oxford City Police Court, Friday 23 June 1876 (JOJ, 24 June 1876)

Edward Beale, Osney was charged on remand with embezzling sums of money whilst secretary of the Amalgamated Society of Railway Servants (Oxford 463). The evidence was that he received money from Mr Browning, treasurer and the money was not forwarded onto the London headquarters. It was a complicated case, and was found not proven. The case was dismissed.

129.   Oxford City Police Court, 27 August 1878 (JOJ, 31 August 1878

Joseph Nutt, secretary of Court Duke of Cornwall, AOF (Oxford 478) was summoned for not producing the accounts of the club. A summons was issued by the trustees, but he did not appear at court and a warrant issued.

> 129.1. Oxford City Police Court, 7 January 1879 (JOJ, 11 January 1879)
> Joseph Nutt, a plumber and glazier of St Clement's was charged with having between 10 December 1877 and 10 June 1878 embezzled divers sums of money whilst secretary of the Court Duke of Cornwall, AOF (Oxford 478), and falsifying accounts. The minimum amount missing was £41 15s 7d for the years 1876 and 1877. Nutt had received the money from members at the court room of the Coach and Horses public house. Nutt claimed any omission from the books was on busy nights and would have been accidental and not intentional. He was committed to the Assizes for trial with bail of £50 and two sureties of £25.

129.2. Oxford Assizes (JOJ, 18 January 1879)
Joseph Nutt appeared charged with embezzlement of three sums of money and falsifying accounts. These were specimen charges. Money had been paid to Nutt, and membership cards made up but the subscriptions were not entered into contribution book. The case was adjourned to the next Assizes as extra charges were to be added. However, no further reports have been traced.

130.   **Oxford City Police Court, 28 February 1882 (JOJ, 4 March 1882)**

Thomas Gardner, a carpenter of Adelaide Villas, Adelaide Street, and an agent for the Integrity Life Assurance and Sick Benefit Society, Bath District (Oxford 497), appeared charged with embezzlement. Integrity Life was a collecting society. The case was adjourned to the Quarter Sessions.

> 130.1. Oxford City Quarter Sessions, 3 April 1882 (JOJ, 8 April 1882)
> Thomas Gardner was charged with the embezzlement of funds between 16 January and 6 February 1882 from Integrity Life Assurance and Sick Benefit Society (Oxford 497), He was appointed agent and collector in August 1881 and was paid part by commission and part by bonus, collecting from house to house. A shortage of £2 10s 8½d was found between what he collected and what was deposited with the society. He was determined not guilty by a jury and The Recorder commented that he hoped the jury were right.

131.   **Bullingdon Petty Session Division, Oxford, 7 July 1888 (JOJ, 14 July 1888)**

William Busby summoned the secretary of the Summertown St John's Unity Benefit Society (Oxford 540) wanting reinstatement to the society and the payment of sickness benefit. He had been excluded from the society for being drunk on club day. It was a complex case and was adjourned.

> 131.1. Bullingdon Petty Session Division, Oxford, 21 July 1888 (JOJ, 28 July 1888).
> The case of William Busby was considered and an order for him to be reinstated to the society was made by the Justices.

132.   County Court, Oxford (WG, 30 May 1891)

The secretary of Royal Liver Friendly Society was summoned due to the failure to pay £7 to a widow on the death of her husband, Mr A. Kilby. He was insured for £14. He had ill health at the time of taking out the policy and it was argued he did not declare it. His wife had been paid half by the society. The court found in favour of plaintiff, Mrs Kilby and the society was required to pay the remainder due.

133.   City Court, 25 May 1895 (JOJ, 21 December 1895)

Eliza Whetton, widow of George, appeared and sought a decision regarding £100 claim on a life policy affected by the husband in accordance with the rules of the College Servants' Provident Institution (Oxford 474), of which he was a member. There was no unwillingness on the part of the society to pay the amount but both executors and the widow had claimed the amount. The court found in favour of the widow.

134.   Crown Court, Oxford, 31 October 1895 (JOJ, 2 November 1895)

The bankruptcy hearing of Charles Titian Hawkins, an accountant of 12 Broad Street, Oxford and wine and spirit merchant of 42 Cornmarket Street was heard. His home was at 'Mayfield', Summertown. There was extensive public interest in the case as his debts totalled £55,000. Hawkins stated he was involved in the Summertown Benefit Society (Oxford 540) but he had forgotten in what capacity. He thought it may have been trustee. He received £332 10s of society money in two lots but he had no account of it. He stated he received the money about one year 'before he was ill' and put it into his bank account. Mr Ivory mortgaged his property and Hawkins received some money from him for the benefit society. There were further hearings on 19 November and 14 January 1896. As a registered society, the Summertown Benefit Society was a preferred creditor but there is no report on how much money was refunded to the society.

Piddington

135.   Serious sexual assault at Piddington (BH, 14 June 1878)

Eliza Edwards, a domestic servant of Cauble Farm, Piddington left home at
about 6.15 p.m. to attend Piddington club feast on the evening of 4 June 1878.
She stayed at the feast and while there did not see the defendants, George
Claridge (17) and Robert House (16), both of Brill. She returned home at 9.00
p.m. over the fields. The young men approached her after one and a half miles
and raped her. She had never seen them before. Both men were committed for
trial at the Assizes.

> 135.1. Oxfordshire Summer Assizes, 5 July 1878 (JOJ, 6 July 1878)
> Robert Howse and George Claridge, were indicted with rape upon
> Eliza Edwards of Piddington on 4 June 1878. She had been at
> Piddington feast and on her way home the prisoners threw her down
> with violence. Her clothes were torn and covered in dirt. There
> was evidence of early complaint but the doctor's evidence was
> inconclusive. The case continued.

> 135.2. Crown Court, Saturday 6 July (JOJ, 13 July 1878)
> The case of Howse and Claridge continued and both were found guilty
> of attempted rape. They were sentenced to 18 months imprisonment.

136.   Bicester Petty Session Division, 11 June 1897 (BicA, 18 June 1897)

A report headed 'Club Feast Sequels' reported upon Frank Reynolds, a
labourer of Piddington who was summoned for being Drunk and Disorderly at
Piddington on 1 June 1897. He entered a not guilty plea. Police stated that at
8.00 p.m. they saw the defendant drunk and using bad language. He had been
disturbing the Piddington club (Piddington 550) feast earlier in the day and
had a black eye. The defendant went home several times, taken by his father
but returned each time. Reynolds gave evidence and stated that he attended
club day as his father had carried the flag during the parade for many years.
He took his part in a quarrel about who should perform the duty that year. His
own brother was very drunk and gave him the black eye. Reynolds asserted he
had not drunk for months until that day and then he only drank a small amount.

He has been tee-total since. He stated it was his brother who should be before the court. Reynolds was found guilty and fined 2s with 9d costs or seven days imprisonment in default.

Rotherfield Greys

137.   **Henley Petty Session Division, 16 February 1854 (JOJ, 18 February 1854)**

William Marsham, a hired farm servant claimed two weeks wages from his employer, Mr C. House of Rotherfield Greys, he being unwell during that period. Mr House attended and explained Marsham was a hired servant for a year. He had been unwell and had asked to go home as he was a member of a benefit club, to which he should become chargeable. This was granted and he was absent about two weeks. On his return he claimed his wages for that time. House objected as he was not allowed to perform any labour according to his club's rules when claiming sickness benefit. In Mr House's view, his illness was not such to incapacitate him of all labour. The chairman said Marsham had been unwisely advised to make a claim on Mr House who had treated him with kindness. Marsham was ordered to pay 4s costs and return to his service.

138.   **Oxfordshire Quarter Sessions, Oxford, 5 July 1866 (JOJ, 7 July 1866)**

Charles Alleway was indicted for unlawfully wounding George Smith at Rotherfield Greys on 21 May. On the day in question there was a club feast after which the prisoner was seen to strike Smith with a thick stake of wood. Immediately before the assault, Alleway had been talking to a deaf and dumb boy in an abusive manner and when Smith protested, he was struck. Alleway was found guilty of common assault and was sentenced to four months imprisonment.

Salford

139.   **Chadlington Petty Session Division, Chipping Norton, 2 August 1871 (JOJ, 12 August 1871)**

George Betteridge was charged by John Jeffries with being drunk and quarrelsome, and refusing to quit his public house in Salford club day (Salford

558) held on 21 July. Betteridge was fined and ordered to pay costs, together totalling 11s.

Sandford on Thames

140. **Bullingdon Petty Session Division, Oxford, 2 September 1871 (JOJ, 9 September 1871)**

Joseph Bennett, a dyer of St Clement's was summonsed by the Inland Revenue for using a Whitechapel Cart without a license. A trap was seen being driven between Littlemore station and Sandford with a man and boy riding in it next to Bennett. Bennett denied using it for that purpose, but said he went to Sandford Independent (Hand and Heart) Life Society club dinner (Sandford on Thames 559). The bench considered the case and they gave him a mitigated penalty of £5, the lowest fine they could impose and recommended the fine be reduced to £1 by the Board of Commission.

141. **Bullingdon Petty Session Division, Oxford, 26 October 1878 (JOJ, 2 November 1878)**

Richard Nutt and Thomas Wakefield of Sutton Courtenay were summoned for being drunk and riotous at Sandford on Thames on 8 October 1878, club feast day. The case was dismissed on the payment of 8s costs.

142. **Bullingdon Petty Session Division, Oxford, 2 June 1888 (JOJ, 9 June 1888)**

Ambrose Rowlands, a labourer of Sandford on Thames was summoned for being drunk on a highway on 21 May 1888. He pleaded guilty. Rowlands had been at the Sandford Independent (Hand and Heart) Life Society (Sandford on Thames 559) dinner and had been very troublesome for some time. It was reported that 'he wanted to fight everyone'. His employer, Mr Cannon of Sandford, gave a good reference and Rowland promised to be a tee-totaller. He was fined 1s with 9s costs.

Shenington

143. **Banbury Petty Session Division, 30 June 1859 (JOJ, 2 July 1859)**

John Anderson of Shenington preferred a complaint against his man-servant, John Bennett, for absenting himself from his service. Bennett had been given leave to go home for club day with strict instructions to return at a certain time. However, he stayed home some days longer and was very abusive and insolent when he did return. For this, the Magistrates ordered him to be discharged from his service and to forfeit all wages due to him.

144. **Banbury Petty Session Division, 18 June 1868 (JOJ, 20 June 1868)**

Alexander Hillman and Thomas Harvey were charged with assault on a police officer at Shenington club day. They were described as 'old offenders' and were found guilty. Each was fined £1 with 17s costs or 14 days imprisonment in default.

145. **Banbury Petty Session Division, 2 June 1870 (JOJ, 4 June 1870 and BanA, 9 June 1870)**

James Robbins summoned John Ward and Elijah Hitchcox, the stewards of the Shenington Amicable Society (Shenington 561) for failing to pay 7s sick pay for the last week of his sickness. Robbins had been in the club for 20 years and in January 1870 he had a bad arm. He was seen leading a horse along a road to pick up a cart when receiving sickness benefit and the monies were withheld as it was interpreted by the club officials that he was working. It was observed he was also in the public house until 11.00 p.m. although there was nothing in the rules that prevented it. The case was upheld and the court ordered the Stewards to pay the 7s and 10s costs.

146. **Fatality at Shenington club feast (JOJ, 22 June 1878)**

There was a fatality at Shenington club feast held on Monday and Tuesday, 17 and 18 June 1878. On the latter day at about 4 p.m. some men who had been drinking together saw a Bath chair outside the Bell Inn. One of the party, George Roberts, a blacksmith was placed in the chair and others pushed it. Before they had gone many yards the chair was upset and Roberts fell on his head, breaking his neck. He was picked up but was dead. An inquest was due the following week.

Shilton

147.   Swing boat accident (JOJ, 18 June 1892)

The Shilton club feast was held on Whit Tuesday, 7 June 1892. There was a swing-boat accident when a rope broke and a man, John Smith was injured.

Shipton under Wychwood

148.   County Court, Chipping Norton, 11 April 1872 (JOJ, 20 April 1872)

Philip Coombs, plaintiff, issued a suit against Robert Longshaw, both of Shipton-under-Wychwood. Longshaw was secretary to the Shipton-under-Wychwood Friendly Society (Shipton under Wychwood 569), to which both belonged. It was alleged Coombs was 4s in arrears with his payments, but Coombs stated his son had paid Longshaw. This was denied and the case was dismissed.

Somerton

149.   Bicester Petty Session Division, Friday 11 June 1897 (18 June 1897)

In a report headed 'Club Feast Sequels', it was reported that William Eaglestone of Lower Heyford was charged with being drunk and disorderly at Somerton Friendly and Benefit Society (Somerton 581) club day on 1 June 1897. He entered a not guilty plea. At 6.30 p.m. the Police had been called by Mr Eagle, farmer, to put the defendant off his premises which he did. The club band was playing at Eagle's Home at the time. The defendant refused to go home and returned to the village. At 9.30 p.m. near to the station he was seen very drunk and it was reported that 'he wanted to fight everyone'. At 9.40 p.m. he was outside the public house in the road shouting and still offering to fight. Eaglestone was found guilty and ordered to pay a 2s fine with 9d costs or serve seven days imprisonment in default.

Souldern

150.   **Ploughley Petty Session Division, Bicester, 13 May 1864 (JOJ, 21 May 1864)**

John Finch of Souldern charged the officials of the Souldern Friendly Society (Souldern 583) in that the club refused to pay him weekly sick pay of £3 5s due to a change of rules that were not agreed by a general meeting. The Justices found in favour of Finch and the stewards were ordered to pay him the full amount and also pay 8s 6d costs.

151.   **Ploughley Petty Session Division, Bicester, 14 June 1867 (JOJ, 29 June 1867)**

John Paine of Croughton was charged with assaulting Police Constable Wharton on 29 May 1867 at Souldern Friendly Society (Souldern 583) club day. Paine was lying in the road but when the police constable went to pick him up, he struck PC Wharton in the face. Paine was fined £1 with 9s 6d costs or 21 days imprisonment in default. He was committed to prison as he could not pay.

152.   **Ploughley Petty Session Division, Bicester, 27 June 1884 (JOJ, 5 July 1884)**

James Jarvis of Souldern appeared at court in custody, charged with assaulting James Finch of Souldern at Souldern Friendly Society (Souldern 584) club day on 30 May 1884. The defendant was summoned some time ago by the complainant for offences under the Game Laws. On meeting the complainant at club day, he assaulted him and absconded to Nuneaton where he was later arrested. Jarvis pleaded guilty and was fined 5s with £2 12s costs.

153.   **Incident at club day (BicA, 7 June 1901)**

The 'District Tattler' column of the newspaper reported that a tradesman's daughter lost a gold watch and chain as it fell out of her waistband at Souldern Friendly Society (Souldern 584) annual feast held the previous Wednesday. It was picked up by an attendant of the swings who was due in court the next day.

153.1. Bicester Petty Session Division, 7 June 1901 (BicA, 14 June 1901)

A full account appeared in the *Bicester Advertiser* of alleged watch stealing at Souldern club day. Andrew Buckland of Botley was charged with stealing a gold watch and chain valued at £6 9s 6d on 2 May 1901, the property of Fanny Jarvis of Souldern. Several witnesses were called and the case was committed to the Quarter Sessions for trial. No outcome of the case can be traced.

Stadhampton

154.   Watlington Magistrates, 7 June 1890 (BOA, 13 June 1890)

Thomas Moores, a beer retailer was summoned for selling liquor on the highway adjoining his beer off-licensed premises on Brookhampton Hand and Heart Friendly Society (Stadhampton 589) club day on 27 May 1890. The club and band had called at his house for 20 years and it was custom to draw beer. Moores stated he thought there was no impropriety in keeping an old custom. He was found guilty and fined £5.

Standlake

155.   Fatal incident at club day (JOJ, 6 June 1781)

Standlake Club feast was held on Wednesday 6 June 1781 at the Chequers Inn. A Coroner's Inquest was held on 9 June 1781 because on club day William Burford threw Thomas Huckwell into a furnace in the village and he died. The inquest found that both were good friends and Burford did not know that there was water in the furnace. It was accepted it was an accident.

Steeple Aston

156.   **Wootton North Petty Session Division, Deddington, 5 June 1852 (JOJ, 12 June 1852)**

James Preston of Steeple Aston, a labourer, was charged with assault on the landlord of the Red Lion, Steeple Aston on 5 May 1852, club day. Preston was drunk. He was bound over for a Breach of the Peace for twelve months.

157.   **Wootton North Petty Session Division, Woodstock, 6 February 1854 (JOJ, 14 May 1854)**

David Mole of Middle Barton summoned the Stewards of the Steeple Aston Friendly Society (Steeple Aston 615) to pay £3 10s for outstanding sick pay. The case was dismissed.

158.   **Wootton North Petty Session Division, Deddington, 1 June 1860 (JOJ, 9 June 1860)**

Joseph Fenemore, Frederick Markham, Benjamin Bolton and James Nelson, labourers of Steeple Aston, were charged with being drunk and disorderly at the Steeple Aston club day on 3 May 1860. All pleaded guilty, and were cautioned with each to pay 1s 6d costs.

159.   **Wootton North Petty Session Division, Deddington , 2 June 1871 (JOJ, 17 June 1871)**

Joseph Fenemore of Steeple Aston, a labourer, and Joseph Mobbs of Middle Aston, a labourer, pleaded guilty to being drunk and fighting at Steeple Aston on 24 May 1871, club feast day. Both were members of the Heyford and Aston Friendly society. Each was fined 3s with 15s 6d costs, and were bound over to keep the peace in the sum of £10. Both were liable for expulsion from the society on their conviction.

160.   **Wootton North Petty Session Division, Deddington, 16 June1871 (JOJ, 24 June 1871)**

William Burgin of Steeple Aston, beerhouse keeper, was charged with permitting gambling on his premises at Steeple Aston on 24 May 1871, being club day. Police Constable Horn stated that at 3 o'clock in the afternoon several men were playing skittles on Mr Burgin's premises. All the landlords in the area had been cautioned about allowing such practices with gambling. PC Horn reported that the place was fitted out as a skittle alley, with hurdles around it and he saw two men playing. After they finished, he heard Burgin say, 'I'll play you for a pint'. They played and after the game the man went and filled beer in a can from Mr Burgin's. Other examples of obtaining beer following a bet were given. Mark Lewis, a policeman of four years, was a witness for Burgin. He denied any money or beer had exchanged hands by gambling. The case was held over for a month to gain opinion.

161.1. Wootton North Petty Session Division, Deddington, 8 September 1871 (JOJ, 23 September 1871)
Mark Lewis of Deddington was charged with committing wilful perjury on 14 July regarding ongoing charges against William Burgin. Lewis gave evidence for the defence that Thomas Louch was only at the beerhouse alley playing skittles in the afternoon. Five hours evidence was taken. The case was adjourned for two weeks, and Lewis was bailed in the sum of £20 with surety of £20. Lewis was an off-duty Police Constable at the time of the incident.

161.2. Wootton North Petty Session Division, Deddington, 22 September 1871
A case of perjury against Mark Lewis of Deddington was carried over from last session. Lewis was committed for trial at the Assizes. Bail was granted at £40 with two written sureties of £20 each. Six hours of evidence was taken.

160.3. Oxfordshire Lent Assizes (JOJ, 9 March 1872)
There was a full case report of trial. At the conclusion, Lewis was acquitted and discharged by the court.

161.   Wootton North Petty Session Division, Deddington, 28 July 1871 (5 August 1871)

William Burgin of Steeple Aston, beerhouse keeper and his wife Hannah, were charged with assault by Thomas Louch of Steeple Aston, a witness against him in an ongoing case. Louch was also charged with assaulting Burgin and refusing to leave the beerhouse. Charges against Burgin were dismissed by the Justices. Louch was found guilty on both accounts and was fined 19s 6d, including costs in each case or 14 days imprisonment in default.

162.   Wootton North Petty Session Division, Deddington, 3 June 1881 (JOJ, 18 June 1881)

James Parsons, a carpenter of Steeple Barton was charged with being drunk and disorderly at Steeple Aston club day on 18 May 1881. He was fined 2s 6d with costs of 13s 6d.

Stowood

163.   Bullingdon Petty Session Division, Oxford, 23 October 1869 (JOJ, 6 November 1869)

John Collett, secretary of the Stowood Friendly Society (Stowood 628) and landlord of the Royal Oak, Stowood was charged by William Savin, a stableman of Bletchingdon, with a breach of rules of the society. Savin had been a member for more than 30 years and he had been expelled from the society for non-payment of subscriptions. The expulsion was confirmed by the court but the society was told to improve and be more particular about entries in the minutes of such occasions in the future.

Thame

164.   Bullingdon Petty Session Division, Oxford, 14 August 1869 (JOJ, 21 August 1869)

The secretary and treasurer of the Thame Permanent Hand in Hand Friendly Society (Thame 648) were charged with expelling Thomas Green, a member from the society contrary to the rules. Green was convicted in April of obtaining money from the club under false pretences, a breach of the club rules, and was expelled. The Justices considered the case and ordered Green's reinstatement to the society or pay £10 and 10s costs in lieu. The plaintiff's solicitor said Green had been a member of the society for more than 50 years and it might be better for the society to pay him the £10 rather than reinstate him.

165.   **Bullingdon Petty Session Division, Oxford, 22 May 1869 (BH, 28 May 1869)**

Francis Batchelor, a labourer of Thame, was charged with assaulting Police Constable Savin on 19 May 1869 at Thame club feast and being drunk and riotous in the street. At 3.00 p.m. Batchelor kicked Police Constable Savin. He was ordered to pay a fine and costs of 25s or serve 21 days imprisonment with hard labour in default. John Batchelor, brother of Francis was also charged with assaulting Police Constable Martin at Thame Police Station the same day. It was stated James had been teetotal for six or seven weeks before the club feast. The Justices decided 'the best that they could do was to make him a teetotaller for a bit longer' and he was sentenced to 21 days imprisonment.

166.   **Theft by club official (JOJ, 15 February 1879)**

It was reported that for several years, William Scadding of the Court British Queen of AOF (Thame 640), deceived auditors and had misappropriated £500. He absconded but Police obtained a warrant for his apprehension. Scadding was adjudged bankrupt on 13 June 1879 but no outcome of the alleged defalcation can be found.

Scadding was court secretary but had been replaced by the time of publication of *The Foresters Directory* in March 1879. Reported funds of Court British Queen were shown as having reduced from £1,194 to £540 in the year to the end of December 1878. No record of Scadding being expelled can be located in the AOF quarterly reports as would be expected.

Warborough

167.   **County Court, Wallingford, 4 May 1871 (JOJ, 13 May 1871)**

T. Bailey, a carrier of Warborough, sued the stewards of the Prince of Wales Friendly Society (Warborough 657) to receive 18s he was entitled to. The society dissolved a few months before and divided the funds among the members. The society kept 18s per member for enrolment into the new society. Bailey said he had no intent of enrolling in the new club and claimed the money. The Judge remarked on the unsatisfactory manner of the evidence given by Bailey. He said he was sure Bailey intended to rejoin and so dismissed the suit.

Wendlebury

168.   County Court, Bicester, 3 June 1898 (BicA, 10 June 1898)

An article appeared in the Bicester Advertiser entitled, 'Another claim for sick pay on Wendlebury Benefit Society'. Alfred Clements of Bicester, formerly a highway surveyor was plaintiff in a case against the president, Edwin Lapper and secretary, Mr Hathaway of the Wendlebury Benefit Society (Wendlebury 676). He claimed £3 18s arrears of sick benefit. Hathaway initially refused to take the oath as no such role as secretary of the society existed but after discussion, he eventually did. The society was unregistered. It was stated the club funds were exhausted on 7 March 1898 and the club had 'died'. It was formally declared dissolved on 9 March. The plaintiff stated he had been a member for 40 years and he never received notification of the dissolution of the society. It was said he had not paid his quarterly subscription of 3s 6d as this was normally deducted from sick payments when made. Lapper stated there had been a public notice of dissolution in the press. A new club had been started (Wendlebury 677). The Plaintiff alleged the old club was dissolved to get rid of him as a burden. The court could not order the sick money to be paid as there was only 1d left in the funds. Lapper offered to pay the plaintiff the 1d remaining. No costs were awarded and the costs of the society had to be met by the witnesses.

Westcott Barton

169.   Wootton North Petty Session Division, Deddington, 13 June 1884 (JOJ, 21 June 1884)

Samuel Newman pleaded guilty to being drunk and riotous at Barton club. He was fined 15s 6d or 14 days imprisonment in default.

170.   Wootton North Petty Session Division, Deddington, 12 May 1889 (JOJ, 18 May 1889)

Mr Gillam of the Fox Inn, Westcott Barton was granted an occasional license to sell beer in a field and barn on club day.

171.   Tragedy at Middle Barton (JOJ, 10 August 1895)

An inquest was held at the Three Horseshoes, Steeple Barton into the death of Mark Gibson, 45, a road contractor. Gibson had been the treasurer of the Barton Friendly Society (Westcott Barton 678) for four years. On 31 December 1894 the balance of the accounts was £89 in the treasurer's hand. Gibson could not account for the money. He was a prominent member of the Methodist chapel and a parish councillor. He committed suicide by shooting himself.

Weston on the Green

172.   Embezzlement by secretary

In 1894 it became apparent that Mr E. Hicks, secretary of the Weston on the Green Friendly Society (Weston on the Green 680), was unable to account for approximately £200 of the society's funds. As an unregistered society, recourse through the courts could not be sought unless the offence of larceny could be proved. As in many cases, Hicks had held the money lawfully but had then misapplied it to his own use and larceny was impossible to prove. Hicks had controlled the funds of the society since it began in 1875. When it was discovered there was a shortfall in the funds, Hicks had claimed it was invested in Post Office savings. The solicitors' account of Mallam & Co. recorded the progress of recovering the position by Haman Porter, the new secretary, supported by Mr Crouch, an honorary member between 1894-1899. There is no evidence Hicks was prosecuted for his embezzlement.

Wheatley

173.   City Court, Oxford, 19 May 1849 (JOJ, 26 May 1849)

Henry Quarterman, a steward of Wheatley Tradesmen's Hand in Hand Benefit Society (Wheatley 693) was charged with embezzlement of £19 17s 8d. The case was adjourned to 9 June for the society to consider turning the debt into a loan.

> 173.1. County Court, 4 August 1849 (JOJ, 11 August 1849)
> Henry Quarterman, a former steward of the Tradesmen's Hand in Hand Benefit Society (Wheatley 693) was charged with embezzlement

of £19 17s 8d. The case was adjourned for one week. Quarterman claimed he had entered into an agreement with the society to replay at 2s 6d a week.

173.2. County Court, 11 August 1849 (JOJ, 18 August 1849)
Henry Quarterman, one of the stewards of the Tradesmen's Hand-in-Hand Benefit Society (Wheatley 693) appeared charged with embezzlement. It was reported that by neglect he had gained all three keys of the box and obtained the money. Quarterman was convicted and fined £5, with an order to repay £19 7s 8d within a fortnight.

174.   **Bullingdon Petty Session Division, Oxford, 2 March 1867 (JOJ, 9 March 1867)**

James Ring, a mail contractor, summoned the officers of the Wheatley Tradesmen's Hand-in-Hand Benefit Society (Wheatley 693) for refusing to pay him sick pay. The Justices ordered the club to pay.

175.   **Bullingdon Petty Session Division, Oxford, 18 February 1871 (JPJ, 25 February 1871)**

James Munt, a labourer of Wheatley was charged with assaulting Mr Beck of Wheatley Station Hotel and kicking Police Sergeant Wyatt in the execution of his duty on 30 January 1871. This resulted from a brawl. There was a club dinner of Court Constitution, AOF (Wheatley 681) and Munt entered the club room at the Station Hotel where he was not welcome. The landlord, Beck attempted to eject him. The police were called and the police officer was attacked. The case was adjourned for seven days as it was alleged there were witnessed who would testify Beck was the aggressor. The case of assault on police was dismissed. No outcome of the case can be located.

176.   **Bullingdon Petty Session Division, Oxford, 26 July 1873 (JOJ, 2 August 1873)**

The secretary of Wheatley Hand in Hand Benefit Society (Wheatley 693) was summoned by three members, William Williams, Andrew Lambourn and William Woods, for illegally expelling them from the club. The secretary raised no objection to their reinstatement and the club was ordered to pay 10s costs for each defendant.

177.   Bullingdon Petty Session Division, Oxford, 12 July 1873 (JPJ, 19 July 1873)

Richard Davis, a tailor, summoned the secretary of the Wheatley Tradesmen's Hand-in-Hand Benefit Society (Wheatley 693) for failing to pay £1 4s sickness benefit. He also claimed he had been illegally expelled from the society. The decision of court was that Davis should be reinstated and he should receive the amount claimed.

178.   Bullingdon Petty Session Division, Oxford, 17 June1882 (JOJ, 24 June 1882)

James Munt, a labourer of Wheatley was summoned for refusing to quit the Red Lion at Wheatley, when ordered to do so on 12 June 1882. Thomas Hunt, landlord, said Munt came to the Red Lion drunk and began to abuse him due to the removal of the club box from the King's Arms to his house. It was alleged Munt called him a rogue, swore at him and tore out some of his whiskers. Munt was repeatedly asked to leave but he refused and the Police were called. Munt was fined 5s with 12s 9d costs or 14 days imprisonment with hard labour in default.

179.   Bullingdon Petty Session Division, Oxford, 11 June 1887 (JOJ, 18 June 1887)

Samuel Williams, a licensed victualler of Wheatley was summoned for having six unjust quart and five unjust pint measures on 2 June 1887. An unidentified Wheatley Friendly Society were dining at William's premises on Whit Tuesday and Whit Wednesday. They met in a galvanized iron shed at the rear of the premises. Some of the cups belonged to the club and 60 were hired for the occasion. Members of the friendly society appeared for the defence and stated the club purchased three 18-gallon casks of beer. The cups were used for serving. The court noted this was not the first offence. Williams was found guilty and fined 6s plus costs. It is unclear to which friendly society in Wheatley this case relates.

180.   Bullingdon Petty Session Division, Oxford, 11 January 1890 (JOJ, 18 January 1890)

Foster, a stonemason and bricklayer of Garsington summoned the secretary of the Wheatley Tradesmen's Hand-in-Hand Benefit Society (Wheatley 693). He had been a member for 27 years and had been sick but had been expelled from the society. The magistrates reinstated Foster.

181.   Bullingdon Petty Session Division, Oxford, 21 October 1893 (JOJ, 28 October 1893)

William Washington and Joseph Munt, labourers of Wheatley, were summoned for being drunk and disorderly and refusing to quit the Crown Inn on 17 October 1893 where a club feast was being held. The landlord, Edwin Scott, said the men came to his public house and used very bad language and threatened to fight a fiddler who was playing for dancing. He kept asking them to leave for an hour. Police Inspector Smith said the men belonged to 'the gang' at Wheatley who were a rowdy, disorderly lot. They were found guilty and fined 2s with 4s costs each, or seven days imprisonment with hard labour in default. It is unclear to which friendly society in Wheatley this case relates.

Witney

182.   Witney Petty Session Division, 1 August 1844 (JOJ, 3 August 1844)

The Justices considered a dispute between the stewards and a member of an un-named benefit society in the town. The member, who was not named, had received sickness benefit but had been charged with a breach of the rules and expelled from the club. The case was brought before the magistrates at Oxford who decided in favour of the member. The magistrates at this session recorded that the parties had met and settled the matter out of court.

183.   Death from snake bite after club feast, 2 June 1874 (JOJ, 6 June 1874)

It was reported in *Jackson's Oxford Journal* that Fanny Wiggins, 18, whose parents lived in Witney, attended Minster Lovell feast the previous Wednesday. On returning, she sat down on the grass and fell asleep at Maggots Grove. She awoke, having been 'stung" on the neck. The next day she went to Hailey club feast. On Friday, she was at work at the Mill when her neck swelled up. She died on Tuesday 2 June 1874 and it appears she was bitten by a viper.

184.   Witney Police Court, 10 June 1903 (WG, 13 June 1903)

The *Witney Gazette* reported a 'Serious Charge against a Witney Tradesman'. Francis Solomon Barnes, a plumber of Corn Street, was charged on 10 June 1903 with unlawfully withholding money to the amount of £200 belonging to Court Windrush, AOF (Witney 706). Barnes had been secretary of the club since its formation in 1890. Following a bank audit, it was found the deficiency ran over several years. A meeting had been held between Trustees of the society, their solicitors and Barnes on the previous Wednesday. Barnes stated he did not think the deficiency was as large as £200 and that it was nearer £130-150. He stated he had used the money in his business. Further charges were reported likely the following week. Bail was granted with two sureties of £200, and £200 from the prisoner.

184.1. Witney Police Court (WG, 20 June 1903)
There was a further appearance by Barnes at court. It was stated he had been secretary of Court Windrush (Witney 706) since 5 January 1891. His duties included attending all committee meetings and keeping accounts. The Foresters district auditor had attempted to inspect the books but Barnes had delayed the process. Barnes had produced a balance sheet as at December 1902 showing £342 10s 4d. The auditor had determined it should have been £172 6s 1½d. The amount held in the Post Office bank and cash in hand of treasurer was £189 11s 1d, showing a deficiency of £182 15s 0½d. Barnes had made false accounts. The defendant's solicitor stated he had a full explanation but would not go into it at that hearing. The case was adjourned with bail as before.

184.2. Witney Police Court (JOJ, 4 July 1903)
There was a further hearing of a 'Charge against a Witney Tradesman'. It was stated the defendant had agreed the deficiency identified. The trustees had accepted the full amount owed by Barnes and it had been paid that day. The trustees of Court Windrush (Witney 706) carefully considered the matter and came to the conclusion a large amount of money had been 'muddled away', with no wilful intent to defraud the members of the AOF. It was suggested the trustees were partly to blame as they should have accompanied the treasurer to deposit or withdraw money. However, they had not been told of withdrawals. The request from the trustees was that the charges be withdrawn. The

Magistrates stated it was one of the most serious cases they had to deal with. They had thought of fining Barnes but decided against it and stated Barnes had a narrow escape.

Wolvercote

185.   Bullingdon Petty Session Division, Oxford, 9 June 1883 (JOJ, 16 June 1883)

In a report entitled 'Successful claim on a friendly society', the widow of Charles Warmington summoned the officials of the Independent Mutual Brethren Friendly Society, Wolvercote Lodge (Wolvercote 723) for non-payment of £15 4s due to her. The claim was allowed by the Justices.

Woodstock

186.   County Court, 23 January 1857 (JOJ, 31 January 1857)

Charles Hanniss, a harness maker of Woodstock alleged he was illegally excluded from the New Angel Friendly Society (Woodstock 734) by holding the club meeting at the Marlborough Arms Inn, contrary to the rules. Henry Haynes, publican and member of the committee, had moved to the Marlborough Arms from the New Angel, as had the club. However, the rules had not been amended with the Registrar of Friendly Societies. Hanniss was ordered to be reinstated by the Justices and the club was ordered to pay the sum of £5 12s 8d costs.

187.   Woodstock Borough Petty Session Division (JOJ, 16 January 1875)

A prosecution under the Licensing Act was brought to court in that on 7 December 1874, nine men were found at the King's Arms Inn, Woodstock at midnight. The King's Arms was kept by Joseph Haynes, Mayor of Woodstock. The case 'excited a considerable degree of interest in the town'. Closing time was 11.00 p.m. It was a Police prosecution and it was reported that the landlord faced a separate prosecution the following Monday. It was a quarterly meeting of the Court Loyal Blenheim, AOF (Woodstock 727). There was a great deal of business and new members to induct on the night in question and the committee sat until about midnight. After business, a bowl of rum punch was drunk and it was this that was found by Police. The landlord stated no-one had paid and he had treated them to it. All the nine defendants were club members and all pleaded guilty. The case was adjourned to the following Monday for sanction.

187.1. Woodstock Petty Session Division, 18 January 1875 (JOJ, 23 January 1875)
Alderman Haynes, the Mayor of Woodstock and landlord of the King's Arms, appeared at court for keeping a public house open after 11.00 p.m. on 7 December 1874. Haynes claimed ignorance of the licensing laws and was acrimonious towards the Police. He was found guilty and fined 20s with 13s 6d costs. The deferred action of others defendants resulted in seven being fined 2s 6d each with between 9s and 10s costs.

Wroxton

188.   Banbury Petty Session Division, 3 June 1869 (JOJ, 5 June 1869)

Charles Warmington of Drayton was charged with being drunk and fighting at Wroxton club feast. He was fined 5s with 10s costs.

Appendix 3   Bands deployed at Club Days and Hospital Sundays

This appendix comprises details of 266 musical bands that performed at friendly society club days and Hospital Sunday event between 1836 and 1914. They have largely been identified from newpaper reports and two deanery magazines (Chipping Norton and Deddington). The list is structured alphabetically by band. This section is not a comprehensive record of all such bands in Oxfordshire but provides an extensive record of the variety that were engaged by friendly societies. The first identified use of band on club day in Oxfordshire was the Burford Band (Bands 70) that performed at Burford club day on Whit Monday, 23 May 1836 (JOJ, 28 May 1836).

Name: The name of the band in alphabetical order as it appears in the sources, including alternative or additional elements in parentheses. Where the place of origin of the band is not obvious or is from outside the county, clarification is given within parentheses immediately after the name of the band. Reference to other entries within this appendix is also located here.

Place: For each band, the place of performance is recorded in alphabetical order.

Reference: After each place, the specific details are recorded. The first part of the reference relates to the source, mostly newspapers but also deanery magazines and other publications (see list of abbreviations). It is followed by the date of publication (not the date of the club day) and the final number in parentheses refers to the calendar entry of the friendly society responsible for hiring the band where that information is available.

HS: The initial HS within the reference parentheses indicates it was a Hospital Sunday parade.

1.   **1st London Rifle Brigade Band**
      i.   Woodstock JOJ, 7 August 1886 (727).

2.   **1st Oxfordshire Rifle Corps Band**
      i.   Beckley IOOFMU Magazine 1860 (87).

3.   **1st Warwickshire Militia Band**
      i.   Banbury BG, 4 July 1867 (65).

4. **2nd Battalion, Oxfordshire Light Infantry Band**
   i. Chipping Norton JOJ, 30 June 1894 (HS, 194 and 198).
   ii. Thame TG, 22 May 1883 (644).

5. **2nd Oxfordshire Rifle (Volunteer) (Corps) (Brass) Band**
   i. Adderbury WT, 25 May 1883 (8).
   ii. Charlbury JOJ, 2 July 1881 (175); JOJ, 1 July 1882 (175).
   iii. Chesterton BicA, 13 June 1884 (185).
   iv. Chipping Norton JOJ, 30 June 1878 (198).
   v. Deddington BG, 4 June 1885 (240); BG, 14 May 1891 (236).
   vi. Shenington BG, 12 June 1884 (561).
   vii. Shipton under Wychwood JOJ, 12 July 1884 (566).

6. **2nd Warwickshire Militia Band**
   i. Banbury BG, 9 July 1863 (65).

7. **3rd Oxfordshire Rifle (Volunteer) Band**
   i. Banbury BG, 8 July 1869 (65); BG, 7 July 1870 (72); BG, 6 July 1871 (65); BG, 8 July 1875 (72).

8. **Adam's Oxford Band**
   i. Bicester BG, 31 May 1849 (101).

9. **Adam's Sax Horn Band**
   i. North Leigh, JOJ, 26 May 1855 (449).

10. **Adderbury and Bloxham Band** (see also Bands 50, Bloxham Band)
    i. Cropredy BG, 23 June 1859 (230).

11. **Adderbury and King's Sutton Band** (see also Bands 138, King's Sutton Band)
    i. Bodicote BG, 30 May 1861 (129).

12. **Alderminster Brass Band** (Warwickshire)
    i. Sibford Gower BG 13 June 1878 (576).

13. **Alderminster Steel and Hone's Band** (Warwickshire) (see also Bands 126, Hone's (Adderbury) **Band)**
    i. Shenington BG, 15 June 1876 (561).

14. **Alkerton Band** (see also Bands185, Perkin's Alkerton Band)
     i.   Shenington BG, 6 June 1901 (561).

15. **Alvescot and Burford (Brass) Band** (see also Bands 70, Burford
     Band)
     i.   Broadwell WE, 16 June 1870 (140); WE, 8 June 1871 (140).
     ii. Langford WE, 2 June 1870 (409).

16. **Alvescot (Brass) Band**
     i.   Bampton WE, 9 June 1870 (39); WE, 1 June 1871 (39); WE,
          25 May 1872 (39).
     ii. Broadwell WE, 25 May 1872 (140).
     iii. Clanfield JOJ, 9 June 1860 (212);JOJ, 21 June 1862 (212); JOJ,
          13 June 1868 (213); WE, 7 June 1870 (213); JOJ, 10 June 1871
          (213).

17. **Ambrosden (Brass) Band**
     i.   Arncott BicA, 16 May 1913 (16).
     ii. Weston on the Green BicA, 7 June 1895 (680).

18. **Appleton (Brass) Band** (see also Bands 19, Appleton and Bampton
     Band)
     i.   Bampton 7 June 1873 (39).
     ii. Fencott and Murcott BG, 8 June 1854 (281).
     iii. Iffley JOJ, 28 June 1873 (384); JOJ, 27 June 1874 (384).

19. **Appleton and Bampton Band** (see also Bands 18, Appleton Band,
     and Bands 22, Bampton Band)
     i.   Bampton WE, 12 June 1873 (39).

20. **Aston (Brass) Band**
     i.   Aston WG, 3 May 1885 (22); WG, 26 May 1888 (22); WG,
          19 May 1894 (22); WG, 8 June 1895 (22); WG, 12 June 1897
          (22); WG, 24 May 1913 (22).
     ii. Bampton WG, 9 June 1881 (29); JOJ, 3 June 1882 (29); JOJ,
          19 May 1883 (29); WG, 12 June 1897 (30); JOJ, 4 June 1898
          (30); JOJ, 9 June 1900 (30).

21. **Bampton Ancient Order of Foresters Band**
     i.   Bampton WG, 8 August 1903 (32).
     ii. Eynsham JOJ, 24 May 1902 (270).

22.   **Bampton (Brass) Band** (see also Bands 19, Appleton and Bampton
       Band)
       i.   Aston BG, 6 June 1844 (24); WG, 9 June 1906 (22);WG, 5
              June 1909 (22).
       ii.   Bampton JOJ, 13 June 1840 (28); BG, 4 June 1846; WE, 9
              June 1870 (28); WG, 26 May 1888 (39); WG, 15 June 1889
              (39); WG, 23 May 1891 (39); WG, 19 May 1894 (39); WG,
              1 June 1901 (30); WG, 28 May 1904 (30); WG, 17 June 1905
              (30).
       iii.   Clanfield WE, 2 June 1870 (211).
       iv.   Eynsham WG, 25 May 1907 (273).
       v.   Kidlington JOJ, 14 May 1894 (393).
       vi.   Standlake WG 23 May 1908 (595).

23.   **Bampton Foresters Band**
       i.   Bampton JOJ, 1 June 1901 (30); WG, 8 August 1903 (HS, 32);
              WG, 5 June 1909 (32).

24.   **Bampton Military Band**
       i.   Bampton JOJ, 1 June 1844 (28).

25.   **Banbury and Bloxham Sax-Horn Band** (see also Bands 30,
       Banbury Sax-Horn Band, and Bands 51, Bloxham Sax-Horn Band)
       i.   Bloxham JOJ, 13 June 1857.
       ii.   Drayton JOJ, 16 May 1857 (259).

26.   **Banbury (Brass) Band** (see also Bands 238, United Banbury and
       Bloxham Band)
       i.   Deddington BG, 24 May 1888 (236); JOJ, 15 June 1889 (240
              and 246); DDM, July 1895 (240).
       ii.   Hanwell BG, 5 June 1862 (326).

27.   **Banbury Battalion Oxfordshire Light Infantry Band**
       i.   Fritwell BicA, 25 May 1888 (297).

28.   **(Banbury) Britannia (Brass) Band, also Banbury Foundry Band,**
       Britannia Foundry Band, Britannia Works Band, Samuelson &
       Co. Band
       i.   Adderbury BG, 9 June 1859 (6); JOJ, 8 June 1861 (6); BG, 7
              June 1866 (6); BG, 12 June 1873 (6).

ii.   Banbury BG, 5 July 1860 (79); BG, 4 July 1861 (79); BG, 3
       July 1862 (79); BG, 5 July 1866 (85).
iii.   Bloxham BG, 23 May 1861; BG, 1 June 1871 (114).
iv.   Bodicote BG, 12 June 1873 (129); BG, 27 May 1880 (129).
v.   Deddington JOJ, 14 June 1873 (240); BG, 8 June 1876 (240);
       JOJ, 2 June 1900 (236); BG, 16 June 1892 (240).
vi.   Drayton BG, 18 May 1865 (259).
vii.   Fritwell BH, 2 June 1876 (297)
viii. Great Tew BG, 13 June 1878 (318).
ix.   Hanwell BG, 6 June 1878 (326).
x.   Hook Norton BG, 16 May 1872 (368); BG, 28 May 1874
       (368); BG, 20 May 1875 (368).
xi.   Shenington BG, 12 June 1873 (561); BG, 4 June 1874 (561).
xii.   Sibford Gower BG, 7 June 1866 (576); BG, 10 June 1865
       (576): BG, 4 June 1874 (576).
xiii. Steeple Aston BH, 14 May 1869 (615).

Banbury Foundry Band (see Bands 28, Banbury Britannia Brass Band)

29.   **Banbury (Volunteer) Rifle (Corps) Band**
i.   Adderbury BG, 2 June 1881 (6); BG, 5 June 1884 (6); BG, 4
       June 1891 (8); BG, 2 June 1892 (8 and 10); BG, 6 June 1895
       (8).
ii.   Banbury BG, 5 July 1860 (60); BG, 9 July 1863 (79); BG, 7
       July 1864 (65); BG, 6 July 1865 (65); BG, 4 July 1867 (85);
       BG, 9 July 1868 (65); BG, 3 July 1873 (72); BG, 9 July 1874
       (65).
iii.   Bodicote BG, 5 June 1879 (127); BanA, 7 June 1879; BG, 16
       June 1881 (127).
iv.   Deddington BanA, 29 May 1880; BG, 24 May 1883 (240);
       JOJ, 14 June 1884 (240); JOJ, 11 June 1887 (236); BG, 31 May
       1888 (240); BG, 13 June 1895 (240).
v.   Drayton BG, 14 May 1863 (259).
vi.   Great Bourton BG, 8 June 1876 (131)
vii.   Shenington BG, 5 June 1884 (561).
viii. Sibford Gower BG, 14 June 1877 (576)
ix.   Steeple Aston BH, 11 May 1887 (615).
x.   Woodstock JOJ, 6 August 1892 (727).
xi.   Wroxton BG, 30 May 1861 (750).

30.   **Banbury Sax-Horn Band** (see also Bands 25, Banbury and
        Bloxham Sax-Horn Band)
        i.   Bloxham JOJ, 13 June 1857; BG, 23 May 1861.

31.   **Banbury Town Band**
        i.   Fringford JOJ, 13 June 1903 (293).

32.   **Banbury United Band**
        i.   Banbury 3 July 1856 (79).

33.   **Barton (Brass) Band** (also known as **Squire Hall's Band**) (see also
        Bands 216, Steeple Barton Brass Band)
        i.   Bodicote BG, 4 June 1863 (129)
        ii.   Steeple Aston JOJ, 6 May 1865 (615); BH, 6 June 1873 (614).
        iii.   Westcote Barton JOJ, 5 July 1873 (678).

34.   **Beckley (Brass) Band**
        i.   Beckley JOJ, 3 August 1889 (87).
        ii.   Bicester JOJ, 14 June 1879 (107).
        iii.   Bletchingdon BicA, 18 June 1886 (111); BicA, 25 May 1888
               (111); BicA, 30 May 1890 (112); BicA, 31 May 1901 (112).
        iv.   Chesterton JOJ, 14 June 1879 (185); BicA, 6 June 1890 (186).
        v.   Cowley JOJ, 17 June 1865 (227); JOJ, 22 May 1869 (227);
               JOJ, 11 June 1870 (227).
        vi.   Eynsham JOJ, 6 June 1903 (273).
        vii.   Headington JOJ, 29 July 1893 (HS, 331, 332, 336, 338, 339
               and 428); JOJ, 11 August 1894 (HS, 331); JOJ, 2 September
               1899 (HS, 336).
        viii. Oxford JOJ, 28 June 1873 (540); JOJ, 11 July 1874 (540).
        ix.   Stratton Audley BicA, 24 May 1907 (629).
        x.   Wendlebury BicA, 30 May 1890 (676).
        xi.   Weston on the Green BicA, 25 May 1888 (680); BicA, 31 May
               1901 (680).
        xii.   Wolvercote JOJ, 4 June 1898 (722).

35.   **Benson (Brass) Band**
        i.   Benson SON, 11 June 1887 (89); BOA, 14 June 1889 (89);
               BOA, 30 May 1890 (89).
        ii.   Drayton St Leonard BOA, 6 June 1890 (260).

36.   **Berkshire Volunteer Band**
   i.   Hook Norton BG, 31 May 1900 (369).

37.   **Berkshire Yeomanry Band**
   i.   Dorchester WT, 2 June 1882 (251).

38.   **Berrick** (and Roke) **Temperance Brass Band** (see also Bands 194,
      Roke Temperance Band)
   i.   Lewknor SON, 7 June 1890 (551).
   ii. Warborough BOA, 30 May 1902 (656).

39.   **Bibury Band** (Gloucestershire)
   i.   Bampton JOJ, 25 May 1861 (39).

40.   **Bicester (Brass) Band**
   i.   Banbury BG, 7 July 1855 (79).
   ii.   Bicester JOJ, 14 July 1855 (103).
   iii. Bladon BH, 19 June 1867 (109).
   iv.   Bletchingdon BH, 21 May 1875 (111); BicA, 21 May 1880
         (111).
   v.   Chesterton BicA, 25 June 1886 (185); BicA, 25 June 1887
         (185).
   vi.   Deddington BG, 8 June 1876 (246).
   vii. Fringford JOJ, 5 May 1855 (101 and 294).
   viii. Fritwell BH, 25 May 1877 (297).
   ix.   Hethe BicA, 30 May 1880 (361).
   x.   Kidlington JOJ, 3 June 1876 (394).
   xi.   Kirtlington BH, 21 June 1867 (403); BicA, 28 May 1880 (403).
   xii. Launton BH, 11 June 1875 (410); BH, 2 June 1876 (410); BH,
         15 June 1877 (410); JOJ, 14 June 1879); BicA, 10 June 1887
         (410).
   xiii. Piddington BicA, 10 June 1881 (549).
   xiv. Souldern BG, 3 June 1880 (584).
   xv.   Stoke Lyne BicA, 23 May 1879 (617).
   xvi. Weston on the Green BH, 25 May 1877 (680); BicA, 21 May
         1880 (680).
   xvii. Woodstock BH, 28 June 1867 (734).

41.   **Bicester Excelsior Band**
   i.   Bletchingdon BicA, 10 June 1892 (112).
   ii. Chesterton BicA, 29 May 1890 (186).

iii.   Fritwell BicA, 22 May 1890 (297).
iv.   Hethe BicA, 22 May 1890 (361).
v.   Wendlebury BicA, 10 June 1892 (676).

42.   **Bicester** (Oxfordshire) **Rifle (Volunteer) Corps Band**
i.   Charlton on Otmoor BicA, 5 May 1882 (181); BicA, 11 May 1883 (181).
ii.   Chesterton BicA, 1 June 1888 (185).
iii.   Kirtlington BicA, 17 June 1881 (403); BicA, 9 June 1882 (406); BicA, 29 May 1890 (403).
iv.   Launton BicA, 17 June 1881 (410); 15 June 1888 (410).
v.   Lower Heyford BG, 25 May 1865 (614).
vi.   Shenington BG, 1 June 1882 (561).
vii.   Steeple Aston JOJ, 6 May 1865 (613); BG, 11 May 1865 (614).
viii.   Souldern BicA, 3 June 1881 (584); BG, 1 June 1882 (584).
ix.   Stratton Audley BicA, 6 June 1884 (629); BicA, 29 May 1885 (629); BicA, 29 May 1890 (629); BicA, 10 June 1892 (629).
x.   Wendlebury BicA, 14 June 1889 (676).
xi.   Woodstock JOJ, 14 July 1866 (734).

43.   **Bicester Temperance Brass Band**
i.   Stratton Audley BicA, 29 May 1896 (629).

44.   **Bicester Town Band**
i.   Hethe BicA, 7 June 1895 (361).
ii.   Stratton Audley BicA, 7 June 1895 (629).

45.   **Bishopstone Brass Band** (Buckinghamshire)
i.   Thame JOJ, 7 June 1890.

46.   **Blenheim (Brass) Band**
i.   Woodstock JOJ, 12 July 1873 (734); JOJ, 2 August 1873 (727); JOJ, 11 July 1874 (734, 735, 737 and 744); JOJ, 1 August 1874 (727); JOJ, 10 July 1875 (727); JOJ, 12 July 1879 (744).

47.   **Bletchingdon Drum and Fife Band**
i.   Bletchingdon BicA, 18 June 1886 (113).
ii.   Woodstock JOJ, 7 July 1894 (HS, 632).

48.   **Bloxham Amateur Brass Band**
i.   Bloxham BG, 1 June 1871 (119).

49. **Bloxham and Bodicote Band**
    i.   Bodicote BG, 3 June 1858 (126).

50. **Bloxham (Brass) Band** (see also Bands 10, Adderbury and Bloxham
    Band, and Bands 204, Shutford and Bloxham Band, and Bands 238,
    United Banbury and Bloxham Band)
    i.   Adderbury BG, 4 June 1846 (123); BG, 3 June 1847 (123);
          BG, 12 June 1873 (1); BG, 5 June 1884 (9); BG, 7 June 1888
          (6); BG, 2 June 1892 (6); BG, 8 June 1893 (6); BG, 7 June
          1894 (6); BG, 6 June 1895 (6); BG, 4 June 1896 (6); BG, 8
          June 1899 (6); BG, 7 June 1900 (6).
    ii.   Banbury BG, 7 July 1864 (85); BG, 6 July 1865 (85).
    iii. Bloxham BG, 19 May 1864 (119); BG, 1 June 1882 (119); BG,
          5 June 1884 (114); BG, 24 May 1888 (114); BG, 29 May 1890
          (119); BG, 14 May 1891 (118); BG, 9 June 1892 (118); BG, 25
          May 1893 (119); JOJ, 19 May 1894 (119); JOJ, 30 May 1896
          (119); JOJ, 12 June 1897 (119); BG, 2 June 1898 (119); BG,
          25 May 1899 (119); DDM, July 1899; BG, 30 May 1901 (119);
          BG, 22 May 1902 (122).
    iv.   Bodicote BG, 23 June 1859 (129); BG, 4 June 1863 (126); BG,
          24 June 1886 (129); BG, 1 June 1893 (129).
    v.   Charlbury JOJ, 21 June 1862 (175).
    vi.   Chipping Norton JOJ, 11 July 1857 (205).
    vii. Deddington JOJ, 6 June 1896 (240); JOJ, 3 June 1893 (246);
          BG, 4 June 1896 (240).
    viii. Enstone JOJ, 6 June 1885 (540).
    ix.   Duns Tew JOJ, 7 May 1892 (262).
    x.   Hook Norton BG, 9 June 1892 (365).
    xi.   North Newington BG, 1 June 1865 (455); BG, 21 May 1885
          (452).
    xii. Souldern BG, 6 June 1901 (584).
    xiii. Steeple Aston BH, 27 May 1870 (614).
    xiv. Wardington BG, 4 June 1863 (660).
    xv.   Wiggington BG, 15 June 1876 (701); BG, 13 June 1878 (701).

51. **Bloxham Sax-Horn Band** (see also Band 25, Banbury and Bloxham
    Sax-Horn Band)
    i.   Deddington JOJ, 17 May 1856.

52. **Bloxham Temperance Band**
    i.   Bloxham BG, 14 May 1891 (118); BG, 25 May 1893 (119).

53.   **Bloxham Wesleyan Mission Band**
i.   Bloxham BG, 14 May 1891 (118).

54.   **Blunsdon and St Leonard's Band** (Wiltshire)
i.   Clanfield WG, 26 May 1894 (213).

55.   **Blunsdon Band** (Wiltshire) (see also Bands 54, Blunsden and St Leonard's Band)
i.   Clanfield WG, 27 May 1899 (213).

56.   **Bodicote (Brass) Band**
i.   Adderbury BG, 7 June 1888 (10).
ii.   Banbury BG, 5 July 1855 (59).
iii.   Bodicote BG, 24 June 1886 (127); BG, 9 June 1887 (127); BG, 28 May 1891 (127); BG, 16 June 1892 (127); BG, 1 June 1893 (127); BG, 24 May 1894 (127); BG, 1 June 1899 (127); BG, 6 June 1891 (127); BG, 6 June 1901 (127).
iv.   Bloxham JOJ, 1 June 1901 (122).
v.   Bourton BG, 13 June 1889 (131); BG, 29 May 1890 (131).
vi.   Deddington BG, 8 June 1876; BG, 24 May 1888 (246); JOJ, 15 June 1889 (240 and 246); BG, 29 May 1890 (246); JOJ, 30 May 1891 (246); BG, 16 June 1892 (246)
vii.   Duns Tew JOJ, 5 May 1888 (262).
viii. Hanwell BG, 13 June 1889 (326).
ix.   Hook Norton JOJ, 31 May 1890 (368); BG, 19 May 1892 (368).
x.   North Newington BG, 29 May 1884 (452).
xi.   Somerton JOJ, 6 June 1891 (581).
xii.   Westcote Barton JOJ, 30 May 1891 (678).

57.   **Brackley (Brass) Band** (Northamptonshire)
i.   Bloxham JOJ, 4 June 1898 (122).
ii.   Fringford BicA, 7 June 1901 (293 and 295).
iii.   Fritwell BicA, 4 June 1909 (297).
iv.   Stratton Audley BicA, 20 May 1910 (629).

58.   **Brackley Temperance Band** (Northamptonshire)
i.   Hethe BicA, 11 June 1897 (361).

59.   **Brackley Town Band** (Northamptonshire)
i.   Hethe BicA, 31 May 1901 (361).

ii.   Stratton Audley BG, 15 June 1911 (629).

60.   **Brailes (Brass) Band** (Warwickshire)
i.   Bodicote BG, 30 May 1861 (126).
ii.   Churchill JOJ, 12 June 1909 (209).
iii. Hook Norton JOJ, 5 June 1897 (365); BG, 26 May 1898 (365); BG, 25 May 1899 (365); BG, 31 May 1900 (365); JOJ, 21 May 1904 (369).
iv.   Kingham JOJ, 3 June 1905 (397).
v.   Sibford Gower BG, 5 June 1845 (576).
vi.   Wroxton BG, 9 June 1898 (752); BG, 1 June 1899 (752); BG, 6 June 1901 (752); BG, 15 June 1911 (752).

61.   **Bridge Street Mills Band** (Witney)
i.   Hailey WG, 27 May 1893 (322); JOJ, 27 May 1899 (321).
ii.   Witney WG, 27 May 1899 (HS); WG, 11 May 1892 (HS, 721); WG, 11 May 1895 (HS).

62.   **Brill (Brass) Band** (Buckinghamshire)
i.   Fritwell BicA, 30 May 1890 (297).
ii.   Hethe BicA, 20 May 1910 (361).
iii. Piddington BicA, 6 June 1884 (549).

Britannia Foundry Band (see Bands 28, Banbury Britannia Brass Band)

Britannia Works Band (see Bands 28, Banbury Britannia Brass Band)

63.   **Brize Norton (Brass) Band**
i.   Bampton WE, 9 June 1881 (39); JOJ, 3 June 1882 (39).

64.   **Broadwell Band**
i.   Langford JOJ, 8 June 1861 (409).

65.   **Brook's String Band** (Oxford)
i.   Woodstock 22 January 1887 (727).

66.   **Buckingham (Brass) Band**
i.   Banbury JOJ, 11 July 1840 (59); JOJ, 7 July 1855 (59); BG, 3 July 1856 (59).
ii.   Deddington JOJ, 17 June 1848 (242).

67. **Buckingham Militia Band**
    i.   Cowley JOJ, 14 June 1862 (227).

68. **Buckinghamshire Yeomanry Band**
    i.   Banbury BG, 7 July 1853 (59); BG, 6 July 1865 (60).
    ii. Fringford BG, 11 May 1854 (294).

69. **Burford and Hailey Band** (see also Bands 70, Burford Band and
    Bands 112, Hailey Band)
    i.   Minster Lovell JOJ, 18 June 1859 (436).

70. **Burford (Brass) Band** (see also Bands 15, Alvescot and Burford
    Band, and Bands 69, Burford and Hailey Band)
    i.   Bampton JOJ, 19 May 1866 (39); JOJ, 24 May 1902 (39).
    ii.   Burford JOJ, 28 May 1836 (143); JOJ, 17 May 1856 (143);
          JOJ, 25 May 1861 (144); JOJ, 7 September 1861 (145) (the
          band was engaged for club day 1862 and the following six
          years); WG, 2 June 1888 (146); JOJ, 22 June 1889 (146); WG,
          7 June 1890 (146); WG, 30 May 1891 (146); JOJ, 18 June
          1892 (146); WG, 3 June 1893 (146); WG, 26 May 1894 (146);
          JOJ, 15 June 1895 (146); JOJ, 6 June 1896 (146); JOJ, 11 June
          1898 (146); JOJ, 3 June 1899 (146); WG, 16 June 1900 (146);
          WG, 8 June 1901 (146); JOJ, 31 May 1902 (146).
    iii. Charlbury JOJ, 5 July 1851 (175); JOJ, 5 June 1852 (171); JOJ,
          3 July 1858 (175).
    iv.   Leafield JOJ, 9 June 1855 (412); JOJ, 13 June 1857 (412); JOJ,
          25 June 1859 (412); JOJ, 6 June 1861 (412).
    v.   Ramsden BG, 23 May 1850 (554).
    vi.   Shilton WG, 4 June 1910 (563); WG, 1 June 1912 (563).
    vii. Witney JOJ, 15 June 1889 (715).

71. **Burford Town Band**
    i.   Bampton WG, 1 June 1901 (39).

72. **Byfield Band** (Northamptonshire)
    i.   Banbury JOJ, 11 July 1840 (79).

73. **Calvert (Brickworks) (Brass) Band** (Buckinghamshire)
    i.   Fringford JOJ, 4 June 1904 (293); JOJ, 16 June 1905 (293 and
          295); BicA, 19 June 1908 (293).
    ii.   Hethe BicA, 5 June 1903 (361).

74. **Caversham Drum and Fife Band**
    i.   Shiplake HA, 15 June 1878 (565).

75. **Church of England Temperance Society Drum and Fife Band**
    i.   Deddington BG, 13 June 1895 (237); BG, 4 June 1896 (237).

76. **Chacombe (Brass) Band** (Northamptonshire) **(see also Bands 205, Shutford and Chacombe Band)**
    i.   Banbury BG, 5 July 1855 (85).
    ii.   Bodicote BG, 23 June 1859 (126).

77. **Chalgrove (Brass) Band**
    i.   Chalgrove TG, 16 June 1908 (168).
    ii.   Garsington JOJ, 6 June 1903 (304); JOJ, 28 May 1904 (304).
    iii. Great Haseley TG, 28 May 1907 (312).
    iv.   Warborough BOA, 31 May 1901 (656).

78. **Charlbury (Brass) Band**
    i.   Banbury JOJ, 11 July 1840 (86); JOJ, 2 September 1843 (86).
    ii.   Chadlington JOJ, 5 April 1856 (164).
    iii. Charlbury JOJ, 3 June 1854 (173); 4 July 1857 (175); JOJ, 15 June 1899 (170).
    iv.   Eynsham JOJ, 24 May 1902 (279); JOJ, 24 May 1902 (279); JOJ, 6 June 1903 (270); WG, 25 May 1907 (270); WG, 5 June 1909 (273).
    v.   Hailey WG, 1June 1901 (320); WG, 9 June 1906 (319).
    vi.   North Leigh JOJ, 14 June 1856 (448); JOJ, 10 June 1899 (451); WD, 13 June 1903 (448); WG, 12 June 1909 (448).

79. **Cheltenham Town and Promenade Band** (Gloucestershire)
    i.   Chipping Norton JOJ, 14 June 1884 (198).

80. **Chesterton (Brass) Band**
    i.   Adderbury BH, 19 June 1868.
    ii.   Chesterton BicA, 15 June 1906 (185); BicA, 31 May 1907 (185); BicA, 11 June 1909 (185); BicA, 16 June 1911 (186).
    iii. Kirtlington BH, 26 June 1868.
    iv.   Weston on the Green BicA, 8 June 1806 (680); BicA, 12 June 1908 (680); BicA, 20 June 1910 (680).

81.   **Chetwode (Brass) Band** (Buckinghamshire)
    i.   Hethe BicA, 29 May 1885 (361).
    ii. Launton BicA, 12 June 1885 (410).
    iii. Stratton Audley BicA, 2 June 1882 (629); BicA, 18 June 1886
       (629).

82.   **Chilton (Brass) Band** (Buckinghamshire)
    i.   Aston Rowant TG, 25 May 1858 (25); TG, 14 June 1859 (25).
    ii. Little Milton TG, 7 June 1859 (469).
    iii. Thame TG, 14 June 1859.

83.   **Chinnor (Brass) Band**
    i.   Kingston Blount HSOS, 18 May 1894 (399).
    ii. Tetsworth TG, 18 June 1889 (638).
    iii. Thame TG, 10 June 1884 (642); TG, 7 June 1887 (644).
    iv. Watlington JOJ, 11 June 1881 (663); WT, 2 June 1882 (663);
       WT, 18 May 1883 (663); TG, 29 June 1886 (644, 663 and 671).

84.   **Chipping Norton Brass Band**
    i.   Charlbury CNDM, August 1881 (175).
    ii. Sarsden CNDM, July 1882 (209).
    iii. Woodstock JOJ, 19 May 1883 (744).

85.   **Chipping Norton Quadrille Band**
    i.   Charlbury JOJ, 3 July 1880 (175).

86.   **Chipping Norton** (Rifle) **Volunteer Band**
    i.   Ascott under Wychwood CNDM, August 1881 (18).
    ii. Charlbury JOJ, 30 May 1885 (172).
    iii. Churchill JOJ, 27 May 1899 (209); JOJ, 9 June 1900 (209);
       JOJ, 13 June 1903 (209).
    iv. Milton under Wychwood JOJ, 25 May 1907 (432).

87.   **Claydon Musicians**
    i.   Fringford JOJ, 28 April 1860 (294).

88.   **Combe (Brass) Band**
    i.   Charlbury JOJ, 16 June 1860 (175).
    ii. Hailey WG, 6 June 1903 (319); WG, 4 June 1904 (319).
    iii. North Leigh WG, 13 June 1903 (451); WG, 11 June 1904
       (448); WG, 10 June 1905 (451).

    iv.   Shipton under Wychwood JOJ, 30 May 1857 (569).

    v.   Woodstock JOJ, 7 July 1894 (HS, 325).

89.   **Compton Brass Band** (Long Compton, Warwickshire)

    i.   Milton under Wychwood JOJ, 29 May 1858 (433).

90.   **Deddington Amateur Brass Band**

    i.   Deddington BG, 11 June 1846 (242).

91.   **Deddington (Brass) Band**

    i.   Deddington Smedley-Stevenson (2007), 18 May 1842; BG, 11 June 1857 (239); JOJ, 17 May 1856 (239).

    ii.   Sibford Gower BG, 6 June 1861 (576).

92.   **Deddington Congregational Band**

    i.   Deddington BG, 13 June 1895 (246).

93.   **Deddington Fife and Drum Band**

    i.   Adderbury BG, 7 June 1866 (1).

    ii.   Bloxham 24 May 1866 (114).

94.   **Deddington Reed Band**

    i.   Deddington BG, 8 June 1876 (242).

95.   **Dinton** (Excelsior) **(Brass) Band**

    i.   Thame TG, 30 May 1893 (643); HSOS, 18 May 1894 (644); HSOS, 14 June 1895 (644); JOJ, 30 May 1896 (644).

96.   **Dorchester (Brass) Band**

    i.   Benson WT, 18 June 1886 (89).

    ii.   Dorchester JOJ, 31 May 1851 ; WT, 18 June 1886 (251); WT, 25 May 1888 (254); BOA, 16 June 1893 (254); BOA, 8 June 1900 (251); BOA, 31 May 1901 (251); BOA, 24 May 1897 (254); BOA, 16 May 1913 (251).

    iii.   Wolvercote JOJ, 6 June 1903 (722); JOJ, 9 June 1906 (722).

97.   **Eastleach Band** (Gloucestershire)

    i.   Hailey WG, 1 June 1901 (319).

    ii.   Minster Lovell JOJ, 1 June 1901 (437).

98. **Eynsham (Brass) Band**
    i.   Combe JOJ, 15 June 1878 (219).
    ii. Eynsham JOJ, 20 September 1890 (HS, 279).

99. **Faringdon (Brass) Band**
    i.   Bampton WG, 8 June 1895 (39).
    ii. Burford JOJ, 17 May 1856 (144).

100. **Fieldtown Band** (Leafield) (see also Bands 143, Leafield Band)
    i.   Bampton JOJ, 24 May 1902 (30); JOJ, 9 June 1906 (30).

101. **Fifield (Brass) Band**
    i.   Fifield CNDM, July 1884 (282); CNDM, July 1885 (282);
        CNDM, July 1886 (282); CNDM, June 1891 (282); CNDM,
        June 1899 (282); JOJ, 16 June 1900 (282).
    ii. Filkins WG, 6 June 1903 (286).
    iii. Milton under Wychwood CNDM, July 1884 (433); CNDM,
        July 1886 (433); JOJ, 9 June 1906 (432).
    iv. Shilton WG, 8 June 1901 (563); JOJ, 31 May 1902 (563).

102. **Finstock (Brass) Band**
    i.   Finstock CNDM, July 1886 (288); JOJ, 12 May 1894 (288).
    ii. Stonesfield OHC, STON I/ii/b/2, 1887 (626).

103. **Forest Hill and Shotover Band**
    i.   Chesterton BicA, 10 June 1898 (186).
    ii. Stoke Lyne JOJ, 22 July 1899 (617).

104. **Forest Hill Brass Band**
    i.   Stratton Audley BicA, 31 May 1901 (629).

105. **Fowler's Sax-Horn Band** (Thame)
    i.   Thame JOJ, 26 May1866 (648); TG, 14 June 1870 (651) .
    ii. Watlington TG, 5 June 1866 (668).

106. **Freeland (Brass) Band**
    i.   Cogges WE, 20 May 1880 (215).
    ii. Combe JOJ, 28 May 1887 (221).
    iii. Eynsham JOJ, 20 September 1890 (HS, 601).
    iv. Leafield WG, 26 May 1894; JOJ, 3 June 1899 (416).

    v.   North Leigh JOJ, 14 June 1890 (451); WG, 11 June 1892 (448).

    vi.   Stanton Harcourt WG, 8 June 1895 (606).

    vii.   Stonesfield OHC, STON/I/ii/b/2, 1875 (626); OHC, STON/I/ii/b/2, 1876 and 1888 (626)

    viii. Witney WG, 23 May 1891 (HS, 715).

107.   **Fritwell (Brass) Band**

    i.   Deddington JOJ, 14 June 1873 (246).

    ii.   Fritwell JOJ, 1 June 1861 (296).

    iii.   Somerton JOJ, 27 July 1867 (582).

108.   **Garsington (Brass) Band**

    i.   Garsington JOJ, 29 May 1880 (303); WT, 18 May 1883 (304).

    ii.   Stadhampton WT, 1 June 1883 (304).

    iii.   Headington JOJ, 11 August 1894 (HS, 331).

109.   **Great Horwood Band** (Buckinghamshire)

    i.   Hethe BicA, 8 June 1906 (361); BicA 24 May 1907 (361); BicA, 4 June 1909 (361); BicA, 31 May 1912 (361).

110.   **Great Milton (Brass) Band**

    i.   Dorchester WT, 29 May 1885 (254).

    ii.   Great Milton WT, 13 June 1884 (314).

    iii.   Stoke Talmage WT, 13 June 1884 (619).

111.   **Grimmett's Quadrille Band**

    i.   Oxford JOJ, 2 August 1862 (474).

112.   **Hailey Band** (see also Bands 69, Burford and Hailey Band)

    i.   Charlbury BG, 23 May 1850.

113.   **Hanborough Band**

    i.   Eynsham JOJ, 20 September 1890 (HS, 280).

114.   **Hanborough Primitive Methodist Brass Band**

    i.   Eynsham JOJ, 20 September 1890 (HS, 270).

115.   **Headington (Brass) Band**

    i.   Bletchingdon BicA, 6 June 1884 (111).

    ii.   Charlbury JOJ, 2 July 1881 (170); JOJ, 1 July 1882 (170).

    iii. Chesterton BicA, 28 May 1880 (186); BicA, 28 May 1883 (185).

    iv. Cowley WT, 18 May 1883 (227); JOJ, 30 May 1885 (227); JOJ, 15 June 1889 (227); JOJ, 31 May 1890 (227).

    v. Garsington WT, 18 May 1883 (303).

    vi. Great Milton TG, 29 May 1888 (314).

    vii. Headington JOJ, 2 June 1849 (328); JOJ, 29 July 1893 (HS, 331, 332, 336, 338, 339 and 428); JOJ, 11 August 1894 (HS, 331).

    viii. Islip JOJ, 2 June 1849 (390); JOJ, 31 May 1851 (390).

    ix. Kirtlington JOJ, 10 June 1887 (328); BicA, 21 June 1889 (406).

    x. Steeple Aston JOJ, 31 May 1862 (613); BG, 5 May 1864 (614).

    xi. Upper Heyford BG, 27 May 1858 (614).

    xii. Weston on the Green BicA, 10 June 1881 (680).

116. **Headington Drum and Fife Band**
    i. Bletchingdon BH, 21 May 875 (113).
    ii. Headington JOJ, 11 August 1894 (HS, 331).

117. **Headington No. 1 Brass Band**
    i. Garsington JOJ, 26 May 1883 (303).

118. **Henley Brass Band**
    i. Burford JOJ, 2 June 1860 (144).
    ii. Henley on Thames JOJ, 2 June 1849 (340).

119. **Henley Drum and Fife Band**
    i. Rotherfield Peppard HC, 28 May 1909 (HS, 306).

120. **Henley Town Band**
    i. Nettlebed HSOS, 9 June 1911 (443).

121. **Henley Working Men's Institute Band**
    i. Shiplake HA, 26 May 1877 (565).

122. **High Wycombe (Brass) Band** (Buckinghamshire)
    i. Crowmarsh Gifford WT, 18 May 1883 (232).
    ii. Stokenchurch TG, 4 June 1901 (621).

    iii.   Thame JOJ, 10 June 1871 (651); JOJ, 7 June 1884 (644); TG, 2 June 1885 (644); TG, 29 June 1886 (643); TG, 7 June 1887 (643).

123.   **Highworth Brass Band** (Wiltshire)
    i.   Clanfield WG, 6 June 1903 (213).

124.   **Highworth Town Band** (Wiltshire)
    i.   Clanfield WG, 8 June 1901 (213); JOJ, 31 May 1902 (213); WG, 4 June 1904 (213); WG, 24 June 1905 (213).

125.   **Holton (Brass) Band**
    i.   Great Milton TG, 1 June 1875 (314).
    ii.   Tetsworth TG, 24 June 1862 (637).
    iii.   Thame TG, 18 June 1878 (644).
    iv.   Wheatley TG, 14 June 1870 (693).

126.   **Hone's** (Adderbury) **Band** (see also Bands 13, Alderminster and Hone's Band)
    i.   Adderbury BG, 12 June 1873 (9).
    ii.   Bloxham BG, 24 May 1866 (119).

127.   **Hook Norton (Brass) Band**
    i.   Adderbury BG, 3 June 1897 (6); BG, 7 June 1900 (8).
    ii.   Bloxham JOJ, 6 June 1896 (118); BG, 25 May 1899 (122).
    iii.   Enstone JOJ, 6 June 1896 (264); CNDM, July 1900 (264).
    iv.   Hook Norton BG, 10 May 1894; BG, 30 May 1895 (368); BG, 21 May 1896 (365); JOJ, 5 June 1897 (368); BG, 18 May 1899 (368); JOJ, 21 May 1904 (368); JOJ, 10 June 1905 (368).
    v.   Salford JOJ, 28 July 1900 (558).
    vi.   Swerford JOJ, 3 June 1899 (630); JOJ, 9 June 1900 (630).
    vii.   Wroxton BG, 24 May 1894 (752).

128.   **Horley (Brass) Band**
    i.   Deddington JOJ, 3 June 1893 (240).
    ii.   Hanwell BG, 6 June 1901 (326).
    iii.   Hook Norton BG, 15 May 1902 (365).
    iv.   Shenington BG, 6 June 1895 (561).
    v.   Wroxton BG, 11 June 1896 (752).

129. **Hornton Brass Band**
    i. Hornton JOJ, 15 July 1893 (374).

130. **Horton** (cum Studley) **(Brass) Band**
    i. Bletchingdon BicA, 29 May 1896 (112).
    ii. Chesterton BicA, 17 June 1892 (185 and 186); BicA, 12 June 1903 (186); BicA, 3 June 1904 (185 and 186).
    iii. Fringford BicA, 15 June 1900 (293 and 295).
    iv. Great Milton TG, 3 June 1890 (314); TG, 2 June 1891 (314); TG, 14 June 1892 (314); HSOS, 26 May 1893 (314); TG, 22 May 1894 (314); TG, 11 June 1895 (316).
    v. Islip BicA, 8 June 1900 (389); BicA, 16 June 1905 (388 and 389); JOJ, 25 May 1907 (389).
    vi. Kidlington JOJ, 15 June 1895 (396).
    vii. Kirtlington BicA, 19 June 1908 (404).
    viii. Wendlebury BicA, 31 May 1901 (677); BicA, 5 June 1903 (677); BicA, 20 May 1904 (677); BicA, 16 June 1905 (677); 24 May 1907 (680).
    ix. Weston on the Green BicA, 29 May 1895 (680); BicA, 22 May 1890 (680).

131. **Ickford (Brass) Band** (Buckinghamshire)
    i. Great Milton JOJ, 6 June 1903 (316).
    ii. Headington JOJ, 29 July 1893 (HS, 331, 332, 336, 338, 339 and 428); JOJ, 11 August 1894 (HS, 331).
    iii. Postcombe HSOS, 29 May 1896 (551).
    iv. Thame TG, 14 June 1892 (643).

132. **Iffley Band**
    i. Garsington JOJ, 5 June 1852 (459).
    ii. Nuneham Courtenay JOJ, 5 June 1852 (302).

133. **Islip (Brass) Band**
    i. Islip BicA, 6 June 1879 (389); BicA, 6 June 1884 (389); BicA, 3 June 1887 (389); BicA,18June 1886 (389); BicA, 11June 1897 (389); BicA, 10 June 1892 (389).
    ii. Kidlington BicA, 19 May 1865 (396); JOJ, 13 June 1874(396); JOJ, 5 June 1875 (396); JOJ, 3 June 1876 (396).
    iii. Kirtlington BH, 21 June 1867 (406); BicA, 28 May 1880 (406); BicA, 12 June 1885 (403); BicA, 25 June 1886 (403); BicA, 10 June 1887 (403).

    iv.   Stadhampton SON, 2 June 1888 (589); SON, 15June 1889 (589).

    v.   Wendlebury BicA, 9 June 1860(676); BH, 1 June 1877; BicA, 21 May 1880 (676); BicA, 10 June 1881 (676); BicA, 6 June 1884; BicA, 18 June 1886 (676).

    vi.   Weston on the Green BicA, 30 May 1890 (680).

    vii.   Woodstock JOJ, 1 July 1865 (737).

134.   **Kay's (Brass) Band also J. Kay's Brass Band, Mr Kay's Band** (Banbury)

    i.   Adderbury BG, 2 June 1881 (9).

    ii.   Bloxham BG, 5 June 1879 (114 and 119); BG, 10 June 1897 (119).

    iii.   Bodicote BG, 13 May 1880; BanA, 29 May 1890 (127).

    iv.   Claydon BG, 27 May 1880 (214); DDM, June 1895 (214).

    v.   Hook Norton CNDM, July 1884 (368).

    vi.   North Newington BG, 2 June 1881 (452).

135.   **Kempsford Band** (Gloucestershire)

    i.   Alvescot WE, 28 May 1874 (13).

136.   **Kent's Witney Band**

    i.   Bampton BG, 4 June 1846.

137.   **Kidlington (Brass) Band**

    i.   Banbury JOJ, 11 July 1840 (85).

    ii.   Eynsham WG, 25 May 1907 (279).

    iii.   Islip JOJ, 9 June 1855 (390).

    iv.   Kidlington JOJ, 17 June 1854 (396); JOJ, 16 June 1855 (396); JOJ, 14 June 1856 (396); JOJ, 13 June 1857 (396); JOJ, 25 June 1859 (396); JOJ, 14 June 1862 (396); JOJ, 12 June 1869 (396); JOJ, 11 June 1870 (396); JOJ, 3 June 1899 (396); JOJ, 4 June 1904 (396).

    v.   Somerton JOJ, 21 June 1856 (582).

    vi.   Weston on the Green BicA, 5June 1903 (680); BicA, 20 May 1904 (680).

    vii.   Woodstock JOJ, 7 July 1894 (HS, 727).

138.   **King's Sutton (Brass) Band** (Northamptonshire) **(see also Bands 11, Adderbury and King's Sutton Band)**

    i.   Adderbury BG, 3 June 1897 (8); BG, 8 June 1899 (8).

    ii.   Bodicote BG, 24 May 1894 (129); BG, 17 June 1897 (127).
    iii. Bourton DDM, July 1898 (131); DDM, July 1900 (131).
    iv. Deddington Smedley-Stevenson (2007), 18 May 1842; BG, 24 June 1886 (236); BG, 30 May 1891 (249); JOJ, 1 June 1901 (249).
    v.   Duns Tew BG, 16 May 1901 (262).
    vi. Fritwell BicA, 29 May 1896 (297).
    vii. Hanwell BG, 1 June 1899 (326); BG, 31 May 1900 (326).
    viii. Hook Norton BG, 15 May 1902 (368).
    ix. North Newington BG, 25 May 1899 (452).

139.   Kingston Lisle Band
    i.   Clanfield WG, 1 June 1912 (213).

140.   Kirtlington Band of Hope Fife and Drum Band
    i.   Kirtlington BicA, 17 June 1881 (406).

141.   Lane End (Brass) Band (Buckinghamshire)
    i.   Crowmarsh Gifford WT, 2 June 1882 (232); WT, 6 June 1884 (232).
    ii.   Kingston Blount TG, 6 June 1871 (398).
    iii. Stokenchurch TG, 10 June 1879 (621).
    iv. Watlington TG, 2 June 1874(663); JOJ, 13 June 1876 (671); TG, 29 May 1877 (663); JOJ, 7 June 1879 (663).

142.   Langford Band
    i.   Langford JOJ, 5 June 1869 (708).

143.   Leafield (Brass) Band (see also Bands 100, Fieldtown Band)
    i.   Bampton WE, 20 May 1880; JOJ, 9 June 1900 (39); WG, 9 June 1906 (30).
    ii.   Cogges WE, 9 June 1881 (215).
    iii. Finstock CNDM, July 1881 (288); CNDM, July 1892 (288).
    iv. Hailey WG, 19 May 1894 (319); WG, 25 May 1907 (320); WG, 21 May 1910 (319); WG, 17 June 1911 (321); WG, 1 June 1912 (321); WG, 17 May 1913 (319 and 320); WG, 6 June 1914 (321).
    v.   Kidlington JOJ, 16 June 1877 (396).
    vi. Kingham JOJ, 26 May 1900 (397).
    vii. Leafield WG, 26 May 1894; WG, 16 June 1900 (417 and 418); JOJ, 1 June 1907 (417).

   viii. Milton under Wychwood JOJ, 1June 1901 (432); WG, 6 June 1903 (432).

   ix. Minster Lovell WG, 27 May 1899 (437); WG, 13 June 1908 (437); WG, 5 June 1909 (437); WG, 4 June 1910 (437).

   x. North Leigh WE, 6 June 1878 (451); WG, 11 June 1892 (451); WG, 13 June 1908 (448).

   xi. Oxford JOJ, 27 May 1899 (486).

   xii. Shipton under Wychwood Miller (1983), 24May 1893; JOJ, 6 June 1903 (571).

   xiii. Stonesfield OHC, STON I/ii/b/2, 1880, 1882, 1883, 1890 and 1891 (262); JOJ, 4 June 1892 (626).

   xiv. Witney WG, 11 June 1892 (HS).

144. **Leamington Band** (Warwickshire)
   i. Bloxham BG, 8 June 1876 (114).
   ii. Claydon BG, 2 June 1881 (214).

145. **Leamington Military Band** (Warwickshire)
   i. Bodicote BG, 31 May 1877 (127).

146. **Leamington Sax-Horn Band** (Warwickshire)
   i. Banbury BG, 4 July 1861 (65); BG, 4 July 1872 (65); BG, 9 July 1874 (72); JOJ, 6 June 1872 (65).

147. **Lechlade (Brass) Band** (Gloucestershire)
   i. Bampton JOJ, 21 May 1864 (28); JOJ, 30 May 1874 (39); JOJ, 4 June 1898 (39).

148. **Little Compton Band** (Warwickshire)
   i. Chipping Norton JOJ, 29 June 1861 (190); JOJ, 5 July 1862 (205).

149. **Little Milton Band**
   i. Dorchester WT, 2 June 1882 (254).

150. (Long) **Crendon (Brass) Band (Buckinghamshire)**
   i. Forest Hill JOJ, 1 June 1861 (292).
   ii. Thame JOJ, 25 May 1861 (648); SON, 26 May 1888 (644); TG, 18 June 1889 (643); TG, 3 June 1890 (643); TG, 26 May 1891 (644).
   iii. Watlington JOJ, 13 June 1840.

iv.   Wheatley TG, 30 May 1899 (688).

151.   **Marsh Gibbon (Brass) Band** (Buckinghamshire)
i.   Bletchingdon BicA, 20 May 1910 (112).
ii.   Fringford BicA, 11 June 1909 (293 and 295).
iii. Fritwell BicA, 20 May 1910 (297).
iv.   Kidlington JOJ, 11 June 1870 (394).
v.   Kirtlington BicA, 16 June 1911 (404).
vi.   Launton BH, 5 June 1874 (410).
vii. Stratton Audley BicA, 3 June 1887 (629); BicA, 4 June 1909 (629).

152.   **Marston Band**
i.   Charlton on Otmoor BG, 13 June 1844 (183).
ii.   Horton cum Studley TG, 14 June 1859 (382).

153.   **Middleton Cheyney Band**
i.   Bodicote BG, 28 May 1891 (129).

154.   **Middleton Stoney Fife and Drum Band**
i.   Somerton BicA, 24 May 1895 (581).

155.   **Milton Brass Band**
i.   Dorchester WT, 6 June 1884 (254).
ii.   Thame TG, 29 May 1877 (644).

156.   **Minster** (Lovell) **(Brass) Band**
i.   Bampton WG, 15 June 1889 (29).
ii.   Burford JOJ, 11 June 1887 (146).
iii. Cogges WE, 9 June 1870 (216).
iv.   Cowley WT, 18 June 1886 (227).
v.   North Leigh JOJ, 14 June 1890 (448).
vi.   Witney WG, 31 May 1890 (HS, 715); WG, 16 May 1891 (HS).

157.   **Mixbury Band**
i.   Bloxham BG, 19 May 1864 (114).

158.   **Monks Risborough Brass Band** (Buckinghamshire)
i.   Thame JOJ, 27 May 1893 (644).

159. **Moredon Band** (Wiltshire)
  i.   Alvescot WG, 8 June 1895 (437); WG, 6 June 1803 (11); WG, 6 June 1914 (11).

160. **Nephalite** (Temperance) **(Brass) Band (Watlington)**
  i.   Dorchester BOA, 10 June 1892 (251).
  ii. Little Haseley TG, 3 June 1890 (420).
  iii. Stadhampton TG, 7 June 1892 (591).
  iv. Watlington JOJ, 22 May 1880 (668); TG, 29 June 1886 (668); TG, 7 June 1887 (668); WT, 25 May 1888 (668); TG, 18 June 1889 (668); BOA, 26 May 1893 (591 and 668); TG, 11 June 1895 (672); JOJ, 4 June 1898 (672).

161. **North Leigh (Brass) Band**
  i.   Finstock JOJ, 7 June 1867 (288).
  ii. Hailey JOJ, 22 June 1867 (320).
  iii. Kidlington JOJ, 10 June 1871 (396); JOJ, 15 June 1872 (396).
  iv. North Leigh JOJ, 18 June 1870 (451).

162. **North Newington Band**
  i.   North Newington BG, 1 June 1865 (454).

163. **North Oxfordshire** (Conservative) **Band**
  i.   Somerton BG, 4 June 1891 (581); JOJ, 3 June 1893 (581); BicA, 1 June 1894 (581).
  ii. Tadmarton BG, 4 June 1891 (634).

164. **Northampton Band**
  i.   Banbury BG, 9 July 1863 (60).

165. **Oakley (Brass) Band** (Buckinghamshire)
  i.   Arncott BicA, 20 May 1904 (16); BicA,12 June 1907 (16).
  ii. Great Haseley JOJ, 9 June 1900 (312); JOJ, 1 June 1901 (312); JOJ, 24 May 1902 (312); TG, 9 June 1903 (312); TG, 31 May 1904 (312); TG, 20 June 1905 (312); TG, 16 June 1908 (312); TG, 8 June 1909 (312); TG, 7 July 1910 (312); TG, 20 June 1911 (312).
  iii. Great Milton JOJ, 20 June 1903 (315); HC, 3 June 1904 (316); TG, 20 June 1905 (316); TG, 12 June 1906 (316); TG, 28 May 1907 (316); TG, 16 June 1908 (316); TG, 15 June 1909 (316); TG, 20 June 1911 (316).

    iv.   Little Milton SON, 18 June 1892 (421).

    v.   Stadhampton TG, 2 June 1891 (589).

166. **Old Barton Band**
    i.   Westcote Barton 3 July 1873 (678).

167. **Old Watlington Band** (see also Bands 249, Watlington Band)
    i.   Watlington TG, 29 June 1886 (675).

168. **Oxford Adult Schools Band**
    i.   Eynsham 20 September 1890 (HS, 325).

169. **Oxford Brass Band**
    i.   Bicester JOJ, 22 July 1847 (98).

170. **Oxford City Band**
    i.   Fritwell BicA, 29 May 1885 (297); BicA, 18 June 1886 (297); BicA, 3 June 1887 (297).
    ii.   Tetsworth TG, 18 June 1889 (637).

171. **Oxford City Rifle (Corps) Band**
    i.   Cowley JOJ, 2 June 1860 (227).
    ii.   Oxford JOJ, 23 June 1866 (540).
    iii.   Thame TG, 9 June 1868 (648).
    iv.   Woodstock JOJ, 29 June 1867 (737).

172. **Oxford Excelsior Band**
    i.   Eynsham WG, 5 June 1909 (270).

173. **Oxford Hungarian Band**
    i.   Fritwell BicA, 8 June 1900 (297); BicA, 31 May 1901 (297); BicA, 23 May 1902 (297); BicA, 5 June 1903 (297); BicA, 24 May 1907 (297); BicA, 12 June 1908 (297).
    ii.   Kirtlington BicA, 12 June 1914 (407).

174. **Oxford Institute (Brass) Band**
    i.   Bletchingdon BicA, 26 May 1899 (112).
    ii.   Standlake JOJ, 23 September 1900 (HS, 595).
    iii.   Witney WG, 19 may 1894 (HS, 706).

175. **Oxford Militia Band**
i.   Chipping Norton JOJ, 4 July 1868 (205).
ii. Cogges WE, 8 June 1876 (216); WE, 24 May 1877 (216).
iii. Deddington JOJ, 13 June 1857 (242); JOJ, 29 May 1858 (242).
iv. Oxford JOJ, 20 July 1872 (478); JOJ, 25 July 1874 (482, 514, 506 and 513).
v.   Shipton under Wychwood JOJ, 10 August 1878 (566); JOJ, 13 August 1881 (566).
vi. Thame TG, 6 June 1882 (644).

176. **Oxford University Brass Band**
i.   Bicester 24 July 1847 (98).

177. **Oxford University Rifle Corps Band**
i.   Deddington JOJ, 14 June 1873 (242).

178. **Oxford Yeomanry (Brass) Band** (see also Bands 182, Oxfordshire Yeomanry Band)
i.   Kidlington JOJ, 11 July 1878 (734).
ii. Woodstock JOJ, 13 June 1863 (396).

179. **Oxfordshire Light Infantry Band**
i.   Fritwell BicA, 14 June 1889 (297).
ii. Thame JOJ, 19 May 1883 (644).

180. **Oxfordshire Militia Band**
i.   Chipping Norton JOJ, 6 July 1872 (198); JOJ, 28 June 1873 (198); JOJ, 11 July 1874 (198).
ii. Deddington BG, 11 June 1857 (242).
iii. Iffley JOJ, 16 July 1870 (384).
iv. Shipton under Wychwood CNDM, September 1883 (566).

181. **Oxfordshire Rifles Band, also Oxford County Rifle Corps Band**
i.   Chipping Norton JOJ, 29 June 1861 (191).
ii. Iffley JOJ, 6 July 1869 (384).

182. **Oxfordshire Yeomanry (Brass) Band** (see also Bands 178, Oxford Yeomanry Band and Bands 190, Queens Own Oxfordshire Yeomanry Cavalry Band)
i.   Chipping Norton JOJ, 1 July 1843 (190).
ii. Eynsham JOJ, 12 May 1855 (276); JOJ, 5 April 1856 (276).

    iii.   Woodstock JOJ, 24 July 1874 (744); JOJ, 9 July 1881 (744).

183.   **Padbury Band** (Buckinghamshire)
    i.   Hethe BicA, 29 May 1899 (361); BicA, 8 June 1900 (361); JOJ, 24 May 1902 (361).
    ii.   Stratton Audley BicA, 6 June 1879 (629).

184.   **Peppard Band**
    i.   Nettlebed HSOS, 8 June 1906 (443); HSON, 24 May 1907 (443) .
    ii.   Rotherfield Peppard HC, 28 May 1909 (154).

185.   **Perkin's Alkerton Band** (see also Bands14, Alkerton Band)
    i.   Shenington BG, 29 May 1902 (561).

186.   **Prescott's Quadrille Band**
    i.   Banbury BG, 5 July 1855 (83).

187.   **Preston Bissett Brass Band** (Buckinghamshire)
    i.   Hethe BicA, 10 June 1892 (361).

188.   **Princes Risborough Brass Band** (Buckinghamshire)
    i.   Aston Rowant TG, 13 June 1865 (25).

189.   **Pyrton Band**
    i.   Bampton JOJ, 21 May 1864 (39).

190.   **Queens Own Oxfordshire Yeomanry Cavalry Band** (see also Bands 182, Oxfordshire Yeomanry Band)
    i.   Charlbury JOJ, 21 May 1864 (39).

191.   **Ramsden**
    i.   Bampton WG, 31 May 1890 (39).
    ii.   Cogges WE, 25 May 1872 (215); WE, 28 May 1874 (215); WE, 20 May 1875 (215); WE, 8 June 1876 (215); WE, 24 May 18 77 (215); JOJ, 30 May 1885 (216); JOJ, 19 June 1886 (216); WG, 15 June 1889 (216); JOJ, 31 May 1890 (216); WG, 23 May 1891 (216).
    iii.   Hailey WG, 19 May 1894 (321); WG, 1 June 1901 (321); WG, 16 June 1903 (320); WG, 4 June 1904 (321); WG, 17 June 1911 (320); WG, 17 May 1913 (321); WG, 6 June 1914 (320).

iv.   Hanborough JOJ, 3 June 1893 (325).
v.   Kirtlington JOJ, 13 June 1903 (404); BicA, 24 June 1905
      (404); BicA, 15 June 1906 (404); BicA, 31 May 1907 (404);
      BicA, 11 June 1909 (404); BicA, 20 May 1910 (404).
vi.   Leafield JOJ, 3 June 1899 (418); WG, 16 June 1900 (418); JOJ,
      1 June 1907 (418).
vii. North Leigh JOJ, 18 June 1870 (451); WG, 11 June 1904
      (451); WG, 10 June 1905 (448); WG, 13 June 1908 (451);
      WG, 11 June 1910 (448).
viii. Stanton Harcourt JOJ, 27 May 1899 (601, 602 and 606); JOJ,
      9 June 1901 (601); WG, 1 June 1901 (601); JOJ, 6 June 1903
      (601); WG, 25 May 1907 (601); WG, 13 June 1908 (601); WG,
      10 June 1911 (601); WG, 17 May 1913 (601).
ix.   Witney WG, 23 May 1891 (HS, 715); WG, 11 June 1892 (HS,
      216); WG, 19 May 1894 (HS, 715); WG, 8 June 1895 (HS,
      706).
x.   Woodstock JOJ, 14 July 1866 (737).

192. **Reading Temperance Band** (Berkshire)
      i.   Watlington JOJ, 11 June 1881 (668); WT, 2 June 1882 (668);
            WT, 18 May 1883 (668); WT, 6 June 1884 (668).

193. **Redditch Rifle Corps Brass Band** (Worcestershire)
      i.   Thame TG, 14 June 1870 (648).

194. **Roke Temperance Band** (see also Bands 38, Berrick and Roke
      Temperance Band)
      i.   Warborough BOA, 8 June 1900 (656); BOA, 16 June 1905
            (656).
      ii.   Watlington HSOS, 16 June 1905 (672); HSOS, 9 June 1911
            (667).

195. **Royal Berkshire Militia Band**
      i.   Banbury 34 July 1873 (65).

196. **Royal Berkshire Quadrille Band**
      i.   Banbury 8 July 1875 (65).

197. **Royal Berkshire Yeomanry Band**
      i.   Dorchester WT, 25 May 1883.

Royal Thame (Brass) Band (see Bands 230, Thame Royal Brass Band)

198.	**Rugby Steam Shed Band** (Warwickshire)
   i.	Banbury BG, 6 July 1871 (72).

Samuelson and Co. Band (see Bands 28, Banbury Britannia Brass Band)

199.	**Shenington (Brass) Band**
   i.	Adderbury BG, 8 June 1893 (8).
   ii.	Shenington BG, 5 June 1890 (561); BG, 9 June 1892 (561);
      BG, 1 June 1893 (561); BG, 4 June 1914 (561).
   iii.	Wroxton 31 May 1888 (752).

200.	**Shilton (Brass) Band**
   i.	Bampton WG, 19 May 1894 (30); WG, 23 May 1891 (30);
      WG, 8 June 1895 (30).
   ii.	Brize Norton WE, 8 June 1876 (139); WG, 9 June 1906 (137).
   iii.	Shilton WG, 19 May 1894 (563); WG, 27 May 1899 (563);
      WG, 6 June 1903 (563); WG, 11 June 1904 (563); WG, 25
      May 1907 (563); WG, 13 June 1908 (563).
   iv.	Shipton under Wychwood JOJ, 4 August 1860 (570).

201.	**Shipton** (under Wychwood) **(Brass) Band**
   i.	Ascott under Wychwood JOJ, 8 August 1857 (20).
   ii.	Bampton BG, 3 June 1852 (38).
   iii.	Burford JOJ, 14 June 1884 (146); WG, 6 June 1885 (146).
   iv.	Charlbury BG, 10 June 1852 (173); BG, 2 June 1853 (171).
   v.	Chipping Norton JOJ, 11 July 1857 (205).
   vi.	Leafield JOJ, 25 June 1859 (415).
   vii.	Milton under Wychwood JOJ, 2 June 1855 (433); JOJ, 24 May
      1856 (433).
   viii.	Shipton under Wychwood JOJ, 9 June 1855 (569); JOJ, 4
      August 1860 (570); JOJ, 26 July 1862 (570); JOJ, 25 July 1863
      (570); JOJ, 11 August 1866 (570); CNDM, July 1882.

202.	**Shipton Drum and Fife Band**
   i.	Shipton under Wychwood CNDM, July 1882.

203.	**Shipton Oliffe Band**
   i.	Burford 18 June 1881 (146).

204.   **Shutford and Bloxham Band** (see also Bands 50, Bloxham Band)
   i.   Hook Norton BG, 3 July 1862 (368).

205.   **Shutford and Chacombe Band** (see also Bands 76, Chacombe
         Band, and Bands 206, Shutford Band)
   i.   Banbury BG, 3 July 1856 (85).

206.   **Shutford (Brass) Band** (see also Bands 204, Shutford and Bloxham
         Band, and Bands 205, Shutford and Chacombe Band)
   i.   Banbury JOJ, 6 July 1844 (79); BG 7 July 1853 (85); BG, 5
          July 1860 (85); BG, 4 July 1861 (85).
   ii.   Cropredy BG, 4 May 1877 (230); BG, 20 May 1880 (230); BG,
          5 June 1884 (230).
   iii.   Enstone JOJ, 16 June 1906 (264).
   iv.   Fritwell BicA, 10 June 1892 (297).
   v.   Great Tew BG, 7 June 1894 (318); BG, 6 June 1895 (318); BG,
          4 June 1896 (318); BG, 9 June 1888 (318); BG, 8 June 1899
          (318); BG, 7 June 1900 (318); BG, 6 June 1901 (318); BG, 9
          June 1910 (318).
   vi.   Hanwell BG, 6 June 1861 (326); BG, 5 June 1879 (326).
   vii.   Hook Norton CNDM, June 1885 (368).
   viii. North Newington BG, 29 May 1879 (452); BG, 10 August
          1886 (452); DDM, June 1901 (452).
   ix.   Shenington BG, 8 June 1899 (561).
   x.   Shutford BG, 8 June 1876 (574); BG, 13 June 1878 (574); BG,
          19 June 1879 (574); BG, 16 June 1881 (574); BG, 12 June
          1884 (574); BG, 10 August 1886 (574); BG, 8 June 1893 (574);
          DDM, July 1896 (574); DDM, July 1898 (574).
   xi.   Swerford JOJ, 8 June 1901 (630); JOJ, 6 June 1903 (630); JOJ,
          3 June 1905 (574).
   xii.   Wiggington BG, 25 May 1893 (702).

207.   **Sibford (Brass) Band** (Sibford Gower)
   i.   Adderbury BG, 2 June 1892 (9); BG, 8 June 1893 (9); BG, 7
          June 1894 (9); BG, 6 June 1895 (9); BG, 4 June 1896 (9); BG,
          3 June 1897 (9); BG, 8 June 1899 (9): BG, 7 June 1900 (9).
   ii.   Bloxham BG, 13 June 1889 (114); BG, 29 May 1890 (118);
          JOJ, 27 May 1893 (118); BG, 17 May 1894 (118); BG, 28 May
          1896 (118).
   iii.   Enstone JOJ, 6 June 1903 (264).
   iv.   Fritwell BicA, 18 May 1894 (297).

> v.   Hook Norton BG, 26 May 1898 (368); BG, 15 May 1902
>   (368); JOJ, 30 May 1903 (365); JOJ, 21 May 1904 (365).
> vi. Shenington BG, 7 June 1900 (561); BG, 8 June 1911 (561).
> vii. Sibford Gower BG, 10 June 1886 (576); BG, 9 June 1887
>   (576); BG, 7 June 1888 (576); BG, 6 June 1889 (576); BG,
>   5 June 1890 (576); BG, 4 June 1891 (576); BG, 8 June 1893
>   (576); BG, 31 May 1894 (576); BG, 30 may 1895 (576); DDM,
>   July 1898 (576); BG, 7 June 1900 (576); BG, 6 June 1901
>   (576).

208.   **Sibford Temperance Band** (Sibford Gower)
    i.   Sibford Gower BG, 8 June 1911 (576); BG, 4 June 1914 (576).

209.   **Souldern Brass Band**
    i.   Hethe 1 June 1877 (362).

210.   **Speen Brass Band**
    i.   Stokenchurch SON, 23 May 1891 (620).

    Squire Hall's Band (see Bands 33, Barton Brass Band)

211.   **St Thomas', Oxford Band**
    i.   Bletchingdon 17 June 1905 (112).

212.   **Standlake (Brass) Band**
    i.   Bampton BG, 27 May 1847; BG, 8 June 1854.
    ii. Witney JOJ, 20 September 1890 (HS, 715).

213.   **Stanton Harcourt (Brass) Band**
    i.   Hanborough 18 June 1892 (325).
    ii. Woodstock JOJ, 1 July 1865 (734).

214.   **Stanton St John (Brass) Band**
    i.   Arncott BicA, 29 May 1896 (16).
    ii.   Charlton on Otmoor BicA, 5 May 1896 (181).
    iii. Great Haseley JOJ, 27 May 1899 (312).
    iv.   Headington JOJ, 15 July 1899 (HS, 331).
    v.   Kirtlington BicA, 2 June 1893 (403).
    vi.   Sandford on Thames JOJ, 7 July 1900 (559).
    vii. Stanton St John JOJ, 15 July 1899 (610).
    viii. Stratton Audley BicA, 26 May 1899 (629).

ix.   Wendlebury BicA, 18 May 1894 (676).

x.   Weston on the Green BicA, 14 June 1889 (680).

215.   **Steeple Aston (Brass) Band**
i.   Deddington BG, 11 June 1846 (239); JOJ, 14 June 1884.
ii.   Fritwell BG, 12 June 1884 (297).
iii. Kirtlington BicA, 9 June 1882 (403); BicA, 28 May 1883 (406)
      BicA, 25 June 1886 (406).
iv.   Weston on the Green BicA, 18 June 1886 (680).

216.   **Steeple Barton Brass Band** (see also Bands 33, Barton Brass
Band)
i.   Westcote Barton 6 July 1861 (678).

217.   **Stokenchurch Church Institute Brass Band**
i.   Stokenchurch SON, 11 June 1892 (621).

218.   **Stokenchurch Temperance (Brass) Band**
i.   Stokenchurch TG, 4 June 1901 (620); HC, 27 May 1904 (620).
ii.   Watlington HSOS, 27 May 1904 (672); HSOS, 8 June 1906
      (672); TG, 28 May 1907 (668).

219.   **Stonesfield (Brass) Band**
i.   Eynsham WG, 5 June 1909 (279).
ii.   Finstock CNDM, June 1898 (288); CNDM, June 1900 (288).
iii. Hailey WG, 6 June 1903 (321).
iv.   Hanborough JOJ, 28 May 1904 (325).
v.   Kirtlington BicA, 7 June 1901 (403).
vi.   Leafield JOJ, 1 June 1907 (414).
vii. Minster Lovell WG, 6 June 1903 (437); WG, 28 May 1904
      (437); WG, 9 June 1906 (437); WG, 25 May 1907 (437).
viii. North Leigh JOJ, 8 June 1901 (451); WG, 12 June 1909 (451);
      WG, 11 June 1910 (451).
ix.   Stonesfield JOJ, 6 June 1896 (626); JOJ, 4 June 1898 (626);
      JOJ, 4 June 1904 (626); JOJ, 3 June 1905 (626); JOJ, 6 June
      1908 (626).
x.   Tackley JOJ, 20 July 1895 (632).
xi.   Woodstock JOJ, 7 July 1894 (HS, 626).

220.   **Stow on the Wold Brass Band** (Gloucestershire)
i.   Bampton BG, 3 June 1852 (28).

221. **Stow Rifle Volunteer Corps Band** (Gloucestershire)
   i.   Salford JOJ, 23 July 1881 (558).

222. **Summertown (Brass) Band**
   i.   Islip BicA, 2 June 1882.
   ii.   Kidlington JOJ, 14 June 1879 (396).

223. **Swalcliffe Band**
   i.   Banbury JOJ, 11 June 1840 (54).

224. **Swanbourne Band** (Buckinghamshire)
   i.   Hethe BicA, 20 May 1904 (361); BicA, 16 June 1905 (361).

225. **Swindon (Brass) Band** (Wiltshire)
   i.   Clanfield WG, 2 June 1888 (213); WG, 7 June 1890 (213).

226. **Tadmarton Oddfellows Band**
   i.   Tadmarton BG, 6 June 1895 (634).

227. **Tetsworth Brass Band**
   i.   Great Milton TG, 27 May 1899 (316); TG, 12 June 1900 (316) TG, 4 June 1901 (316).
   ii.   Little Milton TG, 30 May 1899 (421).
   iii. Postcombe HSOS, 18 May 1894 (551); HSOS, 10 June 1898 (551).

228. **Thame (Brass) Band** (see also Bands 230, Thame Royal Brass Band)
   i.   Banbury BG, 4 July 1861 (60); BG, 3 July 1862 (60).
   ii.   Benson JOJ, 1 June 1839 (89); WT, 2 June 1882 (89); WT, 18 May 1883 (89); WT, 6 June 1884 (89).
   iii. Headington JOJ, 2 June 1849 (335).
   iv.   Thame JOJ, 13 June 1840 (648); JOJ, 21 May 1864 (648); JOJ, 10 June 1871 (648); TG, 25 May 1875 (644); JOJ, 26 May 1883 (642); TG, 5 June 1906 (HS).
   v.   Watlington JOJ, 22 June 1878 (668).

229. **Thame Rifle Corps Band**
   i.   Benson JOJ, 25 May 1861 (89).
   ii.   Thame TG, 17 June 1862 (648); TG, 2 June 1863 (648).

230.　**Thame Royal (Brass) Band also Royal Thame (Brass) Band (see also Bands 228, Thame Brass Band)**
  i.　Benson JOJ, 10 June 1854 (89); JOJ, 23 May 1857; JOJ, 2 June 1860 (89).
  ii.　Bicester JOJ, 13 July 1844 (98).
  iii.　Bloxham BG, 29 May 1879 (119); BG, 17 May 1883 (119).
  iv.　Henley on Thames JOJ, 2 June 1849 (352).
  v.　Kingston Blount TG, 6 June 1871 (401).
  vi.　Little Milton JOJ, 23 May 1857 (421).
  vii.　Headington JOJ, 1 June 1850 (335).
  viii.　Henley on Thames JOJ, 29 May 1847 (352).
  ix.　Oxford JOJ, 27 August 1842 (506).
  x.　Thame JOJ, 10 June 1854 (648); JOJ, 2 June 1855 (648); JOJ, 12 July 1856 (640); JOJ, 23 May 1857 (648); JOJ, 18 June 1859 (648); TG, 5 June 1860 (648); JOJ, 1 August 1874 (643); JOJ, 29 May 1875 (644); JOJ, 14 June 1879 (644); JOJ, 29 May 1880 (644); TG, 25 May 1880 (644); TG, 14 June 1881 (644); TG, 6 June 1882 (644); TG, 22 May 1883 (643).
  xi.　Watlington JOJ, 14 June 1851; TG, 25 May 1858; TG, 14 June 1859; TG, 18 June 1878 (668).

231.　**Thame Royal Sax-Horn Band**
  i.　Thame JOJ, 17 June 1865 (648).

232.　**Thame Temperance Band**
  i.　Watlington JOJ, 14 June 1851 .

233.　**Tingewick Brass Band** (Buckinghamshire)
  i.　Fritwell BicA, 6 June 1879 (297); BicA, 21 May 1880 (297); BicA, 2 June 1882 (297).

234.　**Tingewick Temperance Band** (Buckinghamshire)
  i.　Fritwell BG, 12 June 1879 (297); BanA, 29 May 1880 (297).

235.　**Titcombe's Witney Brass Band** (see also Bands 257, Witney Brass Band)
  i.　Bampton WG, 27 May 1893 (30 and 39); WG, 12 June 1897 (39).
  ii.　Cogges WE, 28 May 1874 (216).
  iii.　Hailey WG, 27 May 1893 (321); WG, 8 June 1895 (715).
  iv.　Minster Lovell WG, 27 May 1893 (437).

    v.   Standlake WE, 16 June 1870 (600).

    vi. Witney WG, 27 May 1893 (HS, 715); WG, 11 May 1895 (HS).

236.   **Twyford Band** (Buckinghamshire)
    i.   Fringford BicA, 12 June 1914 (293 and 295).
    ii. Stratton Audley BicA, 5 June 1914 (629).

237.   **Tysoe Band** (Warwickshire)
    i.   Shenington BG, 11 June 1874 (562); BG, 3 June 1875 (562).

238.   **United Banbury and Bloxham Band** (see also Bands 26, Banbury Band, and Bands 50, Bloxham Band)
    i.   Banbury BG, 3 July 1862 (85).

239.   **Waddesdon (Brass) Band** (Buckinghamshire)
    i.   Arncott JOJ, 9 June 1860 (17); BG, 8 June 1882 (16); BicA, 30 May 1890 (16).
    ii. Bicester JOJ, 11 August 1900 (99).
    iii. Chesterton BicA, 2 June 1893 (185 and 186); BicA, 18 May 1894 (185 and 186); BicA, 7 June 1895 (186).
    iv. Islip BicA, 22 May 1890 (389); JOJ, 6 June 1903 (389).

240.   **Waddesdon Old Band** (Buckinghamshire)
    i.   Arncott BicA, 31 May 1901 (16).
    ii. Chesterton BicA, 14 June 1895 (185 and 186); BicA, 18 June 1897 (185).

241.   **Waddesdon** (Old) **Prize Band** (Buckinghamshire)
    i.   Arncott BicA, 5 June 1903 (16); BicA, 31 May 1912 (16).
    ii. Piddington BicA, 7 June 1901 (550).

242.   **Waddesdon Temperance Band** (Buckinghamshire)
    i.   Arncott BicA, 3 June 1898 (16); BicA, 16 June 1905 (16); BicA, 24 May 1907 (16); BicA, 20 May 1910 (16).

243.   **Wallingford (Brass) Band**
    i.   Dorchester WT, 25 May 1888 (251); JOJ, 6 June 1903 (251); BOA, 24 May 1907 (251); BOA, 12 June 1908 (251).

244.   **Wallingford Militia Band**
    i.   Wheatfield TG, 9 June 1863 (469).

245.   **Wantage (Brass) Band**
i.   Bampton JOJ, 19 May 1866 (28); WE, 8 June 1876 (39); WE, 24 May 1877 (39); WE, 13 June 1878 (39); WE, 5 June 1879 (39); JOJ, 19 May 1883 (39); WG, 30 May 1885 (39).

246.   **Wantage Militia Band**
i.   Bampton WE, 20 May 1875 (39).

247.   **Warwickshire Militia Band**
i.   Banbury BG, 5 July 1866 (65).

248.   **Warwickshire Yeomanry Band**
i.   Banbury BG, 5 July 1860 (65); BG, 3 July 1862 (65).

249.   **Watlington (Brass) Band** (see also Bands 167, Old Watlington Band)
i.   Brightwell Baldwin TG, 4 June 1901 (132); TG, 9 June 1903 (132).
ii.   Chalgrove TG, 25 June 1878 (167).
iii.   Marsh Baldon SON, 30 May 1891 (427).
iv.   Watlington JOJ, 13 June 1840 (668); JOJ, 8 June 1844 (674); JOJ, 17 May 1845 (674); JOJ, 14 June 1851; JOJ, 6 June 1868 (668); TG, 26 May 1872 (668); TG, 2 June 1874 (668); TG, 29 May 1877 (668); JOJ, 22 June 1878 (668); JOJ, 7 June 1879 (668); JOJ, 11 June 1881 (668); JOJ, 3 June 1882 (668); WT, 18 May 1883 (668); WT, 18 June 1886 (668); JOJ, 4 June 1887 (668); TG, 14 June 1892 (668).

250.   **Watlington Excelsior (Brass) Band**
i.   Watlington HSOS, 23 May 1902 (668); HSOS, 5 June 1903 (668); HC, 27 May 1904 (668); HSOS, 16 June 1905 (668); HSOS, 8 June 1906 (668); HSOS, 24 May 1907 (668).

251.   **Watlington Town Band**
i.   Drayton St Leonard BOA, 19 May 1893 (260).
ii.   Stadhampton SON, 8 June 1889 (591); SON, 6 June 1891 (591).
iii.   Watlington TG, 9 June 1868 (668); TG, 7 June 1887 (668); WT, 25 May 1888 (668); SON, 15 June 1889 (668); TG, 11 June 1895 (672).

252.   **The Welcome Brass Band**
    i.   Dorchester WT, 18 June 1886 (254).

253.   **West Wycombe Brass Band** (Buckinghamshire)
    i.   Stokenchurch SON, 11 June 1887 (621).

254.   **Wheatley (Brass) Band**
    i.   Bletchingdon BG, 8 June 1882 (111 and 113).
    ii. Headington JOJ, 11 August 1894 (HS, 331).
    iii. Little Milton SON, 3 June 1893 (421).
    iv. Marston JOJ, 11 June 1892 (428).
    v. Wheatley TG, 14 June 1870 (684); JOJ, 6 August 1892 (686); JOJ, 15 July 1893 (686).

255.   **Wick** (Rissington) **Brass Band**
    i.   Burford BG, 12 June 1851 (143); JOJ, 29 May 1858 (143); JOJ, 28 May 1859 (144).
    ii. Langford JOJ, 19 May 1866 (409).
    iii. Milton under Wychwood JOJ, 6 June 1857 (433).

256.   **Witney Amateur Brass Band**
    i.   Chipping Norton JOJ, 5 July 1862 (204).
    ii. Witney JOJ, 13 July 1844 (703).

257.   **Witney (Brass) Band** (see also Bands 235, Titcombe's Witney Brass Band)
    i.   Bampton BG, 28 May 1846 (28); BG, 27 May 1847.
    ii. Burford JOJ, 6 June 1847 (144); JOJ, 29 May 1880 (146).
    iii. Chipping Norton BG, 4 July 1844; Lewis (1988), 1856 (205); JOJ, 11 July 1857 (205); JOJ, 29 June 1861 (205).
    iv. Cogges WE, 20 May 1875 (216); JOJ, 22 May 1880 (216); JOJ, 9 June 1881 (216).
    v. Deddington BG, 23 May 1844 (242).
    vi. Hailey JOJ, 22 June 1867 (321); WE, 24 May 1877; WG, 7 June 1884 (321).
    vii. Leafield WE, 24 May 1877; WG, 26 May 1894.
    viii. Milton under Wychwood CNDM, July 1886 (433); JOJ, 9 June 1900 (432); JOJ, 24 May 1902 (432).
    ix. Minster Lovell WE, 24 May 1877 (437); WG, 19 May 1894 (437).
    x. North Leigh WE, 6 June 1878 (451); JOJ, 8 June 1901 (448).

xi. Stanton Harcourt WE, 20 May 1875 (604); WE, 8 June 1876 (604); WE, 13 June 1878 (604).

xii. Stonesfield JOJ, 1 June 1850 (626); JOJ, 3 June 1871 (626).

xiii. Witney WE, 24 May 1877; WE, 5 June 1879; WG, 23 May 1891 (HS, 715); WG, 19 May 1894 (HS); WG, 25 May 1907 (HS); WG, 6 June 1914 (HS).

258. **Witney Militia Band**
i. Bampton BG, 15 June 1856.

259. **Witney Reed and Brass Band**
i. Charlbury JOJ, 3 July 1880 (170).

260. **Witney Rifle Corps Band**
i. Charlbury JOJ, 11 July 1863 (175).
ii. Chipping Norton JOJ, 10 July 1880 (198).

261. **Wolverhampton Rifle Corps Band**
i. Banbury BG, 3 July 1873.

262. **Woodstock (Brass) Band**
i. Stonesfield JOJ, 11 June 1870 (626).
ii. Woodstock JOJ, 9 July 1859 (734).

263. **Woodstock Drum and Fife Band**
i. Woodstock JOJ, 11 July 1868 (737).

264. **Wootton Band**
i. Woodstock JOJ, 7 July 1894 (HS, 744).

265. **Wroxton Brass Band**
i. Shenington BG, 20 May 1880 (561).

266. **Wycombe Sax-Horn Band**

i. Stadhampton JOJ, 6 June 1857 (589).

Appendix 4   A list of societies registered by the Registrar of Friendly Societies for Oxfordshire

This appendix is a list of all Oxfordshire societies listed in order of their registration number allocated for the county by the Registrar of Friendly Societies from 1 to 392 (excluding 389). It provides their corresponding number in the Calendar of Oxfordshire friendly societies. Register number 389 and those above 392 were allocated to working men's clubs.

Registered numbered societies			
Register No	Name of Society	Place	Calendar No
1	Stokenchurch Friendly Society	Stokenchurch	622
2	Mechanical Benefit Society	Oxford	515
3	Deddington Friendly Society	Deddington	239
4	Stadhampton Associated Providential Benefit Society	Stadhampton	593
5	Brookhampton Benefit Society	Stadhampton	588
6	Garsington Benefit Society	Garsington	302
7	Friendly Society of Tradesmen	Bicester	100
8	The Loyal Union Friendly Society	Neithrop	442
9	The Industrious Society	Oxford	496
10	Whitchurch Friendly Society	Whitchurch	698
11	Wheatley Associated Providential Benefit Society	Wheatley	689
12	Bensington Friendly Society	Benson	89
13	Standlake Friendly Society	Standlake	598
14	Summertown Friendly Society	Oxford	541
15	The Beneficial Society	Banbury	54
16	Reformers Friendly Society	Banbury	79
17	Iffley Friendly Benefit Society	Iffley	386
18	Red Horse Friendly Society	Shipton under Wychwood	569

19	Nuneham Courtenay Friendly Society	Nuneham Courtenay	459
20	Stanton St John Providential Benefit Society	Stanton St John	609
21	Headington Quarry Friendly Society	Headington	335
22	Tetsworth Seven Years' Friendly Society	Tetsworth	639
23	The United Relieving Officers and Masters of Workhouses Superannuation Society	Thame	653
24	Steeple Aston Friendly Society	Steeple Aston	615
25	Old Friendly Society	Bicester	105
26	Friendly Union Tradesmen's Society	Oxford	492
27	Reform Union Friendly Society	Henley on Thames	357
28	Hethe Friendly Society	Hethe	361
29	Britannia Club Benefit Society	Headington	328
30	Chipping Norton Friendly Society	Chipping Norton	191
31	Kidlington Friendly Society	Kidlington	396
32	Tradesmen's Union Society	Chipping Norton	205
33	Henley Congregational Benefit Society	Henley on Thames	345
34	Deddington Union Beneficial Society	Deddington	242
35	Ascott-under-Wychwood Friendly Society	Ascott under Wychwood	19
36	Enstone Friendly Society	Enstone	265
37	Shutford Provident Institution and Friendly Society	Shutford	575
38	Tradesmen's Society	Oxford	543
39	College Servants' Benefit Society	Oxford	473
40	Thame Friendly Society	Thame	647
41	Ramsden Friendly Society	Ramsden	554
42	Thame Friendly Benefit Society	Thame	646
43	Oxford Friendly Institution	Oxford	524
44	Hand-in-Hand Friendly Society	Witney	710

45	Wroxton Friendly Society	Wroxton	754
46	Oxford Phoenix Benefit Society	Oxford	529
47	Watlington United Friendly Society	Watlington	675
48	Standlake Friendly Society	Standlake	599
49	Minster Lovell Friendly Society	Minster Lovell	435
50	Reform Mechanics Society	Henley on Thames	356
51	United Christian Benefit Society	Banbury	84
52	Bampton Friendly Society	Bampton	28
53	Horley Friendship and Unity Benefit Society	Horley	372
54	(Conservative) Friendly Society	Banbury	59
55	Tradesmen's Benefit Society	Banbury	82
56	Iffley New Benefit Society	Iffley	387
57	Heyford and Aston Friendly Society	Steeple Aston	613
57	Lower Heyford and Steeple Aston Friendly Society	Steeple Aston	614
58	Chalgrove Friendly Society	Chalgrove	166
59	Adderbury Amicable Friendly Society	Adderbury	1
60	Eynsham Friendly Society	Eynsham	271
61	Union Society of Chipping Norton	Chipping Norton	206
62	South Oxfordshire Friendly Society	Henley on Thames	359
63	Fritwell District Benefit Society	Fritwell	296
64	Curbridge Friendly or Savings Club	Curbridge	234
65	Henley Provident Society	Henley on Thames	346
66	Combe Friendly Society	Combe	218
67	Heart and Hand Benefit Society	Newington	447
68	Bull Club	Charlbury	169
69	Burford (Old) Friendly Society	Burford	143
70	Minster Lovell Friendly Society	Minster Lovell	436
71	Thame Permanent Hand in Hand Friendly Society	Thame	648
72	Stonesfield Friendly Society	Stonesfield	626

73	Civis Society	Oxford	472
74	(Blanket Hall) Friendly Society	Witney	703
75	South Stoke Mutual Benefit Society	South Stoke	586
76	Great Tew Friendly Society	Great Tew	318
77	Souldern Friendly Society	Souldern	583
78	Marston Friendly Society	Marston	430
79	Wheatley Tradesmen's Hand-in-Hand Benefit Society	Wheatley	693
80	Beckley Friendly Society	Stowood	628
81	North Stoke Friendly Benefit Society	North Stoke	456
82	Studley and Horton Benefit Society	Studley	382
83	United Brethren Benefit Society	Eye and Dunsden	269
84	Woodcote Friendly Society	Woodcote	725
85	Hand in Hand Benefit Society	Crowmarsh Gifford	233
86	Sibford Gower Friendly Society	Sibford Gower	578
87	Hand-in-Hand Benefit Society	Dorchester	254
88	Collins End Friendly Society	Whitchurch	695
89	Brookhampton Hand and Heart Friendly Society	Stadhampton	589
90	Brize Norton Friendly Society	Brize Norton	135
91	Banbury Sick Fund Society	Banbury	52
92	Banbury Refuge for the Afflicted	Banbury	51
93	Islip Friendly Institution	Islip	389
94	Sampson Tent	Banbury	81
95	Loyal Union Friendly Society	Bloxham	123
96	Cuxham United Friendly Society	Cuxham	235
97	Chipping Norton Tent	Chipping Norton	192
98	Forest Hill Benefit Club Society	Forest Hill	291
99	Caversham Friendly Society	Caversham	150
100	New Union Friendly Society	Chipping Norton	202
101	Crown Inn Friendly Society	Wheatley	682

102	Heart and Hand Benefit Society	Great Milton	317
103	Stokenchurch Friendly Society	Stokenchurch	623
104	Tetsworth Friendly Society	Tetsworth	637
105	Thame Permanent Hand in Hand Friendly Society	Thame	649
106	Subscription Fire Engine Society	Steeple Aston	616
107	Church Hanborough Friendly Society	Hanborough	323
108	New Street Friendly Benefit Society	Chipping Norton	201
109	Good Intent Lodge, Oxford Independent Order of United Brothers	Oxford	493
110	Oxfordshire Friendly and Medical Society	Charlbury	178
111	Hand in Hand Benefit Society	Little Milton	421
112	Holy Guild and Friendly Society of St Joseph and Our Blessed Lady, for the Catholic Congregation of Radford and Heythrop	Heythrop	364
113	Thame Temperance Provident Society	Thame	650
114	Wenman Independent Friendly Society	Thame	654
115	Woodstock District Branch, IOOFMU	Woodstock	741
116	Shutford Friendly Society	Shutford	573
117	Loyal Wellington Lodge	Oxford	514
118	Loyal Marlborough Lodge	Woodstock	732
119	Good Intent Lodge	Wroxton	750
120	Loyal Valentia Lodge	Kirtlington	405
121	Henley United Friendly Society	Henley on Thames	347
122	Tradesmen's Beneficial Society	Adderbury	10
123	(Loyal) British Queen Lodge Benefit Society	Banbury	72
124	Duns Tew Friendly Society	Duns Tew	262
125	Loyal Drake Lodge, Loyal Drake Benevolent Sick Society	Bicester	103
126	Broadwell Friendly Society	Broadwell	140

127	General Beneficial Society	Banbury	71
128	Temple of Friendship Lodge	Wardington	659
129	New Angel Friendly Society	Woodstock	734
130	Woodstock Friendly Society	Woodstock	742
131	Somerton Friendly Society	Somerton	582
132	St Clements Union Friendly Society	Oxford	532
133	British Queen Benefit Society	Banbury	55
134	Banbury Mutual Cattle Assurance Association	Banbury	49
135	Banbury and Neithrop Clothing Society	Banbury	50
136	Banbury Hail Storm Assurance Association	Banbury	47
137	Loyal Amicable Foresters Benefit Society	Charlbury	175
138	Fifield Loyal United Benefit Society	Fifield	285
139	Loyal Tree of Friendship	Burford	149
140	United Britons Friendly Society	Banbury	83
141	Chalgrove Friendly Society	Chalgrove	167
142	Royal Albert Friendly Society	Brize Norton	139
143	Christian Mutual Benefit Society	Banbury	58
144	Burford Mutual Benefit Society	Burford	144
145	Fountain of Friendship Benefit Society	Adderbury	9
146	Loyal Good Samaritan Lodge	Henley on Thames	351
147	Banbury District of IOOFMU	Banbury	43
148	United Burial Friendly Society	Dorchester	257
149	Loyal Coker Friendly Society	Bicester	102
150	Bloxham Friendly Society	Bloxham	116
151	Banbury Working Man's Co-operative Friendly Society	Banbury	53
152	The Victoria Club	Bampton	38
153	Headington Benefit Society	Headington	333
154	Valentia Club	Bletchingdon	113

155	Deddington General Friendly Institution	Deddington	240
156	Conservative Friendly Society	Banbury	60
157	Friendly Society of Carpenters and Joiners	Oxford	490
158	Hanwell Amicable Society	Hanwell	326
159	Aston Friendly Society	Aston and Cote	21
160	Charlton Friendly Society	Charlton on Otmoor	182
161	Amicable Society of Tradesmen	Ambrosden	15
162	Peppard Union Society	Rotherfield Peppard	557
163	Union Society of Oxford	Oxford	545
164	Burford Friendly Institution	Burford	142
165	Sociable Society	Oxford	536
166	Deddington New Friendly Society	Deddington	241
167	Bletchington Friendly Society	Bletchingdon	111
168	Chipping Norton Friendly Society	Chipping Norton	190
169	Minster Lovell Friendly Society	Minster Lovell	434
170	King's Arms Friendly Society	Witney	712
171	Cropredy Benefit Society	Cropredy	229
172	Deddington Friendly Society	Deddington	238
173	Bicester Friendly Society	Bicester	92
174	Charlbury Old Club	Charlbury	171
175	Charlton Friendly Society	Charlton on Otmoor	181
176	Standlake Benefit Society	Standlake	597
177	Kidlington Friendly Society	Kidlington	395
178	Thame Friendly Society	Thame	645
179	Dorchester Friendly and Beneficial Society	Dorchester	252
180	Kingston Friendly Society	Kingston Blount	400
181	Mapledurham Friendly Society	Mapledurham	425

182	Bloxham Amicable Society	Bloxham	114
183	Banbury Female Friendly Society	Banbury	44
184	Adderbury Friendly Society	Adderbury	3
185	[Blue Boar] Friendly Society	Woodstock	726
186	Banbury Friendly Society	Banbury	45
187	Witney Friendly Society	Witney	719
188	Northfield End Friendly Society	Henley on Thames	352
189	Killingworth Castle Friendly Society	Wootton	747
190	The Sociable Friendly Society	Witney	717
191	Drayton Friendly Society	Drayton	259
192	Alliance Benefit Society	Wootton	745
193	Hand-in-Hand Friendly Society	Eynsham	276
194	Stokenchurch Friendly Society	Stokenchurch	624
195	Chipping Norton United Provident Society	Chipping Norton	194
196	The Victoria Club	Bampton	39
197	Court British Queen	Thame	640
198	Court Pride of the Thames	Henley on Thames	341
199	Tradesmen's Beneficial Friendly Society	Bloxham	125
200	Ascott-under-Wychwood Friendly Society	Ascott under Wychwood	20
201	Sibford Benefit Friendly Society	Sibford Gower	576
202	Hand-in-Hand Benefit Society	Combe	223
203	Loyal Good Intent Lodge	Oxford	506
204	United Christian Benefit Society	Chipping Norton	207
205	Headington Quarry Benefit Society	Headington	334
206	United Brethren Benefit Society.	Woodstock	736
207	Dorchester Friendly Society	Dorchester	253
208	Court Loyal Oxonian	Oxford	482
209	Sovereign Benefit Society	Woodstock	735

210	Charlbury New Friendly Benefit Society	Charlbury	170
211	Summer Town Benefit Society	Oxford	540
212	Horley General Insurance Society	Horley	373
213	Weston-on-the-Green Friendly Society	Weston on the Green	679
214	Heart and Hand Benefit Society	Great Haseley	313
215	Hook Norton United Provident Society	Hook Norton	368
216	Arncott Friendly Institution	Arncott	17
217	Bladon Benefit Society	Bladon	109
218	Elder Brothers Friendly Society	Charlbury	173
219	New United Friendly Society	Chipping Norton	203
220	Kidlington Benefit Society	Kidlington	394
221	Oxford District of IOOFMU	Oxford	522
222	Sandford Independent (Hand and Heart) Life Society	Sandford on Thames	559
223	Oxford Arms Friendly Society	Kirtlington	406
224	Court Loyal Britannia	Banbury	64
225	United Glovers Benefit Society	Woodstock	739
226	Central Oxfordshire Friendly Society	Oxford	469
227	Barton Friendly Society	Westcote Barton	678
228	NOT OXFORDSHIRE – This was Lillingstone Lovell Friendly Society, Buckinghamshire. Until 1844 it was a detached part of Oxfordshire under the control of the Royal manor of Kirtlington. This friendly society was established in 1860 but mistakenly registered in Oxfordshire.		
229	Fox Friendly Society	Stanton Harcourt	603
230	Chadlington Friendly Society	Chadlington	160
231	Wroxton Friendly Society	Wroxton	755
232	United Christian Benefit Society	Wardington	661
233	Woodleys Mutual Benefit Society	Wootton	748
234	Marston Friendly Benefit Society	Marston	429
235	Refuge Friendly Society	Mollington	441

236	Loyal Farmers' Home Lodge	Beckley	87
237	Loyal Havelock Lodge	Headington	338
238	King and Queen Friendly Benefit Society	Wheatley	684
239	Burford Mutual Benefit Society	Burford	145
240	Headington Quarry seven years Benefit Club	Headington	336
241	Crown Inn Friendly Society	Wheatley	683
242	Old Guildhall Club	Chipping Norton	204
243	Loyal Prince of Wales Lodge	Oxford	509
244	Garibaldian Benefit Society	Goring	308
245	Somerton Friendly and Benefit Society	Somerton	581
246	Stratton Audley Benefit Society	Stratton Audley	629
247	Combe New Friendly Society	Combe	222
248	Piddington Friendly Society	Piddington	549
249	Crown Inn Friendly Society	Witney	708
250	Kirtlington Provident Friendly Society	Kirtlington	403
251	Launton Provident Society	Launton	410
252	Leafield Friendly Society	Leafield	415
253	Sanctuary Loyal Oxonian	Oxford	534
254	Hensington United Brethren Benefit Society	Hensington	360
255	Combe Friendly Society	Combe	219
256	The Church Benefit Society of Mixbury	Mixbury	438
257	Salford Friendly Society	Salford	558
258	Ducklington Friendly Society	Ducklington	261
259	Forest Hill (with Shotover) Benefit Society	Forest Hill	292
260	Finstock Independent Friendly Benefit Society	Finstock	288
261	Hornton Friendly Society	Hornton	377
262	Court Duke Of Cornwall	Oxford	478

263	(United) Beckley Friendly Society	Beckley	88
264	Great Bourton Friendly Society	Bourton	131
265	Sturdy's Castle Friendly Society	Tackley	633
266	Shillingford Friendly Society	Warborough	658
267	Prince of Wales Friendly Society	Warborough	657
268	Shutford Friendly Society	Shutford	574
269	Hand-in-Hand Benefit Society	Dorchester	255
270	Hornton New Insurance Society	Hornton	378
271	Sibford New Friendly Society	Sibford Gower	579
272	United Brethren Benefit Society	Woodstock	737
273	Ramsden Friendly Society	Ramsden	555
274	Loyal Walton Lodge	Oxford	513
275	Standlake Friendly Society	Standlake	600
276	Chadlington New Friendly Society	Chadlington	161
277	Eynsham Seven Years Benefit Society	Eynsham	275
278	Good Intent Lodge Friendly Society	Wroxton	751
279	Court Temple of Friendship	Hornton	374
280	Sanctuary Duke of Cornwall	Cowley	533
281	College Servants' Provident Institution	Oxford	474
282	Bodicote Friendly Society	Bodicote	126
283	Conservative Friendly Society	Banbury	61
284	Kingston Friendly Society	Kingston Blount	401
285	Court British Lion	Bloxham	119
286	Court Pride of the Hill	Shiplake	564
287	Reformers United Friendly Society	Banbury	80
288	Prince of Wales Club	Clanfield	213
289	Court Royal Crown	Banbury	67
290	Loyal Volunteer Lodge	Goring	309
291	North Leigh Friendly Benefit Society	North Leigh	451
292	Eynsham Friendly Society	Eynsham	272

293	Heart in Hand Benefit Society	Stanton St John	607
294	Oxford District Widow and Orphan Society	Oxford	523
295	South Oxford Working Men's Club and Institute	Oxford	538
296	Court Alexandra	Bampton	31
297	Hand and Heart Benefit Society	Woodstock	729
298	Court Hearts of Oak	Iffley	384
299	Court Prince of Wales	Clanfield	211
300	New Friendly Medical and Benefit Society	Enstone	266
301	Broughton and North Newington Benefit Society	North Newington	452
302	King's Arms Friendly Society	Tackley	632
303	Court Constitution	Wheatley	681
304	Court Loyal Blenheim	Woodstock	727
305	Fox Friendly Society	Stanton Harcourt	604
306	Court Hampden	Watlington	665
307	Court Noble	Caversham	152
308	Tadmarton Junior Benefit Society	Tadmarton	636
309	Woodstock United Permanent Benefit Friendly Society	Woodstock	744
310	Wheatley Friendly Society	Wheatley	691
311	Court Robin Hood	Deddington	236
312	Court Royal Oxonians	Dorchester	251
313	Loyal Oxonian Juvenile Foresters	Oxford	507
314	Studley Hand in Glove Benefit Society	Horton cum Studley	383
315	Loyal Old Elm Tree Lodge	Chipping Norton	198
316	Loyal Wenman Lodge	Thame	643
317	Loyal Mansfield Lodge	Fringford	295
318	Loyal Garibaldi Lodge	Witney	715
319	Horley Friendly Society	Horley	371

320	Labourers' Accident and Burial Society	Oxford	499
321	Loyal Bud of Hope Lodge, Juvenile Branch	Henley on Thames	350
322	Loyal St Peter's Lodge	Caversham	155
323	Court Allnut	Goring	306
324	Court Loyal Oxonian	Bicester	99
325	Queen of England Lodge	Eynsham	280
326	Sanctuary Noble	Caversham	158
327	New Bladon Friendly Society	Bladon	110
328	Arncott Benefit Society	Arncott	16
329	DUPLICATE. This was a duplicate registration in error by the Registrar of Oxon 304, Court Loyal Blenheim, Woodstock, Ancient Order of Foresters. No separate papers or records exist under reference Oxon 329 at The National Archives.		
330	Oxford District Agricultural Labourers' Union Sick and Benefit Society	Oxford	520
331	Crowmarsh Friendly Society	Crowmarsh Gifford	232
332	New Friendly Medical and Benefit Society	Enstone	267
333	Court British Lion Juvenile Branch	Bloxham	120
334	Court Hayman	Stokenchurch	620
335	Loyal Old Elm Tree Lodge, Juvenile Branch	Chipping Norton	199
336	North Arms Friendly Society	Wroxton	752
337	Garsington New Independent Friendly Society	Garsington	304
338	Garsington New Benefit Society	Garsington	303
339	Court Pride of the Thames Juvenile Sick and Funeral Society	Henley on Thames	342
340	Langford United Benefit Society	Langford	408
341	United Brethren Friendly Society	Woodstock	738
342	Combe Friendly Society	Combe	220

343	Wiggington Labourers' Friendly Society	Wiggington	702
344	Finmere Friendly Society	Finmere	287
345	Clanfield Provident Society	Clanfield	210
346	Fritwell Provident Society	Fritwell	299
347	Christian Mutual Aid (Benefit) Society	Witney	705
348	Shenington Amicable Society	Shenington	561
349	Stonesfield Permanent Mutual Benefit Society	Stonesfield	627
350	Finstock United Benefit Society	Finstock	289
351	Working Women's Benefit Society	Oxford	547
352	Leafield Independent Friendly Benefit Society	Leafield	416
353	Chipping Norton United Provident Juvenile Society	Chipping Norton	193
354	Ramsden Working Men's Benefit Society	Ramsden	556
355	Old George Benefit Society	Leafield	417
356	Lewknor Friendly Society	Lewknor	419
357	Hethe Benefit Society	Hethe	363
358	Legal Provident Institution	Bampton	36
359	Banbury Juvenile Foresters Friendly Society	Banbury	48
360	Marston Good Intent Benefit Society	Marston	431
361	Oxford United Brethren Friendly Society	Oxford	530
362	Emmer Green Juvenile Foresters Friendly Society	Caversham	154
363	Wootton Jubilee Benefit Society	Wootton	749
364	Banbury Friendly Societies Medical Association	Banbury	46
365	Juvenile branch of Loyal Wychwood Forest Lodge	Shipton under Wychwood	567
366	Loyal British Queen Lodge, Juvenile Branch	Banbury	73

367	Cropredy United Temperance Friendly Society	Cropredy	231
368	Bloxham Old Friendly Society	Bloxham	118
369	Bampton Self-Help Society	Bampton	30
370	Hope of Iffley Juvenile Foresters Friendly Society	Iffley	385
371	Bicester Juvenile Foresters Friendly Society	Bicester	94
372	Loyal Havelock Lodge, Juvenile Branch	Headington	339
373	Oxford District Juvenile branch	Oxford	521
374	Adderbury Juvenile Foresters Friendly Society	Adderbury	4
375	Cowley Benefit Society	Cowley	225
376	Brookhampton Hand and Heart Juvenile Friendly Society	Stadhampton	590
377	Eynsham Permanent Benefit Society	Eynsham	273
378	Great Haseley Friendly Society	Great Haseley	312
379	Oxford Juvenile Society	Oxford	527
380	Fifield Friendly Society	Fifield	283
381	Mixbury Benefit Society	Mixbury	439
382	Chalgrove Friendly Society	Chalgrove	168
383	Loyal Oxonian Juvenile Friendly Society	Oxford	508
384	United Society of Nephalites	Watlington	672
385	New Inn Permanent Benefit Society	Eynsham	279
386	Great Milton Friendly Society	Great Milton	316
387	Nettlebed Juvenile Sick and Funeral Society	Nettlebed	445
388	Weston-on-the-Green Friendly Society	Weston on the Green	680
390	Shipton Friendly Society	Shipton under Wychwood	571
391	Noble Juvenile Foresters Friendly Society	Caversham	157
392	Fringford Benefit Friendly Society	Fringford	293

Appendix 5   A list of societies established before 1800

This appendix is a list of all known societies in Oxfordshire that were established prior to 1800 in order of year of formation.

Calendar No.	Place	Name of Society	First known date	Last known date
712	Witney	King's Arms Friendly Society	1750	1794
743	Woodstock	Woodstock New Friendly Society	1757	1794
62	Banbury	Constitutional Friendly Society	1758	1794
545	Oxford	Union Society of Oxford	1758	1826
488	Oxford	Elderly Society	1758	1862
674	Watlington	Watlington Old Club	1759	1852
395	Kidlington	Kidlington Friendly Society	1760	1805
475	Oxford	Commercial Society	1761	1762
597	Standlake	Standlake Benefit Society	1761	1866
468	Oxford	(Bowling Green club)	1762	1762
464	Oxford	Amicable Society	1762	1762
495	Oxford	Industrious Society	1762	1762
537	Oxford	(Sot's Hole Club)	1762	1762
494	Oxford	(Greyhound Club)	1762	1762
467	Oxford	(Blue Boar club)	1762	1762
471	Oxford	Civil Society	1762	1762
489	Oxford	Freemen Society	1762	1762
516	Oxford	(New Wheatsheaf Club)	1762	1762
546	Oxford	Useful Society	1762	1834
171	Charlbury	Charlbury Old Club	1762	1870
190	Chipping Norton	Chipping Norton Friendly Society	1765	1885
626	Stonesfield	Stonesfield Friendly Society	1765	1913
159	Chadlington	Chadlington Friendly Society	1766	1794
244	Deddington	King's Arms Friendly Society	1768	1794
115	Bloxham	(Bloxham Friendly Society)	1769	1804
2	Adderbury	Adderbury Friendly Society	1769	1804
143	Burford	Burford (Old) Friendly Society	1769	1859

173	Charlbury	Elder Brothers Friendly Society	1769	1863
544	Oxford	Unanimous Society	1770	1809
182	Charlton on Otmoor	Charlton Friendly Society	1771	1825
472	Oxford	Civis Society	1773	1869
68	Banbury	Friendly Society of Shag Weavers	1774	1794
180	Charlbury	White Hart Club	1777	1805
179	Charlbury	Star Friendly Society	1778	1794
587	Spelsbury	Spelsbury Friendly Society	1779	1794
217	Combe	Combe Friendly Society	1780	1794
367	Hook Norton	Hook Norton Friendly Society	1780	1794
229	Cropredy	Cropredy Benefit Society	1783	1830
111	Bletchingdon	Bletchington Friendly Society	1783	1888
376	Hornton	Hornton Friendly Society	1784	1794
415	Leafield	Leafield Friendly Society	1785	1864
247	Deddington	Red Lion Friendly Society	1786	1795
265	Enstone	Enstone Friendly Society	1786	1864
717	Witney	The Sociable Friendly Society	1789	1789
258	Drayton	Drayton Friendly Society	1789	1815
747	Wootton	Killingworth Castle Friendly Society	1791	1880
253	Dorchester	Dorchester Friendly and Beneficial Society	1793	1855
40	Banbury	Amicable Society	1794	1794
63	Banbury	Constitutional Union Friendly Society	1794	1794
323	Hanborough	Church Hanborough Friendly Society	1794	1854
238	Deddington	Deddington Friendly Society	1795	1795
27	Bampton	Bampton Friendly Society	1795	1804
241	Deddington	Deddington New Friendly Society	1795	1824
598	Standlake	Standlake Friendly Society	1795	1831
296	Fritwell	Fritwell District Benefit Society	1796	1866
645	Thame	Thame Friendly Society	1797	1797
327	Hanwell	Hanwell Friendly Society	1799	1799

Appendix 6   A list of the branches of the Affiliated Orders in Oxfordshire

This appendix is a list of all Affiliated Order branches in Oxfordshire, listed in order of friendly society and then by date of establishment. It provides their corresponding number in the Calendar of Oxfordshire friendly societies.
An * in the last known date column indicates the branch continued beyond 1918.

Ancient Order of Foresters

Calendar No.	Place	Branch No.	Name of Society	First known date	Last known date
370	Horley	1928	Court Old House at Home	1846	1858
479	Oxford	2317	Court Isis	1849	1852
640	Thame	2683	Court British Queen	1855	1907
65	Banbury	2805	Court Prince of Wales	1856	*
341	Henley on Thames	2880	Court Pride of the Thames	1857	*
482	Oxford	2991	Court Loyal Oxonian	1858	*
64	Banbury	3112	Court Loyal Britannia	1859	1862
119	Bloxham	3167	Court British Lion	1859	*
478	Oxford	4338	Court Duke Of Cornwall	1864	*
374	Hornton	4783	Court Temple of Friendship	1865	*
564	Shiplake	5044	Court Pride of the Hill	1867	*
211	Clanfield	5191	Court Prince of Wales	1868	1874
67	Banbury	5156	Court Royal Crown	1868	*
384	Iffley	5183	Court Hearts of Oak	1868	*
31	Bampton	5298	Court Alexandra	1869	1869
665	Watlington	5372	Court Hampden	1869	*
681	Wheatley	5308	Court Constitution	1869	*
152	Caversham	5534	Court Noble	1870	*

236	Deddington	5490	Court Robin Hood	1870	*
251	Dorchester	5546	Court Royal Oxonians	1870	*
727	Woodstock	5428	Court Loyal Blenheim	1870	*
507	Oxford		Loyal Oxonian Juvenile Foresters	1871	1875
306	Goring	5726	Court Allnut	1872	*
620	Stokenchurch	6047	Court Hayman	1874	*
99	Bicester	5947	Court Loyal Oxonian	1874	*
120	Bloxham	3167	Court British Lion Juvenile Branch	1875	1927
127	Bodicote	6277	Court Hand in Hand	1876	*
375	Hornton		Temple of Friendship, Juvenile branch	1877	1895
342	Henley on Thames		Court Pride of the Thames, Juvenile Sick and Funeral Society	1879	1913
8	Adderbury	6599	Court Hand and Heart	1879	*
601	Stanton Harcourt	6686	Court Welcome	1880	*
591	Stadhampton	6697	Court Hampton	1880	*
153	Caversham	6772	Court Saunders	1881	*
331	Headington	6829	Court Napoleon	1881	*
315	Great Milton	6961	Court Admiral Massingberd (and from 1893) Court Ashurst	1882	*
172	Charlbury	7148	Court Wychwood Forest	1883	*
498	Oxford		Juvenile Society of Oxford District	1884	1914
484	Oxford	7166	Court St Frideswide	1884	*
147	Burford	7226	Court Loyal Priory	1884	*
154	Caversham		Emmer Green Juvenile Foresters Friendly Society	1885	1907
237	Deddington		Court Robin Hood, Juvenile branch	1885	*

4	Adderbury	6599	Adderbury Juvenile Foresters Friendly Society	1885	*
592	Stadhampton	6697	Juvenile Court Hampton	1886	1900
157	Caversham		Noble Juvenile Foresters Friendly Society	1886	1914
722	Wolvercote	7514	Court Fair Rosamund's Bower	1886	*
264	Enstone	7451	Court Victoria	1886	*
391	Kidlington	7607	Court Denford	1887	1888
48	Banbury		Banbury Juvenile Foresters Friendly Society	1887	1910
381	Horspath	7626	Court Victoria's Jubilee	1887	*
307	Goring	5726	Court Allnut, Juvenile branch	1889	*
270	Eynsham	7753	Court The Abbey	1889	*
365	Hook Norton	7826	Court Pride of Hook Norton	1889	*
610	Stanton St John	7748	Star of Stanton	1889	*
224	Cowley	7724	Court Knight of the Temple	1889	*
697	Whitchurch		Pride of Whitchurch, Juvenile branch	1890	1892
696	Whitchurch	7732	Pride of Whitchurch	1890	1892
94	Bicester		Bicester Juvenile Foresters Friendly Society	1890	1903
706	Witney	7846	Court Windrush	1890	*
128	Bodicote		Court Hand in Hand, Juvenile branch	1890	*
385	Iffley	5183	Hope of Iffley Juvenile Foresters Friendly Society	1890	*
481	Oxford	7932	Court Lord Nelson	1891	1895
32	Bampton	8000	Court The Bush	1891	*

453	North Newington	7934	Court Saye and Sele	1891	*
594	Standlake	8039	Court Star of Standlake	1892	*
332	Headington		Court Napoleon, Juvenile branch	1893	1895
508	Oxford	2991	Loyal Oxonian Juvenile Friendly Society	1894	1912
443	Nettlebed	8324	Court Pride of Nettlebed	1894	*
33	Bampton		Court The Bush, Juvenile Branch	1895	1895
445	Nettlebed		Nettlebed Juvenile Sick and Funeral Society	1895	1912
392	Kidlington	8545	Court Duke of York	1895	*
483	Oxford	8593	Court Princess Christian	1896	*
611	Steeple Aston	8883	Court Robin Hood's Pride	1899	*
485	Oxford	8877	Court Victoria	1899	*
388	Islip	9035	Court Edward the Confessor	1901	*
480	Oxford	9047	Court King's Coronation	1902	1905
728	Woodstock		Court Loyal Blenheim, Juvenile branch	1904	*
256	Dorchester		Juvenile Court Royal Oxonian	1907	1907
612	Steeple Aston	9597	Court Royal Queen Mary	1912	*
411	Leafield	9610	Court Wychwood Forest	1912	*
625	Stonesfield	9513	Court Black Head	1912	*
324	Hanborough	9407	Court King George	1912	*
301	Garsington	9438	Court Ivanhoe	1912	*
330	Headington	9602	Court Alice Blacklair Cutler	1912	*
572	Shutford	9583	Court King George	1912	*
66	Banbury	9437	Court Queen Mary	1912	*

Ancient Order of Shepherds (A higher order of the Ancient Order of Foresters)

Calendar No.	Place	Branch No.	Name of Society	First known date	Last known date
534	Oxford	2991	Sanctuary Loyal Oxonian	1863	1863
533	Oxford	4338	Sanctuary Duke of Cornwall	1870	1890
158	Caversham	5534	Sanctuary Noble	1874	1880

Derby Midland United Order of Oddfellows

Calendar No.	Place	Branch No.	Name of Society	First known date	Last known date
106	Bicester	47	The Star of Hope Lodge	1889	1891

Independent Order of Oddfellows Manchester Unity

Calendar No.	Place	Branch No.	Name of Society	First known date	Last known date
704	Witney	3604	Bud of Friendship Lodge	1836	1850
506	Oxford	1703	Loyal Good Intent Lodge	1838	*
72	Banbury	2429	(Loyal) British Queen Lodge	1840	*
542	Oxford	2661	Temple of Friendship Lodge	1841	1850
522	Oxford		Oxford District of IOOFMU	1841	*
514	Oxford	2662	Loyal Wellington Lodge	1841	*

70	Banbury	3311	Fountain of Liberty Lodge	1843	1846
195	Chipping Norton	3609	Chosen Lodge	1843	1846
35	Bampton	3436	England's Glory Lodge	1843	1847
176	Charlbury	3522	Loyal Churchill Lodge	1843	1848
740	Woodstock	3336	Victoria Lodge	1843	1850
98	Bicester	3651	Coker Lodge	1843	1850
248	Deddington	3473	Widows Hope Lodge	1843	1850
655	Thame	3229	Wenman Lodge	1843	1852
149	Burford	3471	Loyal Tree of Friendship	1843	1852
659	Wardington	3655	Temple of Friendship Lodge	1843	*
351	Henley on Thames	3388	Loyal Good Samaritan Lodge	1843	*
750	Wroxton	3656	Good Intent Lodge	1844	1867
87	Beckley	3138	Loyal Farmers Home Lodge	1845	*
278	Eynsham	3201	Macclesfield Lodge	1846	1846
732	Woodstock	3927	Loyal Marlborough Lodge	1846	1869
664	Watlington	4213	Castle Lodge	1847	1850
709	Witney	4440	Fountain of Friendship Lodge	1850	1850
405	Kirtlington	4291	Loyal Valentia Lodge	1850	1861
741	Woodstock		Woodstock District, IOOFMU	1852	1868
43	Banbury		Banbury District, IOOFMU	1852	*
338	Headington	4820	Loyal Havelock Lodge	1859	*
509	Oxford	4902	Loyal Prince of Wales Lodge	1860	*
715	Witney	5261	Loyal Garibaldi Lodge	1864	*
513	Oxford	5385	Loyal Walton Lodge	1866	*
309	Goring	5527	Loyal Volunteer Lodge	1867	*

523	Oxford		Oxford District Widow and Orphan Society	1869	1913
643	Thame	5734	Loyal Wenman Lodge	1869	*
198	Chipping Norton	5964	Loyal Old Elm Tree Lodge	1871	*
295	Fringford	5904	Loyal Mansfield Lodge	1872	*
280	Eynsham	5994	Queen of England Lodge	1873	1818
156	Caversham	5995	Loyal St Peter's Lodge	1873	*
199	Chipping Norton		Old Elm Tree Lodge, Juvenile branch	1876	1912
566	Shipton under Wychwood	6221	Loyal Wychwood Forest Lodge	1877	1968
731	Woodstock	6471	Loyal Chaucer Lodge	1882	1882
503	Oxford	6556	Loyal Borough Lodge	1883	*
428	Marston	6571	Loyal Duke of Albany Lodge	1883	*
567	Shipton under Wychwood		Loyal Wychwood Forest Lodge, Juvenile branch	1889	1910
510	Oxford	6899	Loyal St Giles Lodge	1889	*
73	Banbury		Loyal British Queen Lodge Juvenile branch	1889	*
74	Banbury	6893	Loyal Good Intent Lodge	1889	*
634	Tadmarton	6883	Empress of India Lodge	1889	*
521	Oxford		Oxford District Juvenile branch	1891	1914
339	Headington		Loyal Havelock Lodge, Juvenile branch	1891	1914
686	Wheatley	7068	Loyal Jubilee Lodge	1891	*
687	Wheatley		Loyal Jubilee Lodge, Juvenile branch	1892	1914
595	Standlake	7158	Loyal Harcourt Lodge	1892	*
596	Standlake		Loyal Harcourt Lodge, Juvenile branch	1893	1914
511	Oxford	7323	Loyal St Lawrence Lodge	1895	1914

630	Swerford	7346	Loyal Masons' Arms Lodge	1895	*
163	Chadlington	7372	Loyal Pride of Chadlington Lodge	1896	1914
188	Chinnor	7393	Loyal John Hampden Lodge	1896	*
122	Bloxham	7421	Loyal Old Friendly Lodge	1897	*
249	Deddington	7474	Ye Old Castle Lodge	1898	*
700	Wiggington	7524	Loyal Wiggington Lodge	1899	*
200	Chipping Norton	7512	Loyal Pride of the Old Elm Tree Female Lodge	1899	*
369	Hook Norton	7510	Loyal General Gordon Lodge	1899	*
504	Oxford	7604	Loyal Charlotte Toynbee Female Lodge	1900	1912
404	Kirtlington	7695	Loyal Major Dashwood Lodge	1902	*
156	Caversham	7757	Loyal Stephen Bristow Lodge	1903	1910
41	Banbury	7800	Banbury Cross Female Lodge	1903	1914
505	Oxford	7889	Loyal College Servants Lodge	1904	1912
177	Charlbury	8015	Loyal Evenlode Lodge	1907	*
733	Woodstock	8299	Loyal Marlborough Lodge	1912	*
560	Shenington	8586	Shenington Amicable Lodge	1912	*
298	Fritwell	9007	Fritwell Lodge	1912	*
580	Somerton	8666	Jersey Lodge	1912	*

Independent Order of Oddfellows South London Unity

Calendar No.	Place	Branch No.	Name of Society	First known date	Last known date
355	Henley on Thames	46	Pride of Henley Lodge	1879	1913

Independent Order of Rechabites Salford Unity

Calendar No.	Place	Branch No.	Name of Society	First known date	Last known date
192	Chipping Norton	230	Chipping Norton Tent	1840	1849
81	Banbury	732	Sampson Tent	1844	1847
57	Banbury	134	Cadbury Tent	1872	1910
349	Henley on Thames	1836	Hope of Henley Tent	1888	1910
343	Henley on Thames	671	Excelsior Juvenile Tent	1888	1910
354	Henley on Thames	2294	Onward and Upward Female Tent	1893	1910
69	Banbury	1499	Forward Juvenile Tent	1897	1910
539	Oxford	2835	Star of Hope Tent	1898	1912
228	Cropredy	4198	Advance Tent	1912	1914

Nottingham Ancient Imperial United Order of Odd Fellows

Calendar No.	Place	Branch No.	Name of Society	First known date	Last known date
103	Bicester		Loyal Drake Lodge, Loyal Drake Benevolent Sick Society	1846	1891

Order of the Sons of Temperance

Calendar No.	Place	Branch No.	Name of Society	First known date	Last known date
470	Oxford	361	City of Oxford Subordinate Division	1873	1910
196	Chipping Norton	618	Four Shires Subordinate Division	1884	1910
96	Bicester	711	Bicester Subordinate Division	1889	1913
694	Wheatley	704	Ye Merrie Bells Subordinate Division	1889	1914
337	Headington	721	Headington Subordinate Division	1890	1910
487	Oxford	725	East Oxford Subordinate Division	1890	1912
721	Witney	759	Witney Subordinate Division	1892	1913
226	Cowley	829	Cowley Excelsior Subordinate Division	1896	1910
424	Lower Heyford	843	Lower Heyford Subordinate Division	1897	1913
300	Fritwell	865	Fritwell Subordinate Division	1898	1910
42	Banbury	994	Banbury Cross Subordinate Division	1902	1910
548	Piddington	820	Piddington Division	1905	1913
669	Watlington	1308	Nephalite Subordinate Division	1908	1914
151	Caversham	1484	Caversham Subordinate Division	1910	1910
585	Souldern	865	Souldern United Division	1911	1913
517	Oxford	181	Onward Section, Cadets of Temperance	1886	1886

Appendix 7   A list of surviving flags and banners

Friendly Society	Location	Calendar no.
Bletchingdon Friendly Society	In private hands, Bletchingdon	112
Chalgrove Friendly Society	St Mary's Church, Chalgrove	165
Finstock Independent Friendly Society	Finstock Local History Society	288
Loyal Mansfield Lodge, IOOFMU, Fringford	Fringford Village Hall	295
Court Ashurst, AOF, Great Milton	The Neighbour's Hall, Great Milton	315
Sibford Gower Friendly Society	Holy Trinity church, Sibford Gower	576
Sibford Gower Friendly Society	Holy Trinity church, Sibford Gower	576
Court Star of Standlake, AOF, Standlake	Oxfordshire Museum Service	594
Loyal Marlborough Lodge, IOOFMU, Woodstock	Oxfordshire Museum Service	733

INDEX OF SUBJECTS

INDEX OF PLACES

INDEX OF PERSONS